Teaching Process Writing
with
Computers

REVISED EDITION

EDITED BY
RANDY BOONE

© 1989, 1991 ISTE
ISBN 0-924667-93-1

TABLE OF CONTENTS

KEYBOARDING

REVIEWS

INTRODUCTION

A short 5 years ago a search through the Educational Resources Information Center (ERIC) bibliographic databases returned only a handful of references in the area of computers and writing. Today the list is significantly longer. Word processing in particular is a topic of much interest in the the language arts journals and research literature.

Word processing, one of the most popular innovations to enter school curricula in recent years, has moved rapidly into elementary and secondary classrooms throughout the country. Student use of word processing software to compose and print compositions is increasing in elementary, middle, and high schools that have computers (Bruce, Michaels, & Watson-Gegeo, 1985; Carey, 1985; Olds, 1985; Pollitt, 1984). Several word processing programs are being promoted specifically for use in educational settings while many educational publishing houses now offer a word processing program or system of their own, designed or packaged for school use.

Language teachers, drawing on research of the past decade, see the word processor as a powerful new tool to help student writers, especially in the revision phase of the writing process. A look at the composition process reveals why word processing holds potential for assisting student writers through the labor of writing.

Most writers agree and the literature on writing confirms that writing is not a single act, but rather an on-going process consisiting of several progressive stages (Graves, 1983; Haley-James, 1981; Hink, 1985). Rarely will any two authors' writing processes follow identical paths, yet three basic stages seem to occur in almost everyone's writing. These stages are most often categorized as prewriting, composing, and revising.

Prewriting is defined as a stage for generating ideas and harnessing the inner stream of consciousness through planning, organizing, and analyzing prior to the actual writing. It is the motiviation for writing. A child who draws a picture before beginning to write is engaging in a form of prewriting. **Composing**, the middle stage, is perhaps best viewed as the time when the writer sits down and engages in the task of writing. It may be thought of as the process of making one's thoughts concrete. The final stage of the writing process, **revision**, includes not only the correction of mechanical and grammatical errors, but more importantly, a *re-vision* or second look at the content of the piece of writing.

These stages, however, are not locked into a rigid linear progression. This model of the composition process assumes that writing is generative. That is, as one writes, new ideas continue to be generated, thus causing a writer to make changes halfway through a story, a paragraph, or even in midsentence. Interruptions to re-think an idea, compose a quick paragraph, rewrite, or edit, may occur during the prewriting, composing, or revising stages, and are an inherent part of the process. Moving through any of the three stages,

newly generated ideas may cause the writer to make a quick transition to one of the other two stages. Revision and prewriting, for example, often interrupt the composing phase. Each of these three stages, then, contains a recursive implementation of the same three stages. Each stage allows the entire model to function within itself.

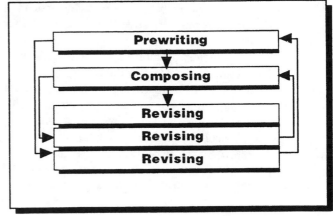

Recursive model of the writing process.

It is this generative nature of writing, the recursive process of revision, that taps the power of the computer word processing program. The word processor, in addition to providing a flexible medium for correcting errors, allows an author to experiment with different ideas and techniques, such as sentence combining, without laborious recopying. Electronic text manipulation permits new ideas to be viewed on screen in a temporary form, providing a realistic image of what is being written without the finality of ink or pencil on paper.

From a Piagetian point of view, one might expect that if a student were able physically to construct and reconstruct a piece of writing much as a child might build and rebuild structures with blocks, a new ability to visualize the writing would develop. Many teachers see the word processor as a vehicle for delivering this concretization of text construction and reconstruction for student writers.

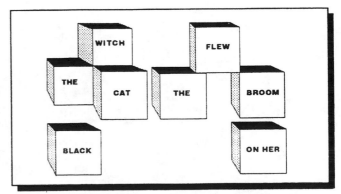

Construction and reconstruction of text in a Piagetian context of concretization of abstract ideas.

Yet the effect of word processing on children's writing behaviors is not fully known. Although assumptions that beneficial writing behaviors will be encouraged by the use of a word processor need to be corroborated more thoroughly through research, much of the information on word processing and writing is positive and encouraging. Effective research should concentrate on computer use within existing, successful writing pedagogies. Process writing, or more specifically teaching writing through a process approach is a popular and seemingly very effective theoretical model for teaching writing.

The research articles, position papers, and product reviews that follow are all related either directly or indirectly to teaching writing through the process approach with the aid of a computer. Much of the information is given over specifically to word processing and word processors. Auxiliary programs, such as spelling checkers, grammar checkers, and idea generators, which may be beneficial to the writing process are also discussed and reviewed both as technical tools in themselves, and in their roles or functions in the writing process.

References

Bruce, B., Michaels, S., & Watson-Gegeo, K. (1985). How computers can change the writing process. *Language Arts, 62*, 143-149.

Carey, R. (1985). *Patterns of microcomputer use by secondary school students at home and school.* Unpublished doctoral dissertation, University of Oregon, Eugene.

Graves, D. (1983). *Writing: Teachers and children at work.* Exeter, NH: Heinemann Educational Books.

Haley-James, S. (1981). Revising writing in the upper grades. *Language Arts, 58*, 562-566.

Hink, K. (1985). Let's stop worrying about revision. *Language Arts, 62*, 249-254.

Olds, H. (1985, March). A new generation of word processors. *Classroom Computer Learning*, pp. 22-25.

Pollitt, A. (1984). Warming to the wonders of the word processor: An English teacher's introduction to the computer. *The Computing Teacher, 11*(9), 48-49.

RESEARCH & POSITION PAPERS

The successful incorporation of computer based tools such as word processors into educational settings will be determined more by the method by which the computer use is employed, rather than the features of the tool itself. Unlike current computer assisted instruction, which has a fixed content and instructional strategy, word processors may be integrated into many different pedagogies at many levels or degrees of usage. It is up to the educator to decide how best the tool can assist the educational process.

The articles that follow discuss the use of word processors as a composition tool within the process model of writing instruction.

COMPUTERS AND THE LANGUAGE ARTS   Edited by Lynne Anderson-Inman

Microcomputers and the Improvement of Revision Skills

by Ernest Balajthy, Robert McKeveny and Lori Lacitignola

One of the principal obstacles to effective revision is the drudgery involved in rewriting. The painful experience of rewriting by hand, or even retyping, discourages students from making the changes needed to improve their compositions. Students think of classroom revision as punishment for not catching "mistakes" the first time. As a result, students often develop a negative attitude toward revision.

Microcomputers have already begun to revolutionize writers' concepts of revision. Used as a tool to free students from the mechanical burdens of recopying, word processing programs can provide a writing environment where revision is both encouraged and easily accomplished. This increased ease of editing has helped students develop a more positive attitude toward writing (Piper, 1983; Rodriguez, 1984).

There is also evidence to suggest that using word processing programs for writing and revision will affect the quality of student compositions. Instead of limiting their changes to the more superficial tasks of correcting misspellings or punctuation errors, students using word processors are often motivated to deal with higher level aspects of writing such as coherence and idea content. For example, in evaluating the effects of word processing software combined with training and teacher directions, Collier (1983) found increases in the number and complexity of operations students used to revise their compositions. Students using word processors made two-thirds more substitutions and reordered their sentences twice as often as students not using word processors.

The Teacher's Role

It is important, however, for teachers to realize that simply making word processors available to students will not automatically improve their writing or revision skills. Unfortunately, writing instruction in some classes has been replaced by instruction in the mechanics of word processing—how to adjust margins or print double-space, for example. There is a clear failing in such instruction. Word processing must supplement writing instruction, not replace it. Teachers still need to teach students the writing process, guide their construction of compositions and provide feedback helpful for revision. Word processors are simply tools that facilitate student output and encourage students to experiment with language.

This experimentation with language, viewing written text as fluid rather than static, is the key concept instructors should communicate to students. When word processors were first introduced into classrooms, many teachers believed children would just naturally carry out such experimentation. After all, they reasoned, it is easy to change a sentence or paragraph to see how an alternate construction reads. It is easy to move paragraphs to see if a different organizational pattern might improve the composition. Since these revisions are easy to do, won't all students do them?

Unfortunately, writing instruction in some classes has been replaced by instruction in the mechanics of word processing. . .Teachers still need to teach students the writing process. . . .

After several years researching the effects of word processors in the classroom, educators have found that students do not automatically engage in such in-depth experimentation (Hansen & Wilcox, 1984). While there is a statistically significant difference in the amount of writing and revision done by children using word processor than by those using pencils, this difference is often so small that it is of little educational significance. Instead of thoughtfully analyzing and revising composition structure, students using word processors will often limit their changes to superficial, mechanical alterations, unless taught by teachers to do more sophisticated revisions.

It is even possible that the computer itself inhibits experimentation. Perl (1980) noted that writers need to skim their text in order to maintain control over the evolution of ideas. And Harris (1985), in a study of six students using word processing, found that the small amount of text allowed on a monitor at one time seems to deter students from making large-scale organization changes. This finding is supported by observations that many students prefer using hard-copy printout to analyze overall composition structure.

It seems clear that "the instructor cannot remain passive and let the students figure out for themselves how they will write on the machines" (Hansen & Wilcox, 1984, p.3). Teachers must target their attention to at least two factors: modeling the revision process and monitoring student revisions.

Modeling revision. Teachers have long known the importance of modeling the thought processes involved in improving text by revision (Norton, 1985). This modeling should also occur in classes where word processors are used. For example, class discussion may focus on revisions by professional authors and show examples of the changes made between their first drafts and final copies. In addition, student compositions can be projected on a screen using an opaque projector, allowing the teacher to talk through the thought processes involved in improving early drafts.

Use of the word processor and large monitors (or projection systems) facilitates the modeling of revision strategies. Changes can be made in the text to illustrate specific types of revision, and the modified text can be neatly printed within seconds. Sections of text can be easily moved from one part of the composition to another and new paragraphs can be added as quickly as they can be typed into the computer.

Teachers may carry out such modeling in small groups or whole-class situations. Copies of compositions to be discussed can be distributed for prior reading so that informed discussion takes place and students have immediate access to the entire composition. Students can also be assigned to work in pairs or small peer groups to provide feedback and suggestions to one another. In individual conferences with the teacher, students can bring their disks and make suggested changes instantly.

Monitoring revision. Feedback on the appropriateness of revisions is also central to successful use of word processors. High school students and even at-risk college students often lack the language and conceptual sophistication to choose correctly from written alternatives. If students cannot tell which way of making a statement is more effective, they certainly cannot be expected to feel successful experimenting with language. Using a word processor will not suddenly confer linguistic or conceptual knowledge upon students. The teacher's critique and constant monitoring of production remains vital. Graves' (1976) work with the development of the writing process has shown that adults must work with students *during* writing rather than only *after* the written material has been produced.

Students can also play a role in monitoring the revision process. Assigning students to work in small groups to share disks and files encourages peer feedback. They can work together to organize and polish their written work, providing group evaluations of clarity and coherence as well as suggestions about usage (Schwartz, 1985). Groups also give writers a sense of audience, which leads to increased reading-writing integration within the classroom.

Teaching Revision Skills. A variety of exercises can be created with word processors to encourage the kinds of revision students ought to employ as they write. Each exercise can be stored in a word processing file on disk. Instructors might want to keep a master disk of such exercises and have students make personal copies for themselves so the exercises can be completed without altering the original.

For example, one file might include paragraphs of expository text with the sentences typed in jumbled order. Students read the paragraphs and decide on an effective sentence order, then they rearrange the sentences using the word processor's MOVE commands. Another file might contain a sample composition that lacks connectives and transitions. Students can then insert these items to provide structural coherence to the composition. Pairing students to work on these exercises encourages discussion and promotes closer analysis. Final copies of the results can be printed and submitted to the instructor. Even better, the teacher can meet with the students and discuss results as they appear on the monitor, having the students make necessary corrections or changes on the spot.

Software designed to teach effective revision skills can also be used. *Electric Writing: Editing on Paper and Screen* is a double-sided disk of text files containing editing exercises.

Skills on this disk include deleting letters and words, correcting misspelled words, ordering sentences in paragraphs, replacing words, inserting punctuation, combining sentences and ordering paragraphs. These files are designed for use with the *Bank Street Writer* or the *Milliken Word Processor*. In the exercises, the student helps an imaginary children's magazine editor. The editor gives hints on how to delete, insert, correct and move text, then the student follows those directions to edit article-like compositions. The program reinforces word processing and revision skills.

Students carry out tasks similar to the following: In an exercise deleting sentences that do not belong in the text, the student is given preliminary instruction on what makes a sentence essential or non-essential to a paragraph. The teacher then provides copies of an article containing errors of essential and non-essential sentences in paragraphs. Students are instructed to delete the nonessential sentences in each paragraph. After the students correct the errors on paper, they use the word processor to edit an identical file from the *Electric Writing* disk. Results can be printed on paper or submitted to the teacher for feedback on the disk.

The New Jersey Reading Association Microcomputer Committee makes two disks of exercises available to reading teachers, *NJRB BSW #1* and *NJRB BSW #2*. The disks are similar in format to the *Electric Writing* disks described above, and both are compatible with *Bank Street Writer*. Teachers seeking other ideas for exercises that employ word processing revision capabilities can check word processing manuals specifically designed for classroom use, such as *The Milliken Word Process* and *Bank Street Writer*. Richards' (1984) and Milone's (1985) books on word processing activities for the classroom offer many ideas that can be used to develop exercise disk files, as does the *Activity Book for the Bank Street Writer* (Scholastic, 1984).

A second possible role for software when teaching revision is to analyze text. Spelling checker programs such as *Bank Street Speller*, *Milliken's Spelling Checker*, *Sensible Speller*, and *Webster's New World Spelling Checker* identify misspellings in text and enable students to command automatic corrections. After typing text, the student loads a spelling checker into the computer. The program then reads the text and uses its bank of stored words (a software dictionary) to identify possible misspellings. The spelling checker then enables the student to make any necessary corrections by highlighting the word in the text and providing a sequence of commands to change the spellings. The process is repeated for all misspelled words.

Grammar checking programs can be used to check students' use of appropriate grammar. *Sensible Grammar* checks for punctuation errors and misused phrases under categories such as cliche, pompous, vague, and redundant. It works with many ProDOS word processing programs (*AppleWorks*, *Apple Writer*, *pfs: Write*, etc.) or with ASCII files. *Ghost Writer*, also available for a number of word processors, checks for homonym errors but is actually more of a style analyzer. Students can check their writing samples for a variety of transitions, overly long sentences, passive verbs, nominalization and repetitive use of words.

Also available for post-writing analysis are grammar checkers built into larger, more integrated packages. *Writer's Helper*, for example, is an integrated series of programs designed to assist writers in defining a topic and writing coherently about that topic. The style analyzer contained within the program assesses sentence length and text difficulty and checks for errors in grammar, punctuation, and usage. The MECC Composing Information Series is a similar set of integrated programs including *MECC Writer, MECC Write Start, MECC Speller*, and *MECC Editor*.

DLM has recently published a text analysis program within its adventure story program *The Writing Adventure*. Its proofreading subprogram scans children's word processed stories to identify a variety of possible errors, such as use of who-whom, its-it's, and so forth. The grammar checker is designed to pinpoint sections of text with a high probability of inappropriate usage. The relevant grammar rules are displayed on the monitor with examples of accurate and inaccurate usage. As with all these grammar checking programs, final determination as to whether a change should be made is up to the writer.

Thesaurus software can be used to supply writers with synonyms. Caution should be exercised, however. These programs are often far more awkward and time-consuming to use than a printed thesaurus and frequently offer fewer synonyms. In addition, use of thesaurus software can lead to stilted writing and misspelled words.

While text analysis programs cannot provide the quality of feedback possible from a trained teacher, they can serve two important functions: First, spelling checkers and style analyzers can perform a preliminary analysis of targeted features, allowing students to correct obvious errors before submitting a composition for review. Second, these programs can be used to perform analyses of written work that the teacher will not have time to correct in detail.

Conclusion

In any effective writing process approach to teaching composition, the teacher's role will remain crucial as modeler and monitor. With easy-to-learn word processing programs available, microcomputers will inevitably play an increasingly central role in writing instruction. Integrated packages such as *The Writing Adventure* and *Writer's Helper*, which guide students through choosing topics, organizing their ideas, writing and revision, are already available. Such programs will free teachers from the more mundane tasks associated with writing instruction and allow students greater independence and more personalized guidance as they write.

Computers cannot replace teacher feedback on writing. They do serve to make the teacher's job easier, encourage increased writing and closer revision, provide limited analysis of composition quality and establish an effective setting for peer discussion and group feedback.

Dr. Ernest Balajthy, State University of New York—College at Geneseo, Geneseo, NY 14454; Robert McKeveny, Warsaw
Elementary School, Warsaw, NY 14569; and Lori Lacitignola, Pavilion Central School, Pavilion, NY 14525.

References

Collier, R. M. (1983). "The word processor and revision strategies." *College Composition and Communication, 34*, 149-155.

Graves, D. H. (1976). "Research update—language arts textbooks: A writing process evaluation." *Language Arts, 53*, 645-651.

Hansen, C. & Wilcox, L. (1984). "Adapting microcomputers for use in college composition." Paper presented at the Delaware Valley Writing Council, Villanova, PA. (ERIC Document Reproduction Service No. 247 609).

Harris, J. (1985). "Student writers and word processing: A preliminary evaluation." *College Composition and Communication, 36*, 323-330.

Milone, M.N. (1985). *Every teacher's guide to word processing*. Englewood Cliffs, NJ.

Norton, D.E. (1985). *The effective teaching of language arts*. Columbus, OH: Charles Reston.

Perl, S. (1980). "Understanding composing." *College Composition and Communication, 31*, 363-369.

Piper, K. (1983). "Word processing in the classroom: Using microcomputer-delivered sentence combining exercises with elementary students." Paper presented at National Educational Computing Conference, Baltimore, MD.

Richards, M. (1984). *Word processing activities for kids*. Reston, VA: Reston Publishing.

Schwartz, H. (1983). *Interactive writing: Composing with a word processor*. New York: Holt, Rinehart, and Winston.

Schwartz, L. (1983). "Teaching writing in the age of the word processor and personal computers." *Educational Technology, 23*, 33-35.

Scholastic. (1984). *Activity book for the bank street writer*. New York: Scholastic.

Software

Bank Street Speller. Scholastic, Inc.

Bank Street Writer. Scholastic, Inc.

Electric Writing: Editing on Paper and Screen. Creative Publications.

Ghost Writer. Minnesota Educational Computing Consortium.

MECC Editor, MECC Speller, MECC Writer, MECC Write Start. Minnesota Educational Computing Consortium.

Milliken Word Processor. Milliken Publishing Co.

NJRA BSW #1, NJRA BSW #2. New Jersey Reading Association Microcomputer Committee.

Sensible Grammar. Sensible Software.

Sensible Speller. Sensible Sortware.

Sensible Checker. Milliken Publishing Co.

Webster's New World Spelling Checker. Simon & Schuster Computer Software.

The Writing Adventure. DLM Teaching Resources.

IN SUMMARY

Microcomputers and the Improvement of Revision skills

- Writing with a word processor can affect the quality of student compositions.

- Word processing must supplement writing instruction, not replace it. Teachers must still teach the writing process.

- Modeling and monitoring by the teacher of activities during the revision stage of the writing process is critical.

- Revision skills can be effectively taught using a word processor through practice exercises created by the teacher or purchased from software publishers.

COMPUTERS AND THE LANGUAGE ARTS   Edited by Robert Shostak

Assessing Our Assumptions
by Elizabeth B. Leonardi and Janet L. McDonald

In the past 12 months I have read dozens of articles describing how effective the microcomputer is in teaching writing. Most were good pieces discussing specific techniques for accomplishing a variety of writing activities using word processing software. Each article espoused a favorite activity: prewriting, freewriting, editing, keyboarding. Each article seemed to imply that using its singular approach would practically guarantee success in the classroom. I sensed that something was missing.

The ideas I had been reading about seemed disjointed, separate pieces of an instructional puzzle whose pattern I could not clearly discern. None of the articles seemed to offer a complete instructional algorithm based on sound principles of teaching; that is, until Elizabeth Leonardi and Janet McDonald submitted the feature of this month's column. Here, for the first time, I was able to see practitioners taking the time to analyze the instructional problem by examining the basic assumptions of the teaching-learning task and offering instructional solutions that mode sense. It is an article which deserves your careful attention because it moves so successfully from theory to practice.

In many ways, teaching is a process of identifying, then connecting, two points. One point represents the goal of instruction, the knowledge we wish our students to attain. The other represents the point from which the students can proceed, their prior knowledge. Connecting the points is a matter of devising a logical sequence of steps which build from the students' foundation of knowledge toward the goal. Learning will not take place unless three assumptions of the teaching process are valid: that the goal is meaningful and attainable; that the assessment of student knowledge is accurate; and that the steps are indeed logical, sequential, and appropriate in terms of scope.

Normally experience enables us to establish the validity of our assumptions. But teaching writing using a word processor is still too new a process for our assumptions to have been thoroughly tested and established. We would therefore be remiss if we failed to continuously examine our procedures by consciously identifying and evaluating the assumptions we have made about utilizing the word processor in the English classroom.

First Assumption
Undermining the sequence of teaching writing using word processing software is the assumption that the software itself is so easy to use that students need only minimal instruction in how to manipulate its editing features prior to using it. But to require students to write using a system with which they are only minimally familiar is to ask them to attend to two learning tasks at once. Doing so typically results in their using only the most simple surface-level revisions such as changing spelling and

punctuation and deleting and adding words; they do not permit the manipulation of significant units of text. Beginning users who do attempt to rearrange sentences and paragraphs or change major units of text do so by shifting their attention from the writing process to the editing process. They risk sacrificing the primary task of writing to the secondary task of using a word processor.

To avoid such task confusion, we should begin our use of the computer in writing with use of the computer in its first capacity, as a computer. The microcomputer, equipped with word processing software, is a tool to be mastered before it is applied. This means instructing students in machine fundamentals such as booting the system, and in word processing fundamentals such as entering and editing text and retrieving files. Thus, word processing competency is removed from the sequence of writing instruction into the position of prerequisite knowledge. As a consequence, word processing instruction need not be regarded as an integral part of the English curriculum. We can invite other disciplines to assume the task of machine instruction while we emphasize machine application.

Second Assumption
A second assumption we make when incorporating word processing in our writing instruction is that the nature of the writing task itself is of little importance. But one writing task may enable us to more fully capitalize on the tool's potential than another. The choice of the writing assignment is critical if we are to do more than simply substitute the computer for the pen. Since the value of word processing in teaching writing is usually attributed to its ability to facilitate revisions, it would seem logical to select writing tasks which encourage students' willingness to revise. Thus we couple students' willingness to revise with a tool which does so easily.

For students to be willing to revise, they must be committed to the writing task. Such a commitment is more often linked to the desire to express an idea than to the need to fulfill an assignment. So the first step in incorporating the microcomputer within the sequence of writing instruction is to encourage students to write for the sole purpose of generating ideas. This encouragement could take the form of brief but frequent freewriting exercises or a weekly journal in addition to regularly graded writing assignments. Such tasks allow students to write without being inhibited by a concern for form, and the teacher to respond without having to evaluate. In time, they should provide a source of thoughtful if unpolished writing.

Having developed a source of material in need of revision, we can use the microcomputer in its second capacity, as a typewriter. Ask your students to select one piece of the ungraded writing which they like, to enter that selection on the microcomputer, save it on disk and obtain several printed copies. It would be inappropriate at this point to ask students to also revise their compositions, for although we have redefined the selection as prewriting, we have yet to either introduce the need to revise or provide the direction for doing so. If you wish to avoid the issue of keyboarding ability, the compositions can be entered by students in a keyboarding class or by volunteers after school.

Third Assumption

The inclination to introduce revision prematurely is indicative of the third of our assumptions, that students know how to revise; they simply don't. As a consequence, we rarely consider *defining* revision as an essential step. Our failure to define revision, coupled with our tendency to edit students' grammatical errors, leads students to equate revision with editing. Rather than envision a reader who has prior knowledge and revise according to that imagined reader's need for comprehension, students typically envision a reader who is essentially an evaluator and revise according to that reader's concern for form. Even students who are able to manipulate significant units of text with relative ease restrict their use of word processing software to changing spelling, punctuation, and words. Such limited use of the computer's capacity may reveal an inability to revise, not a refusal to do so.

To clarify the purpose of revision, another essential step in writing instruction is to foster a sense of audience. That sense can be encouraged by identifying a specific audience whose prior knowledge and lack of comprehension can be made explicit. By asking students to share the computer-generated copies of their compositions with a group of their classmates, you introduce their peers as an audience. Through group discussion of each composition, that audience's prior knowledge and lack of comprehension becomes apparent. Finally, by directing each group to help its members discover the subject of each composition, identify the existing and missing details necessary for comprehension and focus, and select a pattern of development, you define revision as a process of rethinking and reformulating a composition.

With revision thus defined, we can use the microcomputer in its third capacity: as an editing tool. Students should begin by recalling the rough draft previously saved on disk. By asking them to revise an existing draft rather than write a second draft, you introduce them to the potential power of the computer. Revising with a pen requires that they change some of a composition while reproducing the rest. But the computer enables them to attend exclusively to those areas in need of revision. The capacity of the computer is further revealed as students attempt to incorporate the changes recommended by the group. Rewriting with a pen requires that students commit themselves "in ink" to a proposed change. The computer frees students to experiment. Revisions can themselves be revised with a few keystrokes. Once all the changes have been made,

students need only to save their second drafts and print copies. If they are instructed to save each draft under a different name, they'll have legible, accessible records of the evolution of their compositions.

Fourth Assumption

We accept the students' second drafts as the final product to evaluate only if we assume that the appropriate goal for use of the microcomputer in writing instruction is an acceptable written product. To accept this assumption is to impose upon ourselves limitations which, prior to the advent of the microcomputer, were imposed by time. Time limits the number of revisions we can ask our students to make. We are therefore forced to accept as adequate any student writing which fulfills an assignment without grossly violating the rules of syntax. Writing instruction is reduced to teaching the rules of grammar and providing the opportunity to write. As a consequence, those students who write poorly at the beginning of the year are likely to remain poor writers, those who write well will continue to write well, and those who improve are likely to do so as a consequence of maturing rather than instruction.

Since use of a word processor significantly reduces the time it takes to revise, we no longer need to sacrifice teaching to time. We can use the computer to improve our students' control and understanding of the writing process, not only asking them to revise, but to revise more than once. With more revision comes more opportunity for us to teach and, consequently, more opportunity for our students to learn. The computer becomes more than an editing machine; it becomes a teaching implement.

Reassessing the Assumptions

Our assumptions have led us to accept the microcomputer as an integral part of writing instruction but prevented us from exploiting its potential as a teaching tool. If our students are to fully benefit from the technology, its addition to our writing curriculum must be a sequential process which builds on their prior knowledge of the computer as a word processing machine. Having established that our students can competently manipulate the software's editing features, we can couple development of prewriting with the use of the computer as a typewriter and copy generator. Having taught our students that revision is a process of rethinking and reformulating an essay, we can couple establishing a peer audience with use of the computer as an editing tool. Finally, having emphasized the writing process, we can couple our students' capacity as writers with use of the computer as a writing instrument. Then it will be time again to reassess our assumptions.

Elizabeth Leonardi, Old Peck Hill Rd., RD #3, Box 59C, Gloversville, NY 12078; and Janet McDonald, ED 109, State University of New York-Albany, 400 Washington Ave., Albany, NY 12222.

IN SUMMARY

Assessing Our Assumptions

- Teaching students how to use a word processor perhaps should be taught separately from composition instruction so as to avoid task confusion by the student.

- Selection of writing tasks that naturally encourage students to make changes in their writing complements the key power of using a word processor, that is, revision.

- Clarification for students of the purpose of content revision as opposed to editing for errors is necessary.

- The time saved by revising with a word processor rather than recopying by hand, allows students to revise more often. Consequently, with more revision comes more opportunity to learn.

Peer Conferencing, Computers, and Persuasive Writing: A Recipe to Encourage Revision

by Jane M. Ritter

Reprinted from Proceedings of the 6th Annual "Extending the Human Mind: Computers in Education" Summer Conference, *The Center for Advanced Technology in Education (CATE)*, Eugene, Oregon.

The marriage of computers and writing instruction has received the blessings of many, including teachers of writing, developers of curriculum, and designers of computer hardware and software. Although research on the effects of children's use of word processors to write and revise continues to produce variable results, it is still commonly accepted that "computers are, or will be, the means by which our students will produce most of the formal writing they do as their productive careers span into the 21st century" (Bridwell & Duin, 1985, p. 116). This belief is reflected in curricular changes being adopted at schools throughout the country that introduce strands in keyboarding skills and the use of word processors. If word processors are to be successfully incorporated into the elementary writing curriculum, then the goal of research in this area must be to identify strategies that take best advantage of the technology to effectively instruct children as they write. One must first have an understanding about the processes involved in writing and then determine how the word processor might be incorporated into writing instruction to facilitate those processes. Insight into these processes is gained by examining various models of the writing process.

Models of the Writing Process

Several models of the writing process have been proposed to identify the subprocesses of writing and to describe the interaction among those subprocesses. They generally fall into one of two groups: linear stage models and recursive process models. Linear stage models describe the writing process as a linear series of stages through which writers pass as they approach completion of a written product (Britton, Burgess Martin, McLeod, & Rosen, 1975; Rohman & Wlecke, 1964). These stages include prewriting (planning), composing (writing), and revising (editing). Recursive process models describe a recursive interleaving of the writer through many subprocesses, including planning, remembering, generating, monitoring, reviewing, evaluating, and revising (Flower & Hayes, 1981; Graves, 1975; Nold, 1981). In the recursive models, subprocesses can occur simultaneously or can interrupt any other subprocess at any point during the act of writing. Recursive models reflect the current shift in emphasis from product to process in writing instruction. Although revision is named as a subprocess in both linear and recursive models, its definition varies greatly between the two types of models.

The Subprocess of Revision

In the linear models of the writing process, revision is presented as the final stage of the process and consists of the editing of surface features of the text to correct errors. In recursive models, revision can occur at any time and can interrupt any other process. Revision in this context involves reviewing, evaluating, and changing content and ideas. It requires that the writer detect and resolve discrepancies between what has been written, or the inprocess text, and a set of abstract representations of goals and plans for the finished product, or the intended text (Bryson, Lindsay, Joram & Woodruff, 1986). The process approach to writing, currently employed in many writing classrooms, is based on recursive models of the writing process. Teachers who employ a process approach encourage children to continually review their writing and revise as necessary. For young writers, however, revision is a skill that does not come naturally (Pufahl, 1984). Revision must be taught.

All revisions are outcomes of evaluations (Flower & Hayes, 1981). According to Hilgers (1984), successful revision results from "a series of correctly made evaluations the result in a 'yes...continue' decision...coupled with correctly made evaluations that result in a 'no...change' decision" (p. 367). The writing conference has been widely used as one method to elicit evaluations and to motivate revisions.

The Writing Conference

During the ideal writing conference, the writer and his or her teacher orally discuss the piece of writing, exchanging ideas about how the text might be interpreted, where problems might exist, and how those problems might be resolved. Recent research on conferencing reveals, however, that typical teacher-student conferencing tends to be a unilateral communication dominated by the teacher (Florio-Ruane, 1986; Freedman & Sperling, 1985). The content and direction of the conference depend on how closely the student's text already matches the teacher's schema for the topic being written about (Michaels, Ulichney, & Watson-Gegeo, 1986).

Although a certain amount of control by the teacher is necessary to impart new information during instruction, too much control may result in a loss of ownership by the writer over the piece of writing. Students quickly begin to form hypotheses on what the teacher wants to see in their writing and then write for the teacher to evaluate rather than to communicate their ideas (Dyson, 1984). In other words, the student writer "throws the teacher a bone to pacify him, knowing full well that his theme does not at all represent what he can do" (Moffett, 1983, pp. 193-194).

One solution to the problem of teacher dominance is the use of peer group conferences in which a group of peers collaborate to discuss and evaluate each other's writing. Peer conferencing has become an established pedagogical method in many writing programs and has been promoted by many writing specialists (Calkins, 1980; Flynn, 1984; Freedman, 1981; Graves, 1983). The group interaction supplies the writer with the necessary feedback and reflects the variety of opinions and interpretations that exist within a group of readers. The teacher can continue to monitor the group conferences, actively participating from time to time to model appropriate conferencing techniques and to introduce new evaluative criteria.

Another problem with many writing conferences is that the writer simply forgets much of what was discussed during the conference and often incorporates only what was discussed at the end of the conference. Some teachers suggest that children maintain lists during the conference to remind themselves of what was discussed.

Computers and the Writing Process

One major problem associated with the writing process still needs to be addressed: the tedium of the recopying that is necessary to incorporate revisions and still produce a legible paper. Recopying hand-written text is a tedious burden that discourages writers from revising substantially (Shaugnessy, 1977). This aspect of the writing process is the one most often mentioned when touting the advantages of using computers to write.

The computer does indeed eliminate much of the tedium associated with the recopying that is a necessary part of revising. It provides children with a tool to easily insert, delete, and move text. "Not having to re-copy helps writers to compose freely, focusing on what they want to say...the ease of revision encourages writers to experiment and to view their writing as dynamic" (Daiute, 1983, p. 139).

Nonetheless, expectations of computers in the writing process have been unreasonably high. One cannot expect children who have little or no experience with revising to spontaneously take advantage of the word processing functions that facilitate revision (Bridwell & Duin, 1985; Pufahl, 1984). One cannot focus on the computer alone, isolated from the context in which it is used. Recent research concludes that the instructional methods used to teach writing determine to what extent student writers make use of the word processor (Collier, 1983; Evans, 1986; Sommers, 1985).

It seems then that the ideal situation in which to teach revision is one which motivates students to write and revise by providing a genre of writing that inherently demands revision, a variety of feedback about what they have written, a method for remembering the feedback, and access to tools that make revision operations easy to perform. The computer plays a role in all of these when one employs a computer-facilitated group conferencing technique with children who are doing persuasive writing.

A Computer-Facilitated Group Conferencing Technique

Using computer-facilitated group conferencing, the writer and a group of conferencers, sometimes including the teacher, gather around the computer to read and discuss a piece of writing. The writer first reads his or her text aloud with no interruptions from the group. Next, group members provide the writer with feedback, focusing on the content of the writing. Questions and comments ought to emphasize such things as completeness of ideas, clarity, logical organization, and effective word choice. Surface features such as spelling and punctuation must be addressed only if they interfere with the meaning of the text. Compliments should be voiced along with suggestions.

In addition to orally discussing the piece of writing, paraphrased conference comments are also typed directly into the text at an appropriate point. The appropriate point is determined by the writer and the student who made the comment. The writers themselves paraphrase the comments into brief phrases that are sufficient to remind them of the discussion that occurred during the conference. This method provides the writer with an abridged record of the conference discussion as well as indicating where revisions might be placed. More importantly, the oral interaction during the conference and paraphrasing of comments by the writer increases the involvement of the writer in the writing process.

Persuasive writing is an excellent domain in which to teach this method. Afflerbach (1985) found that sixth and seventh-grade children who were assigned informational reports of a persuasive nature were much more likely to revise than if the reports were purely informational. Following peer group conferences, these students felt a need to gather more information and revise their papers to defend their positions. Students who once approached revision with "funereal enthusiasm" began to view revision as a purposeful part of the writing process.

Many questions have been asked about the effectiveness of children's use of computers to write and revise. Does the computer influence the way children write and revise? Does the computer encourage children to use more sophisticated revision strategies than they would normally use with pencil and paper? Does the computer affect children's perceptions or attitudes about writing and revising? Does the computer have an effect on the quality of writing that children produce? It has become clear that it is insufficient to ask those questions about computers in isolation from the context in which they are used. Those same questions must be asked about computers as components of a sound teaching technique.

References

Afflerbach, P. "Overcoming children's reluctance to revise informational writing." *Journal of Teaching Writing, 4,* (1985). pp. 170-176.

Bridwell, L.S., & Duin, A. "Looking in-depth at writers: Computers as writing medium and research tool." In J.L. Collins & E.A. Sommers (Eds.), *Writing on-line: Using computers in the teaching of writing.* Upper Montclair, NJ: Boynton/Cook, 1985. pp. 115-133.

Britton, J., Burgess, A., Martin, N., McLeod, A., Rosen, H. *The development of writing abilities.* London: Macmillan Education, 1975.

Bryson, M., Lindsay, P.H., Joram, E., & Woodruff, E. "Augmented word-processing: The influence of task characteristics and mode of production on writers' cognitions." Paper, American Educational Research Association, San Francisco, CA, April, 1986.

Calkins, L.M. "Children learn the writer's craft." *Language Arts, 57,* (1980), pp. 207-213.

Collier, R. "The word processor and revision strategies." *College Composition and Communication, 34,* (1983), pp. 149-155.

Daiute, C. *Writing and computers.* Reading, MA: Addison-Wesley Publishing Company, 1983.

Dyson, A. "Learning to write/Learning to do school: Emergent writers' interpretations of school literacy tasks." *Research in the Teaching of English, 18,* (1984), pp. 233-264.

Evans, B. "The integration of word processing and composition instruction in fifth and sixth grades." Paper, American Educational Research Association, San Francisco, CA, April, 1986.

Flower, L. & Hayes, J. R. "A cognitive process theory of writing." *College Composition and Communication, 32* (1981), pp. 265-387.

Flynn, E. "Students as readers of their classmates' writing: Some implications for peer critiquing." *The Writing Instructor, 3,* (1984), pp. 20-128.

Freedman, S. "Influences on evaluators of expository essays: Beyond the text." *Research in the Teaching of English, 5,* (1981), pp 245-255.

Freedman, S., & Sperling, R. "Written language acquisition: The role of response and the writing conference." In S.W. Freedman (Ed.), *The acquisition of written language: Response and revision.* Norwood, NJ: Ablex, 1985, pp. 106-130.

Graves, D. "An examination of the writing processes of seven-year-old children." *Research in the Teaching of English, 9,* (1975), pp. 227-241.

Graves, D. *Writing: Teachers and children at work.* Portsmouth, NH: Heinemann, 1983.

Hilgers, T. "Toward a taxonomy of beginning writers' evaluative statements on written compositions." *Written Communication, 1,* (1984), pp. 365-383.

Michaels, S., Ulichney, P., & Watson-Gegeo, K. "Social processes and written products: Teacher expectations, writing conferences, and student texts." Paper, American Educational Research Association, San Francisco, CA, April, 1986.

Moffett, J. *Teaching the universe of discourse.* Boston: Houghton Mifflin, 1983.

Nold, E. "Revising." In C.H. Frederiksen, & J.F. Dominic, (Eds.), *Writing: The nature, development, and teaching of written communication.* Hillsdale, NJ: Lawrence J. Erlbaum, 1981, pp. 67-79.

Pufahl, J. "Response to Richard M. Collier, 'The word processor and revision strategies.'" *College Composition and Communication, 35,* (1984), pp. 91-93.

Rohman, G., & Wlecke, A. "Pre-writing: The construction and application of models for concept formation in writing." (U.S. Office of Education Cooperative Research Project No. 2174). East Lansing, MI: Michigan State University, 1964.

Shaugnessy, M.P. *Errors and expectations: A guide for the teacher of basic writing.* New York: Oxford University Press, 1977.

IN SUMMARY

Peer Conferencing, Computers, and Persuasive Writing:
A Recipe to Encourage Revision

- The process approach to teaching writing encourages students to continually review their writing and revise as necessary. Revision must be taught, however, it does not always occur naturally with or without a computer.

- Peer conferencing is an established method for facilitating revision in many successful writing programs.

- During a computer-facilitated group conference, paraphrased comments may be typed into the text of a piece of writing as a record for the writer's reference when returning to the piece to revise.

- Persuasive writing can provide students with a need to gather more information and revise more than when writing an informational composition.

Learning to Write with a New Tool: Young Children and Word Processing

by Jessica Kahn

For two years I have been observing young emergent writers as they learn to use word processing in the context of a process approach to writing instruction. My purpose has been to document some of the ways in which word processing influences their newly developing writing practices. What follows are some observations on the word processing experiences of second and third grade students learning to write in classrooms using different interpretations of process writing.

Developmentally, this age is fascinating, for seven-and eight-year-olds have started to shed the egocentrism and confidence of first graders (Calkins, 1986). They are beginning to look outside themselves for evaluation, less certain of their own perfection. This can be used to advantage by a skilled writing teacher, making second and third grade an appropriate time for children to begin conferencing with each other about their writing. Conferencing helps seven- and eight-year-olds evaluate their writing from a reader's perspective, making it easier to see where revisions might be necessary. As children learn about drafting and revising their drafts, they begin to form a concept of writing for an audience.

Children, however, are hampered in their writing by the difficulties of transferring thought to paper. These difficulties have more to do with small motor coordination and the permanence of pencil marks on paper than with the ability to compose a meaningful sentence. In other words, at this stage in their development children are burdened simultaneously by mechanical and compositional concerns during the writing process. For this reason it is particularly helpful to understand how the computer fits into emergent writers' practices. How do young children feel about writing with a computer as opposed to writing with pencil and paper? How does writing with a computer influence their emerging skills or their attitudes toward the writing process?

For the last two years I have been involved in an ethnographic study of teachers and children learning to write with word processing. Since the research is based on the assumption that the context in which writing occurs shapes the ways in which writing is practiced, a brief description of the two different classrooms follows.

The teacher of the second grade classroom chose to primarily use computers with her language arts group, which meets for an hour and a half each morning. In addition to three district-mandated writing assignments, the second grade teacher asks her students to write pieces every week, usually on topics drawn from their reading assignments. After students write their first drafts (either in their journals or on the computer), the teacher checks them for usage, spelling, and punctuation, and then the

children correct their drafts. The children who work at the computer sometimes do their corrections on the word processor and then print their finished pieces. The children who do their drafting in journals either recopy their pieces with pencil and paper or type their corrected drafts into the computer so that the stories can be made into books.

Although similarly constrained by district-mandated writing projects, the third grade teacher has adopted a structure somewhat more compatible with process writing for her language arts group. She sometimes allows the children to choose their own writing topics and has taken a great deal of class time to teach the steps of the writing process directly. For example, when the children are expected to write an opinion paper, she teaches prewriting by providing them with a ditto on which they can jot down their ideas—pros on one side, cons on the other and conclusions at the bottom. Most writing projects in this class take several weeks to complete. During this time each child reads his/her piece to another child, and the teacher conferences with each student, pointing out problems in mechanics and expression. As skills improve the children are expected to seek out an "editing expert" in the class for help with mechanics, and as the year progresses, the teacher increasingly expects the children to take charge of their writing.

These two classrooms are described in some detail in order to place children's experiences writing with word processors within the context of a larger writing curriculum, reflecting individual teacher expectations. Understanding the dissimilarities between the two classrooms makes the similarities in the children's word processing experiences more striking, and helps to account for some of the differences in their behavior and attitudes.

Observations of students in these two classrooms revealed some interesting commonalties in the ways in which word processing was incorporated into the writing process. All of the children seemed to think that word processing was easier than writing with pencil and paper. Furthermore, they reported that pressing keys was more fun because, in the words of a second grader, "It doesn't hurt my hand." The children seemed to write for longer periods of time at the computer, and they knew that they were doing so. The pieces written at the computer were longer and possessed fewer of the gaps in meaning that often characterize children's writing. Students at both grade levels said they never wrote such long pieces with paper and pencil because, as one child said, "It wears me out."

In addition, the children accepted the idea of making changes more readily when word processing. Once the students realized that they did not have to do battle with an eraser, they were quick to ask, "What else needs to be fixed?" The third graders learned to use the spelling checker incorporated into *Bank Street Writer III*, and they loved it. The spelling checker highlights any word which does not appear in its dictionary and offers a list of alternate spellings. The children were good at recognizing the correct spelling if it appeared on the list, and thanked the computer when it replaced the misspelled word with the correct one.

Students in both grades loved the printouts. They seemed to care a great deal about the appearance of their written work, and judging from their use of the spelling checker, cared a great deal about correct spelling. Their satisfaction with the printouts and their willingness to return to the computer when another child noticed a mistake suggest that the students valued perfection and were striving toward that goal in their writing. Perhaps the children did not strive for the same perfection when writing with pencil and paper because it was so difficult to achieve. Word processing became a tool that made it easier to get things right.

Although both the second and third graders in this study found that word processing helped them to write for longer periods of time, write longer pieces, and take more interest in revising and correcting those pieces, there were also differences in the ways in which the two groups used word processing. The second graders were less interested in the word processing system, grateful for what it enabled but not extensively *curious* about extra keys and additional features. It was sufficient for them to be able to get their writing done. In the second grade, the children generally wrote a piece during one sitting at the computer, and so had little need for saving or retrieving what they had written. It was not surprising, therefore, that they seemed vague about the purpose of saving and retrieving their compositions. They all, however, remembered how to print, and loved to get hard copies of their work.

The third graders revised more extensively and spent a larger number of class periods on one piece of writing. They seemed to have mastered saving and retrieving their pieces, probably because they had to do it more often. It also seemed that the third graders approached the computer more systematically than the second graders, relying less on "magical explanations" of computer functions. Within the third grade, word processing experience had been made a desirable commodity. Students who began the year with prior computer experience were designated "computer experts." Perhaps because computer expertise was clearly valued, the children were eager to learn how to get special effects such as underlining, indenting, and paginating to create books. The students even demonstrated an understanding and appreciation for the workings of the spelling checker and learned to predict which words would not be in the dictionary (e.g., proper names and makes of automobiles).

The children I observed clearly found that word processing facilitates the writing process. This seemed to have a ripple effect on the children's writing practices and their attitudes toward writing. For example, there were 24 entries in the Young Authors Contest from the third grade class, eight of which were first drafted on the word processor. From the 24 entries there were eight winners, four of which had drafted their papers on the computer. Is there something about drafting a story on the computer that is reflected in improved quality? I asked the third grade teacher whether she had an explanation for why these children won the contest. She said that she thought their pieces were fuller and contained fewer "potholes" than the pieces which were drafted with pencil and paper. Potholes are those gaping conceptual holes where the writer has failed to supply bridges from one side to another. Frequently they occur because a child does not have the patience or energy to write out every idea. As I watched the children write at the computer, I noticed that they circled back in their writing, adding phrases or whole sentences, revising as they composed. It seems that word processing helps children to eliminate potholes because it is easier to go back and add a sentence on the computer screen than it is to do so on paper.

Similarly, word processing affects how young students experience the writing process. For example, a poll of some of the students in this study revealed that they preferred to write with word processing because "it gives me more time to think." Let us speculate about where that additional time to think might come from. When children write with word processing they do not have to worry about their handwriting. Specifically, they do no have to think about spacing their letters, keeping them on the lines, or shaping them correctly. The children also never have to think about allowing time to copy their pieces over on "good paper." Calkins (1986) suggests that the goal of teaching writing to second graders is "fluency and voice." Facilitating the mechanical process of producing text frees up time for children to think about the messages they intend to convey, thus helping them develop both fluency and voice. In this way, word processing helps teachers and children to improve the quality of writing in a classroom.

But—and this is a crucial point—the primary responsibility for teaching writing is always the teacher's. Teachers are learning how to teach process writing. They are supporting children's writing attempts by providing helpful prewriting activities. In classrooms where the teaching of process writing is an evolving art, the computer is a valuable addition. It makes it easier for children to achieve fluency in their writing and it allows them to make revisions as they write. In short, it supports and facilitates the practices that these teachers are trying to encourage.

Jessica Kahn, Graduate School of Education, University of Pennsylvania, 37th & Walnut Streets, Philadelphia, PA 19104.

Reference

Calkins, L. (1986). *The Art of Teaching Writing*. Portsmouth, NH: Heinemann Educational Books, Inc.

Software

The Bank Street Writer III. Scholastic Software, 730 Broadway, New York, NY 10003. Available for Apple IIc, IIe, IIGS; IBM PC; and Tandy 1000, all with 128K.

IN SUMMARY

Learning to Write with a New Tool:
Young children and Word Processing

- Young children are burdened by both mechanical and compositional concerns during the writing process.

- Writing projects can take as long as several weeks to complete.

- The children valued perfection in their compositions and showed a willingness to return to the computer when a mistake was found.

- Word processing seemed to help children eliminate conceptual holes in their stories.

COMPUTERS AND THE LANGUAGE ARTS   **Edited by Lynne Anderson-Inman**

Writing with Word Processors for Remedial Students

by Susan B. Neuman and Catherine Cobb-Morocco

Student: I don't know what to write about. I hate school.
Teacher: Why don't you write about why you hate school?
Slowly the student writes: The reason I do not like school is because when I have to get to school early at 8:45 and get out at 2:45.
Teacher: Why don't you like that?
Student: I don't know. I just don't like school.
Teacher: You must have a reason for not liking school. What's tough about getting to school early?
Student: I have to wake up at 5:00 or 4:00.
Teacher: Then tell me, "I have to wake up at...."
The student writes, "I have to get up at 4:00 or 5:30." That's all I want to write Mrs. F because that's all I can think of.

This dialogue illustrates the way many remedial students approach the writing process. They tend to regard writing as an unpleasant chore, a task to be completed as quickly as possible or not done at all. For remedial students who spend many hours per week in tutorial or resource room settings working on their reading and writing skills, the "out of ideas feeling" comes frequently (Johnston & Allington, 1985). By the time they reach fourth and fifth grade, most of these students are convinced they lack the ability to write and in many cases believe they have nothing to say.

An increasing number of teachers and researchers are exploring the use of word processors as writing tools for students with poor writing skills (Behrman, 1984; Daiute, 1985). The hope is that the computer will be a more engaging tool than the pencil, that it will cramp the hand less than conventional writing tools and make revision easier. Presumably, if students are more willing to write and are able to write and revise more easily, the overall quality of their written products will improve.

To learn more about how resource room teachers use word processing to improve the writing skills of remedial students, we have been conducting a two-year study of five elementary-level resource room teachers. Through observations and interviews, we have gathered data on the instructional interactions of these teachers with 14 remedial students: seven boys and seven girls. The students are from diverse socioeconomic and ethnic backgrounds and bring to the resource room varying degrees of difficulty with the writing process.

Analysis of the results from the first year of this study led to four conclusions about effective writing instruction for remedial students using the computer. These four conclusions are shared below, illustrated with examples and dialogue from participating classrooms.

1. Initial keyboarding and word processing skills should be taught separately from writing instruction.

Students need training in computer usage and word processing before being able to use the technology as a tool to write. The teachers in our study found this to be true in two areas. First, the students had to be familiar with the keyboard. Although it was not necessary that students learn to touch type, their skills in keyboarding needed to be sufficiently refined so that they no longer had to hunt and peck for letters—only peck. Five minutes of practice, two days a week using *Stickybear Type* helped students increase their typing speed to a rate more commensurate with the flow of their ideas (Neuman and Morocco, 1987). Second, the students needed some initial skills in word processing, such as use of the delete, insert, save, and print functions. Without these initial skills, attention tended to be drawn away from the writing task to matters related to the machine. Here is one example.

Teacher: Last session you wrote about the foods you like to eat. I'd like you to finish that today.
Kurt: I don't have to type this, do I?
Teacher: Yes, you do.
Kurt: This is going to take me years to do it. Can anyone type this for me?
Teacher: No. You can type it for you.
Kurt types "I cook turkey."
Kurt: I'm through. Absolutely, totally.
Teacher: Now you have to go to the transfer menu.
Kurt: Oh, man.

We found that in settings where students had been given separate practice sessions to familiarize them with the keyboard, keyboarding fluency developed much more quickly than it did for students whose skills were simply allowed to evolve. Although some students were able to acquire keyboarding facility in the latter context, most were not. A few students who were still unable to locate keys quickly after several months evidenced some computer phobia—an extreme reluctance to write on the computer. One student would angrily call the computer "Stupid!" possibly attempting to project his own feelings of inadequacy onto the computer.

Word processing is not easy for elementary-level remedial students. It involves a number of operations that at first do not appear to make sense. For example, the delete function is difficult because it requires a student to position the cursor one letter beyond the actual letter he or she is trying to erase. Other functions, such as saving text, need to be taught explicitly so that students will develop confidence in their use of the machine. For instance, forgetting to save a file led one student to say: "I'm writing on the papers because I have to.... I put my things on that computer that day . . . I'm never going to touch that again."

The teacher's role as helper and troubleshooter is critical during this early stage. His or her ability to help students with some of the mechanics of word processing will allow young writers to continue to focus on the writing task. For example, when students become discouraged with the new writing tool, the sensitive teacher can help the writer perform the desired function, then acknowledge that the first stages of learning to write with a new tool are the most difficult.

2. Students should be taught strategies for generating and organizing their own ideas.

The most effective teachers in our study did not tell children what to write. Instead, they provided students with a context for discussion and helpful procedures or "hooks" for getting them started in the writing process. These procedures included both conversational approaches and cognitive strategies. Conversational approaches included such activities as joint brainstorming, having the student tell a story, or encouraging the student to recall personal experiences. Cognitive strategies provided students with new ways to gather and organize information. For example, when one student had difficulty describing the tea room in a story, "Tea at the Ritz," the teacher suggested that she draw a map of the room, showing what people would see as they walked in. The student then placed the map beside her at the computer and was able to compose the description.

The word processor was of assistance to remedial students in generating their own ideas for writing in several ways. For example, the computer encouraged students to take risks as they began to write. Because beginning attempts could be easily erased as the students thought of additional ideas, there was less hesitancy in getting started. In addition, use of word processing meant that students often began to compose sooner than before, i.e., prewriting and first draft attempts often merged during the writing sessions.

The teachers also developed a number of creative techniques to facilitate student planning on the computer, techniques which led to ideas for further writing. Using the computer for brainstorming was one of these techniques. In the following example, the student was asked to brainstorm on the computer by writing whatever words came to mind. He slowly wrote two complete sentences, then apparently ran out of ideas.

Teacher: When you get stuck, just write "blank." The thing is, you can't stop writing.
Student: Yea, but I don't have nothing else to write about.
Teacher: Then you know what to do? (Stands over him and types "blank.") Tell me a word that you're thinking of in your head, any word.

Student: Autobiographies (Teacher types this).
Teacher: What does that make you think of?
Student: Working (Teacher types this).
Teacher: Another word.
Student: Unnormal powers. (When the student sees these words on the monitor, he comments:) I wish I could have unnormal powers.
Teacher: When you write, you can.

After several more minutes of discussion on "unnormal powers" the notes were printed out. On the next day, the student used these notes as the basis for writing about his own "unnormal powers."

The resource room teachers in this study found that there was a public quality about the computer's screen. Students' early ideas were accessible for teachers and other students to discuss because the writing was legible and available for all to see. The monitor also functioned as a neutral ground where students and teachers could brainstorm together, the resulting words and phrases all appearing as one activity. In addition, the teachers felt it was easier to interact with students about their writing when they were at the computer. The teachers were drawn to talking with the students as they wrote and provided encouragement to keep students thinking. Reading and rereading text on the screen became a primary way of maintaining the students' engagement in writing. It also enabled the teacher to praise the content of the text and to encourage expansion.

3. Students' attention should first be focused on composing their ideas, not editing their text.

Remedial students tend to be anxious about spelling and mechanics. They are often concerned about "saying it right." Unfortunately, paying so much attention to the mechanics of writing often makes it difficult for students to pay attention to what they want to say. The mechanical issues tend to draw these students away from what should be their major focus: generating and writing ideas. Here is a typical example:

Student: How do you spell "reason"?
Teacher: Think. REASON.
Student: R-E-A-S-O-N?
Teacher: Good.
Student: I don't know what to write now.

The teachers who acknowledged spelling concerns but handled them quickly (usually by encouraging the students to use invented spelling) helped students maintain a high level of involvement in writing. This is not to suggest that these teachers ignored spelling accuracy. Rather, they assured students that spelling would be attended to at a later time. When students had completed their compositions, spelling checkers (*Bank Street Speller*, 1984) were used to help correct their work. In addition, students were encouraged to develop personal word files of frequently misspelled words to be used for later reference and study.

Too much emphasis on revision can also have negative effects on content. The word processor, with all its flexibility, makes editing and revising text particularly attractive. In fact, it may make the revision process too attractive. Our observations indicated that many students would begin to revise and edit their writing too early. This was unfortunate because it led some students to write short, technically correct pieces of writing which lacked spontaneity. For other students, the word processor's capacity for easy deletion resulted in a pattern of constantly generating and then erasing text.

Observations revealed that it was most effective for editing to be approached in two steps. After students had written their stories, they printed draft versions. The teachers and students then conferenced together, making corrections on their printed drafts. Following the conferences, students returned to the word processor to edit and publish final copies. In this way, mechanics and spelling issues were held in abeyance until students' ideas had been written down.

For example, an area in which this two-step approach to editing was found to be extremely helpful was in the teaching of sequencing. Remedial students often have difficulty sequencing their ideas into a logical order. Use of the "move" procedure on the word processor provided these teachers and students with a new remedial technique for this area of difficulty. First, students were encouraged to write down their ideas as the thoughts came to mind. While conferencing, the teacher would help each student specify which activities came first, second, third, etc. Students were then encouraged to organize the text sequentially by rearranging the sentences using the "move" procedure.

4. Students can be helped to manage their writing anxiety and lack of confidence.

The teachers who praised students' writing, verifying their role as authors, created a positive writing environment for those who might otherwise be anxious and insecure. Comments such as, "That's so interesting" and "She is such a writer!" reflected the teachers' opinions that their students were capable of generating good writing. Students' willingness to engage in writing was very closely tied to having a warm and nonjudgmental person who responded with genuine interest to their ideas. This attitude enabled the students to feel that they had something of value to communicate to others.

This sense of achievement was also fostered by activities that allowed the students to "become like writers" (Smith, 1983). In one class, for example, the students each published a book of stories. These books were final versions of stories written on the computer. In addition to the stories, each book included an autobiography, a dedication, and a table of contents. The computer written stories from another resource room were proudly hung on the bulletin board in the students' regular classroom. The word processor allowed students to produce work that was more professional looking and therefore more valued. One student, who was just beginning to feel successful as a writer, cheerfully exclaimed, "I wrote a great story. It is 57 lines long." While we know that sheer productivity does not indicate good writing, these comments reflect the student's positive attitude toward the writing task.

Conclusion

This column has described four major guidelines for helping remedial students learn to write with word processors. Our observations indicate that effective teachers were those who explicitly taught basic word processing and keyboarding skills, gave students strategies for generating their own ideas, encouraged students to focus their attention on composing rather than editing, and helped students manage their anxiety by encouraging and praising their ideas.

The word processor was used as a significant instructional resource by the five resource room teachers we observed. It allowed them to provide new opportunities for writing and to teach new strategies for revision. But the word processor's features alone did not facilitate improved writing. Rather, it was the teacher's approach that fostered effective use of the computer. Teachers who brought a working knowledge of the writing process to the instruction of their remedial students used the unique features of the word processor to enhance student learning and extend their repertoire of good writing skills.

Susan B. Neuman. College of Education, University of Lowell, One University Ave., Lowell, MA 01854; and Catherine Cobb-Morocco, Education Development Center, 55 Chapel St., Newton, MA 02160.

References

Behrman, M. (1984). *Handbook of Microcomputers in Special Education.* San Diego: College Hill Press.

Daiute, C. (1985). *Writing and Computers.* Reading, MA: Addison-Wesley Publishing Co.

Johnston, P. & Allington, R. (1985). The congruence of classroom and remedial reading instruction. *The Elementary School Journal, 85(4),* pp. 465-477.

Neuman, S. and Morocco, C. (1987). Two hands is hard for me. *Keyboarding and Learning Disabled Children* (at press).

Smith, F. (1983). Reading like a writer. *Language Arts. 60(5),* pp. 558-67.

IN SUMMARY

Wrtiting with Word Processors for Remedial Students

- Initial keyboarding and word processing skills should be taught separately from writing instruction.

- Students should be taught strategies for generating and organizing their own ideas.

- Students' attention should first be focused on composing their ideas, not editing their text.

- Students can be helped to manage their writing anxiety and lack of confidence.

- The teacher's approach rather than features of the word processor facilitated improved writing.

Should Students Use Spelling Checkers?

by Janice Adele Meyer

Reprinted from Proceedings of the 6th Annual "Extending The Human Mind: Computers in Education" Summer Conference, *The Center for Advanced Technology in Education (CATE),* Eugene, Oregon.

"Yes!!"—say high school students who are now suffering from withdrawal symptoms because their spelling checker software was taken away at the conclusion of my research.

"Yes!"—say the participating high school teachers who saw some gains, which they considered to be impressive, in the writing skills and spelling achievement of their students who used spelling checker software.

"Maybe"—say some educators who are waiting for volumes of research to determine either the positive or negative aspects of spelling checker software usage.

"No! !"—say some teachers. "They're a crutch just like calculators in math."

Research on The Use of Spelling Checkers

A search of the literature revealed no empirical studies specifically regarding the effects of spelling checkers, used in conjunction with word processing, on the spelling achievement of students even though word processing programs and their enhancements, including orthographic aids, are rapidly growing in popularity.

Word processing programs are now being used more in the language arts curriculum because of the advantages they appear to offer writers (Bradley, 1982; Daiute, 1985; Green, 1984; Schwartz, 1982). Why has word processing become so important in the area of writing skills? Writing is done in the schools for the purpose of helping students "discover what it is they learn. In the act of trying to put down words, students can discover their ideas, sharpen their thoughts, and order their thinking" (Marcus, 1984, p. 54). This process has often been considered "drudge work" because of the many corrections, sometimes numerous and messy, and refinements necessary to perfect writing. Now writers can use computers to do the drudge work. Student writers can turn over to the computer the task of storing information, assisting in the correction of misspellings, recopying, and reformatting the text. While the computer is doing all these tasks the writer is freed to think (Daiute, 1983; Schwartz, 1982).

Secondly, spelling should be an integral part of writing. It should be taught in a meaningful context—the writer's expressed thoughts (Allred, 1984; Manning, 1981)—not as some subject in isolation. Some educators question why so much emphasis is put on correct spelling when writing experts are telling them students who are in the prewriting and writing stage should not be hampered in their creative thinking by mechanical concerns such as spelling. Writing experts and spelling authorities both stress correct spelling, especially in the post writing aspect of the composition process. Peters (1985) believes correct spelling should be emphasized because: (1) poor and careless spelling causes communication to suffer because a lack of precision brings about misinformation or misunderstanding of the message intended; (2) good spelling continues to be considered a sign of literacy; (3) some children and adults are freed to write only when they have learned to spell correctly; and (4) the writing of poor spellers may be simpler in vocabulary and less precise in meaning because they are not confident in the use of new words found in their vocabulary. Allred concludes that "Accurate spelling is important at all levels of written composition because it greatly influences a writer's creativity and effectiveness" (1984, p.8).

Thirdly, computers have become an important teaching tool in spelling instruction (Allred, 1984; Balajthy, 1986; Garsh, 1984). Computers have been and are being used to teach spelling. They are used for drill-and-practice and tutorial computer-assisted instruction as well as to individualize students' spelling programs. Computer software can provide for a variety of student learning styles. For the visual learner, the visualization of spelling works on the computer monitor is extremely important, especially considering the fact that most spelling authorities believe spelling is mainly a visual task (Allred, 1977; Fitzgerald and Loomer, 1984). Recently, spelling software has been enhanced with speech synthesis which may benefit auditory learners.

What Are Electronic Spelling Checkers And How Might They Assist Students With Their Writing Skills and Spelling Instruction?

In order to understand how spelling checkers may benefit students in the area of writing skills and spelling instruction it is necessary to understand the concepts upon which spelling checker software is based. In general, spelling checkers are microcomputer software containing built-in dictionaries of correctly spelled words. The text created by the writer on a word processor is analyzed by the spelling checker and compared with words in the internal dictionary to find a matching word. If this match is not found, the text word is reported as a possible misspelling. When a word is reported as being possibly misspelled, various possibilities for the correct spelling are typically presented to the writer. If desired, new words may be added to the internal dictionary, thereby individualizing or customizing the dictionary in such a manner as to serve as the writer's own personal vocabulary directory. In this way, names and technical terms can be added to augment the basic dictionary.

There are basically two types of spelling checkers used in an educational setting: resident (integrated) spelling checkers and nonresident (stand-alone) spelling checkers (Eiser, 1986; Janus, 1986). Resident programs reside in the computer's memory along with the word processing program. With such a resident program the user can "toggle" back and forth between the main program (the word processor) and the resident program (the spelling checker) by using two predefined keystrokes. There are four common modes of checking which may be offered by a resident spelling checker: (a) interactive, (b) single, (c) full screen, or (d) full document. Any or all of these four may be used when the spelling checker is active. After all checking is done by the resident spelling checker program, the user then returns to the word processor in order to print out a corrected copy.

Nonresident (stand-alone) programs are used during the revision or editing stage of the writing process after writers have completed their writing and saved the file to disks. In order to use this type of spelling checker it is necessary to quit the word processor and load the spelling checker into the computer's memory. The words in the document are then "read" alphabetically and checked against each word in the spelling checker's dictionary. Those that do not match are counted and displayed on the screen as questionable words to inform the user that the word is possibly misspelled. The next step with this type of spelling checker is for the program to highlight each questionable word and to ask the writer what should be done about the particular word. It then presents possible options, such as "Ignore the highlighted word," "Add to the auxiliary dictionary," or "Suggest an alternative." The original word processor must be rebooted and the correct file called up if the writer wishes to print the correct version.

Although microcomputer spelling checkers were originally developed solely as a tool to check spelling, this research indicated that they may also be a beneficial tool for spelling instruction. Some microcomputer spelling checkers can provide a multisensory approach to learning, which is necessary in spelling instruction if all students are to be taught according to the teaching style by which they learn best. If spelling is primarily a visual exercise, as is often asserted, then students whose visual sense is weak can learn to spell if visual training is provided by the spelling checker. Also, the use of microcomputer spelling checkers combines the kinesthetic-tactile learning modality with a visual approach when the computer keyboard is used to input data. Finally, if speech synthesis is added to the spelling checker program, the auditory modality enters into the learning process and offers training in auditory perception and auditory discrimination which supplements the visual and kinesthetic-tactile aspects of learning.

Possible Benefits Of Electronic Spelling Checkers

This research project explored the effects of electronic spelling checkers on the spelling achievement of a group of randomly selected high school students. The study sought to determine if students who used an electronic spelling checker, in conjunction with a word processing program, showed: (a) greater gains in spelling achievement than students who used

word processors without spelling checker, (b) an increase in expressive vocabulary; (c) an increase in functional spelling skills; and (d) a decrease in specific types or categories of spelling errors. The study also attempted to determine what relationship, if any, exists between keyboarding skills and improvement of spelling achievement when students used spelling checkers.

Spelling Achievement

The greatest gains in spelling achievement were made by the poorer spellers in the experimental group, i.e., the group that used spelling checkers. The poorer spellers, (those scoring below 69% on a standardized spelling achievement test), made an average gain of 6 percentage points. The poorest speller went from 49% on the pretest to 62% on the posttest, a gain of 13 percentage points.

Expressive Vocabulary

A comparison of the initial and final expressive writing samples indicated that the experimental group, with an increase of 145.94 total words and 48.00 unique words, showed a greater mean gain than the control group which exhibited an increase of 63.64 total words and 8.73 unique words. This comparison suggests that the use of a spelling checker may assist in the expansion of an expressive vocabulary used for writing purposes.

Functional Spelling Skills

Raw scores and percentages indicated that, on posttests, the experimental group made fewer misspellings than the control group even though they wrote more total and unique words. The control group, by contrast, made more misspellings although they wrote fewer total and fewer unique words. This was a reversal of the pretest scores.

Specific Types of Spelling Errors

Substitutions, omissions, additions and transpositions were analyzed in the research. The results indicated that certain types of errors, such as substitutions and omissions, seem to decrease when a spelling checker is used.

Typing Speed and Spelling Achievement

A comparison of spelling achievement for slow and fast typists in both groups indicated that for both groups combined, the experimental and control groups, fast typists made higher mean scores for both the pretests and posttests.

Conclusions Based On This Research

One of the most important conclusions of this exploratory research is that the use of a spelling checker program neither definitely assists nor hinders spelling achievement on a standardized spelling test. There are other implications from this research which are perhaps educationally significant even though data analyses did not find them to be statistically significant. This includes the suggestion that a spelling checker program assists in increasing written expressive vocabulary. There is the possibility, also, that an increase in functional spelling skills may occur with the use of a spelling checker, particularly with certain categories of spelling errors. In addition, a specific relationship may exist between typing abilities and spelling achievement thus enabling fast typists to show greater gains in spelling achievement than slow typists.

Should Students Use Spelling Checkers?

This study shows that a spelling checker certainly has no negative effect on student performance on any of the various categories analyzed, if anything, it may have a positive effect on increasing the expressiveness of students' written vocabulary by encouraging them to write more freely and by diminishing certain categories of spelling errors. Secondary school teachers should feel no hesitation in permitting or even encouraging their students to use spelling checkers in conjunction with word processing software on microcomputers.

References

Allred, R.A. (1977). *Spelling: The application of research findings.* Washington, DC: National Education Association.

Allred, R.A. (1984). *Spelling trends, content, and methods.* Washington, DC: National Education Association.

Balajthy, E. (1986). Using microcomputers to teach spelling. *The Reading Teacher, 39* (5), 438-443.

Bradley, V. (1982). *Improving student work with microcomputers. Language Arts,* 59, 732-743.

Daiute, C. (1983). *The computer as stylus and audience. College Composition and Communication, 34*(2), 134-145.

Daiute, C. (1985). *Writing and computers.* Reading, MA: Addison-Wesley.

Eiser, L. (1986, November/December). I luv to rite! *Classroom Computer Learning,* pp. 50-57.

Fitzgerald, R.J., & Loomer, B. (1984). Best ways to teach spelling. *The Reading Teacher, 37,* 679.

Garsch, T. (1984). Spelling instruction gets a boost from the microcomputer. *Electronic Education,* 4, 16, 53.

Green, J. (1984). Computers, kids, and writing: An interview with Donald Graves. *Classroom Computer Learning,* 4, 62-65.

Janus, S. (1986). Spell it write: The latest in orthographic aids for Apple II word processing. *A+, 4* (7), 49-61.

Manning, M.M., & Manning, G.L. (1981). *Improving spelling in the middle grades.* Washington, DC: National Education Association.

Marcus, S. (1984, October). Computers in the curriculum—Language arts. *Electronic Learning,* pp. 55-64.

Peters, M.L. (1985). *Spelling: Caught or taught?* London: Routledge & Regan Paul.

Schwartz, M. (1982, November). Computers and the teaching of writing. *Educational Technology,* pp. 27-29.

IN SUMMARY
Should Students Use Spelling Checkers?

- Spelling check software contains built-in dictionaries against which text from a word processing document is compared. Words not found in the dictionary are reported as possible misspellings.

- Spelling should be an integral part of writing. It should be taught in a meaningful context, not as a separate subject in isolation.

- Computer assisted instruction software, some with electronic speech capability, has become an effective teaching tool in spelling instruction.

- There are two basic types of spelling checkers used in educational settings: resident or integrated systems, and nonresident or stand alone software.

- Although spelling checkers have not been shown to significantly increase student achievement on a standardized spelling test, scores indicate that poorer spellers made larger gains in spelling achievement than did average or good spellers.

COMPUTERS AND THE LANGUAGE ARTS

The Reading-Writing Connection:
Classroom Applications for the Computer, Part I

by Lynne Anderson-lnman

Have you ever stopped to think about thinking? The role of thinking in the language arts curriculum is a critical one, primarily because the *communication of thought* serves as a glue for the entire discipline. Although we tend to view the language arts curriculum as some combination of separate subjects (e.g., reading, writing, and spelling), these distinctions often obscure their fundamental similarities. All of the language arts—reading, writing, listening, and speaking—are language-based processes through which human thoughts are communicated. And *instruction* in the language arts is that blend of activities used by teachers to improve the skills needed for effective communication.

With this in mind, it is unfortunate that instruction in reading and instruction in writing are so frequently presented in isolation; separate from each other and from the context of communication. Instead of recognizing that reading and writing are related endeavors and mutually beneficial activities, the prevailing tendency is to see them as distinctly different processes, at opposite ends of some continuum. Writing is usually viewed as the process of putting meaning *onto* the printed page (production) and reading as the process of getting meaning *from* the printed page (reception).

Although this view is certainly not incorrect, it is somewhat superficial. When one explores what the writer actually has to do in order to put meaning onto a page, it becomes increasingly clear that a tremendous amount of reading is required in order to write well. This reading is of two types. First, there is the reading that a writer does in order to assimilate the varied and complex features of good writing. Such exposure leads to familiarity with different types of discourse and text structures, as well as an internalization of the stylistic devices and conventions used in any given type of writing. The writer in us seems to acquire this specialized knowledge from reading in much the same way that children acquire the complex and idiomatic rules of grammar from listening to others speak (Smith, 1983).

Second, there is the reading that a writer does in order to check on the clarity and meaningfulness of what is being written. Because writers are most often writing for an audience other than themselves, the material being written needs to be complete, and presented in a logical, organized fashion. The only way to ensure this is to read and reread what is written, looking for conceptual gaps and possible areas of confusion. Successful writers are able to put themselves in the shoes of their intended audience and read as if reading with *their* eyes. This form of critical and evaluative reading is difficult, but absolutely crucial if the words on the printed page are to convey meaning.

In a similar manner, what the reader has to do in order to gain meaning from the printed page involves skills not unlike those of the writer. To comprehend what has been written, the reader must construct meaning from the writer's words, looking for relationships among the different parts of the text. This is not a passive endeavor, but rather one in which the reader works to combine his/her own background knowledge on the subject with the ideas or information presented by the writer. Thus, reading comprehension is an active process of creating meaning *from* text, similar to the active process of creating meaning *with* text.

The key to the similarity of these processes is that both are productive. In reading as well as writing, the learner produces (and usually revises) something that did not previously exist. Since the skills required are similar, instruction in one context can impact performance in the other. In short, instruction in writing can improve performance in reading, and instruction in reading can improve performance in writing (Stotsky, 1983).

Unfortunately, the mutually beneficial nature of reading and writing is seldom taken advantage of in today's curricula. This is where the computer can play an important role. Because of its word processing capabilities and its abilities to prompt and respond to reader interaction, the computer can create an environment for communication that enhances both reading and writing skills.

The remainder of this column is devoted to exploring two ways in which the computer can help bridge the gap between reading and writing instruction. In the first, the computer is used as a tool to facilitate an approach to reading instruction centered around student writing. In the second, the computer is used to help students produce reading materials which combine text and graphics. A third application will be the focus of a future column: using computers to facilitate interactive reading and writing experiences.

Language Experience Approach

Popular for decades as a method for teaching beginning reading, the Language Experience Approach consciously builds on the interrelated nature of listening, speaking, reading and writing. Because it uses the students' own language to create reading materials, the materials are familiar in vocabulary and sentence structure. For this reason, the approach has also found favor with teachers of illiterate and non-English speaking adults as well as teachers of students from disadvantaged and minority cultures. Although individual teachers implement the method differently, the key features remain consistent.

Using this approach, either the teacher or students generate a topic for writing. Following a discussion on the topic, students dictate sentences to be included in the story. The teacher records the ideas on the chalkboard or large chart paper, taking care to use the students' own words and syntax. The resulting story is read aloud by the teacher, and then students and teacher take turns reading all or parts of the story. Individual copies of the story are prepared and duplicated for the students and follow-up activities are provided to improve word recognition and comprehension skills.

The strength of the Language Experience Approach to reading instruction is its use of students' own oral language as the foundation for both writing and reading. Students quickly learn that thoughts can be translated into speech, speech into writing, and that one's own words can be read. In other words:

What I can think about, I can talk about.
What I can say, I can write.
What I can write, I can read (Allen, 1966).

This approach, whether used as the foundation of a reading program or as a supplement to another approach, can be facilitated by introducing a computer for recording, and eventually reading, students' stories. For recording class-dictated stories, the word processing program *Magic Slate* works nicely because it can be set to write with only 20 or 40 characters per line, resulting in letters large enough to be read by a group using a single large monitor.

Using a word processing program to record language experience stories has certain advantages over the chalkboard or chart paper method. First is the efficiency with which language experience stories can be recorded and printed. Traditional recording methods are somewhat time consuming; letters large and clear enough to be read by a group or class of students take time for the teacher to print—time that students often spend fidgeting and forgetting what *they* wanted to include in the story. Typing the same sentences into a computer takes only a fraction of that time, leaving more of the period for reading and rereading the story and providing follow-up activities. Furthermore, preparing word processed stories for duplication does not require recopying from the board or chart; just the press of a few keys when a printer is attached. If working with a small group, multiple copies can be printed on the spot and distributed during the same class period for individual reading.

The second advantage is the ease with which stories can be revised. Because changes are difficult to handle with traditional recording methods, even minor revisions or corrections are discouraged (e.g., adding a word for clarification or changing the order of two sentences). Such insertions and reordering of parts are, of course, easy to accomplish with a word processing program, and doing so communicates something extremely important to students about writing. When students initiate and guide the modification of a language experience story by suggesting minor improvements, they learn very early that stories are not static, but rather entities that can be molded to achieve better communication.

The third advantage is the possibility for individualization. A group experience story is the product of multiple students and,

A sample screen created using Story Maker.

by necessity, usually lacks any personalizing details. When using a word processing program, however, the teacher can easily insert different students' names (or other identifying information) into a story and print out individualized copies for the various members of a reading group. In cases where students propose multiple story lines for a single beginning, it is even possible to have more than one story in creation at the same time.

The potential role for a computer in facilitating the Language Experience Approach is not limited to its capacity as a word processor. With the arrival of synthesized speech, programs such as *Talking Text Writer* and *Kidtalk* allow teachers to consider creative ways for computer-assisted reading of students' experience stories. For example, because a talking word processor can provide immediate auditory access to what has been written, students are able to practice reading and rereading language experience stories on their own. When a word or phrase is problematic, the computer can repeat it as often as necessary. With the eventual addition of voice recognition and speech-to-text capabilities, the computer may free even very young students to both write and read language experience stories in total independence.

Combining Text and Graphics

For students of all ages, seeing and reading one's own words in print can be a motivating and personally rewarding experience. When graphics are added to what has been written, the resulting product is appealing to other readers as well. Students have been enlivening their writing with hand-drawn pictures since the advent of crayons, and many a classroom library is augmented with these student productions. What the computer can contribute is a degree of professionalism.

Software to support the production of student-generated reading materials can be loosely classified into three categories, according to the amount of student control over the creation process and the type of reading material produced. For each category the writing process may impact students' reading skills in a different way.

Little Red and the B.B. Wolf

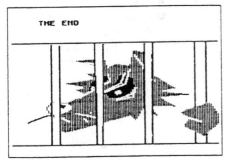

Screens from a fractured fairy tale by Betty Boegehold, with graphics by Joan Auclair. Written and illustrated with Bank Street.

The first category might best be labeled "build-a-book" software. When using these products students are prompted through a series of questions, generally about themselves, family and friends. The answers are then used to personalize a story already provided on the disk. The story is printed out, often on specially provided paper, and materials are included to add graphics and bind the pages into a book. With some of the programs, students can enter the prepared text and make alterations. The *Playwriter* series allows the writer to make minor changes to the text, limited by constraints on the allowable length of additions and modifications.

The "build-a-book" software currently available is best considered for its motivational capability. The resulting products are indeed slick-looking little books and novice writers/readers will feel there is a big payoff for a small effort. As software publishers do a better job of controlling the vocabulary of these stories (so that readability is compatible with the skills of the targeted audience), "build-a-book" software could have a significant role in motivating reluctant writers to produce personalized materials to be read by reluctant readers.

The second category of software allows students to combine text and graphics in the creation of *electronic* books. In these products, the computer screen becomes equivalent to the printed page and students are provided with electronic tools for writing and illustrating their stories, often in dazzling color. One of the simplest and oldest of this genre is *Kidwriter*, a program containing a pool of prepared pictures from which students can select their illustrations and a narrow panel at the base of each screen for written input. Ease of operation makes this program a logical choice for young writers, but the limitations on topics and story length make it inappropriate for more complex creations.

Similarly, *Story Maker* is a program best incorporated into the primary grades. Although it allows students to draw their own illustrations (in addition to selecting from a pool of prepared graphics), the type sizes available are all quite large and therefore generally thought childish by older writers.

The most versatile software in this category is *Bank Street Storybook*. Writers using this program can type text anywhere on the page, in any amount, and they are also provided with a sophisticated yet easy-to-use graphics program for illustrating their electronic creations. What makes the program special is the capability provided for making revisions (to graphics as well as text) and additional features which allow writers control over the pacing of a story. The resulting pages are far more dynamic than those of similar products, providing both writer and reader with experiences in a new electronic medium.

The use of a motivating program such as *Bank Street Storybook* encourages writers to read their creations with an evaluative eye, making adjustments to improve communication and appeal. Such critical reading skills are invaluable to students as they read other authors and work to create meaning from various forms of narrative and expository text.

The third category is software which supports layout for newspaper production. The most popular of this genre in schools is *The Newsroom*, a program which allows budding journalists to write, illustrate, paste up and print pages resembling a newspaper or newsletter. Used to communicate either classroom or school news, the program can promote understanding of the literary conventions in journalism and recognition of text structures conducive to effective reporting. This knowledge can have a beneficial effect on students' skills in reading commercially produced newspapers and interpreting other forms of journalism.

The reading and writing connection can be alive and well in your classroom. If you have found yourself discouraged by the paucity of good software to promote improved reading skills, consider augmenting your reading program with a vigorous program emphasizing student writing. Improving students' skills in written communication will impact their ability to comprehend the written communications of others.

Lynne Anderson-Inman, College of Education, University of Oregon, Eugene, OR 97403.

References

Allen, R.V. and Allen, C., 1966, *Language Experiences in Reading,* Chicago: Encyclopedia Britannica.

Smith, F. (1983). "Reading like a writer." *Language Arts, 60,* (5), pp. 559-579.

Stotsky, S. (1983). "Research on reading/writing relationships: A synthesis and suggested directions." *Language Arts, 60,* (5), pp. 627-642.

Software

Bank Street Storybook; Apple II series, 64K. Mindscape, Inc., 3444 Dundee Rd., Northbrook, IL 60062.

Kidtalk; Mac. First Byte, Inc., 2845 Temple Ave., Long Beach, CA 90806.

Kidwriter, Apple II series, 48K. Gessler Educational Software, 900 Broadway, New York, NY 10003.

Magic Slate; Apple II series, 48K. Sunburst Communications, Inc., 39 Washington Ave.—Rm. EA, Pleasantville, NY 10570.

The Newsroom; Apple II series, 64K. Springboard Software, Inc., 7807 Creekridge Circle, Minneapolis, MN 55435.

Playwriter, Apple II series, IBM, C-64. Woodbury Computer Associates, Inc., 127 White Oak Lane, Old Bridge, NJ 08857.

Talking Text Writer, Apple IIc, IIe, 128K. Scholastic, Inc., 730 Broadway, New York, NY 10003.

Story Maker; Apple II +, IIe, 48K. Bolt, Beranek & Newman, Inc., 10 Moulton St., Cambridge, MA 02238.

IN SUMMARY

The Reading-Writing Connection:
Classroom Applications for the Computer

- Reading and writing, although frequently presented to students separate from each other and seen by many teachers as distinctly different processes, both involve the construction of ideas: writing, an active process of creating meaning *with text*; and reading, an active process of creating meaning *from text*.

- Improvement of students' writing skills will have a positive impact on their ability to comprehend the written communication of others.

- The computer, through the use of various reading and writing programs, can provide an environment for communication that enhances both reading and writing skills for students.

- The language experience approach to reading and writing instruction, a pedagogy based heavily on the student's own vocabulary and experiences, can be greatly facilitated through the use of a computer and a word processing program.

- Programs that allow students to combine text and graphics into a book-like format are best considered for their motivational capabilities.

Desktop Publishing: More Than Meets the Eye

By Shelley Yorke Rose

Reprinted with permission from the March-April 1986 issue of ETC.

True or False? To do "desktop publishing," all you need is a desktop, a computer, printer and software.

Many people (and current publications) seem to believe that the statement above is true. As with any computer application, however, the equipment is merely a means to an end. We are falling in love with computers all over again. The new generation of truly "user-friendly" computers with their iconography and new ways of inputting data has dazzled us and, temporarily, blinded us to the fact that just because we are producing publications using the latest technology and software, we are not necessarily producing publications that people will want to read. The rush is on to communicate, and we are rediscovering the printed word. But is anyone reading it?

In order to produce publications that people will want to read, we need to turn off our computers, shelve that slick software that promises "typeset-quality" results, and do a little homework. How many newsletters have crossed your desk recently that you immediately identified as desktop published? And, how many of those were simply printed in an unrelenting two-column format, with few graphics (or excessive graphics) and no thought to the aesthetics of producing the publication?

What can you do to combine the technology with standard production policies to produce an attractive and readable publication? Read! If you're going to produce a newsletter on a regular basis, invest in some reference materials and talk to a graphic artist, printer and/or your district's communications coordinator (who, more than likely, produces a district newsletter using this or more traditional equipment). Realize that although you may be able to push your software to the limit, you may not be fully aware of how to lay out copy and graphics. Perhaps you have a thing or two to learn about picas, points, fonts and families of typestyles. Do you know how to crop pictures to fit your format? Do you know where the focal point of your page is? Can you "guess-timate" whether your copy will fit your page? Are you considering your readers and including articles of interest to a targeted group?

Editors using the new technology to publish have re-opened Pandora's Box. Those who are still publishing after the dust settles will be those people who have done their homework and are looking beyond style to substance. Right now, we are enamored of the process. But the product must be of value to our readers or even our slickest efforts will fail.

Shelley Yorke Rose, Editor, ETC, Interactive and Instructional Computing Department, Oakland Schools, 2100 Pontiac Lake Road, Pontiac, MI 48054; ph. 313/858-1895.

References

Arnold, Edmund C. (1982). *Editing the organizational publication.* Chicago: Lawrence Ragan Communications, Inc.

Beach, Mark. (1982). *Editing your newsletter: A guide to writing, design and production.* Second Edition. Portland, OR: Coast to Coast Books.

Personal publishing, the magazine of electronic page creation. A Renegade Publication, P.O. Box 390, Itasca, IL 60143; published monthly, $30/year.

White, Jan V., *Graphic idea notebook: Inventive techniques for designing printed pages.* Watson-Guptill Publications, New York, 1980.

Workshops workbook: Writing and editing, layout & design. Photography. Ragan Communications Library, 1985.

IN SUMMARY
Desktop Publishing: More Than Meets the Eye

Producing an attractive, readable newsletter takes more than just making use of a desktop publishing program on a computer. Knowledge of page makeup, graphic art, and typography can be of real value when using even the most sophisticated publishing programs.

Process Writing Research Topics

By Anne Auten

Reprinted with permission from Franklin, S. (Ed.). (1988). Making the Literature, Writing, Word Processing Connection: The Best of Writing Notebook (2nd ed.). Eugene, OR: The Writing Notebook.

Current research in composition reveals that teaching writing as a process rather than a product develops students' writing skills more effectively. The majority of this research, beginning with a benchmark study on the composing processes of twelfth graders (Emig, 1971), has been supported by colleges and universities. We who are intrigued by the use of word processing in the writing classroom have much to gain from the body of knowledge, developed through the past 15 years on college campuses around the country, that documents the benefits of the process approach.

Process-oriented writing programs share a number of basic features (King & Fitterman-King, 1986). Some combination of the following techniques and program benefits can be found in every classroom where the process model has been adopted:

1. **Increased student interest.** Students working with process approaches often seem more active and attentive than those in traditional English/language arts classes. The same holds true when these writing techniques are used in social studies, math, or science. Students are active writers, responders, and collaborators, rather than passive recipients of textbook-based information.

2. **Development of each writer's voice.** First experiences with the process approach can help students overcome the anxiety often associated with writing. After one or two class periods of listening to each other, they also begin to abandon their reticence about reading their work aloud. Within such a frame of acceptance, students can begin to find individual writing voices, and assuming honest effort, the particular styles they develop tend to be lively and energetic.

3. **Writing, thinking, and learning across the curriculum.** Development of supportive interrelationships among reading, writing, thinking, and talking is the major benefit of using the process approach in any subject area. Students in math, science, and other disciplines keep written records of their thinking as they work to understand a particular situation, concept, or theorem. These problem-solving notebooks, or "earning logs," help students deal with difficult material. The logs occasion not only deep and careful thought about content, but also a clearer perception of what is known and what remains to be learned.

> *"NCTE commissions cite an old-fashioned view of language teaching, still held by large and influential segments of the American public, as presenting the greatest obstacle to the process writing approach. This limited view of language tends to retard classroom application of new knowledge from research, and weakens teacher education and staff development efforts."*

It has been suggested in many publications, including this one, that the computer and text processing/analysis programs can provide powerful support for the process approach to writing instruction. Primarily through the energies of graduate students producing doctoral dissertations and that of computer literate college composition teachers, the beginnings of a body of research on computing and composing has developed. Gail Hawisher (1986), in her meta-analysis of 24 writing and word processing studies completed since 1981, reports that despite the dissimilarities of subjects, research methodologies, and analysis tools, a tentative conclusion has emerged from this body of literature. Her conclusion is that "most writers—regardless of age or status—enjoy writing with computers and perceive word processing as a boon to their composing strategies." Not an earth-shaking statement, perhaps, but a beginning.

She goes on to suggest issues for future study, some of which might be taken up by The Johns Hopkins University over the next three years. The university's Center for Social Organization of Schools provided this country's first comprehensive look at instructional uses of computers in schools. Under the direction of Henry Jay Becker, the center completed two national surveys in 1983 and 1985 that sampled over 2,300 elementary and secondary schools in each of those years. Recently the university's Center for Research on Elementary and Middle Schools announced a new cooperative research project: The National Field Studies of Instructional Uses of School Computers. During 1988-89, the project will examine computer use for improving student writing and has invited the collaboration of university researchers for the first time, along with district administrators and classroom teachers.

Although research at colleges and universities contributes clear data on effective ways to teach writing, the number of teachers who use a process approach falls far short of the majority. Some sources estimate that fewer than 20% of practicing English teachers have received training in process approaches to teaching writing, even though such training opportunities are available through regional National Writing Project summer workshops and a proliferation of college and university programs such as those offered by Bard College's Institute for Writing and Thinking in Annandale-on-Hudson, New York.

Why then are so many teachers not practicing process approaches? Perhaps the greatest obstacle is the old-fashioned concept of English and the language arts held by large and influential segments of the American public. This is the consensus of the 1986 Report on Trends and Issues from the six commissions of the National Council of Teachers of English. The commissions, made up of teachers and professors of English at all levels of education, monitor developments in the English curriculum and in the teaching of reading, literature, composition, the English language, and media (including computers). The NCTE Commissions cite narrow curriculum mandates for "basic skills" and standardized testing, which focuses on such skills, as serious obstacles to higher learning today. The commissions attribute these problems to a belief on the part of the public and educational policy makers that studying the English language arts as simply a matter of learning to recognize words on a page and to use "correct" forms in writing and speaking. This limited view of language, a subject central to all learning, commissioners say, tends to retard that classroom application of new knowledge from research. It weakens teacher education and staff development efforts.

It appears that until the evidence is overwhelmingly conclusive that the process approach to teaching writing that appropriately incorporates word processing does, in fact, improve students' writing skills, this "limited view of language" may prevail. University researchers and classroom teachers need to work cooperatively to contribute to that evidence.

Anne Auten, P.O. Box 5017, College of St, Thomas, 2115 Summit Avenue, St. Paul, MN 55102.

References
Emig, J. (1971). *The Composing Processes of Twelfth Graders.* Urbana, IL: National Council of Teachers of English.

Hawisher, G. E. (1986, November). Studies in word processing. *Computers & Composition: A Journal for Teachers of Writing.*

King, D. C., & S. Fitterman-King. (1986, December). *The Tug-of-War is on Between Writing Approaches: Emphasis on Process Challenges the Five-Paragraph Essay. ACSD Curriculum Update.*

IN SUMMARY
Process Writing Research Topics

- A large body of research exists indicating that teaching writing as a process rather than a product helps students develop their writing skills more effectively. This information is important to those teachers who are interested in using word processing as part of the composition activities in their classes.

- It is estimated that fewer than 20% of practicing English teachers have been trained to teach writing by the process approach.

- Narrow curriculum mandates for basic skills and standardized testing, both of which focus on a limited view of language instruction, have been cited as obstacles to the adoption of process oriented writing instruction by many teachers.

- Studies involving the use of word processing in a process oriented approach to composition instruction have not provided conclusive evidence that this combination of technology and instructional approach does significantly improve students' writing skills.

Six Directions for Computer Analysis of Student Writing
by William Wresch

Now that writing with a word processor has become common in many schools, a frequently asked question is, "What comes next?" There are, of course, many answers to that question, including desktop publishing, computer conferencing, and on-line information accessing. Another common answer is computer analysis of student writing.

The last answer is popular for several reasons. Among them is the fact that writing teachers are responsible for improving students' knowledge of standard conventions in spelling, punctuation, and grammar. Writing analysis programs can be helpful to students and teachers in this area. A second reason is the current popularity of writing analysis in business. If students will have ready access to such programs as adults, then it is logical to initiate instruction on their use while students are still in school. (This is essentially the calculator argument restated for writing teachers.) Another strong argument for the introduction of writing analysis programs is independence. If students can be shown by a computer when to use *who* and *whom*, they are able to improve their writing without relying on a teacher. This means that teachers will see student papers with fewer mechanical errors to correct—perhaps a sufficient reason for using writing analysis programs in itself.

An increasing number and variety of computer-based analysis software exists. Although most of these programs use common labels such as style checker or grammar checker, several very different approaches can be taken to the computerized analysis of writing, and existing programs often vary much more than their labels would indicate. Writing analysis programs can be sorted into at least six different categories, each having a very different pedagogical orientation.

Error Checkers

Most of the existing writing analysis programs are error checkers. The term error checker is a generic label for programs that check for homonym confusions, sexist language, usage errors, and infelicitous phrases. This has been the most commercially successful form of computer-based writing analysis software, and from the programmer's perspective, the easiest to develop. An error checking program searches through the writer's text for specific words or combinations of words and prints a message to the writer if one is found. The program doesn't actually analyze text, but rather searches it in the same manner as a spell-checking program.

Error checking programs are popular for the same reason spell checkers are popular. For poor writers, error checkers provide help with basic conventions: When to use *too*, when to use *affect* versus *effect*, and not to say "in our modern word of today." For better writers, error checking programs serve more as a safety net, like combining a belt with suspenders. Better

writers already know how to use language correctly; they just want to make sure they aren't embarrassed by a slip of the tongue (or fingers).

Many programs offer this kind of text analysis. A few of the major programs that have become popular in schools are *Writer's Helper* (Conduit), *Sensible Grammar* (Sensible Software), *RightWriter*, (RightSoft), *Ghost Writer* (MECC), *Writer's Workbench* (AT&T), *Success with Writing* (Scholastic), and *Grammatik II* (Reference Software). While such programs provide a needed service, they are obviously very limited. They may catch errors in phrasing, but they cannot catch errors in grammar (despite the claims of *Sensible Grammar*). Even the grossest sentence structure error goes unnoticed by this type of writing analysis software.

What, then, is their attraction in the classroom? Students love them. When instructors at Colorado State University checked the reaction of their students to *Writer's Workbench*, they found that 76% of their students thought using the computer added to their enjoyment of the writing course (Kiefer & Smith, 1984). Furthermore, 65% said they would look forward to their next writing assignment if it involved using the computer. Why? Among other things, by using error checkers students feel they have a chance to catch errors before a teacher sees them. Although students know not all errors will be caught, and an error fixed is one that won't attract a red pencil.

Teachers seem to like error checking programs for the same reason—fewer mechanical errors to mark and comment on. Perhaps more importantly, there is also a valid instructional rationale for encouraging the use of these programs. Although most teachers do a good job of explaining errors in word usage, students frequently don't seem to learn what has been explained. This may be because the explanation isn't provided at the teachable moment. Students don't need to know, for example, about the difference between *affect* and *effect* every day. They need to know the difference when they try to use one of the words. It is at this moment that an error checker can mark the word and present a sentence or two of explanation. When using an error checker, instruction is available when it has the best chance of sticking.

Reformatters

A different approach to writing analysis is that used by reformatters. Rather than find errors, reformatters make it easier for writers to find their own errors. One of the first programs to try this was *Quill* (DC Heath). This program was a trendsetter in many ways, including its union of prewriting, writing, and revising activities. The program has since been superseded by more sophisticated software, but it did one simple thing that many programs have copied: To help students revise their work,

Quill displayed each sentence of written text alone on the screen. The program didn't say anything about the sentence. It didn't do anything with the sentence. It just printed it there for the student to see.

Why? So students could just look at the sentence and see it—not the paragraph, not the preceding or following sentences, just this one sentence. And it helped. Without other sentences to distract them, students could determine if this sentence was really a sentence, if it made sense, and if it was properly stated. Displaying text sentence by sentence serves as a proofing tool. The clutter of surrounding sentences is temporarily removed so students can better see the editing skills they already possess.

Reformatting text as an aid to editing can be done in many ways. *Ghost Writer* (MECC) prints a graph of each sentence with punctuation and conjunctions displayed but all other words replaced by dashes. The results might look like this:

Sentence 1: _ _ _ _ _, but _ _ _ _ _

The purpose of this type of reformatting aid is to provide writers with a visual picture of each sentence's structure and highlight the connectives used. If certain structures or conjunctions are overused, the graph will make that obvious. Student writers are able to see that on their own and respond.

Other programs have taken similar tacks. *Writer's Helper* (Conduit) prints an outline formed by the first sentence of each paragraph. Students can use this outline to quickly see if they have developed their essay logically, used transitions, or overused a particular opening. Here, for example, is the beginning of an outline *Writer's Helper* created of an early version of the preface to my book *A Practical Guide to Computer Uses in the Language Arts.*

A recent study of writing done in schools (Applebee, 1981) shows that only about three percent of class time is used for writing texts at least one paragraph long.

The study leaves the impression of a nation of workbook users.

National studies notwithstanding, there is writing going on all over this country.

The computer can also be a death knell for programs already in trouble.

Clearly the computer can fill many roles in the English/ language arts classroom.

This is not an outline in the usual sense of the word; it merely shows how each paragraph starts. It is now up to the writer to see whether these initial lines are all coherent. Here, the fourth sentence seems out of place; it might be useful for me to go back and see what I was trying to do there. Maybe I'll decide to change

the beginning of that paragraph, or maybe I'll leave things as they are, but at least the computer's manipulation of my text made me aware of my paragraph openings.

Writer's Workbench (AT&T) highlights *to be* verbs. In each case the idea is to make student writers more aware of what they are doing. Although teachers may still have to help students determine better ways of phrasing their prose, reformatting programs help students recognize potential problems independently.

Audience Awareness Programs

Another kind of program for writing analysis tries to help students reach beyond themselves to their readers. Good writing requires a sense of the audience; their interests, their reading skills, and their needs with respect to written text. Several programs have tried to help student writers understand the needs of readers, and some even offer suggestions on how to consider those needs when editing.

The most common program of this type is the readability formula. The computer is used to calculate such features as the average sentence length and the average word length of a passage. These calculations are then put into a formula and the grade level of the optimal reader is computed. If students produce writing well above or below the level of the projected reader, they are warned. Virtually every style checking program contains at least one readability formula. *Writer's Workbench* contains five!

Although programs which provide writers with an index of passage difficulty do get students to think about their readers, most of the programs offer little advice about how to match the writing to the readers' skills.

One program that malkes a substantial effort to help writers address the needs of readers is *Writer's Helper* (Conduit). In addition to the usual readability formula, *Writer's Helper* includes four other tools to help writers think about readers. One is a measure of diction. How formal is the author? The program calculates formality on a scale of 1-10 and then shows word pairs that might be used to make the tone of the passage more or less formal. Writers who think their audience would benefit from less formal writing can modify their passages by substituting the targeted words with the suggested alternatives.

Most writing courses include some mention of transition sentences or phrases, but few students seem to use this information when writing. *Writer's Helper* highlights all the transitions that are used in a given writing passage and then lists all the transitions that were not used but could have been. The point, of course, is to urge writers to help readers by using appropriate transitions.

Another problem for readers is the writer's use of vague references. *Writer's Helper* highlights such common problem words as *lots*, *many*, and *thing*. Each time the program finds a word identified as a vague reference, it displays the appropriate text on the screen and gives the writer an opportunity to replace it with something more specific.

The fourth audience awareness tool in *Writer's Helper*

focuses on writing style. Based on the distinctions described in the book *Tough, Sweet, and Stuffy* (Gibson, 1966), the program compares the student's writing to the styles used in argumentation (tough), advertising (sweet), and scholarly prose (stuffy). Many characteristics of these writing styles (e.g., use of monosyllables, choice of pronouns, length of sentences) are easily recognized and counted by the computer. Because the program compares students' writing to the characteristics of these three styles, beginning writers can gauge the impression they are likely to have on readers.

For each of the programs in this category, the intent is to help student writers think more fully about the people who will be reading their work and to give them some tools for estimating the effect they will have as authors.

Student Conferencing Utilities

Another way to help students write better is to help them read better. By reading other students' essays and trying to identify their strengths and weaknesses, beginning writers can gradually learn to apply the same editing skills to their own writing. Student conferencing utilities are computer programs which try to help develop these editing skills.

Quill (DC Heath) began the effort by including a Post Office option in its integrated writing program. One thing students were asked to send was comments about each other's essays. Even very young students learned about revising by reading the papers of other students and sending comments.

A more formal example of this approach was developed for *Alaska Writer* (Yukon-Koyukuk School District). In this program, students are given on-line directions for commenting on each other's papers. For example, in one activity they are asked to identify the author's main goal and then mark passages that most fully help meet that goal. Another activity asks students to give holistic scores in six categories (overall, focus, support, organization, conventions, assignment), inserting comments into the paper to support their judgments. The computer is used to guide students in their commenting and as a text editor so that reactions can be placed next to the appropriate passage. This feature also allows the comments to be printed out legibly. No more scrawls in the margins.

The role of the student conferencing utilities is the opposite of what many have come to expect from computers. Rather than doing the analysis work for students, this type of program actually encourages students to analyze their own writing. The computer program may give guidance or supply windows for comments, but it is the students who have to do the careful reading and commenting.

Grading Utilities

While it is crucial that students learn to evaluate their writing independently and make as many improvements as they can on their own, it is also important for teachers to evaluate student writing. A number of teachers have looked to computers for some help in the clerical aspects of writing assessment and grading. Since students are writing on a computer and could just as easily turn in their work on a disk as on paper, why not collect disks and use the computer to help grade them?

The use of grading utilities for providing feedback on student writing has been tried by many people. One approach is to set up word processor macros, redefined key combinations that are usually available with more powerful word processing programs. For example, a teacher might redefine Control-F so that it tells the word processor to print a message about sentence fragments. The message can be fairly long and include a three- or four-line explanation of fragments with an example. Instead of having to mark such an error in the margin of a paper, the teacher would move the cursor to the location in the text where the fragment appears and press Control-F. The complete explanation is then inserted into the paper at the designated point. By creating a number of macros for major errors, teachers can respond with just a keystroke or two to most of the mistakes they are likely to see in students' papers. In addition, students get more feedback and more complete marking than they normally find in their margins.

A large-scale version of this approach is the RSVP Project at Miami-Dade Community College in Miami, Florida (Anandam, 1983). RSVP stands for Response System with Variable Prescriptions, a title that reflects the project's focus on individualized analysis and feedback. Using the RSVP system, errors found on student papers are identified and coded by type: fragment, subject-verb agreement, punctuation, syntax, etc. For each type of error identified, the teacher also selects relevant specific details: omission of end punctuation, misuse of commas, etc. Instead of inserting a few lines of comment into the student's paper, however, each error that is marked results in a page of explanation with appropriate exercises appended to the essay.

Writer's Network (Ideal Learning) is a program currently under development that takes a different approach to grading. First, the program creates a statistical portrait of the essay. When teachers begin grading the paper, they are shown the total number of words in the essay, the number of words per sentence, the level of subordination, and other related information. As the teacher marks the essay using any of the standard error codes, a comment is placed in the student's paper and in both the student and class record. The result is a running total of the kinds of errors made by the student and the class.

These totals can be used in several ways. First, students can be automatically directed to a set of corresponding exercise built into the system. More importantly, the instructor can determine how individual students are doing over a period of time and how the class as a whole is faring. If the class summary shows that eight students have continuing problems with parallelism and six students are misusing semicolons, that pretty well establishes what to do on Monday morning. Teachers can direct their efforts to the writing problems students have actually demonstrated, rather than the problem featured in this week's textbook chapter.

Grading utilities help supply students with more complete

More recently, W. Michael Reed (1987) compared the information supplied by *Writer's Helper* (Conduit) to the grade given by fellow teachers. He found that "the words-per-paragraph ratio was a reliable predictor of essay quality," as was the words-per-sentence ratio.

How can this be? How can a dumb computer, using only a set of numbers, predict something as abstract as quality? Actually, it's quite simple. Look at the result of a writing assessment comparing poor and good 17 year-old writers (Myers, 1980):

	Poor	*Good*
Average number of words per essay	67.3	218.6
Average number of words per sentence	4.4	14.3
Average number of words per paragraph	63.6	135.3

Given such overwhelming differences, it doesn't take much of a computer program to predict with reasonable accuracy which essay is going to get a good grade and which isn't. No wonder Page was able to predict grades so well with his program.

In an actual classroom, however, assigning a grade isn't enough. We hope students will never settle for a paper returned with the comment "B-, add 145 more words for an A." Students should expect, and teachers should be able to supply, a range of responses that include, in addition to a request for additional information, some direction as to what information is expected, where, and why. We don't just grade when we respond to papers; we teach.

But that doesn't mean that computer graders of the kind pioneered by Page should be dismissed. There are times when an overall assessment is all that is needed or desired. The popularity of large-scale assessment of student performance seems to be growing nationwide. Why not save time and dollars by using the computer to do what it has already proven it can do well: large-scale evaluation of student writing? True, one or two percent of the papers may be misjudged, but a sufficiently high percentage would be assessed correctly to result in accurate decision making and recommendation.

Conclusion

Student essays are currently sitting in millions of computers, and many thousands of teachers are trying to determine how best to take advantage of this opportunity for writing analysis. For some it will be a quick check for homonym errors and pompous phrasing. For others it will be peer review of papers through computer conferencing. A few will try to reduce the clerical load by using computer-based grading or feedback. There are still many decisions to be made about how computers can or should be used in writing anlysis. The opportunities are numerous and varied, and the future potential is even more exciting than the present.

IN SUMMARY

Six Directions for Computer Analysis of Student Writing

- Writing analysis programs can be helpful in improving students' knowledge of standard conventions in spelling, punctuation, and grammar. This will provide the students with greater independence from the teacher, and provide the teacher with student papers filled with fewer mechanical errors.

- There are at least six difference types of writing analysis programs available: error checkers, reformatters, audience awareness programs, student conferencing utilities, grading utilities, and automatic graders.

Writing-Related Research: A Review of the Literature

by Cathy Gunn

Reprinted with permission from The Writing Notebook, *Jan./Feb. 1989.*

Development of Children's Writing

According to Smith (1982), as cited by Sinatra and Geisart (1986), "children do not learn language as an abstraction, as an end unto itself, but as a process to achieve other ends." A major problem in writing instruction up to this time is that it has been done as an exercise—an end in itself. McQuade (1986) incorporated Piaget's and Bruner's theories with those of current investigators of writing such as Calkins, Jacobs, Marik, Moffett, Petrovsky, Brozick, and Yates, and writes that "writing of any form requires higher cognitive development" (p. 2).

Sinatra and Geisart (1986) write about the holistic form of writing, stating that the higher thought process of synthesis—evaluation, justification, classifying, grouping, and perceiving how things are alike or different without being told that they are so—is necessary (p. 6). Bloom (1956) supports this holistic theory, defining synthesis as "the putting together of elements and parts so as to form a whole." He goes on to say, "This is the category in the cognitive domain which most clearly provides for creative behavior on the part of the learner.... It is probable that tasks involving synthesis objectives provide a wider kind of experience than those involving mainly acquisition of ideas" (pgs. 162-167). Sinatra and Geisart (1986) state that "teachers can point out how a combination of sounds makes a word, how the combination of functional parts makes a sentence, and how a main idea of a paragraph can be found, but the meaning and relationship of each part to the whole is not there until it is synthesized by each student." They continue, ". . . holistic uses of language focus on how language will be used in real social contexts" (p. 6). This is an important consideration in language learning, having powerful implications for the reading and writing curriculum. It can be the goal for educators not to teach writing, not to teach computers, but to teach writing through the content areas using a computer.

Development of Intermediate Students' Writing

To understand how teaching writing as a process influences students in grades kindergarten through six, one must first investigate the writing development of these age groups. Erikson, as cited in Balajthy (1986), states that:

> The formation of self identity is the crucial developmental task of the adolescent years. One forms one's identity through interaction with one's peers, parents, teachers, and others. The resulting feedback is intensely confusing, generating a great deal of psychological stress as a characteristic of adolescents. As

students approach early adolescence, writing can act as an aid for identity building (p. 12).

Younger children, according to Balajthy (1986), assume that there are absolute rules in writing, that events must be described exactly as they occurred, whether there are components that are tangential to the basic plot. Stories by this age child are usually ended with "happily ever after." But intermediate students begin to display evidence of ability to deal with multiple viewpoints (p. 11).

Intermediate grade students develop the ability to take on different roles as they write. They develop a sense of "voice," which, according to Donald Graves (1983), "is the dynamo of the writing process, the reason for writing in the first place." Children learn to "control a subject, limit it, persuade, sequence information, change their language . . . all to satisfy their own voices, not the voices of others" (p. 31). Graves also calls the voice the imprint of ourselves on our writing, which pushes our writing on (p. 226). Balajthy (1986) writes that intermediate grade students "develop the ability to take on different roles as they write— skill of voice involves complexity, of distancing one's point of view from oneself. The egocentricity of younger children makes this task difficult" (p. 11). Older children can pretend to become that explorer and write about their experiences from another point of view.

Calkins, as cited in Balajthy (1986), writes that the operation of the writing process becomes largely internalized with intermediate grade students. Operations which once had to be carried out concretely with several drafts can now be carried out in the student's mind (p. 11). Children at this age are developing an intuitive feeling about what is effective or ineffective in their writing. They can hear what is right and wrong, and have years of experience of detailed feedback from their teachers and peers.

The younger child is characterized by egocentricity or self-centeredness and younger children focus on themselves, which is as it should be, according to Graves (1983, p. 239). But as children grow older, they decenter, which is defined as the "act of backing off, getting off the center of the problem and seeing it in its broadest terms" (p. 239). This decentering allows children to function at increasingly adult levels (Balajthy, 1986, p. 11). Ganz (1984) writes that influences which work on writing development are seen as a natural process of maturation combined with an expanding involvement in the writing process across the curriculum (p. 5). With all the research evidence on the developmental stages of writing, Busching and Schwartz (1983) feel that no matter what the grade level, teachers should let children become involved with real writing at whatever level of competence and not wait until such time as the teacher feels that children have mastered all the separate skills needed for writing (p. 58).

Writing as a Process

In many ways, the principles and practices of good instruction haven't changed that much over the years, although we've experienced a number of different curricular fashions, according to Jon Madian (1987):

> Schools and districts must realize that they are in the curriculum design business. They will want to explore how technology can support their design and dissemination efforts... teachers will be refining continuously their own curriculum response to current research, best practices, and their own educational experiences (p. 1).

Writing and Thinking, a teacher resource book for teachers (Adelman, 1985), lists three principles upon which writing instruction should be based:

1. Writing is meaningful when it is done for an actual purpose and a specific audience.
2. Writing involves several stages of thinking, trying, and refining, and it is, therefore, best taught as a process.
3. Writers require frequent practice that incorporates feedback about the success of their communication at several points along the way toward a finished product. (p. viii)

Current research in composition reveals that teaching writing as a process rather than a product develops students' writing skills more effectively (Wresch, 1987, p. 33). The shift from product to process has occurred partially because scholars are questioning prior descriptions of good written products, but also because of a need for operational knowledge about writing, since the end result of writing does not necessarily include information about the procedures that the child used to get to the finished product (Humes, 1984, p. 46). Busching and Schwartz (1983) write that "children learn to use language as part of the process of making sense of the world and the language that surrounds them. They do not wait passively to be 'taught'" (p. 1).

"The emphasis in writing has shifted from product to process" (p. 1). Zamel (1983) writes that "researchers and teachers are recognizing that examining product alone tells us very little about what underlies the product... they realize that if we are to have some impact on the product, on the performance, we must inform ourselves about what proceeded it" (p. 195). Zamel continues, "The composition classroom, rather than concerning itself only with learning to write, should be a place where students are writing to learn" (p. 199).

Methods For Writing as a Process

The process approach to writing as outlined by Donald Murray and cited by Wresch (1987) includes the following components:

- **Prewriting:** Oral discussion, brainstorming, reflection, reading
- **Writing:** Organizing ideas, drafting
- **Revising:** Peer review, evaluation
- **Editing:** Spelling check, correcting, research, grammar, selecting words

There are more activities under each heading than those few listed, but they do show the complexity of the process of writing. It begins with rough ideas, initial research, notes, and ramblings; goes through multiple drafts in consideration of its audience, purpose, and organization; and finally is edited for spelling, word choice, style, and layout. What we see as a final document has clearly had a lengthy evolution (Wresch, 1987, p. 1, 2). Other writers have also included the "sharing," "evaluating," and "publishing" components.

This gives us a good working model for writing that tends to take students "out of workbooks and into a wider range of writing assignments, as it encourages them to experiment, revise, and alter their written work" (Wresch, 1987, p. 2). There is no argument over the fact that students need to learn and master certain skills if they are to become proficient writers. Learning to deal with content, organization, style, punctuation, usage, and spelling is also an ongoing process. Encouraged by textbooks that view writing as a series of isolated skills, programs have removed skills from their appropriate context: the writing process itself. Skills should be taught in the context of the writing process rather than through isolated exercises that have no bearing on real communication. The Wisconsin Department of Public Instruction *Guide to Curriculum Planning in English/ Language Arts* (Last, 1986) gives these reasons for doing so:

1. Students have a reason for learning the skills: They are going to apply them immediately.
2. Learning "sticks" when it is connected with purpose.
3. Students see the importance of skills, see their efforts rewarded, when they see greater success in a given piece of writing.
4. Integrating language skills in writing leads to careful planning for the whole class, as well as for individualized instruction. When skills work is tailored to the writing assignment and connected with actual student drafts, the teacher is able to focus on specific problems.
5. Fifty years of research, as well as classroom experience in teaching writing as isolated skills, tell us that the practice does not work. Students do not become proficient writers through the practice of drills (p. 148).

There are times when language skills work should be introduced and reinforced, when the use of supporting exercises may be appropriate, such as:

1. Just before writing, when the practice has meaning because it will be applied immediately.
2. During revising or editing, before the draft is submitted for formal evaluation or "publishing."
3. Immediately after the draft has been evaluated formally,

when students will see the need to practice certain skills they had trouble with, and before they attend to the next writing task (Last, 1986, p. 148).

It is important with all skills work that the student is not overwhelmed by demands in too many areas at one time. Teachers need to prioritize and limit the number of exercises and return to full writing experience as quickly as possible. Daiute (1985) writes that children who learn early that writing is "not simply an exercise gain a sense of power that gives them confidence to write—and write a lot" (p. 5). Benefits of process-oriented writing, as stated by Auten (1987) include:

1. Increased student interest. Students are active writers, responders, and collaborators, rather than listening recipients of textbook-based information.
2. Development of each writer's voice. First experiences with the process approach can help students overcome the anxiety often associated with writing.... Within a framework of acceptance, students can begin to find individual writing voices, and assuming honest effort, the particular styles they develop tend to be lively and energetic.
3. Writing, thinking, and learning across the curriculum. Development of supportive interrelationships among reading, writing, thinking, and talking is the major benefit of using the process approach in any subject area (p. 33).

References

Adelman, L. (1985). *Writing and thinking: A process approach.* Watertown, MA: Mastery Education Corporation.

Auten, A. (1987, April/May). Writing on the college campus. *The Writing Notebook*, 33-34.

Balajthy, E. (1986, August). *Process writing in the intermediate grades: Magical panacea or oversold cliche?* Paper presented at the Conference on Language and Literacy, Genesco, NY.

Bloom, B. (Ed.). (1956). *Taxonomy of educational objectives: The classification of educational goals.* New York: David McKay.

Busching, B., & Schwanz, J. (Eds.) (1983). *Integrating the language arts in the elementary school.* Urbana, IL; National Council of Teachers of English.

Daiute, C. (1985). *Writing & computers.* Reading, MA: Addison-Wesley.

Ganz, A. (1984). *Writers making meaning: How do young writers share experience within the writing process?* Urbana, IL: National Council of Teachers of English.

Graves, D. (1983). *Writing: Teachers and children at work* Portsmouth, NH: Heinemann.

Humes, A. (1984, April). Writing research into practice. *Educational Digest, 49,* 46-49.

Last, E. (1986). *A guide to curriculum planning in English language arts.* Madison: Wisconsin Department of Public Instruction.

Madian, J. (1987, April/May). Curriculum renewal and the Chinese cleaver. *The Writing Notebook,* 1.

McQuade, M. (1986, August). *Implications for teaching report writing using the informal process.* Bronxville, NY. (ERIC Document Reproduction Service No. ED 274 976)

Sinatra, R., & Geisart, G. (1986, January). *Stressing holistic approaches to the teaching of reading and writing using microcomputers.* Paper presented at the Annual Meeting of the Southwest Regional Conference of the International Reading Association, San Antonio, TX.

Wresch, W. (1987). *A practical guide to computer uses in the English/language arts classroom.* Englewood Cliffs, NJ: Prentice-Hall.

Zamel, V. (1983, March). *In search of the key: Research and practice in composition.* Paper presented at the Annual Convention of Teachers of English to Speakers of Other Languages, Toronto, Canada (ERIC *Document* Reproduction Service No. ED 275 152)

Cathy Gunn (1428 E. 20th, Eugene, OR 97403) is a doctoral student in Curriculum and Instruction, with an emphasis on language arts and computers.

IN SUMMARY

Writing-Related Research: A Review of the Literature

- Approaching writing instruction with an emphasis on the process of writing rather than a final product from the student is supported by the professional literature. Current research reveals that teaching writing as a process develops students' writing skills more effectively.

- The process approach to writing instruction involves students in higher order mental tasks such as synthesis, evaluation, justification, classifying, grouping, and perceiving differences.

- There are four generally recognized components to the process approach to writing instruction: (a) Prewriting—oral discussion, brainstorming, reflection, reading; (b) Writing—organizing ideas, drafting; (c) Revising—peer review, evaluation; and (d) Editing—spelling check, correcting research, grammar, selecting words.

- Benefits of process-oriented writing instruction include: (a) Increased student interest; (b) development of each writer's voice; and (c) writing, thinking, and learning across the curriculum.

COMPUTERS IN THE CURRICULUM: LANGUAGE ARTS
Edited by Lynne Anderson-Inman

Computers and First Grade Writing: A Learning Center Approach

By Nancy Kuechle

Writing teachers have long advocated frequent writing as a means to improve writing skills, and computer teachers have been increasingly enthusiastic about the benefits of word processing for teaching the writing process to students of all ages. Use of the computer helps sustain the interest and enthusiasm of youthful authors while supporting a diversity of writing experiences. The product—their own printed page—is new and exciting to students. Described below is a first-grade writing project that combined word processing with a learning center approach to teach beginning writing skills. It produced dramatic results.

The Project

Beginning in November, first graders in the experimental writing program attended the computer lab four days a week for 45-minute periods. During each visit to the computer lab, they completed various activities both on and off the computer. The 12-computer lab was divided into five stations, three using the computer and two not using the computer. The students were divided into five heterogeneous groups. Each group attended a different station each visit. A chart on the wall indicated which group was to attend which station. Before beginning the rotation, the software pieces to be used were introduced to the students, and they were each given a chance to experiment and familiarize themselves with the programs.

The first computer station focused on phonics. *Snoopy's Reading Machine* (Random House) was used initially, as its presentation of words through word families paralleled the spelling approach used in the first grade classes. When all lessons on that program were completed, the MECC *Final Consonants* program and some Logo-based stories were substituted. The goal of the phonics station was to expose the children to phonics rules and correct spelling. Although spelling was not a primary focus of the program, there was the hope that learning phonics would provide students with a foundation for spelling phonetically regular words when writing.

The second computer station used the program *Kidwriter* (Spinnaker). The program allows students to select pre-designed graphics and arrange them on the screen to create a scene. Size, color, position, and background are controlled by the students. When the scene is complete, a simple word processor allows the student to write a story about it. Then both picture and story can be printed. At first, students were so involved in creating their pictures that story length and quality of writing suffered. A teacher-imposed limit of four figures in each scene improved the stories by leaving more time for writing. As their ability to manipulate the program and their familiarity with the graphic capabilities of the software grew, this restriction was lifted. After the stories were printed, misspelled words were corrected by the teacher and the stories were then put into book form for the students to read to themselves and to each other.

The last computer station used the word processing program *Magic Slate* (Sunburst). This program was selected because of its ability to print out in a 40-column (primary print) display. Students learned how to write, delete, and insert characters. For the first exercise they were given sentences to copy, with blanks to fill in. The first week the sentence read "My name is _____ . I am _____ years old." After completing these sentences, the students added another sentence telling something about themselves. As students' abilities to use the word processor developed, the amount of direction they were given decreased. Eventually they were given only a topic sentence, a topic, or occasionally no direction at all. Topics included holidays, classroom happenings, or subjects related to other areas of study (social studies, science, etc.). As with the *Kidwriter* stories, *Magic Slate* paragraphs were corrected for spelling by the teacher for future reading by the authors and their peers.

One of the two non-computer stations was a listening post. Students used headphones to listen to stories recorded on audio cassette while they followed along in their books. This station was designed to familiarize the students with story reading, to allow them to see words correctly spelled, and to improve their reading fluency. A variety of levels and types of stories were used at this station, from easy readers to non-fiction books dealing with subjects studied elsewhere in the curriculum. When the tapes concluded before the end of the period, students could either finish stories begun at the writing station, or draw a picture to illustrate the tape they had just heard.

The final station was a writing station. Students were given a topic to write about and then to illustrate. At this station, students used pencils, crayons, and paper. Again, no emphasis was placed on correct spelling or grammar, although completed stories were corrected by the teacher. The purpose of this station was to help students realize that writing done on computers does not differ from the writing they do using the old-fashioned tools that are readily available to them. While computers and word processors facilitate the writing and editing processes, it was felt that students must still be able to write, and to enjoy writing, using paper and pencils.

The emphasis of this experimental program was on fluency rather than accuracy of writing. Students were encouraged to approximate the spelling of unfamiliar words. No criticism was made for misspelling, and no spelling help was given by the teachers. At the end of each session, students would read their stories to the class and share their illustrations. The audience was always attentive, and the author was usually proud. Children who felt their stories were not their best effort would sometimes read them apologetically, and ask to read an improved version next time. This sharing led to an improvement in quality of the students' reading skills as well as their writing skills.

Results

While it was evident throughout the program that the children enjoyed the various writing experiences and were writing more fluently than before, the true impact of the project wasn't clear until February. At that time a first-grade teacher of another class in the school saw some of the writing that students had produced. She was amazed by the fluency, creativity, and length of the stories being written. While both classes were approximately equal in ability in other domains, the writing skills of the students in the experimental program appeared to be far superior to those of the students who had not participated in the program. To explore whether or not there was an actual difference in writing skill between the two groups, the same writing assignment was given to each class. All students were given a picture of a snowman and asked to write a story about it.

The resulting stories were analyzed using Kellogg Hunt's method for analyzing the maturity level of children's writing. This method breaks down writing into phrases that can stand alone as sentences, known as Terminal units (T-units). "A T-unit is a single main clause plus whatever else goes with it" (Hunt, 1977, p. 92-93). The mean number of T-units written by students in the experimental group was substantially higher than the number of T-units in the comparison group. Stories written by

Mean Number of T-units Across Ability Levels		
Ability	Computer group	Non-computer group
Above average	5.6	3.0
Average	6.5	2.8
Below average	4.5	1.4

Table 1.

Mean Number of Words per T-unit Across Ability Levels		
Ability	Computer group	Non-computer group
Above average	5.7	5.3
Average	5.8	5.0
Below average	5.2	5.0

Table 2.

students who learned to write using the computer learning centers averaged 5.4 T-units, while stories written by the other students averaged only 2.5 T-units. The difference between the number of words per T-unit was not so dramatic. Stories produced by the computer based group averaged 5.5 words per T-unit, while stories written by the other group averaged 5.1 words per T-unit.

Overall, students who interacted with the computer learning centers developed more writing fluency than students who did not have this opportunity. Students in the experimental group wrote stories that were longer and more detailed. In addition, their sentences were slightly more mature, including more frequent use of prepositional phrases and adjectives. There was also a difference in spelling between the two groups. Although the total number of misspellings was high for both groups, the computer using group was more likely to spell sight words correctly. The quality of their misspellings was also better. They were more likely to use (and misspell) difficult words. And the approximations they made were very close to the correct spellings.

In an attempt to examine the benefits of this approach to beginning writing instruction for different groups of students, the results were analyzed by students' reading level. Students were divided into three ability levels: above average, average, and below average. Table 1 presents the mean number of T-units for students in each ability level for both the computer using group and the non-computer using group.

As can be seen from Table 1, computer using students at all three ability levels wrote stories with substantially more T-units than their non-computer using counterparts. It is interesting to note that the average readers in the computer using group actually produced more T-units than did the above-average readers. This was not true of the non-computer group.

Table 2 presents the mean number of words per T-unit for students in each reading level for both the computer using and non-computer using groups. A similar pattern can be seen. Students at all three ability levels produced more words per T-unit, with the average students outperforming the above average students.

Conclusions

The implications are clear. Frequent writing using a computer based learning center approach appears to improve writing skill for students of all ability levels. The impact of this approach appears to be especially beneficial for average readers. The fact that the majority of the writing experiences were computer based probably helped sustain students' interest and enthusiasm. The use of frequent writing and computer based phonics instruction also appears to have had benefits for students' ability to spell or to approximate the spelling of words.

Using learning centers for language arts instruction is not new. As one administrator remarked, "You are doing what primary teachers have been doing for years." The difference lay in the fact that the learning centers in this program used computers to provide students with various reading and writing experiences. The students were highly motivated to do the writing, perhaps because the medium was novel to them. They enjoyed the computer activities and they enjoyed seeing their words in print. Every child in the program appeared to benefit from the activities, learning to write several sentences on any subject, prompted or unprompted. The improvement was especially noticeable for students whose native language was not English. At the beginning of the project many of these children were unsure of what a word was, what individual letters were, or what the space bar on the computer did. By the end of the project they were able to produce nice little stories and were unafraid to express themselves. They worked independently. They wrote!

Nancy Kuechle, Computer Coordinator, Horace Mann School, Beverly Hills, CA 90211.

References

Hunt, K. W. (1977). Early blooming and late blooming syntactic structures. In C. R. Cooper & L. Odell (Eds.) *Evaluating writing: Describing, measuring, judging*. Urbana, IL: National Council of Teachers of English.

Software

Final Consonants, MECC, 3490 Lexington Ave. N., St. Paul, MN 55126-8097.

Kidwriter, Spinnaker Software Corp., 1 Kendall Square, Cambridge, MA 02139.

Magic Slate, Sunburst Communications, Inc., 39 Washington Ave., Pleasantville, NY 10570.

Snoopy's Reading Machine, Random House School Division, 201 E. 50th St., New York, NY 10022.

IN SUMMARY
Computers and First Grade Writing:
A Learning Center Approach

- A learning center approach to the classroom management of computer-based writing instruction produced positive results in a first grade classroom.

- Three computer stations were used, each running a different language arts or writing oriented program. One focused on phonics instruction, another combined graphics and text creating ability for producing an illustrated story, and the third was a student-oriented word processor for writing.

- The students who used the computer learning centers for writing instruction (a) wrote longer stories, (b) used substantially more T-units in their writing, (c) constructed more mature, sophisticated sentences, and (d) were more likely to spell words correctly or have closer approximations in their misspellings.

COMPUTERS IN THE CURRICULUM: LANGUAGE ARTS
Edited by Lynne Anderson-Inman

Speech: The Third Dimension

by Lynne Anderson-Inman, William Adler, Mary Cron, Michael Hillinger, Richard Olson, and Bonnie Prohaska

One of the most exciting advances in computer based language arts instruction is the increasing availability of quality software with voice output. It is no longer unusual for beginning readers and writers to use talking word processors when writing, reading, and sharing their stories. In a classroom equipped with computer technology, students can practice their spelling words and even take their weekly tests with the aid of computerized speech. For a class project, students might write and produce an electronic play in which different characters have distinctly different voices. And down the hall, students with special needs might use drill and practice programs in which instructions and feedback are given orally.

The role of speech in language arts applications varies greatly. For some, speech is an integral and necessary part of the program. For others it is supplementary, even optional. Similarly, the quality of the voice output in today's software varies greatly. In some programs intelligibility is high, matching that of tape-recorded human speech. In others, the sounds are more robotic—machine-like and flat. This wide variation has contributed to a number of misconceptions about voice technology, and in turn confused consumers about the potential of "talking" software. In fact, these variations are not accidental. Instead, they reflect the purpose for which the software was designed, limitations dictated by the technology used, and decisions made by software developers concerning program cost and marketability.

For those interested in the production and use of language arts software with voice output, this article provides a description of the technology, an overview of current applications, a brief look at the research, and a list of considerations for evaluating available programs. Also included are the names and publishers of speech-based language arts software in three categories: talking word processors, computer assisted instruction, and creativity tools.

The Technology

Speech can be added to almost any educational program. Approaches for doing this differ, however, and each approach has its advantages and its limitations. Voice quality is primarily dictated by the amount of computer memory used to process the speech. The three most common ways of adding speech to educational software are (a) digitized speech, (b) encoded speech, and (c) synthesized speech.

The highest quality computer speech is derived from human voice that is recorded, digitized, compressed, and then stored in the computer's memory. To hear the voice, the speech is decompressed, converted back to an analog signal, and then output through a speaker (Figure 1). The amount of memory used for this process is dependent on the amount of compression: the less compression, the more memory intensive and the higher the quality of speech. Unfortunately, the amount of digitized voice that can be stored and processed by a microcomputer is severely limited unless a mass-storage device (hard drive) is used. One second of digitized speech will typically require about 4,000 bytes of memory, but this can easily double. On an Apple IIGS, for example, a second of digitized speech requires approximately 7,000-8,000 bytes of memory.

The process of encoding speech is less memory intensive, but still produces very intelligible speech. Encoded speech, also known as LPC speech (for linear predictive coding), is extremely memory efficient. High-quality voice output can be produced using approximately 175 bytes of memory per second of speech. With this method, human speech is recorded, digitized, and broken into frames that are approximately 25 milliseconds long. A portion of each frame is electronically extracted and the results are then "hand" edited to eliminate errors introduced during the process (Figure 2). Using a special speech synthesis chip, the resulting units are then compared to a computerized mathematical model in order to simulate the original speech signal as closely as possible (Figure 3). When the words requiring speech are known in advance and are defined in number, encoded speech is an effective way for software developers to add high-quality voice without using excessive memory.

In those instances where unlimited speech is required, the appropriate approach for computerized voice output is synthesized speech. Talking word processors, for example, place no limitations on the words a user may wish to have spoken. It is therefore necessary to produce synthesized speech using a text-to-speech translator. Text-to-speech systems translate ASCII

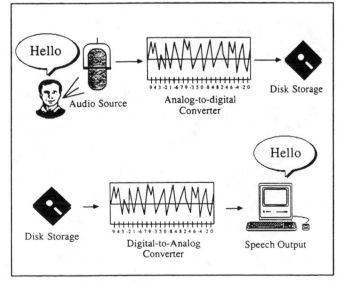

Figure 1. Digitized Speech. (Courtesy Bill Adler, Street Electronics.)

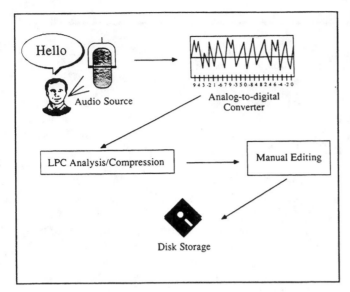

Figure 2. Encoded (LPC) Speech: Recording. (Courtesy Bill Adler, Street Electronics.)

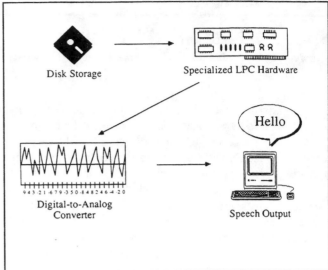

Figure 3. Encoded (LPC) Speech: Playback. (Courtesy Bill Adler, Street Electronics.)

characters (text) into phoneme codes using letter-to-phoneme conversion tables and a set of rules. The phoneme characters are then converted into the digital data needed to make sounds (Figure 4). Exception tables are used to handle the many irregularities of the English language, and additional processing is used to refine the prosody and pronunciation of synthesized speech. As with digitized speech, the quality of synthesized speech is directly related to the amount of memory used: the more complex the text-to-speech algorithm, the more memory required.

Current Applications

Voice output has become a necessary component for certain types of language arts software and a desirable feature in others. The degree to which speech is required in any given program is influenced by the audience for whom the software is intended and the nature of the instructional task.

For pre-literate and low-literacy learners, voice output is frequently essential. Speech that provides orientation messages, program directions, and instructional feedback enables beginning readers to work at the computer independently and to focus on the targeted instructional task. This application helps to solve many of the problems that arise when program instructions and feedback are beyond the reading level of the intended user. As readers acquire more sophisticated skills, the importance of this function is diminished.

For more literate readers, the use of speech can enhance learning by providing an additional information channel. Coupled with the computer's visual display, an auditory explanation can focus attention on the learning activity and expand the amount of information provided at any given time. The instructional impact is increased because the presentation is now multisensory.

For students with delayed language skills or limited proficiency in English, speech can be used to model the sounds of our language. Whether listening to isolated words or complete sentences, the computer based model is under learner control, to be repeated as often as necessary. For children who have difficulty speaking, a talking word processor can even serve as a voice, enabling earlier entry into the speaking world.

For writers, speech output can be a tool for creative expression, adding a third dimension to the usual tools of text and graphics. Writing becomes an interactive and dynamic form of expression when children can hear their creations spoken as well as see them on the page. And dialogue takes on new meaning when a voice can be selected to match the character's age, gender, and personality.

And finally, some subjects simply can't be effectively taught or practiced on the computer without the aid of speech. Spelling is one. The spelling task expected in schools necessitates an oral

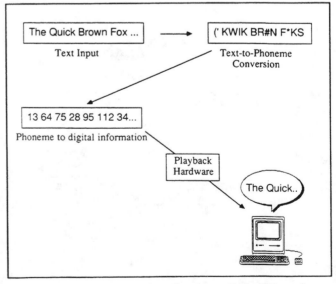

Figure 4. Text-to-Speech. (Courtesy Bill Adler, Street Electronics.)

presentation of the words to be spelled, without accompanying graphics or clues. Although other forms of practice may be fun, if the programs do not require students to write out the words upon hearing them pronounced, they are not practicing spelling, and transfer to the targeted task is usually minimal.

What the Research Says

Only a small amount of research has been conducted on the use of speech-based software in language arts instruction. Although the potential benefits of software with voice output seem to be considerable, the database to support the many claims for its excellence is only beginning to emerge. Furthermore, the variation in voice quality and intelligibility across studies makes interpretation of this database somewhat difficult. Nonetheless, some general conclusions can be drawn from existing studies concerning (a) voice output to support computer assisted instruction in phonics, (b) reading and writing instruction with talking word processors, and (c) speech feedback for reading instruction.

A large percentage of the speech-based programs in language arts use voice output to model the phonetic pronunciation of letters, letter combinations, and/or words. These CAI programs are designed for beginning readers, and the speech is an integral part of the program. Indeed, it is difficult to imagine how phonics software could be effective without the use of speech. Nonetheless, there is relatively little empirical evidence supporting the benefits of speech in this role.

The most thorough study to date was conducted by the Educational Testing Service (ETS) on IBM's *Writing to Read* program. In this program digitized speech is used to introduce phonemes, key words that use the phonemes, and the concept of letter-sound relationships. A study involving thousands of children found that students using the *Writing to Read* program performed significantly better in several reading and writing skills than students in the control groups (Murphy & Appel, 1984). Unfortunately, it is difficult to determine the precise contribution of speech in this study as compared to other program components.

Talking word processors have been recommended as motivational tools for beginning readers and writers. The availability of speech output enables children to hear what they write, thereby reducing their dependence on teachers and hopefully increasing their self-confidence. Studies that have examined the use of talking word processors in writing instruction have found that even very young children benefit from using a word processor combined with synthesized speech (Kurth & Kurth, 1987); that the use of a talking word processor leads to increased editing (Borgh & Dickson, 1986); that talking word processors have a positive effect on collaborative writing (Kurth & Kurth, 1987); and that the motivating effects of unlimited speech output in a word processing environment are more pronounced for less skilled writers (Borgh & Dickson, 1986). Talking word processors also appear to help young nonreaders to develop and read language experience stories (Casey, 1984), and aid in the language acquisition of developmentally delayed children (Meyers, 1986).

And finally, a number of studies have examined the use of computer generated speech feedback during reading instruction. When speech feedback is available, readers can elect to have the computer pronounce words (or parts of a word) that are unknown. Research suggests that access to speech feedback enables poor readers to read passages that are both more interesting and more difficult than would otherwise be possible (McKonkie & Zola, 1987). Furthermore, students who are able to get speech feedback for unknown words have shown increased speed and accuracy on word recognition tests, and improved passage comprehension (Olson, Foltz, & Wise, 1986; Olson & Wise, 1987; Reitsma, 1988). Efforts to explore the optimum form of speech feedback for disabled readers suggest that it may be more effective to provide words segmented at the subsyllable level rather than whole words or words broken into grapheme-phoneme units (Wise, et al, 1989).

Software Selection

The number and type of educational computer programs with speech output is increasing. This trend will continue as memory becomes less expensive and schools begin to purchase hardware with expanded core memory and mass storage devices. Listed below are some considerations to help guide the process of selecting from the growing pool of talking software available for microcomputers. They are divided into three categories: (a) considerations related to the software's purpose; (b) considerations related to software construction; and (c) considerations related to special populations.

Considerations Related to the Software's Purpose

- When speech is used in a program, there should be a specific educational reason for doing so.
- For programs allowing unlimited text entry, synthesized speech is essential because the vocabulary cannot be predicted.
- For programs in which the vocabulary is known and/or high-quality models are needed, digitized and LPC speech are the most appropriate choices.
- For programs in which the words/sentences do not appear on the monitor at the same time (e.g., spelling programs), high-quality speech is essential.
- For talking word processors, programs should be equally capable of reading letters, words, sentences, and entire passages.
- For talking word processors, the ability to add spoken instructional prompts is a desirable feature.
- For creative applications, the pitch, tone, volume, and sex of the speaker should be under user control.

Considerations Related to Software Construction

- Speech quality should be judged by its intelligibility to the student, not the teacher. Adult familiarity with language may enhance the intelligibility of programs that are difficult for children to understand.

- Speech output should be judged in relationship to its role in the program (i.e., the extent to which speech output accomplishes the purpose for which it was included).
- Speech output should not reflect an obvious geographic region or cultural dialect.
- Speech output should include appropriate inflection when serving as a model or asking a question.
- Speech that provides directions, instruction, and/or remediation should be amenable to repetition under student control.
- Speech should be optional when it serves to orient students to the program and/or provide operational directions. Students should be able to bypass instructions if desired.
- Speech should be interruptible, allowing students to exit a program or proceed. A student may have heard as much of an explanation as needed and want to move on.
- Speech-based programs allowing text-to-speech should provide features for handling irregular words not pronounced "according to the rules." When pronunciations for irregular words are inserted by the teacher or student, they should be automatically saved for future use.
- Attention should be given to the amount of "wait-time" between items as a function of providing speech-based feedback. Too much wait-time is frustrating.
- Speech output should not get in the way of achieving the program's objectives. Too much speech can be confusing and counterproductive.
- Speech-based software should work with more than one of the commonly available speech output cards. Schools cannot afford to buy different equipment for every piece of software.

Considerations Related to Special Populations:

- For young students and other nonreaders, speech quality should be exceptionally clear and preferably augmented with graphics.
- For nonnative speakers, speech quality should also be exceptionally clear, with careful attention to the problem sounds of the target population.
- For the visually impaired, speech quality is less important than speed, which can and should be much faster than normal speech. The visually impaired are far more experienced receiving input through their auditory channel and are often frustrated with the slowness of speech-based programs designed for readers who are not visually impaired.

Conclusion

Voice output is fast becoming a necessary component for software in language acquisition, early reading, and special education. It has also emerged as a desirable feature for beginning word processors and language arts CAI programs. Most of the leading educational software developers have now added

voice capability to at least a few of their programs. As this trend continues, speech output will become a standard feature rather than an optional one.

Technological advances in both hardware and software are facilitating this movement. For example, adding high quality digitized speech to any *HyperCard* stack is extremely easy with Farallon's MacRecorder Sound System, an integrated hardware and software package that enables Macintosh users to digitize, edit, and compress any live or prerecorded sound. Furthermore, advances in optical storage technology and the increased availability of CD-ROMs and videodiscs will soon eliminate the memory constraints that accompany high quality speech. In the near future it may no longer be a question of whether to add voice to educational software, but rather a question of whose voice to add.

This article is a summary of the information presented by the authors at a number of regional and national conferences as part of a panel entitled "Producing and Using Speech-Based Software." Authorship, with the exception of first author, is in alphabetical order.

Dr. Lynne Anderson-Inman, Associate Professor, College of Education, University of Oregon, Eugene, OR 97403.

William Adler, Vice President, Street Electronics Corporation, Carpinteria, CA 93013.

Mary Cron, RYMEL, Inc., Palos Verdes Estates, CA 90274 (formerly Vice President of Product Development, First Byte Software).

Dr. Michael Hillinger, LexIcon Systems, Beaver Meadow Road, Sharon, VT 05065 (formerly Executive Editor for Houghton Mifflin, Educational Software Division).

Dr. Richard Olson, Professor, Department of Psychology, University of Colorado, Box 345, Boulder, CO 80309.

Bonnie Prohaska, Rading & Computers, 230 Schenk St., Madison Metropolitan School District, Madison, WI 53715.

References

Borgh, K. & Dickson, W.P. (1986). *The effects on children's writing of adding speech synthesis to a word processor.* Paper presented at the annual conference of American Educational Research Association.

Casey, J. (1984). *Beginning reading instruction: Using the LEA Approach with and without microcomputer intervention.* Unpublished paper.

Kurth, R. & Kurth, L. (1987). *A comparison of writing instruction using word processing, word processing with voice synthesis, and no word processing.* Paper presented at the annual conference of American Educational Research Association.

McConkie, G.W. & Zola, D. (1987). Two examples of computer-based research on reading: Eye movement monitoring and computer-aided reading. In D. Reinking (Ed.), *Computers and reading: Issues for theory and practice* (pp 97-107). New York: Teachers College Press.

Meyers, L. (1986). *The language machine: Using computers to teach language skills*. New York: Teachers College Press.

Murphy, R.T. & Appel, L.R. (1984). *Evaluation of the Writing to Read instructional system 1982-1984*. Princeton, N.J.: Educational Testing Service.

Olson, R., Foltz, G., & Wise, B. (1986). Reading instruction and remediation with the aid of computer speech. *Behavior Research Methods, Instruments, and Computers, 18*, 93-99.

Olson, R. & Wise, B. (1987). Computer speech in reading instruction. In D. Reinking (Ed.), *Computers and reading: Issues for theory and practice* (pp. 156-177). New York: Teachers College Press.

Reitsma, P. (1988). Reading practice for beginners: Effects of guided reading, reading-while-listening, and independent reading with computer-based speech feedback. *Reading Research Quarterly, 23* (2), 219-235.

Wise, B., Olson, R., Ansett, M., Andrews, L., Terjak, M., Schneider, V., Kostuch, J., and Kriho, L. (1989). Implementing a long-term computerized remedial reading program with synthetic speech feedback: Hardware, software, and real-world issues. *Behavior Research Methods, Instruments, and Computers, 21*(2), 173-180.

Language Arts Software with Voice Input
Talking Word Processors

Dr. Peet's TalkWriter, My Words; Hartley Courseware. (Apple IIe or GS with Echo speech synthesis card.)

FirstWriter; Houghton Mifflin. (Apple IIe or GS with Echo speech synthesis card.)

KeyTalk; PEAL Software. (Apple IIe or GS with Echo speech synthesis card.)

KidsTime; Great Wave Software. (Macintosh.)

KidTalk; SmoothTalker, Mi Editor Primario (Spanish), *Listen to Learn;* First Byte. (Macintosh, Apple IIGS, IBM, Amiga, Tandy 1000, Atari ST.)

Language Experience, Recorder Plus; Teacher Support Software. (Apple IIe or GS with Echo or Slotbuster speech synthesis card.)

Primary Editor Plus; IBM. (IBM with headphones or PS2 Speech attachment.)

Pro Words, Larry Skutchan. (Apple II or GS with Echo or Slotbuster.)

Talking Text Writer. Scholastic. (Apple IIe or GS with Echo speech synthesis card.)

WordTalk, Computer Aids. (Apple II or GS with Echo or Slotbuster.)

Computer Assisted Instruction

Breakthrough to Language, Creative Learning. (Apple II series with Echo.)

Crosswords, Marblesoft. (Apple II series with Echo.)

Edmark Reading Program; Edmark Corporation. (Apple II series with Echo.)

Exploratory Play; Representational Play; PEAL Software. (Apple IIe or GS with Echo Muppet Learning Keys.)

Macmillan Phonics; Macmillan Publishing Co. (Apple IIe or GS with Ufonic Voice System.)

Make a Flash, Reading Realities; Teacher Support Software. (Apple IIe or GS with Slotbuster card.)

PALS; IBM. (IBM with InfoWindow.)

Reading Comprehension; Integrated Learning System; Educational Systems Corp. (Apple IIGS, IBM, Tandy 1000 with CD-ROM.

Reading Skills Development Program; American Education Software. (Apple IIe or GS with Echo.)

Sound Ideas Vowels; Sound Ideas Consonants; Sound Ideas Word Attack, Sound Ideas Word Structure, Spelling Speechware, Reading Comprehension; Houghton Mifflin. (Apple IIe or GS with Echo.)

Speller Bee, First Letters and Words, Bouncy Bee Learns Letters, Bouncy Bee Learns Words; First Byte. (Macintosh, Apple IIGS, IBM, Amiga, Tandy 1000, Atari ST.)

Syllasearch; Construct-a-Word; Hint and Hunt; DLM. (Apple IIe or GS with Echo or Supertalker; Apple IIc with Cricket.)

Talking Nouns; Talking Nouns II, Talking Verbs, First Words; Laureate Learning Systems. (Apple IIe or GS with Echo.)

Talking Reader Rabbit, The Learning Company. (Apple IIGS, Tandy 1000.)

Talking Writer Rabbit, The Learning Company. (Macintosh.)

Touch and Learn; Lexia Learning Systems. (IBM with Dialogic speech card and touch screen.)

Voice Reading; Voice English; Chatterbox Voice Learning Systems. (Apple II series or IBM with Echo and Chatterbox Voice Input Card.)

Word Wise; Reading Comprehension; DLM. (Apple IIe or GS with Echo; Apple IIc with Cricket.)

Writing to Read, IBM. (IBM with PS2 Speech attachment.)

Creativity Tools

FirstWriter; Houghton Mifflin. (Apple IIe or GS with Echo+.)

Gateway Stories, Gateway Authoring System, Center for Applied Special Technology. (Macintosh with *Hypercard*.)

Language Experience Series; Teacher Support Software. (Apple IIe or with Slotbuster card.)

Mad Libs, Dinosaur Discovery Kit, Puzzle Storybook, The Storyteller, The Rhyming Notebook; First Byte. (Macintosh, Apple IIGS, IBM, Amiga, Tandy 1000.)

Monsters & Make Believe; Pelican/Learning Lab. (Apple IIe or GS, IBM with Echo card.)

Once Upon A Time, Compu Teach. (Apple II GS or IBM.)

Paint with Words; MECC. (Apple IIe or GS with Ufonic Voice System.)

Playwriter's Theater; Educational Technology. (Apple IIe or GS with Ufonic Voice System.)

Super Story Tree; Scholastic. (Apple IIe or GS.)

Talking Sensible Speller; Sensible Software. (Apple IIe or GS with Echo.)

Talking TouchWindow; Edmark Corporation. (Apple II series with Apple TouchWindow and Echo Card.)

Speech Output Systems

OutSPOKEN, Berkeley System Design. (Macintosh.)

Say It, Brent Partridge. (Macintosh.)

SCAT (Screen Articulator), RC Systems, (Apple II or GS.)

Talking Keys, Brady Graham. (Macintosh.)

Speech Peripherals

Echo speech synthesizer cards for Apple and IBM computers. Street Electronics, P.O. Box 50220, Santa Barbara, CA 93150.

MacRecorder Sound System 2.0. Farallon Co., Inc., 2000 Powell St., Suite 600, Emeryville, CA 94608.

Slotbuster speech synthesis card. Available from Teacher Support Software, P.O. Box 7130, Gainesville, FL 32605.

Ufonic Voice System. Jostens Learning Systems, Inc., 800 Business Center Dr., Mt. Prospect, IL 60056.

IN SUMMARY
Speech: The Third Dimension

- Voice output for computers varies greatly in quality and can be obtained by three different methods: (a) digitized speech, (b) encoded speech, and (c) synthesized speech.

- Talking word processors, talking spelling programs, and other language arts software make use of voice output either as an essential component of the software, such as that designed for pre-literate or low-literacy learners, or as a supplemental mode for enhancing the instructional design of the program.

- The small amount of empirical research that does exist concerning voice output in educational programs suggests (a) the benefits of speech in a phonics program is uncertain, (b) talking word processors can have a positive effect on collaborative writing behaviors, editing skills, and language experience stories, and (c) speech feedback in reading lessons enables poor readers to read passages that are more difficult than would otherwise be possible.

- Technological advances in both hardware and software, including CD-ROM and videodisc, may bring more, higher-quality voice output to educational programs in the near future.

- An extensive list of language arts software with voice output capabilities is included as an addendum to this article.

COMPUTERS IN THE CURRICULUM: LANGUAGE ARTS
Edited by Lynne Anderson-Inman

Revision for the Restless: Peer Editing with the Macintosh

by Barbara G. Erickson

When students reach high school they often bring misconceptions about the writing process and the role of the writing teacher. Questions such as the following suggest the vast amounts of time spent by previous writing teachers correcting their students' mechanical errors:

"Miss Jones, aren't you supposed to edit my rough draft for me?"

"Why didn't you mark my spelling errors?"

"But I've already recopied my essay. Why does it still need revision?"

Peers and Computers

The combined use of peer editors and computers for writing instruction can make these types of questions disappear from the classroom. I have a step-by-step method for teaching students to peer edit and to revise their compositions within the context of a computer-based writing course. Using this method, both writing scores and attitudes toward the revision process have improved for students.

Two years ago I began the implementation of a new computer writing lab at Spring Woods High School in Houston, Texas. The purpose of the writing lab was to teach the writing process to incoming freshmen and to introduce the use of computers as a revision aid within that process. Computers are an ideal form of support for student revision because changes become fun and painless to make. Furthermore, Collins and Sommers (1985) found that students who use word processors for writing tend to make more and better revisions than students who do not use word processors.

The computer writing lab at Spring Woods High School has twenty-five Macintosh computers, networked to six ImageWriter printers. Students were provided with the new *MacWrite* 5.0 word processing program with integrated spelling checker. We also provided *MacProof* 2.0, a text analysis program that checks students' writing for correct capitalization, punctuation, "be" verbs, sexist and racist language, verbals, expansion (transitional words) and abridgment (topic sentences and concluding sentences). We found that for all students, even low-ability groups, *MacWrite* required only 30 minutes of training and *MacProof* required only 20 minutes.

Described briefly below is a 6-day unit designed to introduce students to peer editing and the use of the computer for revision.

Day 1

In the regular English classroom all students are introduced to revision and peer editing using teacher-assigned paragraphs.

The first paragraph provides a vehicle for students to get acquainted with an error checklist, the same checklist that will be used later in the peer editing process. Each student is asked to analyze the following paragraph using the procedures listed in Figure 1.

Good sportsmanship is caused by many things. If you cooperation thats good sportsmanship. If you don't have any fights during a game, that is a good a good game. When you listin to your coach, you should have good sportsmanship to the other team. And you should always follow directions in anything you do. When you play togeather that is good. It shows that you can play the game with others. On your team or on the other team you should never hold gruges you should just play a friendly game.

Peer Editing Checklist

Each peer editing group will mark errors using the checklist below. All group members will sign this peer editing sheet. The original author is responsible for final changes.

I.   Check words.
1. Circle misspellings.
2. Underline "be" verbs.
3. Place in box words that need improving.

II. Check sentences.
1. Place ( ) around fragments and mark with an F.
2. Place ( ) around run-on sentences and mark with R.
3. Put brackets around short, choppy sentences that are related.

III. Check paragraph structure
1. Mark a + if topic sentence is okay, mark an X if it is wrong, and mark a ? if it is weak.
2. Number details that support topic sentence.
3. Mark with a + if clincher sentence is okay, mark with an X if it is wrong, and mark with a ? if it is weak.

Group Members   _____

_____

_____

Figure 1.

Following their individual attempts to correct the paragraph, the teacher uses an overhead projector to generate discussion and demonstrate appropriate marks on the paragraph so that all students can see the correct way to indicate sections needing revision.

Students are then assigned to peer editing groups of three students each. These groups are carefully constructed to include one excellent writer, one average writer, and one weak writer. Having three students in each group works well for two reasons. First, three students can sit side by side, all working on the same essay at the same time. Second, a group of three students can usually complete three evaluations during one class period of 55 minutes. To provide these peer editing groups with practice on marking errors, each group is given three new faulty paragraphs to correct, similar to the first paragraph on sportsmanship (see box on this page). Each student claims ownership for one of the paragraphs and together they edit the paragraphs using the peer editing checklist in Figure 1.

Day 2

Students meet in the computer writing lab. The focus of Day 2 is on making revisions with the assistance of the computer. Using the *MacWrite* word processing program, students call up each of the three paragraphs and make the revisions discussed on the previous day. After these revisions are made, students print their revised paragraphs. This work fills one class period.

Day 3

Students meet again in their regular English classroom. The focus of Day 3 is on learning to make quality revisions, not just superficial changes. The teacher solicits suggestions for revising each of the three paragraphs. These are shown on an overhead projector and the students are encouraged to discuss the changes they feel work best. Through a consensus of opinion, students decide what editing works best for each paragraph.

Day 4

Students are ready to edit their own longer essays. Students again meet in the computer lab. Using the writing process, students are asked to write a short composition, type it into the computer, and print it. Students are then asked to use the text analysis program *MacProof*, circling problems areas on their hard copies and reading the tutorials as necessary. With these areas marked, students return to their regular classroom, alerted to potential problems appropriate for discussion in their peer editing groups.

Days 5 and 6

Students are assigned to new peer editing groups, using the same criteria as before. Using an error checklist similar to Figure 1, students work together to revise each other's essays. This work takes one full class period.

Students return to the computer writing lab to make the final revisions on their essays. Final copies are printed and turned in to the teacher for evaluation.

Revised Attitudes

"Look at my screen, Joe, and tell me what you think."

"This sounds awkward, so I'm improving it as I type."

"No one can help me type because I am making changes as I type my rough draft."

Peer Editing Paragraphs for Revision

Developed by Roberta Young, Coordinator of Special Projects Spring Branch Independent School Dist.

Fear

The most common fear of children is fear of darkness. Some adults are still afraid of the dark. Most people can remember many of their fears related to the darkness. For example, how they got from the light switch to thier bed before the monster under the bed got them. Most children out-grow this fear by the time they are teenagers. Some people remember thinking that was some terible creature living in thier dark closet when the lights were turned on, the creature might just be a jacket hanging on hanger. A dark place like a attic was a place they would avoid because they would imagine a killer was there.

Rock Music

Many adults think that rock music is just noice. Parents object to rock music becuse they think the words advertize drugs and acting bad and are not good. The parents also think that the loud sound of drums and electric guitars will not be good for their children's hearing. Many parents even object to the names of the groups. Like Grateful Dead or Cold Turkey. Younger generatation and older people will just never agree on what is good music. Teens think that "Elevator music" is boring they say it puts them to sleep. Teens think Barry Manilow is a wimp. He is not a dude. Music is just one of those things that create the generation gap.

Big City People

Most people in a big city are bad toward each other. My brother Sam was going downtown on the bus right after he ate supper. It was just last Friday night. He had a realy bad time. First he lost his wallet, someone might have stoled it. He couldn't even get anyone to give him money to call home. Noone would give him any help. He had to walk the people in this big city are realy bad.

As the above student comments reveal, attention to revision went far beyond the well-supervised peer editing process, Using peer editing and the computer to assist revision within a process approach to writing instruction has proven to be successful for us at Spring Woods High School. Following one year of implementation, the percentage of freshmen students who passed their TEAMS (Texas Educational Assessment of Minimum Skills) writing prompt tests rose from 55 percent to 77 percent. More important, perhaps, as revision was subtly integrated into the whole process of writing, students' attitudes toward revision changed.

Barbara Erickson, Spring Woods High School, Spring Branch Independent School Dist., 2045 Gessner, Houston, TX 77080.

References

Collins, J.L. & Sommers, E.A. (1985).*Writing on-line: Using computers in the teaching of writing.* Upper Montclair, NJ: Boynton-Cook, 47-50.

Hall, J.K. (1988). *Evaluating and improving writen expression: A practical guide for teachers.* Boston: Allyn and Bacon.

Software

MacProof 2.0, Automated Language Processing Systems, 190 W. 800 N., Provo, UT 84604.

MacWrite 5.0, Claris Corporation, 440 Clyde Ave., Mountain View, CA 94043.

IN SUMMARY

Revision for the Restless:
Peer Editing with the Macintosh

- The combination of peer editing and the use of a computer can clear up some of the misconceptions students have about the writing process and the role of the writing teacher.

- After a year of writing instruction that included peer editing and computer use (word processing with a text analysis program) the number of students who passed a state writing assessment test rose from 55 to 77 percent.

LESSON IDEAS & PROJECTS

Educational theory and research findings are wasted potential unless positive impact is felt in the classroom at some level. It is a quantum leap, however, from theory into practice. The lesson ideas contained in the following five articles provide detailed practial applications for using computers in the context of the process approach to teaching writing. They serve as an excellent starting point from which to adapt and extend with one's own ideas.

Word Processing and Curriculum Renewal

by Jon Madian

Word processing used in conjunction with sound principles of instruction is revolutionizing how students learn to read and write. Many of the most influential, humane curriculums from Dewey through The National Writing Project, Poets-in-the-Schools, and language experience movement, can achieve much finer articulation when supported by word processing.

The question before us now is, "How can we best use word processing to support instruction?" With the great diversity of populations, objectives, teaching styles, software, and hardware, the problem of redesigning curriculum in order to take full advantage of the word processor is extremely complex. People designing curriculum—and this includes teachers—need the best current information about tools and strategies.

Creative Word Processing in the Classroom newsletter first identified the need to network information on the relationships among reading, writing, thinking, literature, and word processing in 1983. *CWP* now begins its fourth year with several changes, including an increase from three to six issues each school year, more pages per issue, and an exciting increase in support from the educational community. Over a dozen network editors will provide information in their areas including cooperative learning, special education, computer labs, creative writing, responding to student writing, and bilingual education.

It is part of the philosophy of *CWP* to join new products with new instructional strategies. In the past, instruction has been dominated by lessons structured around textbooks and worksheets, often produced by people outside of the classroom. In recent years there has been a greater emphasis upon instruction enriched by literature and by student oral and written expression. With the advent of computer technology, *CWP* sees its role as helping to align computer activities with this enriched, student-oriented curriculum. This year *CWP* becomes both a newsletter and curriculum guide for teachers.

In addition, based upon a decade of staff and curriculum development, *CWP* is now publishing three products through its software development group, Humanities Software. *Key Words*, a linguistically based software program, teaches students spelling, composing, and editing as they learn to touch type. It is especially useful for special education and bilingual students because they type meaningful words and phrases. *Write-On Diskettes* are data diskettes designed to help students learn to compose, revise, and edit more fluently, and to help teachers coordinate writing activities on and off the computer. *Write-On Diskettes* support most word processors used in schools, can generate hard copy, and can be revised easily by students and teachers. *Story Tailor Library* is a library of 12 personalized computer stories for grades K through eight, designed so that students' names and other information can be automatically inserted into the stories and poems. They are written to be interesting as well as technically sound, and cover areas that include basal or beginning reading, holidays, mythology, journal writing, and science.

CWP is a non-profit educational corporation and an open network for curriculum design supported by technology. CWP *welcomes ideas that will enrich and improve language arts instruction. For more information about* CWP *or Humanities Software products contact* Creative Word Processing in the Classroom, *P.O. Box 590727, Box CT, San Francisco, CA 94159: ph. 415/759-9324.*

The following lesson, "Homonyms in Poems," is reprinted by permission from the Spring 1986 issue of Creative Word Processing in the Classroom, Part III–*Writing Lessons Designed for Computer Publishing.*

Homonyms in Poems

Poetry is often a word game. Homonyms provide a wide field for the play of such games. Since learning homonyms is important for developing writing and reading skills, homonym poems are an excellent way to build composing, vocabulary, and spelling skills.

With younger writers, you may want to insist that each stanza or line contains only one form of the homonym. At early stages this avoids confusion. You may also want to have students begin with familiar chant form. Here are some homonym poems, going from the simple to more complex.

I Know I Knew
A gnu never knew
How to spell no
But I know how
to spell knew
What confuses me
Is how to spell gnu

The Ball Turned Into a Dance
I'll never forget
The night we played baseball
On Halloween
The bat screeched
And flew out of my hands
And the ball turned into a dance

A Database of Homonyms

You may want to have your class or school develop a data base of homonyms. This is a fine activity, because students begin discovering them in the world of written and spoken language. I don't know if there's a definitive list of homonyms. People I've spoken with agree that the more you search for them the more you find! Here's a partial list:

aide, aid	forth, fourth
air, heir	four, for
aisle, isle, I'll	route, rout, root
no, know	fur, fir
not, knot	scene, seen
ant, aunt	great, grate
our, hour	see, sea, si
ate, eight	grown, groan
pane pain	scents, cents, sense
bare, bear, bear (carry)	heal, heel
pair, pare	seam, seem
basis, bases	here, hear
pallet, palette, palate	surf, serf
be, bee	idle, idol, idyll
pause, paws	sheer, shear
bridal, bridle	in, inn
peace, piece	sight, site, cite
buy, by, bye	knows, nose
pedal, peddle	slay, sleigh
caret, carrot	lone, loan
peel, peal	soar, sore
cereal, serial	made, maid
presence, presents	soul, sole
chance, chants	male, mail
principle, principal	sum, some
coarse, course	medal, meddle
raise, raze	sun, son
creek, creak	meet, meat
read, reed	sow, sew, so
dear, deer	mind, mined
reign, rein, rain	stake, steak
die, dye	need, knead
right, write, rite	stair, stare
flower, flour	knew, new
rode, road	stare, stair
steal, steel	wait, weight
straight, strait	waive, wave
tacks, tax	waste, waist
tail, tale	weak, week
taught, taut	wear, where
tea, tee	whirled, world
there, they're, their	whole, hole
threw, through	whose, who's
to, two, too	wood, would
tow, toe	won, one
vain, vein, vane	you, ewe, yew

> Someone
> Someone and someone
> sums to a sum
> of two someones
> or is it two sum ones

The following lesson, "Animal Unit," is reprinted by permission from the Spring 1986 issue of Creative Word Processing *in the Classroom, Part II–Eleven Ideas to Spark Writing and Word Processing in Your Classroom.*

Animal Unit

The following assignment sheet is offered as a model for integrating different kinds of writing, with an emphasis on creative, personal journal, and expository research writing. This assignment uses right and left brain functions, so that sensory, cognitive, effective, and intuitive functions stimulate and inform each other.

The assignment sheet was handed out, and students helped set a reasonable due date. About six weeks later it was agreed upon (students wanted more time; the teacher wanted less). She felt they'd focus better if they had more pressure. I felt that to get into the various sections and share their progress with each other, students needed more time.

We did not set up an effective system for students to share, question and learn from each other, although it would have been a natural. Every other day or so, students could make a draft of their work in response to one section and share it with classmates. In this way the student's work serves as a model, and they gain from sharing their progress and providing feedback.

The assignment was discussed when the student assignment sheet was passed out. We created oral and written examples of poems, collaborative stories, and fictitious and factual journals.

When I do this unit again I will add a discussion of the animal's totemic or mythical qualities. In schools where the scientific method of inquiry is emphasized, and where students are familiar with generating and testing hypothesis, I would ask them to apply the scientific method to one area of their animal's behavior or biology. I would ask students to generate a testable hypothesis about their animal, and explain how they would test their hypothesis.

Animal Unit
Student Assignment Sheet

These activities can be done in any order you choose. Some of the activities should be done more than once.

Draw Your Animal In His Natural Environment

(You may wish to look at drawings by other artists to get ideas of how to render the animal.)

Lesson Ideas and Projects

Write At Least Three Of The Following From The Animal's Perspective

1. A nightmare the animal might have.
2. A happy dream the animal might have.
3. A funny dream the animal might have.
4. An essay the animal might write taking a position on an issue that concerns him or her.
5. A letter the animal might write to some other animal or person for a particular purpose—social, political, etc.

Poetry

Write about your animal in at least three of the following forms: acrostic, chant (include sounds and environment), Haiku, cooperative blank verse, or individual blank verse poem.

Research Reports

Write a report that explains factually about your animal's behavior, psychology, and social, biological, and ecological aspects.

Read poems and stories about your animal, and write a description. Explain the problem, the character and setting, and tell your view of the story or poem, particularly as it relates to how your animal is depicted.

Journal

Write a fictitious journal by your animal about two or three consecutive days in his or her life. Try to carry themes forward from day to day.

Write a factual journal expressing why you chose your animal.

Dramatization

Alone, or with a friend or two, dramatize some events that would occur in your animal's life.

Story Writing

Write a story about your animal by yourself.

Write a collaborative story with a friend, including your friend's animal in the story.

Essay written by an Eagle

Poisons used by farmers in areas where we eagles live is proving to be very dangerous to us. My sister died last month because she caught and ate a gopher from Farmer John's field. This gopher had ingested some poison. My dad is now very, very sick and my mom weak because of pesticide used at Sam Smith's ranch. He had killed a fox for the family this winter. The eggs that my wife lay recently are not strong. I know this is due to the pollution in the river waters.

Scientists should create a poison that will not be harmful to eagles. Dumping garbage into rivers should be stopped too. We cannot relocate. This is our land. My ancestors have lived on and over these lands for years and years. The ranges where we roam must not be harmed by farmers' pesticides nor pollution of the rivers.

The eagle is the national emblem of the United States of America. We are proud to represent this grand country. To be sure we continue to exist, we must be helped. We must be protected.

Acrostic

Elegant
And Swift
Gliding through the
Light sky
Eagles fly high

Chant

Screech, screech, screech
The eagle comes attacking
Grabbing, piercing, killing his prey
Then soars away

The Computer As A Writing Tool

by Ellen Joslin

Ellen Joslin presents some excellent exercises for introducing the basic functions of word processors. To create a data disk of these exercises, use your word processor to type in each file and save it with the appropriate file name. You will need to make a copy of the data disk for each student.

Computers are slowly but surely being integrated into the McCulloch Middle School language arts curriculum. All Highland Park seventh graders take a one-semester course in "Computer Literacy," where they are introduced to machine usage, word processors, spreadsheets, data bases, BASIC programming, etc. Our new language arts curriculum requires our eighth graders to use the computer as a tool, so they need to be especially proficient on the word processor. Each fall the language arts teachers allow me two class periods to introduce word processing. In order to fit it all in, I've developed a set of exercises to present the "Seven Steps to Successful Word Processing." Each student buys a disk which contains the exercises for use with our word processor. As the school year passes, they store their compositions on their own disks.

On the old theory of:
1. Tell them what you are going to teach,
2. Teach it,
3. Tell them what they have learned,

we begin by loading a file called "Seven."

**Seven Steps to
Successful Word Processing**

1. Retrieve file
2. Delete text
3. Insert text
4. Save file
5. Print file
6. Move text
7. Composition and creation

File name: "Seven"

I run through this list, defining each of the terms briefly, then cover them thoroughly with the exercises. Retrieval is the first and easiest skill to teach. After learning how to load a program, the class as a group loads the text file titled "Poem." The teacher explains that the students have on their disks a series of eight clues which, if correctly interpreted, will allow them to find *that*

which is lost. Those who can retrieve those clues by following the appropriate directions will raise the Titanic.

Dear Friends:

    I'm lost in the deep, far from light
    But do not weep! Put it right.

    I'll give you clues to find my site.
    Write them down—make sure they're right.

    Take my measure, use your mind,
    And a treasure you will find!!

                  Signed,
                  ??????

File name: "Poem"

CLUE 1:
Write the following letters on a piece of paper.
They are clues to help you find that which is lost!

M I D

Now retrieve CLUE 2

File name: "CLUE 1"

CLUE 2:
Write the following letters on a piece of paper.
They are clues to help you find that which is lost!

E N I

Retrieve CLUE 3

File name: "CLUE 2"

CLUE 3:
Write the following clue on a piece of paper.
It will help you find that which is lost!

THE ? IS AN "A."

Retrieve CLUE 4

File name: "CLUE 3"

CLUE 4:
Write the following letters on a piece of paper.
They are clues to help you find that which is lost!

I E A L E

Retrieve CLUE 5

File name: "CLUE 4"

CLUE 5:
On a piece of paper, write the sentence below.
It's a clue to help you find that which is lost!

I'—/H—D————/—N/?/F—L—/C—L—D/
—IT—N———/F—N—/—E/IF/————/—A—!

Retrieve CLUE 6

File name : "CLUE 5"

CLUE 6:
Write the following letters on a sheet of paper.
They are the clues to help you find that which is lost!

T A I C I D M Y

Retrieve CLUE 7

File name: "CLUE 6"

CLUE 7:
Write the following letters on a piece of paper.
They are clues to help you find that which is lost!

O U C N

Retrieve CLUE 8

File name: "CLUE 7"

CLUE 8:
THIS IS YOUR LAST CLUE!
Put the letters you have written in the blank spaces
in the sentence from CLUE 5. Be sure to put them in
the order you uncovered them.

CLUE 3 is a special clue.

GOOD LUCK!

File name: "CLUE 8"

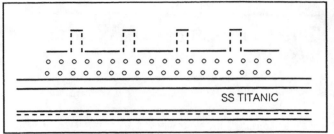

SS TITANIC

After 75 years at the bottom of the sea, the Titanic has been found! File name: (Use the clues to find out!)

The primary purpose of a word processor is to produce and edit text, which involves deletions and insertions. Since there is no penalty for revising on a word processor (no erasures, cross-outs or recopying), students are more willing to rewrite and perfect their work. To teach deletion techniques, direct the student to load "Max."

Directions: Move the cursor to the homonyms in this story. Delete the incorrect one. Only the homonym that fits the story should remain.

Max—the RODE/ROAD Warrior

In the DAZE/DAYS after the GREAT/GRATE war when civilization DYED/DIED and no one defended the WEEK/WEAK THEIR/THERE came a REAL/REEL man. His name was Max. Max was not what he SEAMED/SEEMED to BEE/BE. As a man and BUOY/BOY, he followed the warrior WAY/WEIGH.

THEY'RE/THERE will never again be a hero such as he. THROUGH/THREW war and pestilence, along the desert RODES/ROADS, he fought the savages and ONE/WON. Each TAIL/TALE of daring, each FEET/FEAT of strength was told where good men MEAT/MEET

Who'll RIGHT/WRITE the story of Max and his RAIN/REIGN as king of the highway? Who'll REED/READ and remember when Max defeated the barbarians?

File name: "Max"

The "Skeleton of a Story" is used to show the ease with which text can be inserted. Ideally, a printed copy of the activity (see page 19) is handed out as homework by the classroom teacher, then the students bring it, filled out, to the computer lab ready to make their insertions. When this activity is loaded from the disk, students are sure to note that the blanks have been replaced by parenthesis. This was done to make the whole story fit on one screen.

Lesson Ideas and Projects

Skeleton of a Story

Here are the "bare bones" of a story. By filling in the blanks() in an interesting way, you can make any kind of story you want—mysterious, funny, sad, silly—it's up to you. Be sure to choose an interesting title. When you have finished your story, save the story on your disk and then make a printed (hard) copy of your story.

I always knew my Aunt () was a real (). Why, she (), and one day she (). But even I was surprised when she told us she planned to (). We told her () and begged her not to (), but nothing could (), and so, although we felt (), we watched her ().

() passed. No one heard a () a from Aunt (). We were beginning to wonder if () when suddenly our aunt appeared. She had been () and she seemed very (). ()ly, she told us the whole (). It seemed that she had () and (). Now she was (), and we all felt (). Since then, Aunt () has never (). Instead, she spends her time (). What a () she is!

File name: "Skeleton"

Students will want to save their versions of this story to their personal disks, and the teacher may want a printed (hard) copy for grading, so now is the time to introduce saving and printing text files. Encourage students to review their work on the computer screen and to make and save improvements before printing.

As the students print their work, you might take time to demonstrate some of the print options. Show them centering, left justification, right justification, center justification, and full justification. Printing is seductive; the story comes off the printer looking polished, and kids take pride in showing off their work.

Our final practice exercise shows the students how to move text. There is something exciting about pressing a key and watching a paragraph disappear. It's *aha!* time when the paragraph reappears in another location. Everyone knows nursery rhymes (if they don't, we write them on the blackboard), and it is fun sorting mixed-up ones into correct order.

After completing these exercises the students are ready to create their own composition as assigned by the language arts teacher. Writing assignments can be structured to meet the learning objectives of the language arts department.

Do word processors make better writers? Research indicates an improvement in writing ability. Whether or not this is always true, certainly there is more freedom to edit and more pride in a neatly printed final product.

Directions: AppleWriter II offers a way to move words and paragraphs very quickly. When the arrow in the top left corner of the screen is pointing left the words and paragraphs just deleted can be inserted in a new location. CONTROL D moves the arrow. CONTROL X moves a paragraph.

To correct the nursery rhyme below:
1. Place the cursor two spaces to the right of the word "go"
2. Type CTRL D
3. Type CTRL X
4. Move the cursor two spaces to the right of the word "went"
5. Type CTRL D
6. Type CTRL X
7. Put the rest of the lines of the rhyme in correct order.

Reminder: Because each line of a poem is followed by a RETURN, the computer treats each line as a paragraph. To move a single word type CTRL W.

The lamb was sure to go!
Its fleece was white as snow.
Mary had a little lamb.
Everywhere that Mary went,

Put the rhymes below in correct order.

To fetch a pail of water.
And Jill came tumbling after.
Jack and Jill went up the hill
Jack fell down and broke his crown,

Along came a spider and sat down beside her,
Eating her curds and whey.
And frightened Miss Muffet away.
Little Miss Muffet sat on a Tuffet,

File name: "Rhymes"

Ellen Joslin, Computer Supervisor/Teacher, 9536 Park Highlands Drive, Highland Park I.S.D, Dallas, TX 75238.

Skeleton of a Story

Here are the "bare bones" of a story. By filling in the blanks in an interesting way, you can make any kind of story you want—mysterious, funny, sad, silly—it's up to you. Be sure to create an interesting title. When you have finished your story, save the story on your disk and then make a printed (hard) copy of your story.

I always knew my Aunt _____ was a real_____. Why she,_____ and one day she _____ But

even I was surprised when she told us she planned to _____. After all, she was _____ years old, and

this could be a _____. We told her that _____ and begged her not to _____ but nothing could

_____. Therefore, although we felt _____ we watched her _____.

_____ passed. No one heard a _____ We were beginning to wonder if _____ when suddenly

our aunt appeared. She had been _____ and she seemed very _____. _____ly, she told us the

whole _____. It seemed she had _____ and _____. Now she was _____and we all felt _____.

Since then, Aunt _____ has never _____. Instead, she spends her time _____. What a _____ she is !

An ICCE Copy Me!   *Developed by Ellen Joslin*

Lesson Ideas and Projects

COMPUTERS AND THE LANGUAGE ARTS   Edited by Robert Shostak

Creating Writing Lessons with a Word Processor

by Raymond J. Rodrigues

How would you like to have a computer program which is highly effective both as a writing tool for students and as an instructional tool for teachers? If you haven't discovered it for yourself yet, your word processor is just such a program. In this month's column, Ray Rodrigues explains how you can use any word processing program to create and store lessons that students can later access and work on using the same software. You are shown how, without any knowledge of programming, you can prepare a series of screens to teach a complete writing lesson including exercises in prewriting, writing, rewriting, and evaluation.

The current volatility of the computer hardware and software market has made most major textbook publishers wary of producing writing software; they are not sure whether schools will have the hardware to justify purchasing the software. At the same time, more teachers are wary of purchasing writing software because they have become aware of the shortcomings in software that they have purchased. Yet we teachers need to be the resource people who tell administrators what to purchase. In the face of declining budgets, sound pedagogical decisions become even more important.

At the recent National Council of Teachers of Mathematics convention in San Antonio, one speaker warned participants that they had better be prepared to justify their need for computers, because the next group to start receiving microcomputers would be English teachers. That's one very insightful person.

As we begin to develop our rationales for purchasing microcomputers and software, we might want to consider their most universal applications: word processing, spreadsheets, databases, and graphics packages. For English classrooms, the program that is most essential is the word processor. Deciding to purchase word processing software before all others is economical, helps prepare students for the work place, and is pedagogically sound.

Using a word processor, a teacher can create lessons to take students through writing processes. True, the lessons will not be truly interactive—the program will not read for specific strings and then restructure them into new prompts—but the technique leads students through identical writing steps. All a teacher has to do is create special files that the student can call up and use as lesson guides. Both students and teacher do need to be familiar with the word processor they are using. Stephen Marcus demonstrated the effectiveness of such an approach with his *Activity Files for the Bank Street Writer,* and Paula Reid Nancarrow (1983) and others at the University of Minnesota earlier reported

a similar approach. While the approach is not new, few teachers have realized how very simple it is to use.

To create writing lessons, the teacher has to first determine how to sequence the screen presentations so that students can work their way back and forth through the processes needed to develop a final draft. As a result, each screen must be carefully designed. Preferably, the students should only have a little bit to read on each screen.

At the end of each step, the student can be instructed to press the Open Apple and Down Arrow for the Apple IIe/c, the PgDn key for the IBM-PC, or whatever key brings up the next screen. If the students are accustomed to pressing Return at the end of each paragraph, they should be instructed not to do so when they finish each lesson segment, but to use the appropriate commands to go to the next screen.

Remember that the students may be working through the file when you are not available, so you may want to incorporate instructions that will make their task simple to read and understand. Experiment a little. Urge them to use the full potential of their word processor, rearranging blocks of material, deleting and inserting freely, and moving back and forth from prewriting to their working draft.

At the beginning of each lesson, a set of instructions can direct the students to read through the entire file in order to understand the entire process they will be working through. Throughout the lesson, they can be told to refer back to their previous ideas, notes and drafts, thereby reinforcing the notion of writing as a recursive process. By numbering each segment, you can quickly determine the point at which your students are working when they are in a writing workshop environment.

At the end of the lesson, the students can print the entire lesson. If you want them to just print out what they have written, without the lesson instructions, then you can embed appropriate commands in the lesson commentary itself.

If your word processing files are RAM based, you can load these lesson files in as many computers as you want. If your files are disk based, you will have to provide each student with a separate disk. Whichever you have, the use of lesson files allows you to open your computer writing class to many variations of lessons. You can, for example, create prewriting lessons, peer review files, sentence structure lessons, revising exercises, or anything else that will turn the word processor into a valuable teaching tool. Besides the teaching value, this approach helps you avoid buying expensive software that somehow does not meet your expectations or fit your curriculum.

Raymond J. Rodrigues, Department of Curriculum and Instruction, Box 3AC, New Mexico State University, Las Cruces, NM 88003.

1. WRITING ABOUT CONTRASTING VIEWPOINTS

Very few issues have only one viewpoint. If they did, they would not be issues. Your task is to select a topic and to use readings, research, or personal experience to write about that topic.

Here are some general topics that you might make more specific:
1. Government control vs. individual rights
2. Protection of the environment vs. economic growth
3. Human rights vs. national interests
4. Your choice

What topic would you like to write about?

PRESS THE OPEN APPLE AND DOWN ARROW KEYS

---

2. THINKING OF IDEAS

What are the two sides of this issue?

Side A:

Side B:

PRESS THE OPEN APPLE AND DOWN ARROW KEYS

---

3. What are the arguments for Side A?

What evidence or proof is there?

What are the arguments against Side A?

What evidence or proof is there?

PRESS THE OPEN APPLE AND DOWN ARROW KEYS

---

4. What are the arguments for Side B?

What evidence or proof is there?

What are the arguments against Side B?

What evidence or proof is there?

PRESS THE OPEN APPLE AND DOWN ARROW KEYS

---

5. Do you favor one side or another?

If so, explain why you do.

PRESS THE OPEN APPLE AND DOWN ARROW KEYS

---

6. Now write a controlling sentence for the entire issue. For example, you could write, "Many people believe that....but others argue that...."

PRESS THE OPEN APPLE AND DOWN ARROW KEYS

---

7. Start writing your composition here:

PRESS THE OPEN APPLE AND DOWN ARROW KEYS

---

8. REVIEWING WHAT YOU WROTE...

Using the Open Apple and Up Arrow keys, go back to what you just wrote. Reread what you wrote or have a friend read it for you. Then answer the following questions:
A. Have you treated each side of the issue equally?
B. Have you presented evidence for each side?
C. Do you have a beginning sentence that will grab the reader's attention?
D. Have you ended your composition with a statement that causes the reader to think?

IF THE ANSWER TO ANY OF THESE QUESTIONS IS NO, GO BACK AND REVISE YOUR WRITING TO IMPROVE.

PRESS THE OPEN APPLE AND DOWN ARROW KEYS

---

9. EDITING WHAT YOU WROTE

Make whatever changes you need to leave your reader with a good impression of your ability.

A. Do you vary your sentences, or do they all begin the same way?

B. Check your spelling.

C. Check your punctuation.

D. Check your usage.

PRESS THE OPEN APPLE AND DOWN ARROW KEYS

---

10. Now, if you are satisfied with what you wrote, be sure you SAVE it!

END OF LESSON

Lesson Ideas and Projects

Beyond Merlin and His Magic Staff

by Susan Whisenand

The following article is excerpted from a packet of activities designed for use with FrEdWriter, a public domain word processing program.

Computers process not only words, but thoughts and ideas in ways that seem almost magical. Paragraphs, sentences, and words shift, move, disappear, and reappear with a rapidity that is astounding to the human mind. Magical though it seems, it is within the power of the magician, the writer, to bring about tricks that would make old Merlin stand in awe.

In Search of Young Merlins

Merlin spent many hours in caves, creating mysterious effects and studying ancient tomes. Today that experience can be compared to prewriting as a young learner takes the first steps in the quest to discover where the computer will prove most important in the writing process. If the writing process is examined with the focus on the effective use of computers in writing, a system for creating young Merlins with powerful magic can emerge.

Computer Prewriting

Students make lists, brainstorm ideas, create sentences, and expand on concepts by drawing, painting, coloring, and etching onto the screen their thoughts. Files become recipes, eliciting divergent responses and expanding creativity.

Keyboarding is a problem for the novice typist, but if the expectation is not perfection, then the joy of discovery can develop. Fortunately, several good keyboarding programs are currently available that are appropriate for students at the fourth grade level or up. Ideas may be dictated to adults, older students, or better typists.

Computer Writing

Using interesting ideas from journals and other sources, thoughts are entered into the computer. Work developed from clusters or prompts begins to become a piece of writing. Text can be typed individually or with a partner or helper who knows how to type.

Computer Responding

Now the true power of the young learner begins to emerge. With printouts, cursor movement, flexibility of change, insertion, and deletion, the computer invites the child to play around with old ideas to make them better. If changes are made that the writer doesn't like, out they go. If changes make the writing better, they can be saved permanently or at least until the child wishes to change them again. Young magicians meet and respond to each other's magic touches to the written piece, making suggestions for improvements which do not involve the painful task of rewriting the work over again in handwriting. Teachers and other adults are asked to make suggestions that children now want to hear, because they do want to make their work better and closer to the original purpose for writing.

Computer Revision

The writer uses suggestions to make changes; text is moved around, and new ideas are added and/or eliminated. The writer strives for clarity of purpose in communicating his real intention or point of view. The cursor zips around; the delete, insert, and move functions come alive, and the piece begins to take on its final form.

Computer Editing

Computer and human power combine to give the young writer a chance for excellence. Teachers, parents, and fellow students provide assistance in pointing out spelling, grammatical, and punctuation errors. Again the cursor flashes onto the scene and, obeying its young master, corrects all the mistakes, making the writing ready for publication. All children at this point deserve and need a human helper. It's hard to proofread at any age to find errors, especially if one doesn't know where to look.

Computer Evaluation

There are programs that analyze text for a variety of purposes. They look for certain types of words or phrase combinations. Some ask, through a prompt, for the student to enter appropriate text. The student is then required to respond to the text through a series of leading questions which may lead to rewriting. An excellent way to help students to evaluate their work is to have them print the work out double- or triple-spaced and to reread it for specific purposes, i.e., content, style, interest, spelling, or grammar. The computer does not replace the human evaluator; it only acts as an assistant.

Computer Publishing

Student work deserves recognition. Bulletin board displays, letters, and stories sent over modems, anthologies, parent letters, school newspapers, poems, books, book fairs, and oral readings provide opportunities for commending young writers. Works can be illustrated with borders from software such as *Print Shop* or other clip art programs.

Getting at the Art of Writing

"Dream Focus" is an activity taken from *Beyond Merlin and His Magic Staff*. The activities in this packet are designed to promote writing as an integral part of the art and science of communication. It is hoped the student pages along with the suggestions for teachers will promote writing experiences involving cooperative learning and will reach across the curriculum. If students are freed from the belief that a finished piece of writing is done in 20 minutes and can understand that writing is a process and an art form, the purpose of this packet will be accomplished.

Background

In 1983, California AB 2190 provided initial funding for the Goleta Union School District to develop a model inservice program in writing and problem solving using computers.

The purpose of this project was to train teachers by using district teachers who had expertise in writing and problem solving due to their involvement with the South Coast Writing Project and the Tri County Math Project. Preparation for these staff development programs resulted in the development of model lesson ideas for using the computer in writing and problem solving. The activities given in *Beyond Merlin and His Magic Staff* focus on the writing process. For more information on the packet, contact Judy Connors, Goleta Union School District, 401 North Fairview Ave., Goleta, CA 93117.

A *FrEdWriter* data disk of prompts for each activity in *Beyond Merlin and His Magic Staff is* available from SOFTSWAP. *FrEdWriter* is a public domain word processing program that is also available from SOFTSWAP. For a SOFTSWAP catalog, send $1 to Bruce Fleury, 3225 Petunia Ct., San Diego, CA 92117.

Susan Whisenand, Foothill School, 711 Ribera Drive, Santa Barbara, CA 93111.

DREAM FOCUS

Objective: Students will write a short story that is related to a personal dream.

Grade Level: Fourth through sixth.

Prompted Writing File

FrEdWriter allows you to create prompted writing files. The following screen shots show how the file appears on the screen. Students use the up and down arrows to move around the boxed areas. They can insert their own writing between prompts and print their results with or without prompts.

The prompts are similar to the questions on the worksheet included for this activity. Each prompt is further designed to lead students logistically through the activity. Similar files can be created with any word processor. (See "Creating Writing Lessons with a Word Processor" in the Language Arts column in the February 1986 issue of *The Computing Teacher*.) In *FrEdWriter* the prompts are protected from being accidentally erased or altered.

The worksheet and the prompted writing file provide students with two tools for developing and organizing their thoughts. You can decide how to best use them given the amount and availability of your hardware.

Purpose: Using dreams as a basis, students will have the opportunity to share ideas and feelings that become strange and interesting stories.

Materials/Equipment: Paper, pencils, story written by teacher that relates a childhood dream, computer, word processing program. Optional—Goleta *FrEdWriter* file disk with *Dream Focus* prompts.

Teaching Procedure

Prewriting—directed lesson/30 minutes
1. Teacher tells students about a dream or dream fragment experienced as a child. Describe the feelings the dream evoked.
2. Ask students to think of dreams that they had and to share them in small groups of three people. Students without ideas will think of some once they hear what others have to say.
3. Have students not relating dreams take notes for the student who is telling about his dream. These notes should be given to the dream teller to help with writing the first draft of the dream story.
4. On their own students individually cluster words associated with their dream.

Writing—20 minutes
Using the notes from group members and individual clusters, students write up their dream. Encourage them to add details to make the dream vivid to other readers. The dream should be written as though it was being told out loud. Explain the use of first person as a style of writing. Type rough draft versions into the computer.

Responding—20 minutes
Have students read their dreams out loud to new groups of three. Ask students to give each other feedback as to what the dreams seem to mean and what is easy or hard to understand.

Revision to Publishing— Provide necessary sessions for students to revise and rewrite their stories. Let students work with partners making revisions on the computer. Publish with illustrations in class booklets. Display and encourage students to read the stories during independent reading periods.

A Family Writing Project

by Bruce Fleury

Parents who like to help their kids with schoolwork will love this at-home word processing project. It requires a portable computer, a little instruction, and parents' willingness to get more involved than just checking homework or drilling basic facts. With these three ingredients in place, you're ready for a family writing project!

A portable computer can provide powerful motivation for an enthusiastic family to participate in a student's schoolwork. In a family writing project, portable computers are used in school *and at home* to learn writing skill and technique.

Step 1. At school students become expert at using the computer to write. With an appropriate computer this is readily accomplished with less than an hour of instruction. In class students demonstrate their expertise by using the computer to do their writing lessons.

Step 2. A parent comes to school and checks out a portable computer, which is small (the size of a telephone book), but is a complete system. A full-sized keyboard, an LCD display (the screen), the word-processing software, and memory are all part of a single unit. The system may be battery powered.

The Portable Computer

There are several portable computers available, often called "lap computers," reflecting their compact size. Most have the required features and could be used in this project. However, we found only one in the appropriate price range: the Tandy Model 100 Lap Computer. This computer can be purchased for less than $400. It has a built-in word processor that is simple to use; first grade children write with it on a daily basis. Student writing is displayed on a flat liquid crystal display (LCD), which is part of the single unit system.

Writing and editing are accomplished without the use of special "commands." Letter keys, arrow keys, and the erase key are used in an intuitive process of typing words and changing them until you have the desired final draft ("intuitive" means that the first guess as to how to do something will be correct). The computer memory (24K) is more than sufficient for a family writing project.

The Tandy Model 100's printer connection is accessible outside the computer and needs no additional printer interface. Students easily connect the computer to the printer in order to get a hard-copy printout of their writing. Accessories and enhancements are available to expand the computer's usefulness.

Step 3. At home the student assists the other family members with use of the computer. Parents become involved and assist the student with writing skills (spelling, form, style, etc.). The family writes together. The final draft of everything written by the family is automatically saved in the computer's battery-powered memory.

Step 4. The parent returns the portable computer to school. An enthusiastic parent-teacher discussion about the writing experience usually occurs, which is an additional advantage.

Step 5. At school the family's writing is printed out. Family writing usually consists of purposeful writing such as letters to friends and relatives, as well as creative writing such as stories and poems. Two copies of all family writing is printed; one for the teacher and one for the student to take home.

Family writing often includes letters addressed to the teacher from the parents and students, indicating increased involvement of the family in the student's schoolwork.

Family Stories

Families frequently choose to write about themselves. Brian, a third grader, wrote about his dog Smokey. Here is part of Brian's story:

I have a dog. His name is Smokey. He is a big dog. When he stands up he is 6 feet tall. If he gets out of the yard he won't come back for a long time. We got him when he was a puppy. Now he is 3 years old. He is a brat now. He is a big puppy. He can't wait till his birthday next month. When his birthday comes up I will give him a bone. Smokey got out Saturday and got into a fight. After that Smokey got a rope on his leg. He did not like the rope on his leg....

His mother also wrote:

Dear Mr. Fleury,

This story was written by Brian Jones and edited by Mary Lynn Jones. We spent several hours working on this story. We enjoyed having the portable computer at home to work on. Thank you for the opportunity to share this project together.

Sincerely,
    Mary Lynn Jones

Bruce Fleury, 3225 Petunia Court, San Diego, CA 92117.

Rewriting—Using the Best of Both Worlds

By Larry Lewin

This article is reprinted with permission of the Writing Notebook.

The process approach to writing has become the nearly universal way to teach composition. As teachers, most of us now use the steps of prewriting, drafting, rewriting, and publishing to teach students how to write. And well we should—this approach is as useful for professional writers as it is for those in primary grades.

I have taught high school, middle school, and elementary students writing using this approach. And in the process I have found that of the four steps of this approach, the third—rewriting—is the most difficult to teach students of all ages. Once a first draft has been written, most writers balk at analyzing, evaluating, and critiquing it. Young writers must understand the *purpose* of rewriting, they must be taught *how* to rewrite, and they must be *rewarded* for rewriting.

Rewriting has many different names: editing, proofreading, revising, correcting. I've come to call this third stage "rewriting," both because it sounds good (prewriting... writing... rewriting), and because the word can cover both the revising of content (ideas, organization, style) and proofreading the mechanics (spelling, punctuation, grammar). Both are essential for successful writing, and both are difficult to teach.

I use a combination of traditional methods and new technology (now available to most classrooms) to teach rewriting skills. I strongly recommend using both. Some content considerations can be addressed by software use, but I feel more confident with human input. Mechanics concerns can be taught by teachers and fellow students, but software programs are far more patient and careful. So I use both new and old methods to teach students these two components of rewriting.

Motivating Students to Rewrite

In order to motivate students to rewrite a draft, they must be convinced of the need to rewrite. One way I demonstrate this is to show them a published article, written by me. After seeing their impressed looks, I then show them the stack of written drafts I had to submit before acceptance! This helps prove the point because publication is a suitable reward for the hard work of writing and rewriting. Inviting a published author to the classroom with drafts in hand also works well. I then use the reward of publishing student work (step 4 of the process approach) as often as I can to motivate their rewriting.

Even with the publishing incentive, it still remains difficult for many students to rewrite. They must be taught what to look for in their drafts that need improvement. I have found new software programs that help me teach students this skill. Not only does using software provide them with individualized instruction while freeing me to offer others my help, but the software also does some of the analysis better and faster than I can. It also motivates rewriting—it's still novel, it's quick and clean, and it's almost painless. Even so, I am confident that computer use in the classroom will not replace me—I'm much smarter and more sensitive than even the best software available. Here are some specific ideas and programs to consider.

Young writers must understand the **purpose of** *rewriting, they must be taught* **how** *to rewrite, and they must be* **rewarded** *for rewriting.*

The Writer's Helper (William Wresch, CONDUIT) is a set of 22 mini-programs that work with a word processor (standard Applesoft test files and *Bank Street Writer*) to Find and Organize a Subject (11 prewriting programs) and Evaluate a Writing Project (11 rewriting programs).

To evaluate the content of a writing project, I like the "Outline Document" that shows the lead sentence of each paragraph to easily see transition words and logical sequence development. The "Words in Sentences" miniprogram counts the number of words in each sentence, graphs them, and reveals sentence length variety. A "Readability Index" computes the readability level of the paper against the intended audience level, a job I don't like.

For proofreading the mechanics of a paper, a student can select one of the Word Analysis programs such as "Homonym Checker," "Gender- Related Language," and "Usage Errors."

Of course, rewriting not only means identifying the places that need improvement, it also requires making the improvements. Decisions are made by the student using the information from the *Writer's Helper*. These rewriting decisions are difficult, and the software can't make them. I find students asking me for my opinion quite often at this stage.

"Some content considerations can be addressed by software use, but I feel more confident with human input. Mechanics concerns can be taught by teachers and fellow students, but software programs are far more patient and careful."

Another program I like using is *Ghost Writer* (Robert Bortnick and Thomas Lundeen, MECC). *Ghost Writer* will analyze texts written with the following word processors: *MECC Writer, Apple Writer II, Bank Street Writer*, Milliken's *The Writing Workshop, Magic Window II*, and *PIE Writer*.

Of the seven mini-programs available, I most often use "Paragraph Outliner," which prints the first sentence, shows the number of words in sentences using dashes for each word (except transition words and punctuation, which are printed), and finally prints the complete last sentence of the paragraph. This provides a graphic view of the overall organization and coherence of the paper—an important consideration in content revision.

I also like the "Sentence Length Analyzer," which graphs the number of words in each sentence with dashes (stars mark each fifth word) and prints the total number of words. This is helpful in determining sentence length variety, possible fragments and run-ons, and sentence combining opportunities. Of course, the program can only provide data—the writer must make the editing decisions.

I recently previewed the *Writing Adventure* (DLM), which has a prewriting activity disk, "Story Starter" and a drafting and rewriting disk called "Story Writer." This disk has eight mini-programs in its "Proofing Aid," including commonly misused words, troublesome verbs, adjectives, adverbs, and pronouns. It marks suspect words, so the writer can return to the text for editing.

I am excited by these programs, because they rapidly and loyally provide students with information about their texts—information that can lead to improvements. Best of all, students actually enjoy the process—rewriting is less painful.

These new programs improve the type of analysis found in a method I have used for years—a method I still respect. The "Sentence Opening Sheet" (Stack and Deck, Inc.) is a one-page sheet consisting of four columns that call attention to potential problem areas. Content issues like idea sequence, variety of sentence beginnings, and sticking to the topic are summarized when the student fills in the columns. Proofreading issues of capitalization, run-ons, and fragments are also raised.

Sometimes I prefer using this traditional (precomputer) method, because worksheets remove the issue of hardware shortage, and the student does the analysis. By comparison, the new software method is more intriguing, faster—and it does the analysis.

Another non-computer rewriting technique that I still use is the teacher-student conference. I consider this the most effective rewriting instruction, because it offers one-on-one discussion of the content of a paper. The human teacher is better at this than any software program I've seen.

I use a procedure modified from Donald Graves' book, *Writing: Teachers and Children at Work.* In five minutes I listen to the student read his or her first draft, quote a part I particularly like, ask one or two specific content questions that I was confused about, and listen to the student explain how the confusing parts might be cleared up. The student can then start rewriting as I conference with the next student.

I also like assigning proofreading partners or editing groups. For years teachers have used this method with good results. Regardless of the number of students or whether they are assigned by the teacher or chosen by the students, valuable human feedback is gained, especially when expectations are clearly set, time limits drawn, and some written response from the partners required.

Writing instruction has received a giant boost with the arrival of computer software. It motivates students, it speeds the process, and it's painless. But it can't replace the knowledge, taste, and insights of a human audience. So I use the best of both worlds—and not just as a teacher. I can count on *The Writing Notebook* editor to read this article prior to publication and give me valuable feedback—and you can be certain that I'm running this text through *Sensible Speller*!

Writing Skills with WriteOn!

by Jon Madian

Reprinted with permission from (1986, Nov./Dec.) *The Writing Notebook*.

WRITE ON! from Humanities Software is a collection of 54 writing activity disks designed to use word processing functions (insert, delete, block, move, display, print) to develop composing, revising, and editing skills at grades K-12. All major areas of written language development are addressed: story, poetry, letter, journal, report, and essay writing. While these activities-on-disk are designed to involve students in whole language behaviors, specific mechanical, vocabulary, spelling, revising, and editing skills are also taught.

Primary Literature Collection   K-4

In the **Primary Literature Collection** (grades K-4), the software turns the computer into a wonderfully flexible storyboard for small group or whole class writing activities. Forty of the most popular children's books and poems are bundled with this software and used as the inspiration for student writing patterns. After the teacher reads the story or poem to the students, the students, probably with the teacher, aide, or volunteer typing in their answers, "write" their ideas. Included with the book-inspired writing patterns is a model group journal that students and teacher can modify. This approach to writing for young students capitalizes on children's natural excitement toward learning as they write a story or journal together.

For example, after the class reads *The Runaway Bunny*, children dictate or write their ideas about what they'd turn into in order to run away from their mothers. The following pattern appears on the screen and is repeated for each child in the class or group:

```
"Mommy, I'm going to become a_____,"
said N (child's name goes in N place).

"N (child's name), if you become a_____,
I'll become a_____  and_____,"
said N's mother.
```

Thus, children see their words and names being written or, if they are ready to write at the keyboard, they simply fill in the blanks. Connecting students' ideas to a repeating pattern gives them the repetition they need for comprehension and success, and within the pattern, each child can express his/her unique ideas.

After each child in the group has responded, a printout is made which students illustrate. The activity culminates with each student sharing his or her individual page, or with teacher and students reading from a book containing everyone's illustrated ideas. What child will ever forget *The Runaway Bunny* after this! While all of these primary level programs are designed for group

writing, they also lend themselves to use by individual students working alone or working with another student at the computer.

Elementary Collection   K-5

The **Elementary Collection** also contains several poetry activities designed to teach basic writing and reading skills. The chant, with its easy rhythmic pattern and repetitive structure, is the basic building block. So if students are learning similes, they will respond to a pattern on the screen that looks like this:

```
Fast, fast, fast
I'm as fast as a_____, said N.

Slow, slow, slow
I'm as slow as a_____, said N.
```

As it happens, this particular poetry activity is also keyed to a wonderful picture book called *Quick as a Cricket* by Audrey Wood.

Or if children are working with the "ay" word family, they see all the simple "ay" words on the screen and are given a sample poem or an opening chant:

[AY WORDS: bay, day, gay, hay, jay, lay, may, nay, pay, ray, stay, way, away, slay, tray, clay, today]

```
Complete this chart using as many 'ay" words as possible:

Play, play, play
Please_____
Clay, clay, clay
I_____
Today, today, today
_____
```

Intermediate Collection   5-8
Secondary Collection   9-12

Based on the classroom-tested language experience and writing as a process approaches, WRITE ON! **Intermediate and Secondary Collections** can be used to supplement any phase of the writing curriculum. Prewriting activities stimulate the flow of ideas and help students gather and select writing topics. Organizing activities teach students how to improve their writing through correct sentence, paragraph, and theme structure. Writing activities enable students to practice composing on the computer while emphasizing types of writing style, point of view, etc. Rewriting/correcting activities teach rewriting and editing skills. Publishing activities result in a printed product that can be shared with others.

Next, choose one of the overused words in the word bank below. Write a five-sentence paragraph using that word as many times as you can.

```
WORD BANK
said   feel   walk   run
nice   see    talk   little

MY OVERUSED WORD PARAGRAPH
> >
```

In an activity from Paragraphs 6 called Spicy Woods, students replace overused words with more colorful and descriptive language. Then they write and edit their own overused word paragraph.

DIRECTIONS

Now change the descriptive words in the paragraph below so the brain becomes a lovely, friendly, cute thing.

"It was the most horrible, the most repellent thing she had ever seen, far more nauseating than anything she had ever imagined with her conscious mind, or that had ever tormented her in her most terrible nightmares."

—Excerpted from *A Wrinkle in Time* by Madeleine L'Engle

In this step of an activity called Descriptive Language from the Intermediate Collection WRITING STYLE, *students work with the language used by L'Engle as Meg encounters IT in* A Wrinkle In Time.

The educational power of this collection is the teaching of basic writing skills at the application level using computer functions, and these skills are internalized through whole writing activities. While the educational utility of these activities is rooted in the advantages that word processor functions provide,

these diskettes take into account that students may have limited computer time and that teachers and students may prefer doing some activities with paper and pencil. Included on the teacher side of the disks, along with a teacher activity guide, are activities to be done on hard copy printouts.

This is the first educational software designed to take full advantage of the ideas embodied in desktop publishing—indeed, this is desktop curriculum! Teachers can adapt these activities to meet the needs of their students or to emphasize particular concerns. This collection should be continually growing and self refining. Humanities Software plans an expansion of five diskettes per month with a five year goal of over 250 diskettes. And they expect the new disks to come from needs and strategies identified in the classroom.

Karen Jostad, former Manager of Courseware Design at MECC is the educator and designer behind the *WRITE ON!* collection. She states:

"The *WRITE ON!* diskettes realize their potential each time educators trying to solve particular problems see ways to adapt the strategies in these materials. In the end, we expect this to be a largely teacher authored library. We hope this first collection will help educators see new ways to use word processing."

This approach to computer assisted instruction takes us one step closer to aligning technology with the best current ideas in curriculum design and writing instruction. The *WRITE ON!* collection runs on all major educational word processors that run on the Apple—*Bank Street Writer*, *AppleWorks*, *Apple Writer*, *FrEdWriter*, *MECC Writer*, *The Writing Workshop*, and *Magic Slate*. This collection soon will be available for other computer systems. See the catalogue enclosed in this issue for more information about products and purchase plans.

Process Writing in the One-Computer Classroom

By Kathy Pon

As a K-6 computer teacher, I know I have the time and energy to teach the specifics of word processing as well as to design and carry out writing activities that incorporate the steps of the writing process on a daily basis. In working with the staff at my school and in talking with other teachers, I am also aware that most regular classroom teachers, particularly those with only one computer in their rooms, are more limited as to the time they can spend on these endeavors. However, it wasn't too long ago that I was a regular classroom teacher. I know that there are management and educational techniques that a classroom teacher can use to orchestrate the writing process and the vehicle—word processing itself—and still keep from going crazy.

First of all, a teacher must have a mindset of what steps of the process he or she intends to focus on. For me, although there are seven specific steps, I find it easier to break the process into four: prewriting, writing, editing/revising, and publishing. Second, I make a conscious decision that *all* of the steps will not be performed at the computer in every writing assignment. The computer has its place in all of these steps, but each teacher will have to make personal decisions about when its use is appropriate and convenient. There isn't time for a teacher with 30 students and one computer to put all of the kids on it for every step of the writing process for every writing activity assigned throughout the year. But there are times when using the word processor *is* appropriate and effective.

Prewriting

There are many different kinds of prewriting a teacher may choose to do with students. These range from brainstorming or clustering ideas to researching and participating in sensory experiences. Prewriting may be done in groups, with the whole class, or individually. It can be done with the conventional classroom tools or it can be done on the computer.

I find brainstorming the easiest to do on the computer because students can simply toss out ideas instead of worrying about their classifications. Further, it works well when the class as a whole is sitting in front of the monitor while the teacher or one individual types the ideas generated. Then the teacher need only print the list of ideas, make copies, and distribute it to the class. Now students have their own idea-specific wordbank in front of them, which is particularly helpful for younger kids.

Individual brainstorming files may be created by the teacher. A disk containing directions is loaded into the computer when each student goes for his or her turn. For example:

List six qualities of a good friend. Then, write some ideas telling about a good friend you've had or would like to have. When you save your list, save it with your name in the following way: Kathy.friend.

Each individual saves his or her work on a file disk; the next student simply loads the original directions and continues with the activity.

Clustering is another form of prewriting. It is a way of listing ideas, but grouping them in categories. The computer is well suited for this activity because of its inserting capacity. For example, a student might generate ideas that have to do with autumn. A good place to start is with a few topics such as the following:

Thanksgiving
The Weather
Things in Nature
The Harvest

The student can list ideas under each topic, jumping around from group to group without having to worry whether there is room to add more—there is! This activity is good cognitive skill practice for all students. It can be used in a more advanced way for older students by letting them move text around as their lists grow, putting terms that belong together in groups and then naming the groups. I like to tie this activity in with grammar. Having students cluster terms by nouns, verbs, and adjectives is one way to do this (see Figure 1).

wind	brown	sleeps
turkeys	spicy	falling
pumpkin pie	clear	scatter
leaves	crunchy	whistles
home	yummy	tastes
		smells

Figure 1.

Tying prewriting to what is being studied in grammar is an excellent use of the computer. The following tasks are useful because they are short and they don't tie up the computer for long amounts of time.

> List five words to use for "said." (This list would be printed for groups or individuals studying quotation marks and conversations. They would use the words while writing a conversation.)

> Write five nouns that are names of things you see in the cafeteria. (This might be used as a basis for a creative story that focuses in on nouns.)

> List five words that have the prefix *bi*. (This might be used for writing a poem that uses words with prefixes.)

It's a good idea to keep the computer open with specific tasks such as the following, which are also forms of prewriting:

> Write one or two facts you remember about butterflies.

> Write one fact you've learned about Mr. Lincoln.

The resulting lists can be combined into a class fact list and printed as a resource for students researching and writing reports.

Finally, an effective way to use the computer at the prewriting stage is to write story starter questions and save them in a story starter file. Students can put their cursor in the insert mode and write their answers right after the questions without erasing the rest of the text. Questions would address the major components of the story to be written, such as "Who is the hero *or* heroine?" "Where does the story take place?" and "What good things happen in the story?" When finished, students would again save their work under their own names on a file disk so that the next student need only load up the original task and questions and begin answering them (see Figure 2).

It cannot be emphasized enough that the computer is an excellent tool for use at the prewriting stage. However, when there is only one tool and 30 students, the teacher will need to decide when it will be used at this point (versus another time in the writing process) so as not to tie up valuable classroom time.

Writing

Some would say that when the computer is used at the writing stage, its tool capacity is greatest. After all, students have at their fingertips an instrument that encourages fluency as they write or delete text easily, bypassing horrible eraser marks and crossed out sentences. However, most elementary students don't have the keyboarding skills needed to generate text very quickly. Moreover, most teachers who have one computer in their classrooms don't have the time to allow students onto the computer for very long periods. (If each student took 30 to 40 minutes at a time for writing at the computer, it might be months

---

More Ideas for Writing at the Computer
A Science Fiction Story Starter

Directions: Make sure your cursor is in the insert mode. Then, put your cursor on the first arrow after each question and answer it. When you are finished, move your arrow key to get to the next question. Save your work under your name + Sci (Kathy.Sci).

1. Where on earth or in the universe is the setting of the story?

2. Who is the main character of the story? Describe him or her or it.

3. What happens to the character?

4. Who or what stands in the way of the character?

5. How does he or she or it solve the problem?

6. How does the story end?

Figure 2.

---

before assignments were finished.) Therefore, I advocate for the one computer classroom that most writing at this stage be done with paper and pencil.

At some point during the school year students should generate text directly on the computer so that they see how easily the writing stage can be done. However, with one computer in the classroom and 30 students, a teacher will be doing well to take the entire class through this stage just once.

But there are some one-computer activities I consider sensible and appropriate at this stage in the writing process. Here is my favorite: Have typed into the computer a short poem, ditty, or nursery rhyme with certain sentence parts underlined. Also give students a hard copy of the piece. Their task is to replace the underlined parts with their own words to fit a certain theme. To save time, students first work on their hard copies, then enter their work on the computer. In Figure 3, the tune "Silver Bells" was the blueprint for Halloween Carols. This type of exercise is worthwhile because students can still be creative, but they concentrate on writing certain parts of speech or the syntax of sentences. Also, these can be done in a short amount of computer time. And students get to practice two valuable word processing skills: inserting and deleting text.

Another novel use of the computer is to do a shape poem using words describing a particular concept or idea formed into a shape that echoes it. It helps to begin these ahead of time on paper and pencil because generating them on a computer can sometimes be tricky. This is especially true if the text is in a 40-column setup; often the printout fails to match the screen image.

Finally, I again like to tie writing at the computer to the

> City sidewalks, busy sidewalks.
> Dressed in holiday style.
> In the air there's a feeling of Christmas;
> Children laughing, people passing
> Meeting smile after smile.
> And on every street corner you'll hear. . .
> Silver bells, silver bells.
> It's Christmas time in the city.
> Ring-a-ling, hear them ring!
> Soon it will be Christmas Day.

Figure 3.

grammar being taught in the classroom. By giving students short sentences to expand upon by using interesting adjectives, verbs, or prepositional phrases, you can provide them with a short writing assignment that piques their creativity and teaches a skill at the same time.

Editing

The editing stage incorporates someone's response to the writing, actual editing for mechanics, possible revision of the text or voice of a paper, and even some evaluation of what has been written. The teaching of this skill must not be taken too lightly. As teachers we must constantly model and teach editing to our students. Thankfully, the computer has made the task a bit easier. My experience with students has been that they become quite overwhelmed when faced with editing a whole screen of text, especially if it is the first time the editor has seen the writing. A few strategies to ensure editing is done on every assignment, that it doesn't take too long, and that it isn't too difficult a task for students to do help ease this strain.

I am a great advocate of editing the first draft (usually done on paper) before a student ever gets it on screen. This can be done by the writer, by peers, or by an adult. I like to use an evaluation sheet (see Figure 4) and to concentrate on checking for one or two criteria at a time. Even though this is only a proofreading mechanism for the first draft, it helps students bypass the time wasted in typing mixed up, unorganized text into the computer in the first place. There will be plenty of time to work on computer commands that edit, move, or replace text even if the students type into the computer what seems to be a pretty good draft. There are always typos, words stuck together, paragraphs to be separated, titles and names to be centered, and trite phrases to be replaced.

All these make for useful editing sessions later.

I like to have students edit in one of the following ways:

- First the writer must read through the text. If he or she cannot find any mistakes, a peer checks it over. If they both think they've got a pretty good draft, they are ready for me or another adult to sit with them and go over it.
- Sometimes editing is done for one item at a time by four students in a read-around group. The first reader will edit

only for capitals, the second for punctuation, the third for spelling, and the fourth for usage. By the time I see the manuscript it's a breeze to go through. (I usually like to look at all of my student's text before it is printed, as I believe it's terrible public relations to send work riddled with errors home to parents.)

Of course, the key to this entire process is to give students practice at editing. It's not a bad idea to set up sentences or short paragraphs at the computer that focus in on specific grammar areas as well as the specific commands used to fix the errors. The teachers at my school do a lot of whole-group editing on the overhead, giving students hard copies of the text the teacher is presenting. Again, the class will read through the text and edit for only one item at a time, first on paper and later at the computer.

Publishing

It often seems that, by the time students get to the publishing stage of the writing process, it's time to move on to a new assignment. However, this is the most fun part of the experience for most students, and it should never be left out. The published paper may be hung somewhere for others to see. Perhaps it is read to a PTA or senior citizens group, or just to classmates. Or it may be incorporated into an art project which is set out for Parent Night, displayed in a local bank for the community to see, or placed in the school library for others to enjoy.

One popular option is for students to publish a book (see Figure 5). When a writing is to be published as a book, there are a few decisions that will need to be made:

- Which word processing program will work best?
- What type style would you like?
- Does the program generate graphics that might add to the students' writing? Will the book be a joint or individual effort? Will students print their own work or does an adult need to do it?
- Will another program be needed to do title pages, credits, or an "About the Author" page?
- What about illustrations? Will you use crayon, paint, or photos?
- Will you laminate the pages?
- Will students cover the cardboard covers with fabric, colorful butcher paper, or contact paper?

If you can anticipate these choices ahead of time, there's only fun to be had! Some of my favorite publishing activities include the following:

- Enlarging and illustrating reports about community workers and combining them into a class book on the subject.
- Printing each line in a paragraph of a *fortunately/unfortunately* or *horrible day* paragraph separately so that each

sentence becomes the text for a page in an illustrated book.

- Using a program such as *Print Shop* to print lists beginning with the letters of the alphabet for an "ABC Book of Things That Are Small" or an "ABC Book of Things That Make Us Laugh."
- Printing text written about spiders only 15 characters wide, then folding the text accordion-style and using these strips as spider's legs, attached to construction paper bodies.
- Printing "What Is Peace?" essays in small text so that they may be glued to small doves and hung on mobiles.
- Reading radio shows and plays into a tape recorder to be played back for audiences.

- Saving personal collections of writing to display on a large *me* banner for hanging during Back to School Night.

Not to be forgotten are publications that accept children's writing. Many children's magazines are always looking for original manuscripts and might never get to see the wonderful pieces that pass our desks. We need to be advocates for children in this way.

Word processing and the writing process *can* become a natural part of the one-computer classroom without becoming yet another task for a teacher to do. Moreover, the teacher who does decide to take students through these steps will probably find students enjoying their writing tasks and improving their writing quality and fluency.

Only One Computer? Tips to help you stay sane...

1. Always make sure your tasks, directions, and accompanying task cards are clear and simple. Take a minute to go through the steps yourself to be sure that nothing is left out. Especially at the beginning, students need to know even the simplest directions, such as when to hit or not hit RETURN. Also, make sure *every* student internalizes the rules for computer care and disk handling. This prevents disasters.

2. Pair students at the computer. This gives everyone a chance to get onto the computer in a shorter span of time, enables the less capable to work with the more capable, quickens typing time, and ensures that two minds will be solving each problem that arises. Post the computer schedule every week so that each student can find out when his or her turn is. Leave extra spaces at the end of the week for make-up times.

3. Keep your initial computer tasks limited to about 15 to 20 minutes. That's usually the average time someone can afford to be away from a class assignment. It also allows you to schedule everyone through a particular task in a week's time. Later, as students get more proficient at using the program and at keyboarding, you will find you can make the task more complicated or let them type longer papers.

4. Always station your classroom computer where it won't be too distracting to others, and so the screen will be visible to you. Seat students who might tend to watch what's going on farthest from the computer and those who tend to finish their work sooner and who can give quick aid closest.

5. Don't schedule students onto the computer when you are giving a direct lesson. Rather, have them use it when they are involved with independent practice.

6. Allow the faster students on first, and let those who really need practice wait to use the computer during less academic activities.

7. Train a core of capable students how to use your program and task cards. They can often give aid to someone who is having problems at the computer when you are busy. Also, dedicate an afternoon to teaching some of your adult volunteers how to use your task cards. They can often schedule time to come in and help. Many parents already have computers at home and some knowledge of how to use them. Nonetheless, never assume they know exactly what you want; they often don't.

8. Develop a help signal for students working at the computer to let you know they need assistance. In addition, specific steps should be outlined telling what to do if the pair or individual at the computer needs help (such as asking the computer student aide or doing a computer review game until you can get over to help). These steps should be posted near the computer and every student should be aware of the procedure.

9. Develop a method to keep student data files. Perhaps you can't afford to give everyone in the class a disk, but you can get five disks, one for each seat group or day of the week. Also, remember to delete work from time to time so that disks won't become suddenly filled in the middle of someone's computer time. Back up disks by copying them if the work is important. It's awful to lose 10 students' essays needed for the county speech contest days before the deadline.

10. Teach a trustworthy parent how to print files, as it usually ends up taking a lot of time.

11. If an activity doesn't seem to be working well, don't continue it just because you feel obligated to give everyone a chance. Close down the computer for a day or two and regroup. You'll feel better, the kids will have more success, and you'll end up not hating the computer.

12. Expect at least a couple of disasters to occur as you begin to use the computer in your class. If you can learn to smile about them, they do get more rare, and you do end up having some wonderful end products!

Lesson Ideas and Projects

Creative Writing Evaluation Sheet

Criteria	Dates							
Organization (Makes sense, in order)								
Lively, precise words								
Complete Sentences								
Spelling								
Punctuation								
Capitals (Titles, important words)								
Neatness								
Creative ideas (Did you put much effort into this?)								
Mechanics grade								
Creative grade								
Other comments								

Title _____

Name _____

Figure 4.

How to Make a Book Using the Computer

1. PREWRITING
How will you do it?
- [ ] Clustering
- [ ] Brainstorming
- [ ] Diagramming
- [ ] Visualization
- [ ] In/Out Charts
- [ ] Sentence Strips
- [ ] Will you do this prewriting on the computer?
- [ ] Will you use pencil and paper?

2. WRITING
Which word processing program will you use?
(or will they do pencil and paper first?)
- [ ] *Magic Slate* ?
- [ ] *Bank Street Writer* ?
- [ ] *Appleworks?*
- [ ] *Kidwriter?*
- [ ] *Print Shop* ?
- [ ] *StoryMaker* ?
- [ ] *Newsroom* ?
- [ ] *Mousepaint* ?
- [ ] Will it be a joint or a single effort?

3. EDITING
Will peers do it or will the teacher or will
the individual writer?
- [ ] Will you print out the copy or edit on the computer?
- [ ] Will you edit for specifics or expect the students to do the entire page?

4. PRINTING
Will students be allowed to print their work
or will you or other adults do it?
- [ ] Do you want to enlarge the print?
- [ ] Don't forget titles, credits or title pages.
- [ ] Some may want to include an "About the Author."

5. ILLUSTRATING
How will you do it?
- [ ] Paint
- [ ] Crayon
- [ ] Chalk (Messy unless you laminate the page)
- [ ] Magazine or discarded book pictures
- [ ] Their own photos

6. BOOK COVERS
How will they be done?
- [ ] Cardboard covered with paper, wrapping paper, contact paper, fabric, or artwork
- [ ] Rings
- [ ] Tagboard
- [ ] Laminated construction paper

7. PUTTING IT TOGETHER
(Directions for tied book)

- [ ] Cover the outer cardboard or other book cover first.

- [ ] Use a smaller piece of paper to cover the inside of the book cover.

- [ ] Lay the two covers flat on the table, leaving about 1/8 inch between them. (This will allow the jacket to close all the way.) Use the packaging tape to bind them together.

- [ ] Punch holes in the pages. (You may want to use the gummed hole reinforcers over each of the holes to prevent tearing.)

- [ ] String yarn through the pages first.

- [ ] Mark where the yarn is and punch holes through the covers at those points. A point from a compass works well.

- [ ] Pull the string through first the front cover and then the back cover.

- [ ] Tie the yarn ends together while the book is open on its face. This prevents tying the pages too tight and subsequently difficult page turning.

Figure 5.

COMPUTERS AND THE LANGUAGE ARTS   Edited by Lynne Anderson-Inman

Reading and Writing Interactive Stories

by Maribeth Henney

In past columns we have explored a variety of ways in which the computer can be used to promote the reading-writing connection in language arts instruction (The Computing Teacher, Nov. 1986 & March 1987). One of the most popular and varied of these approaches utilizes computer programs which provide the learner with interactive reading and writing experiences. The value of such experiences is that they promote an environment in which the learner moves back and forth between the role of reader and the role of writer, encouraging recognition that reading and writing are interrelated events. In this month's column Maribeth Henney shares her experiences teaching students to write interactive stories using Story Tree. *For a complete review of the* Story Tree *software refer to the April 1985 issue of* The Computing Teacher.*

—Lynne Anderson-Inman

"Let me write that paragraph so it gives more detail about the ice cream."

"Wouldn't this make more sense if it came before that sentence?"

"I guess I'd better check in the dictionary to find how to spell marmalade."

"Can you give me a simpler word for indicated?"

"I don't think that paragraph adds anything to the story. Let's leave it out."

These comments were made by students writing interactive stories for the computer using Scholastic's *Story Tree*. Interactive stories allow the reader to determine the direction of the story by selecting one of several options at various points in the plot. *Story Tree* provides teachers and students with an authoring system for writing interactive stories. The writer types in one page at a time and specifies what kind of connection or branch to use for subsequent pages. There are three possible types of branches: the writer can develop a *continue* page, which simply connects the current page to the next one; the writer can indicate that there will be a *choice* which means the readers will have two to four choices to select from, each going to a different page; or the writer can tell the program to branch by *chance*, letting the computer select one of two possible directions, favoring one branch over another at a ratio specified by the writer. Each page is given a name, and these names are listed on the story's menu. As the story is developed it is helpful to create a flowchart showing connections between pages, which branches have been completed, and which pages have not yet been written. The program facilitates revisions, and the resulting interactive stories can be printed.

For readers of interactive stories, the choices are what make the story interactive. Since these choices determine the direction the story will take, one story may be read several times but result in different plots each time. The flexibility and unpredictability of interactive stories keep the reader's interest. Described below is a project in which three teachers—myself—and two other researchers taught elementary students to write interactive stories.

The *Story Tree* Project

Students from two fifth grade and two sixth grade classes participated in a project using *Story Tree* for writing interactive stories. The audience for these stories was second and third grade students in the same school. Each classroom was given instruction and work time separately. Because not enough computers were available for each student to work with the program individually, the students worked in groups of two or three, each group writing one story. To save time at the computer, students initially wrote their stories by hand and then entered them into *Story Tree*.

Although the students had previous experience using the computer, they were unfamiliar with *Story Tree*. Introductory instruction included showing students an example of a *Story Tree* story and teaching them procedures for writing pages and making the three types of connecting branches. Following this group instruction, we told students they would be writing for second and third graders. Primary grade students visited the class and read their favorite stories to the older students to familiarize them with material appropriate for young children. Each small group of students then brainstormed topics they might want to write about. After selecting an idea, they concurrently wrote the page (screens) and developed the flowcharts for their stories.

When the stories were completed, the students read through each branch to be sure it made sense. An adult worked with each group to guide students in thinking about the completeness of their explanations, to encourage the use of action and conversation in place of description, and to assist in implementing other aspects of creative writing. For example, emphasis was placed on producing a logical sequence of ideas and including all parts of a plot (introduction, problem, development, climax, problem solution, conclusion). Although instruction had been provided on these topics prior to the project, the instruction given when students thought they were finished with their stories was more effective, resulting in revision of their first attempts.

Students took turns typing pages into *Story Tree*. Although teachers had asked students to correct errors in spelling, punctuation, and grammar on the handwritten pages before entering them into the program, there were still plenty of errors in the typed text to provide students with experience in using the program's editing features. After making a printout, we marked errors and students returned to the computer to make corrections. Final printouts were cut upon, pictures were added, and the pages were laminated and bound into books to be placed in the school's media center for all students to use. Primary-grade students were paired with the intermediate-grade students for reading the stories on the computers, with the older students giving instructions and help when necessary.

Benefits

Using *Story Tree* for a major writing project served as the basis for providing instruction and practice in all the language arts. For example, students used their **oral language** skills as they discussed possible topics and worked cooperatively to write their stories. Students developed **listening** skills as they learned to use the program and considered alternative suggestions made by peers for story plots.

As students developed their stories and made revisions, they were involved in all stages of the **writing process**. During the prewriting stage they brainstormed about what to write, made sketchy notes for developing the story line and characters, obtained background about how to use the program, and learned how to write for younger children. During the composing stage students wrote their stories, taking their audience into consideration. During the revision and editing stages, students reread the written pages to check for story line coherence and clear transitions between pages, then reworded or added pages, to make the text more understandable, and used the printout to identify mechanical errors needing correction.

It was in these latter stages of the writing process that students also developed their **reading** skills, examining their stories for clarity, coherence, and errors in spelling or grammar. A special dimension was added to this task of rereading because the students were writing for second and third graders. Keeping their audience in mind, the students tried to use short sentences and frequently searched for an easier word for a particular idea (e.g., *jail* was substituted for *prison, circus* for *carnival).* Students consulted a thesaurus for synonyms, and in some cases rewording was necessary because a simpler synonym was unavailable. Even with this effort, though, students later found that many of the words were too difficult for the young children who read the final stories.

As students wrote their interactive stories and communicated with other members of their writing groups, the language arts skills were integrated and applied in a meaningful context. When we noticed skill weaknesses or misunderstandings, we provided instruction to remediate students' problems on the spot.

Writing interactive stories helped students recognize the importance of story sequence, cause and effect, main ideas, alternative plots, story grammar, plot development, sentence and paragraph formation, and transitions. In addition, students got a lot of practice in spelling, capitalization, punctuation, using quotation marks, and word usage. Vocabulary was broadened as students shared ideas and searched for different ways to express specific concepts. Higher order thinking skills such as analysis, synthesis, and evaluation were required as students compared plots and solved operational problems, created alternatives and story events, and made decisions about the best ideas or ways to do something.

Students found themselves in a situation where risk-taking was necessary. The program required a different type of writing than they had done before—writing that required developing multiple but related plots. Writing collaboratively with other students was a challenge because students found their ideas were not always in harmony with those of their peers. Students had to agree on a topic, set common goals, and attempt to use similar styles of writing. In order to make progress, competition had to be eliminated and replaced with a spirit of mutual support and respect for each other's ideas, contributions, and abilities. Willingness to let others read their writing and give suggestions was important. In addition, students had to learn they could try something and change it later without feeling failure.

Motivation for this project was high. Students were anxious to get at the task each day, in part because they were working on a topic they had chosen and because they were allowed to accomplish as much as they could each day through whatever process they wanted. There was much opportunity for creativity as they made decisions and solved procedural problems. All students found they had something meaningful to contribute. Some were good at creating the story and writing, some at keeping the flowchart organized, some at typing, some at spelling, some at illustrating, and some at providing group leadership. Because each student helped in a significant way, there was a feeling of success which motivated students to sustain their efforts.

The many benefits of the project were easily observed through daily interaction with the students as they worked, watching their progress, helping when necessary, and listening to the students' own insights about what they were gaining from the project. From an instructional perspective, it was easy to see which students were making improvements in their abilities to write coherently, use the conventions of written language, express ideas clearly, proofread, follow directions, incorporate alternatives and ideas which differed from their own, work cooperatively with others, stay on task, and carry out a series of smaller tasks leading to a large overall goal.

Problems

Although the fifth and sixth grade students in this project learned to use *Story Tree* effectively and the resulting stories were very interesting, some problems were evident. Problems fell into three broad areas: using *Story Tree*, the writing process, and curriculum integration.

Using *Story Tree*. The initial preparation given to students regarding the procedures for using *Story Tree* proved to be quite successful. Students were able to proceed through the different steps as they had been instructed. Having students read a complete interactive story and then work as a class to develop one helped them understand how *Story Tree* works. Even with this solid preparation, however, unforeseen problems did arise.

We considered the tutorial provided in the program's documentation too difficult for the students to follow, so we wrote a simpler guide. This guide told students step by step what to do and provided frequent points where an adult was to check their progress. Only a few students made use of the guide, although they were encouraged to use it to find answers for their questions. Usually students preferred to ask us.

Although students were instructed to develop flowcharts, they still had trouble keeping track of how the page they had just written connected with the others. During the composing process, when students were concurrently writing the story and making the flowchart, keeping track of page connections was fairly easy because students named one page at a time. The problem occurred when students began typing the pages into the *Story Tree* program. They often did not remember that indicating that a certain page led to another page is not the same as actually creating the new page. This confusion resulted in some connections going to the wrong pages and some pages being omitted. The problem was not easily discovered until the first printout when pages were checked against the flowcharts. Much adult guidance was needed to get these problems straightened out. More instruction would have been helpful to make sure students understood how to tell where each page and choice led. It also would have been helpful to provide more instruction on how to use up unwanted pages and how to add extra pages in a story when needed.

Some students were careless about remembering which page names they had already put on their menus. Instead of moving the cursor down to a page name already on the menu, they would type it in again as a new page, thus putting it on the menu more than once. When this extra page was discovered, students had to be helped to select the unwanted page from the menu, change its name, and type in content for the new page. Connections then had to be checked to be sure they were correct. A similar problem occurred when students forgot that all stories went to the same end page. Some even failed to show this on their flowcharts.

The Writing Process. Although students in fifth and sixth grade are fairly proficient in writing, creating an interactive story was different from anything they had done before. They were not only writing a story, but they also had to break the plot into several different threads with differing events, all following the same basic theme and using the same characters. This required the students to conceptualize an overall organization before actually writing the story. Some students had difficulty thinking of a variety of things for their characters to do. They tended to use long strings of *continue* pages, not recognizing points in the story where alternatives could be used to give the reader a choice of direction.

An alternative approach might be to have students write a regular story with a single plot. Then a helper (peer or adult) could read through the story, stopping at certain points to ask "What else could have happened here?" "How else might this character have reacted?" "What would have happened if this didn't happen?" This type of interaction with a basic story line might help the student writer see alternative plots which could result in branches from the main story.

Another suggestion is to begin a story as whole class but have the group break into subgroups to pursue each particular choice and susbsequent branch. As choices continue to occur, subgroups become smaller and smaller until finally individuals are writing branches independently.

Our students frequently had trouble expanding the idea presented on a page. They tended to write the main idea in a one- or two-sentence paragraph and then go on to a new page. We discussed ways to add conversation, use details to describe objects and events and, in general, put some flesh on the main ideas. Students who were doing a good job with this were asked to read their work aloud to the class to provide examples. Some stories did not make sense when read as a whole. Although each page seemed to describe an event and therefore made sense at the time it was written, students often failed to connect ideas from one page to another with logical transitions. This proved to be a difficult concept to teach to some. Even with explanation they did not seem to understand what was lacking in their stories. Teachers choosing to have students write interactive stories should focus special attention on teaching them to recognize gaps in information and to sequence ideas.

Curriculum Integration. When the *Story Tree* project began, the participating teachers agreed there was no way to predict how long it would take to complete the interactive stories. They were willing to allow students the open atmosphere, time, and flexible scheduling necessary to complete this extensive project without pressure to finish prematurely. Some time was allocated to writing interactive stories almost every day. In total, the project required 30 days, although there was quite a bit of variation in the amount of time needed by different students. On the average, 6 days were used for preparatory instruction; 5 to 12 days for writing the handwritten pages and making flowcharts; 12 to 17 days for typing in the stories and editing; and 5 days for sharing stories with the younger children.

As the project progressed, two of the three teachers gave up their regular language arts instructional time for the *Story Tree* work. These teachers realized that the students were still getting much practice in all the language skills and recognized that instruction was being provided as needed. They appreciated the integrated application of language skills in a meaningful context. A third teacher agreed with all this in principle but was concerned that her students might not be receiving the basic language arts skills which would be covered in this grade. She also felt she needed more objective evidence of the students' knowledge of skills for grading purposes. She therefore made time in her daily schedule for a structured language arts period in addition to the time spent writing interactive stories. Although the other two teachers were more comfortable with the type of evaluation associated with a whole language approach to instruction, when the project was completed they also indicated a desire to get back to more structured lessons.

For this project, participating teachers had the help of three researchers (myself and two graduate students). This made the teacher-student ratio unusually low. The teachers discussed ways to teach the reading and writing of interactive stories without this level of support. They decided one strategy would be to teach a small group of students how to use *Story Tree* and then have those students help tutor the rest of the class. A classroom arrangement in which the teacher can set aside time for working with each small group is important if one teacher is to provide students with the individualized feedback needed during editing and revision.

Conclusions

Although many classrooms now have computers, their most frequent use is for drill and practice, in which tasks are shown and can be completed within one working period. In addition, computers are often used as a reward for getting other work finished, in which case the tasks being done on the computer are often completely unrelated to needed instruction. Writing interactive stories is one way to use the computer as an integral part of the language arts program. Although use of such programs as *Story Tree* requires extensive time, the resulting learning is very beneficial. Teachers need to consider the quality of instructional time spent on computers and select worthwhile learning experiences for their students. Students benefit from opportunities to undertake a long-term project requiring the completion of numerous steps and leading to a final goal. Such an experience helps students develop concentration and perserverance, as well as the ability to organize their time effectively.

Dr Maribeth Henney, Professor, Dept. of Elementary Education, N. 107 Lagomarcino Hall, Iowa State University, Ames, IA 50011.

Software

Story Tree. Scholastic. Inc., P.O. Box 7502, Jefferson City, MO 65102.

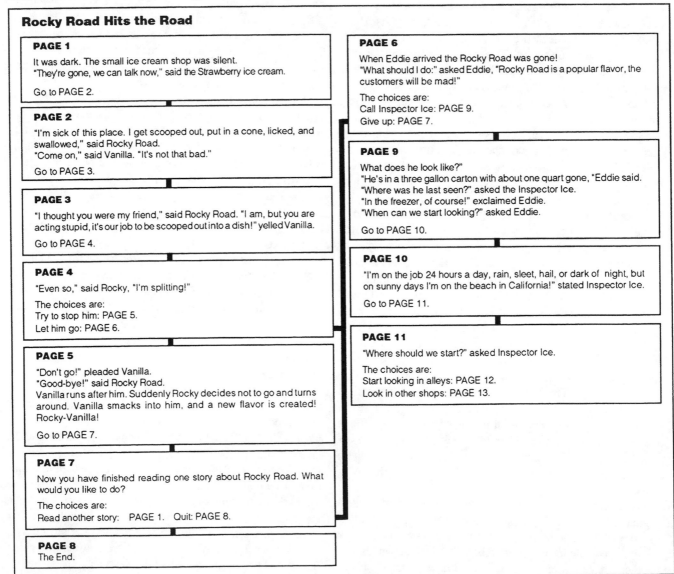

Rocky Road Hits the Road

PAGE 1

It was dark. The small ice cream shop was silent.
"They're gone, we can talk now," said the Strawberry ice cream.

Go to PAGE 2.

PAGE 2

"I'm sick of this place. I get scooped out, put in a cone, licked, and swallowed," said Rocky Road.
"Come on," said Vanilla. "It's not that bad."

Go to PAGE 3.

PAGE 3

"I thought you were my friend," said Rocky Road. "I am, but you are acting stupid, it's our job to be scooped out into a dish!" yelled Vanilla.

Go to PAGE 4.

PAGE 4

"Even so," said Rocky, "I'm splitting!"

The choices are:
Try to stop him: PAGE 5.
Let him go: PAGE 6.

PAGE 5

"Don't go!" pleaded Vanilla.
"Good-bye!" said Rocky Road.
Vanilla runs after him. Suddenly Rocky decides not to go and turns around. Vanilla smacks into him, and a new flavor is created! Rocky-Vanilla!

Go to PAGE 7.

PAGE 7

Now you have finished reading one story about Rocky Road. What would you like to do?

The choices are:
Read another story: PAGE 1. Quit: PAGE 8.

PAGE 8
The End.

PAGE 6

When Eddie arrived the Rocky Road was gone!
"What should I do:" asked Eddie, "Rocky Road is a popular flavor, the customers will be mad!"

The choices are:
Call Inspector Ice: PAGE 9.
Give up: PAGE 7.

PAGE 9

What does he look like?"
"He's in a three gallon carton with about one quart gone," Eddie said.
"Where was he last seen?" asked the Inspector Ice.
"In the freezer, of course!" exclaimed Eddie.
"When can we start looking?" asked Eddie.

Go to PAGE 10.

PAGE 10

"I'm on the job 24 hours a day, rain, sleet, hail, or dark of night, but on sunny days I'm on the beach in California!" stated Inspector Ice.

Go to PAGE 11.

PAGE 11

"Where should we start?" asked Inspector Ice.

The choices are:
Start looking in alleys: PAGE 12.
Look in other shops: PAGE 13.

COMPUTERS IN THE CURRICULUM: LANGUAGE ARTS
Edited by Lynne Anderson-Inman

Collaborative Writing Projects: Lesson Plans for the Computer Age

by William Wresch

For the last several years I have been gathering reports on writing projects demonstrating successful use of the computer by secondary level teachers. In the spring of 1991, a collection of 32 such writing projects will be published in booklet form by the National Council of Teachers of English. The lessons present a wide variety of ways in which the computer can be used, ranging from intensive involvement in a computerized writing lab to occasional use of a single classroom computer. What they have in common is a clear sense of effective writing instruction and a willingness to experiment with new technologies and new techniques. Many of the writing projects reveal an emphasis on *collaboration* between teacher and students and among groups of students. Described below are five of my favorites.

A Rose for Emily: Class Literary Paper

Mary Schenkenberg of Nerinx Hall High School, St. Louis, MO has used the computer to model the process of writing a literary paper. About a week after she assigned students the task of writing an essay on a literary work, she rolled a computer and small monitor into the classroom, attaching it to a large black and white classroom monitor so that all students could see. Students were informed that together they would go through the process of creating a class essay on William Faulkner's "A Rose for Emily," a work they had been reading and discussing for the last two days. Students knew that they were creating a model and that their own paper would be on a different story.

Ms. Schenkenberg first used the computer for brainstorming. Sitting at the computer, ready to type out anything the students suggested, she asked students to toss out ideas for a paper based on the story's point of view. She typed POINT OF VIEW on the blank screen and then waited. After a pause a student voice said, "There's a lot of foreshadowing." The teacher immediately typed FORESHADOWING below POINT OF VIEW. After five minutes the monitor contained the following short but satisfactory list:

"ROSE FOR EMILY"—PAPER IN PROGRESS
POINT OF VIEW
FORESHADOWING
THE SOUTH
WHAT IS THE ROSE
THE TOWN
EMILY

Ms. Schenkenberg then asked the students to select one of the ideas from the list. The class selected EMILY. Since there had been discussion in class about Emily as a parallel to the Old South, this was suggested as a possible theme for the paper. The teacher immediately typed this on the computer and then asked students to look through the story, searching for images or words illustrating Emily's connection with the Old South. She typed as they spoke and at the end of 10 minutes, the monitor was filled with ideas.

She felt it was important for the students to see their ideas and phrases displayed as randomly as they were found or conceived. The students quickly picked up the "anything goes" attitude and the rate of incoming comments accelerated as students looked more and more closely at their texts. In the time remaining, the class developed yet a third list of ideas, and then began putting the ideas into a framework for use as an outline. At the same time, they tried to come to a consensus about the paper's thesis.

By the end of the hour, Ms. Schenkenberg's class had agreed upon a thesis, developed an outline, and generated a substantial amount of content for an essay on "A Rose for Emily." More importantly, the students had a clearer grasp of how a literary paper can be crafted. To quote one of her surprised students, "So that's how writers work!"

Song of Myself: Class Poem

Joan Hamilton of Emerson School, Bolton, MA has tried to build a connection between reading and writing for her eighth grade students by having them write poems modeled after Walt Whitman's "Song of Myself." Computers were used to facilitate brainstorming, encourage revision, and enable the production of a class poem representing the collaborative efforts of multiple students.

After students had read the original Whitman poem, Ms. Hamilton set up six stations in the computer lab. Each was labeled with a beginning line from the poem: *I hear...*, *I understand...*, *I saw...*, *I want...*, *Injustices...*, and *Who are You?* Students were asked to move from computer to computer, adding one idea to each category. For example, at the station labeled "Who are You?", Ms. Hamilton encouraged students to add words, phrases, or ideas that would describe the typical eighth grade student.

The resulting lists were then saved, printed, and made available to all students as they began writing their individual poems. Partners or groups of students were assigned to edit each other's files for correct spelling, and all files were printed out.

When the individual poems were completed, students were given the option of combining their efforts into a class poem. Groups of students determined which parts of individual poems should be included and in what order. Whitman's original poem was used as a model for making these decisions, and the computer made the merging of individual files quick and easy. The final poem was printed, used for a choral reading in class, and displayed on bulletin boards.

Imaginary Worlds: Class Novel

Lee Sebastiani of University Park, PA is a teacher with a love for science fiction, so she involved her entire class in the creation of a science fiction novel. The class began by imagining possible sites for the novel. (A good resource for this task is Lin Carter's *Imaginary Worlds*.) The students brainstormed until they had "created" the planet Titania and even constructed a model of its most distinctive feature, a floating city. To give the novel focus, the students decided to concentrate on one episode of the planet's history, a rebellion of idealistic youths against a despotic technocracy.

The next prewriting step was for students to develop character outlines. Each student was asked to contribute a description of a character for the novel and an illustration related to the character (e.g., a portrait of the character, a map of the character's travels, a diagram of it's living quarters, or a sketch of a vehicle or some other Titanian artifact). Ms. Hamilton encouraged the students to let the characters reflect their own personalities and interests; thereby ensuring an engrossing writing experience and an interesting mix of personalities. For example, one student, herself an accomplished dancer, described a spy who used dance performances to gain access to the rulers' city. Another student, now in medical school, used his knowledge of chemistry and physics to design the system that kept Titania's city afloat.

Following the development of character outlines, each student was asked to imagine an incident of the rebellion and recount it in a 3-5 page story. Students were encouraged to write these incidents in the form best suited to their talents. For example, a student with a gift for realistic dialogue chose to write a transcript of the interrogation of a rebel prisoner.

Computers facilitated the creation of this novel and played several key roles. Most obviously, use of a word processor enabled students to write and revise their contributions easily. Once completed, student sections were combined into a single file and then printed. But there were other roles for the computer as well. Pictures and illustrations were easily scanned into the computer using a digitizer, modified using a graphics program, and inserted into the text. Students with skill using draw/paint programs were able to create their illustrations directly on the computer. For similar projects in the future, additional applications could be useful. For example, details or "specs" about the imaginary world and its characters could be kept in a database for easy retrieval. Teachers with access to a modem might choose to publish the class's work electronically. CompuServe's Science Fiction and Fantasy Forum, for example, offers an exciting opportunity for students to share their creations with interested readers beyond their school audience.

Community Sharing: Class Anthology

Dwight Worman of Webb High School, Reedsburg, WI has expanded the meaning of audience for his students by sharing their published anthology with the community. With the goal of producing a book of student writing, Mr. Worman begins his writing instruction with class discussion and the reading of exemplary models. Students then work through multiple drafts of their papers, using a word processor for composing and editing. When the draft of a paper starts to take shape, it is run through a spell checking program. Upon completion of the spell check, students use a writing analysis program called *Writer's Helper* (Conduit). This program analyzes the students' writing in a number of different ways, printing a hard copy of the analysis upon request. With this hard copy in hand, students begin a more formal stage of revision.

Mr. Worman has integrated computers into all stages of the writing process and feels they have been very helpful. He reports that the quality of writing his students do now is much better than in the precomputer years. Not only do the students produce better writing, but they have learned the skills needed to make effective use of all stages of the writing process.

To share this improved writing, Mr. Worman put together an anthology of his students' work. Each student who contributed to the book received a copy, as did all district administrators and school board members. In addition, each school library in the district received a copy and copies were distributed to multiple locations around town: doctors' offices, realtors' offices, insurance offices, city hall, and the hospital.

Such widespread publication and distribution led to reactions far beyond the class's expectations. There were many positive comments from people in the community who had an opportunity to read all or part of the book while waiting in various offices. At least one young writer even achieved a bit of fame. Matt had submitted a persuasive paper on why the U.S. military should keep the F-15 Eagle fighter plane in its arsenal. Soon after the book appeared in downtown offices, a colonel from a nearby military installation read Matt's paper while waiting for an appointment. He was so impressed that he invited Matt to the base as a special guest, where he was privileged to observe the military exercises being conducted. Subsequent to the visit, a reporter from a newspaper in a neighboring town interviewed Matt and wrote a lengthy article about his writing and the colonel's invitation.

Myth-Making: Team Myths

Jean Bowen of D.C. Everest Junior High, Schofield, WI culminates a unit on mythology by having teams of students collaborate in the writing of their own myths. Students are divided into groups of three and asked to create a new god or goddess and write a nature myth involving the being they have created. (A nature myth is one that explains the existence of some natural phenomenon, such as rainbows, snow, hurricanes, and so forth.) All stages of the writing process—prewriting, composing, revising, and editing—were to be accomplished using the computer. Students were given five days in the computer lab to work on the assignment.

Ms. Bowen deliberated over how many students to have in a group. She decided that three students could fit comfortably around a computer while ensuring an adequate flow of ideas to be combined into one myth. In each group, she tried to include at least one student with computer background. On the first day in the computer lab, there were some obvious reservations about group membership, and some groups were slow in getting started. Some groups began by making lists of potential gods or goddesses, while other groups made lists of potential natural phenomena to write about.

By the second day in the computer lab, groups began functioning as teams, and everyone seemed engrossed in their characters and stories. There was a strong concern over word choice, and the thesaurus was frequently consulted. Enthusiasm grew, and members of one group frequently walked around helping members of other groups. There was lots of positive reinforcement, and Ms. Bowen heard comments such as "It's great"; "It's art"; "I love it. It's so romantic and intriguing."

After six days, the myths were completed and shared with the rest of the class. They were also read by a panel of school personnel, and the top three myths were published in the school's literary magazine, *The Sting*. Ms. Bowen asked for student reactions to using the computer for this project and received favorable reviews. Listed below are some of her students' comments:

"It wasn't only fun, it was an interesting learning experience, probably for all of us, maybe including you, too."

"Being in a group can help you construct better sentences and catch other people's mistakes."

"Using the computer is good because it is kind of a break from having to write just on paper and your hand doesn't get as tired. It's easier to correct because you can move words around and you don't have to use white-out."

"I loved it so much... Combining all of our separate skills helped with the total outcome of the story...Getting out of the classroom itself and having a feeling of freedom was a joy in itself... I like you picking our groups, by the way, because some kids didn't have to feel left out. Thanks."

These five lessons give you some sense of the many types of collaborative writing projects being attempted by secondary teachers using the computer. The lessons also illustrate the variety of ways in which the computer can facilitate and enhance student creation. It can be used to model the writing process, motivate production, support revision, merge individual contributions, correct spelling, add graphics, access information, and enhance publication. Underlying all these roles, however, is the computer's capacity to help students do better writing, both individually and in collaboration with others.

Dr. William Wresch, University of Wisconsin—Stevens Point, Stevens Point, WI 54481.

Waiting to Connect: The Writer in Electronic Residence

by Trevor Owen

The world is waiting to connect.

This isn't news, of course. We have heard it from Shakespeare and Virginia Woolf, Mozart and Joni Mitchell, and every other person whose ideas we have considered when making meaning out of the world. And, when we have been very lucky, we have heard it from within.

At Riverdale Collegiate Institute (RCI) in Toronto, word processing and telecommunications are used for writing in the English classroom and for connecting, or extending, that experience to others, primarily students, writers, and teachers throughout Canada, North America, and the world. Our work in language-based telecommunications, or computer-mediated communication (CMC), is known as "Computer-Mediated Writing."

The Writer in Electronic Residence

Between February and June, 1988, students from Riverdale, British Columbia and elsewhere participated in the first "Writer in Electronic Residence" project with Vancouver poet Lionel Kearns. The students composed original works of writing and posted them, via modem, on a computer conferencing service made available by Simon Fraser University. Kearns offered commentary and his own insights, and encouraged the students' writing and commentary in specific ways. In particular, peer commentary emerged as an important component of these projects.

The English class involved (Ontario grade 10, ages 14 to 16) was housed permanently in the school computer lab. During the project, Kearns arranged to have students from British Columbia participate in the project as well. Individuals from in and around Vancouver were joined by a high school English class (grade 11 and 12) from Cariboo Hill Secondary School in Burnaby, B. C. Taken together, these students generated some 200 pages of original writing and commentary.

Writing, *Not* Computers

Like more traditional writer-in-residence programs, the RCI project assumed that the creative writing process could be encouraged in the classroom by the presence of of a professional writer working directly with the students. It also assumed that computer based word processing and online communication could be used to enhance students' creative writing skills, give students added insights into the craft of writing, and increase their writing productivity.

Language Is The Key

These programs are about writing and communication, and embrace CMC in the English classroom for two reasons: The nature of online interaction is textual, and therefore appropriate to writing and commentary; and the online forum provide a certain equity of use, placing students in control of the medium to broaden the shape and scope of the classroom experience.

We know now that CMC offers meaningful opportunities for language development and proficiency. Students control their own experiences in an atmosphere where tolerance is promoted as a natural result of seeing the world as another might. But we know, too, that a need exists to interpret experience within a meaningful context. A clear example emerged in our first project when the Riverdale students began receiving poems from the students attending Cariboo Hill Secondary. The themes present in their poems were quite similar in many cases, but the images that supported them clearly revealed that a sense of place and region was inherent in the work. Images of urban traffic congestion in one setting gave way to mountains and oceans in another, and the students began to discuss—as a group, within the context of their own classroom—how to respond to the new experience.

To this extent, then, it is clear that CMC offers an oral possibility in addition to a written one, especially when the telecommunicated experience is incorporated into an existing constituency, such as a classroom. We have identified this need to interpret experience within established, participating constituencies as *local shape*.

At Riverdale, we view the telecommunicated experience as a language activity, and we believe that many meaningful opportunities to summon language flow naturally from these links—both online and as a result of having been online. And students agree.

"What a WONDERFUL learning experience it has been," wrote student Yit Yin Tong, who is currently in grade twelve at Riverdale. "It has given me a new perspective on learning, and learning how to learn. With other writers of the world, we have all responded and contributed to one another. I see this as something that has changed my life." She adds that "education shouldn't always be within classroom walls."

Meaning: An Excerpt

I should note that pseudonymous participation is available as an option on this computer conference, and that it extends to all participants, including the writers and teachers.

The following poem, along with its discussion, has been excerpted in various publications, ranging from a Canadian small press literary magazine to papers presented at conferences about computers, distance education, and telecommunications. Its topic, child abuse, is disturbing. However, the discussion it inspires among the participants reveals a good deal about how meaning evolves in the computer-mediated environment. It is offered as an example of how student-controlled discussion can address a controversial issue online.

9752. It Rc 02:28 Tue Apr 5/88 (revised) 54 lines

"To suggest is to create. To name is to destroy."
—Lionel Kearns quoting someone else

did you know
it takes only 10 minutes
on good days

that is
when the child is feeling
particularly trusting &
doesn't bite his or her lips
stubbornly
when there is no need for chocolate promises
or movie passes
but then
it also depends on you...

if you've had one too many
& time is your friend & you'd rather go the distance

or perhaps your big hands
fumble on tiny clasps & zippers
...can't rip the damn thing off—how
would you explain...
so you smooth your affection over chubby arms
smile
say "let's play make-believe"
(2 minutes if it's fun)

finally you have
a naked body on a bed or a sofa or the broadloom
it's your turn
to make it happen
if it doesn't come
it may take a minute or two
and you're in overtime
but it was worth it 'cause the air is heaving
your blood pierces pale skin
your ears club rising whimpers
your eyes are gods & sweep the ceiling

"beautiful" a voice thunders

best part is
that it continues even after
the child is home

on average
on good days
on top
it takes 10 minutes

9752/1. Lionel Kearns 02:13 Fri Apr 1/88 12 lines

Well, okay rc. You have given us something to consider here, with your suggestiveness and your irony. LK

9752/2. Trevor Owen 08:20 Fri Apr 1/88 12 lines

There's a progression in this piece that comes from the "nesting" of lines, which takes you from "here" to "there." I think this form is what makes the "horrible" here possible, because it lets you stick your toe in cold water & make the unfamiliar just familiar enough to go a little further, before you know you're in too deep or, at least, deeper than you might have wanted to go. While you bring us back with this form too (thank you) we are a little changed, which is a good thing to have done to us. TO

9752/3. JK 11:45 Tue Apr 5/88 6 lines

I have been thinking about this poem for weeks. It is obviously about child molesting, but I can't figure out what you are saying about it? There seems to be no criticism of the act even by implication?

I would like to know what your intention was in writing this poem?

752/4. JK 11:47 Tue Apr 5/88 1 line

Are you a child molester?

9752/5 Rc 19:33 Sun Apr 10/88 16 lines

Hello JK:

I am not a child molester. If I were, I do not believe I would write about it unless I felt no shame in my actions.

The intention behind "It" was to disturb the reader. I hope it did not amuse anyone. This poem makes no judgement on child molesting (at least explicitly).

It is merely a painting. You decide how YOU feel about it.

What I would like to add is that it is simple to condemn child molesting. It is difficult to condemn the child molester. If a child trusted you, would he or she not trust your actions as well?

Thanks for your reply. I hope I have cleared some things up for you.

9752/6. Lionel Kearns 00:43 Fri May 6/88 9 lines

What is a poem for? To give you a bit of a jolt. To hang around in your head and make you think about things you would not normally think about. To force you to consider the world or life in a new way. To re-evaluate what is perhaps hidden under the old the old cliches. I think this poem makes it on all these grounds. A poet has to have courage, has to put his or her words at risk. This kind of poem is worth it.
 LK

9752/7. Col 08:02 Tue May 24/88 62 lines

Mother, Stay Home

She sat on her bed
Hating herself
as tears rushed out from her blue-green eyes
Looking around the room,
-She observed how perfect it looked
-How perfect her home looked to the outside world

Remembering the times
when she was younger and would
go outside in the backyard
and sit near the swimming pool with her parents
sipping ice-cold lemonade
and noticing an occasional puff of white cloud

while looking up at the pale blue sky
-the happy times

But then Mother
-her sudden illness
causing her to be in and out of the hospital
Away from home
-which isn't safe when she's not there

And father
-coming into her room those nights
Like tonight
She loathed the sight of him

She had to do something. But what?
Her mother would believe her...Right?

In Rc's poem in discussion '9752' I agree with her reply to your response, J. If you are a child molester you would have to be bold to want to reveal to everyone your hidden identity. In my poem "Mother Stay Home," it deals basically with the same thing. Now think about it J., if someone had incest going on in their family, don't you think that they would be a bit scared to even touch on that topic? That's why I feel that you either think that you're some great critic or you are just not taking this 'Simon Fraser' project seriously. J., why do you insist on putting down people's poems or criticizing them in the worst way?...Col.

9752/8 Rc 09:06 Wed May 25/88 34 lines

Col:

Thank you for the reinforcement. I admit that when I first read J.'s question ("Are you a child molester?") I was taken aback. At first I was indignant. But then I realized that, depending on one's tone and intents, the question could be a very valid one. I am happy to say I am not a child molester. I am even happier to say that I realize I have the potential to molest. No, I am not a monster with a clean grin. What I mean is that we all have the potential to act in endless ways. The attitudes we CHOOSE to keep or discard is what makes us distinctly human. I see the act of child molesting and CHOOSE not to perform it.

It exists (child molesting), but I will be on the look-out for its deep ditch.

When it comes to child abuse, I am quite violent (no pun intended). Vulnerability is dangerous, not only to the one who possesses it, but also to the one who sees it. The media is a great perpetuator of sex. Children are exposed to sex in all stages and forms. Some adults claim that a child seduced him or her. Possibly. But aren't children just mimicking what they see? Do the children realize to the full extent of what they are initiating? I believe not. And here, I believe the responsibility lies with the adult. With the benefits of adulthood (driving, voting, drinking, experience, etc.) comes the responsibility. The adult should prevent child abuse. It is sad that we must teach our children to say no. I feel there is something very wrong about a child TELLING an adult not to molest him or her.

I'm glad you wrote about it in your poem, Col. I think that if we wrote or talked more of "taboo acts" in a NEGATIVE way, we may avoid performing them. Keep writing and thinking!
Rc

Public Forum, A Neutral Floor

Ritz Chow, who currently attends the University of Toronto, has emerged as a writer largely through her participation online over the last three years. The following excerpt is taken from her paper "The Computer-Mediated Writer," presented at the ISTE "Telecommunications In Education" conference in Jerusalem this past August.

The structure of the "Writer-in-Electronic-Residence" conference was especially appealing to me because I could access it from my own room anytime. Often, I signed on at two in the morning when I could no longer read my physics or chemistry texts. I found the conference to be like a drop-in centre. I wrote simply because I knew there was an audience on the other side. The conference provided a public area where I could drop off my writing. My writing was out, not in.

The medium was textual, not vocal, not visual. The emphasis or focus was on the words themselves. I feel that this medium generated unblemished responses from participants because only the writing existed, not the writers. This was especially true for those participants who had only the computer screen as their space of interaction. The black screen afforded the participants a neutral floor.

In my view, Ms. Chow's comments reveal how well writers and students can exist together in a medium that refuses to distinguish between them. Indeed, it is perhaps more to the point to suggest that whatever distinctions are made are more clearly left to us. One student, who chose the name "helga," also commented on this in her evaluation of the project. She also participated on her home, from her home rather than school.

10736. EVALUATION OF THIS PROJECT
10736/7. helga 12:49 Mon Jul 18/88 28 lines

...I found the concept to be somewhat like a living book of poetry and short stories, as we were able to not only read each piece, but discuss it directly with its author or even (!) other readers. To top all that off with anonymity (some with more than others) was sinful. I wonder how different our comments and writing would have been, had they been made face to face.

The program had a strong air of sophistication.... It was an odd pleasure to be taken so seriously, and it in turn encourages (me) to take everyone else the same way.

I was also impressed by the opinions and styles of the "students" (how else can I put it?) especially those who dared comment on other pieces, or submitted their more vulnerable, off-the-wall writings.

My only criticisms are mainly for myself, as I hesitated in entering some of my own pieces due to the fact that I tend to be thin-skinned and defensive. Therefore, and I am beginning to see that this aspect is really in the 'program's' favor, this is not for the self-conscious writer. It is more for the writer who is willing to value criticism, and the giving of criticism. I wonder what the use of writing is without it, yet it is something that takes more than a little getting used to.

Over the past year, Canadian authors David McFadden, Katherine Govier, and Guy Gavriel Kay have participated as writers-in-electronic residence, and the program has begun t be replicated in other school districts. Additional links are currently being established with secondary schools in Ontario and B. C., and schools at all levels in the United States, Europe, and Britain. We are interested in seeing whether the participation of other young writers might continue to develop beyond Riverdale, and if some interaction between these writers—and their schools— might be fostered in meaningful ways.

We think there are some key ideas that may promote this interaction using telecommunications. The projects emphasize task, not technology, and they are language-based, involving participants in actively summoning language appropriate to the tasks at hand, and particular language in particular situations. Accordingly, they seek to empower learners by offering direct and personal access to activities that are relevant now. And they promote equity, seeking to increase access across constituencies by extending our reach out into the world and bringing what we find there back into the classroom to meet existing career goals.

Our next project will operate from January through April, 1990, with novelist Katherine Govier returning for another residency, and poet Lorna Crozier joining us for the first time. Student teaching candidates from the English program at the Faculty of Education, University of Toronto will join us again this year to undertake some of their practice teaching online, while a new mentoring program involving two younger writers will begin.

I said at the beginning that the world is "waiting to connect." What we have called computer-mediated writing offers the possibility that our students can connect directly with others and make meaning in ways they both invent and control.

"The small screen of a computer holds a great view," Ritz Chow notes. "Not only can we glimpse through the computer screen, but the world can gaze back, into our rooms, into our faces, into our worlds."

Trevor Owen, Riverdale Collegiate Institute, 1094 Gerrard ST., E., Toronto, ON M4M 2A1; Bitnet: usernbsp@sfu.

References

Riverdale Collegiate. (1988, August). Computers and word-processing in the English classroom, *3*(1). [Annual documentation of the school's telecommunication activities.]

Chow, R. (1989. August). The computer-mediated writer. Paper presented at the International Society for Technology in Education conference, Telecommunications in Education, Jerusalem, Israel.

Owen, T. (1989) Computer-mediated writing and the writer in electronic residence. In R. Mason and A. Kaye (Eds.) *Mindweave: Communication, computers and distance education* (pp. 208-211). Oxford: Pergamon Press.

The Computing Teacher   (Accepted for Publication 1991-92)

Marrying the Process of Writing with Your Computers

by Richard Smith and Suzanne Sutherland

One of the most exciting developments in the Houston Independent School District is the recent establishment in each of our middle schools of computer laboratories dedicated to facilitating writing instruction. A gift of 1000 Deskpro computers by the Compaq Computer Foundation made possible the 38 labs, each with an average of 27 computers.

Our labs are unique because the students are taught to use the *writing process* to transform their thoughts into writing through six steps. The process begins with prewriting activities, writing a draft, and then discussing the draft; the students revise, edit, and finally evaluate the completed piece. The teachers were shown how to teach the writing process as they learned how to use the computers. Hence, rather than being simply an add-on to traditional instruction, the computers were seamlessly woven into a new state-of-the-art writing curriculum.

Accordingly, a visitor to any of the laboratories steps into an exciting environment where students are engaged in several activities. Teachers help students gather their ideas together, get those ideas down on paper, obtain suggestions for improvement from their fellow students, revise their papers on the basis of that feedback, edit their papers, and then evaluate their efforts. These activities are the key steps of the writing process. A frequent enhancement is publishing the papers in anthologies or newsletters.

How we trained 210 teachers in 21 hours not only to become proficient in teaching the writing process but also to use the computers with ease and to organize their laboratories effectively was an involved process, but it is one that we feel is worth sharing. The teachers were selected by their principals on the advice of their language-arts chairpersons. Although language-arts teachers made up the largest group, the training was open to teachers in any subject area in which writing is used.

Language-arts teachers frequently found themselves working with teachers from areas as diverse as science and social studies.

Training took place in two phases. During the first, the teachers attended a six-hour Saturday inservice covering typical hands-on activities associated with computers, such as handling, formatting, and copying disks. They also learned the basics of computer laboratory management and how to use the word processing program selected for the computers. *Bank Street Writer III* was chosen because of its ease of use and compatibility with the 256K RAM configuration of the Compaq Deskpros. The inservice was conducted by professional trainers from our Bureau of Technology.

The second phase of training was held during five after-school sessions, each lasting three hours. The sessions concentrated on teaching teachers how to use the writing process to improve students' writing. Such training had been offered

before in HISD, but this time it was enhanced with computers. Nobody was quite sure what would happen. We decided that language-arts teachers who used, and were qualified to teach, the writing process would be teamed with experienced computer-using teachers. The writers would teach writing, and the other teachers would assist with the use of the computers.

Each session incorporated reading, personal writing, journal writing, research, response groups, and the use of the computer. What we did not anticipate was the teachers' enthusiasm for using the computers or their need for further technical instruction. Hence, while we originally thought that many of the teachers would opt to write their drafts off-line and then enter them into the computer, we soon realized that those teachers were in the minority. By far, most just plunged into writing directly with the computers.

As they attempted to write, they came up with more and more questions concerning the software and hardware. Accordingly, time that was originally to have been dedicated to teaching the writing process was used instead for instruction in how to use the computers. As a result, the language-arts inservice leaders and their computer-using partners soon became teammates rather than workshop leaders and technical assistants.

On the day following each session, there was a debriefing for all the trainers. What worked, where the time went, how the time would be made up, and what needed more emphasis all came under discussion. Thus, whatever lapses in content had been created during a previous inservice session were taken care of in the next session.

Both inservice participants and their leaders found themselves working double time to fit everything in. By the last session most of the teachers felt comfortable enough with the computers and had learned enough laboratory management techniques to allow them to concentrate fully on the last element of the writing process method, holistic scoring.

During the course of the five sessions the teachers had been working on writing short pieces, improving their drafts through discussion with their peers, and rewriting on the computers. When the teachers decided that what they had written was of high enough quality to be called finished, they were offered the opportunity to publish their papers by using the computers to produce an anthology representative of their training site. Since we had seven concurrent sessions at the end of the training, we had seven very good anthologies of teachers' writing. In fact, seeing their work published gave the teachers the same big thrill it frequently gives students who use word processors for the first time.

So far, our labs have been a big success in every sense of the word. We credit a large part of the success to the training the teachers received and the enthusiastic response it produced!

Here are ten steps we recommend for training teachers to use word processors.

1. Train teachers from a variety of subject areas together. They have a lot to learn from one another.

2. Teach the teachers to integrate word processing with their curriculum according to the findings of research instead of using a variety of word processing activities in haphazard fashion. Doing so will strengthen the effect of the computers. In our case, we selected the *writing process* which has a considerable amount of research behind it along with the backing of HISD's Curriculum Department.

3. Team inservice leaders who are expert in writing with inservice leaders who are expert in the use of computers. With both present, you have all your bases covered.

4. Budget sufficient time for the workshops. Ours took 21 hours. To be honest, we could easily have extended it by another twelve hours. Remember, your inservice participants will want to spend a lot of time on the computers.

5. Debrief your inservice training personnel. Use the information gathered during the debriefing to modify the succeeding workshops. Sticking to a strict schedule will probably prove to be troublesome and actually counterproductive.

6. Pay your teachers to participate in the workshops. Ours were given academic credit during the first phase of the training, which will eventually lead to higher salary, and they were paid $15 per hour during the second phase of the training.

7. Gain the backing of the district and school administrators for the type of computer-related writing instruction given. Without their backing, teachers may find that their newly learned techniques go unappreciated.

8. Use the computers to publish an anthology, a newsletter, or some similar collection of the pieces that the inservice participants have written by the end of the inservice series. Publishing validates writing and goes a long way to making

9. Provide refreshments. Teachers get hungry at the end of the day, especially by 7:30 p.m., when our sessions ended. Refreshments also offer an opportunity for people to get together and talk informally about the inservice.

10. Try getting the group together sometime after the inservice ends. For instance, we are planning a special session for our writing "alumni" during our summer district-wide inservice for all teachers. Keeping in contact with the participants will let them know that you care about what they are doing and what they have learned.

Overview of Workshop Activities
Writing Project
Overview of the Five Writing Sessions
A Fifteen-Hour Workshop

Each session incorporated the following components: reading, personal writing, journal writing, research, response groups, and the use of the computer. Participants enjoyed a variety of experiences that will be applied to their classrooms. The series was designed to give the teachers hands-on experiences with the writing process. Each three-hour session built on the previous sessions.

Session 1
Show not tell
The writing process
Journal writing:
a) response to literature
b) reflection
c) dialogue
Response groups

Session 2
Using the computer
Content dictates form
Writing in the content areas
I search
Journal writing
Response groups

Session 3
Using the computer
Writer's Workshop
Mini-lessons
Publishing
Journal writing
Response groups

Session 4
Using the computer
Reading/writing connection
Journal writing
Response groups

Session 5
Using the computer
Evaluation
Journal writing
Response groups

A Typical Training Session Agenda
Compaq Computer Writing Project
Agenda Day 2
April 17, 1990

Materials for this session:
- Computers
- Disks (blank and *Bank Street Writer* program)
- Handouts (Kirby article and Brainstorming)
- Read aloud (Graves chapter)
- Journals with your dialogues
- Notecards for teachers' questions
- Writing folders

4:00   Computer Practice Time
Labs will be in use at this time.

4:30   Computer Time
How to get started—reminders about booting-up, keying, printing, management, etc.

Response groups
Put participants into response groups.

Discuss experiences
Whole-group discussion of the experiences on the computer. Write questions on notecards.

5:30   Research
Read Dan Kirby's article, "Inside Out." Discuss the assumptions about writing.

6:00   Break

6:15   Wonder About
Read aloud the portion of Donald Grave's book, *Discover Your Own Literacy*, pp. 22-23. (On your own you may want to read all four pages.)

Write (using computer)
Write for 15 minutes about some, *I wonder about*, or some *whys?* or *how comes?* This is free writing. Use of the computer is optional.

Enter (on computer)
If your participants opted to write in longhand, they will now need to enter on the computer.

Save and Print

Response groups
Share and respond to writings in the various groups.

7:00   Content areas
Discuss how the writings can relate to content areas. Have participants share their ideas.

7:15   Journal Learning Log
Ask participants to write a description of what they have learned today.

7:25   PMI
ask participants to talk about the *pluses, minuses*, and *interesting points* of the session.

Practice
Hand out brainstorming activity. Ask participants to try to practice on a computer before the next session.

7:30   Home

* The time allotments for this agenda are only suggestions. Please adjust to meet the needs of your group as you would want the group members to do with their classes.

Suggestions for Further Reading
Calkins, L. (1986). *The art of teaching writing*. Portsmouth, N.H.: Heineman Educational Books, Inc.
Fulwiler, T. (1987). *The journal book*. Portsmouth, N.H.: Heineman Educational Books, Inc.
Graves, D. (1990.) *Discover your own literacy*. Portsmouth, N.H.: Heineman Educational Books, Inc.
Kirby, D., Kiherm, T. (1981). *Inside out.*. Montclair, N. J.: Boynton/Cook.
Macrorie, K. (1988). *The i-search paper*. Portsmouth, N.H.: Heineman Educational Books, Inc.
Nancie, A. (1987). *In the middle*.Portsmouth, N.H.: Heineman Educational Books, Inc.

COMPUTERS IN THE CURRICULUM: LANGUAGE ARTS

Exemplary Writing Projects Using *HyperCard*

Editor's Introduction

The Macintosh computer has been adopted by schools in ever increasing numbers over the last few years. For teachers of writing, the friendly interface and supporting graphics capabilities make the Macintosh an ideal choice for enhancing their students' efforts to get ideas into print. Furthermore, the vast array of software to support all stages of the writing process, coupled with authoring tools like HyperCard, *help extend the realm of writing products considered "doable" by K-12 students.*

To disseminate information about innovative writing projects using the Macintosh computer, Apple Computer, Inc. has recently published the Macintosh Writing Resource Guide. *In this heavily illustrated publication are descriptions of seven successful writing projects from K-12 schools around the country. Accompanying each description is a list of "Teaching Tips," as well as details about the hardware and software used by project participants. In the following article we present two of these exemplary writing projects. Both show imaginative educational uses for* HyperCard, *and both involve students in the production of interactive multimedia.*

Interactive Book Reports and Electronic Yearbooks

Match sixth-graders who want to demonstrate what they've learned about ancient Greece with a teacher who's beginning to experiment with *HyperCard* stacks, and you might get a stack like the Gods and Goddesses Yearbook.

"It starts out with a picture of the children dressed up as gods and goddesses," says teacher Joni Chancer. "When you click on any one of the faces, you see a first-person description of the life and exploits of that god or goddess." Other buttons, she explains, go to a mythological family tree and to a description of ancient Greece.

The idea for the mythology stack evolved from a *HyperCard* yearbook that Chancer had seen. "It was simple," she says. "Just a class picture. When you clicked on a face, you saw a 'Here's about me' description written by that student."

Chancer's own students thought the idea was terrific, and they decided that a similar *HyperCard* yearbook—about gods and goddesses—would be a good vehicle for extending their study of Greek mythology. By developing their stack, the sixth-graders are writing for a real audience, and that's highly motivating. They're also integrating and internalizing what they've learned in their recent studies.

Chancer has noticed that her students are synthesizing what they've learned as they figure out how to present it with *HyperCard*. And they're continuing to come up with new things to add and new connections to make. "Now they're drawing comic book versions of some of their favorite stories in Greek mythology," she says. "Then they'll scan these drawings and make new buttons to connect them to the stack."

Teaching with an integrated curriculum has always been important to Chancer. "But before," she says, "I was the one who made the connections. Now that they're working with *HyperCard*, the children are thinking of the connections themselves."

The sixth-graders' next project is a yearbook stack about themselves. Just like their first one, it will be based on a class picture. Chancer says that buttons will take the viewer to individual descriptions, as well as to prophecies of what each child might be like in 20 years. This time, though, they'll add another element.

"Some of the children have written fantastic poems that they'd like to include, and others want to scan in pictures of their art projects," she says. "So for each child, we'll have a wild card of that child's choice—something special to remember them by."

Although the sixth-graders have been using a Macintosh computer all year for writing and desktop publishing, they've only recently begun using *HyperCard*. According to Chancer, the children learned about buttons and connections by using HyperAtlas (a world geography stack) as well as a stack that Chancer herself developed.

"In terms of knowing the capabilities of *HyperCard*," says Chancer, "working with existing stacks has made all the difference in the world. At first, they loved the way buttons took them to different places, and that started them thinking about ways to classify information. Using other stacks is definitely the way to begin."

The Library, a stack that Chancer developed, is an innovative tool for reporting on books. The students use it to enter information and comments about books they've read, and they also refer to it when they want new book suggestions. Chancer uses the stack herself to keep track of her students' reading progress.

Chancer began exploring the possibilities of using *Hyper-Card* in the language arts classroom while participating in the South Coast Writing Project, an affiliate of the National Writing Project Network. Then she decided to develop a stack that would help reinforce what she'd been teaching in the classroom.

"We have a program of independent reading, and I wanted to make something the children could use as a tool for responding to the books," she says. "I also wanted it to bring together the elements I'm trying to teach: awareness of genre, setting, character descriptions, and plot." Developed with the help of a classroom parent who's also a programmer, the stack is an ambitious first project, according to Chancer, but it does every-

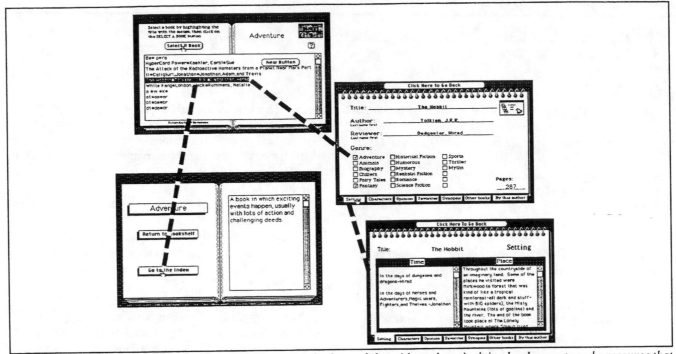

The Library, a stack developed by teacher Joni Chancer, is both a tool that aids students in doing book reports and a resource that can help them to select reading material. Students can choose to examine fields that cover specific genres—such as adventure stories or biographies—select specific titles, and then read their peers' comments about the book's characters, setting, and much more.

thing she wants it to. (For information about getting a copy of this stack, see page 55 of the Software section.)

A child who's looking for reading suggestions can use the stack to browse through descriptions—written by the students—of different literary genres.

"When you click on the icon that says Adventure," Chancer explains, "it takes you to a field that describes—in the students' own words—what that is." Someone looking for specific suggestions within a particular genre can then see a title-by-title list of all the books the children have read. And that's not all.

By clicking on one of the book titles, Chancer says, the child brings up a reference card with basic information about the book. This card, filled out by the first student in the class to read the particular book, also contains buttons labeled with elements such as character, setting, plot synopsis, and favorite quotes. Each of these connects to a scrolling field with room for comments from both the original book reporter and others.

Because each child also keeps a personal reading record on the stack, Chancer is able to see the types of books each one is reading and to follow what each child's interests have been. And, she adds, other students can review a classmate's list to get new suggestions for books to try. "I'd love to have a program like this in a bookstore," she says.

Chancer is convinced that using and developing *HyperCard* stacks made an important contribution to her students' education this year. Citing two things that happen when her students plan what will go into their own *HyperCard* stack, she says, "They make connections and they look for commonalities in the content of what they're presenting. They start thinking, 'Well, this goes

with that. But remember when we first did such and so?'"

Planning a *HyperCard* stack is a way of making those connections, according to Chancer. And when the connections start happening, the students are at the synthesis level of handling information. "That's critical thinking," she says, "and it goes beyond the literal facts and details of information."

One of the main values of *HyperCard*, according to Chancer, is that it encourages students to be responsible for their own education. "They don't feel that I'm giving them the education," she says. "They feel that they own that information. When you take something and turn it around to present it to someone else, then you own it. So for me, *HyperCard* is a tool for facilitating ownership."

Multimedia Helps Students Make Connections

At Cincinnati Country Day School, English teacher Bill Briggeman offers his students the option of writing their research papers in traditional form using a word processor, or in presentation form using a combination of interactive multimedia tools. "Students who choose the traditional option always see the other projects, and they realize very quickly that they've missed something," says Briggeman. "With either option, I require all of my students to use the word processor, and once they understand how helpful the computer is for their essays, they can easily make the leap to *HyperCard* and learn to use it to their advantage."

American literature and interactive multimedia may seem to be an unlikely combination, but students in Briggeman's junior English class are blending the two, and they are very excited with the results. An innovative project uses multimedia to show relationships between the literature, art, and music of various periods in literary history. Briggeman explains that with this project, students begin to appreciate that literature does not exist in isolation, but is related to the major intellectual motifs of an era.

The project involves creating a *HyperCard* stack that includes excerpts from the literature students have read, essays they have written about the literature, paintings selected from videodiscs of art, and musical selections of the period.

To begin the project, students discuss what they have learned from their reading about the characteristics of American literature from the ages of Romanticism, Realism, and Modernism. Then they are asked to apply those characteristics to the art of the three periods by exploring the National Gallery of Art and Louvre videodiscs and selecting three paintings from each period. A *HyperCard* stack index that accompanies the videodiscs allows students to search for paintings by a particular classification, such as artist, style, or time period. This feature presents students with a manageable number of paintings to study, and allows them to focus on the characteristics that relate the art to the literature of the period.

Once they have selected the paintings they will include in their *HyperCard* stacks, students write essays that compare and contrast the features of the paintings with the characteristics of the literature they read in class. Their essays are incorporated into their stacks, along with buttons that will access the paintings they have selected.

The final step of the project is to add music from the different periods. To facilitate this step, Briggeman had one of his students use *HyperSound* and the *MacRecorder* sound digitizer to store short excerpts from eight different compositions on a hard drive. Students were then able to access the musical excerpts and insert them into their stacks.

To create their final presentations, students organized their stacks so that by clicking on the various buttons, they could show the relationships between the literature, art, and music of the periods.

Briggeman describes the result as a presentation that allows students to look at a painting, read about its characteristics, and immediately reference related literature, while they listen to music that is associated with these literary and artistic styles.

He says, "The computer enables the students to understand the concepts of Romanticism, Realism, and Modernism far more vividly, poignantly, and lastingly than ever before. Students loved doing this project and want to do more like it."

Briggeman has his students work in teams on their multimedia projects. He explains that because some students are not comfortable with the technology, he pairs them with students who have more computer experience and can show them how to use the equipment. "This results in a great sharing situation," he says. "The more experienced students are eager to show their partners how to use the technology so that they can contribute equally to the project. It's the best teaching situation possible."

Briggeman's senior English students use *HyperCard* for their research projects, too. These students read several novels during the year, including Joseph Conrad's *Heart of Darkness* and Dante's *Inferno*.

Briggeman explains that in order to fully appreciate these novels, students must have background information about the settings and time periods in which the novels take place. "Rather than presenting my 40-minute introductory lecture on the novel," he says, "I have them do an investigative research project."

To initiate the research project, Briggeman has students brainstorm about what background information they might need to understand the novels. He creates a list of their ideas and has each student pick one to research in the library. "This helps students understand the historical context of the book," he says. "The students discover valuable information that helps them make important connections about the literature and the time in which it was written, and they are connections I would probably not have included in a lecture."

After students have done individual research, the members of each team combine their information into a *HyperCard* stack presentation, which must include an essay that meets the senior English writing requirements. They can also include maps, tables, and time lines. Briggeman says, "It's amazing what they find out." For example, students researching *Heart of Darkness*, which takes place in Africa from 1870 to 1915, discovered that the Kodak camera was invented during that time. They learned about Stanley Livingston's expeditions and were able to include in their *HyperCard* stacks examples of maps, charts, and articles from that time about the expeditions. They learned about the policies of the imperialist armies of Africa, and they included time lines and maps in their stacks showing the changes that resulted from the conferences held by the European powers for the purpose of dividing Africa into countries.

Teams of students who chose Dante's *Inferno* for their project did investigative research on the Italian Renaissance. To illustrate how the project helps students make connections between the literature and history of the period, Briggeman relates, "One group of students brought in piles of art history books and said, 'We can't find a picture that doesn't include a Christian symbol.' This led to their understanding of the importance of the Christian church during that time."

Students also did research on the politics of the period. One student presented information about what was known concerning math, the solar system, and the universe at the time. Another researched the daily life of the people and wrote a creative story about what he had discovered. "When this team of students combined all of their essays and information into one *HyperCard* stack," says Briggeman, "they had a nice background of information for the time period and setting of the Inferno."

Briggeman evaluates the electronic papers using the same criteria he would use for any written essay. He resists being swayed by the glitzy style of some of the multimedia presentations. Instead, he looks at the written components and determines how effective the organization is, and whether the arguments are clearly substantiated. He says that he often finds that the electronic papers that are all text are just as well done as those with lots of graphics.

Briggeman also notes that grading an electronic paper takes more time than grading a traditional paper, but that, because each electronic paper is done by a team of students, the total grading time required is much the same.

Briggeman plans to expand the use of multimedia in his English classes. Next year he will begin to implement a project involving poetry with his junior class. He will have students select poems and write literary analyses. Then they will use audiovisual equipment to create videotapes of images described in the poems. The videotapes will be transferred to videodiscs so that the images can be accessed through *HyperCard*.

A copy of the Macintosh Writing Resource Guide *can be ordered for $15.00 from LIST Services, Inc., 10810 Harney Street, Suite 202, Omaha, NB 68154; 402/334-4991; Applelink X0225.*

COMPUTERS IN THE CURRICULUM: LANGUAGE ARTS

Patrick's Visual: A Book Report Using Presentation Software

by Dan Lake

Patrick, my fifth-grade son, bounded in the door one spring afternoon and announced that he had to do a "visual" for school.

"What do you mean, a *'visual'*?" my wife and I asked.

"Something 'visual' to use with a book report," was Patrick's response. After some prodding and pushing, we ascertained that he wanted to do something for the book he was reading presently: *Kon Tiki.*

"I've got it!" my wife announced. "You can do a salt map!"

"No," I said. "He can do a slide show!"

The rest of this article describes Patrick's project, but it does more than that: It illustrates, first hand, how a new computer use became "integrated" into Patrick's classroom, and into his school building.

Step One: A Visit to Dad's Office

One Saturday morning I went into my office to do some filing and writing. I took Patrick with me so that I could teach him *Slide Shop.* After I spent one half-hour of showing him its use, Patrick wanted to handle the mouse and the Apple IIGS himself. I couldn't keep him away from it. He played with the program, creating graphic screens called "slides," and creating a short "script" consisting of transitions between four simple screens with drawings of trees and some words. He seemed to pick up the use of the program easily, and I asked him if he completed his book *Kon Tiki* yet. He assured me that he was and that it was a very good book. We decided to take the *Slide Shop* software home, where I maintained another IIGS for telecommunications work.

Step Two: Planning the Book Report "Visual"

Patrick had read his book, but had no idea how to plan a "slide show," or organize himself for a book report. I told him to pick 15 (an arbitrary number) of the most exciting events or places from his reading and list them in the order in which they appeared in the book. He did this in about 20 minutes.

I then asked him to consider that he would be doing a drawing (with some words) to accompany each event or place he chose, and that perhaps he should narrow the number of his choices to 10. He did this.

I then started to draw a map of South America on his screen, to show him how to draw an object, fill it with black, and then use the eraser and a white block to refine it. He didn't like my map and erased it, saying he could do a better job. I let him go, and walked away.

Over a period of three days, my son spent about two hours creating the 10 screens for his "visual." I watched from the background, giving occasional encouragement and showing

him how to make a white box within a blue background so he could frame text on his screen. I demonstrated the cut-and-paste method of carrying portions of his screen over to the next screen. He continued, and created the book report "slide show" in Figure 1.

Step Three: Enlisting the Aid of His Teacher

The day came when Patrick presented to his teacher what he was going to do. That afternoon, he came home to tell us that he couldn't do the "slide show." I asked why he was not able to do it. The reply was that the teacher didn't know what it was, and had told him to make something that could "hang on the wall." When questioned, Patrick informed us that his teacher had expressed some reservations about word processing and computers in general, and had even discouraged the use of word processing software by some of the children. He thought she didn't "like" computers.

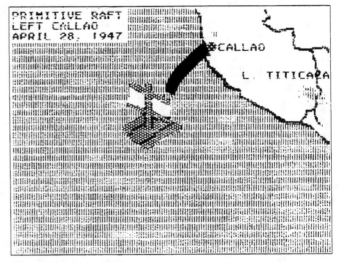

Figure 1.

Step Four: Enlisting the Aid of His "Other" Teacher

In truth, Patrick had many teachers. They worked in a team, splitting several of the fifth-grade curricular areas. Patrick also worked in a small group with a Creative Problem Solving class designed for youngsters needing extra challenges during their day. I knew the teacher of this class and knew that she was very comfortable with computers. I approached her and told her what Patrick had created. I asked her if she would look at it and consider approaching his reluctant teacher. She did look at it, and immediately contacted not only the other teacher, but also the custodian who customarily moved and hooked up large screen monitors to computers. The "show" was arranged!

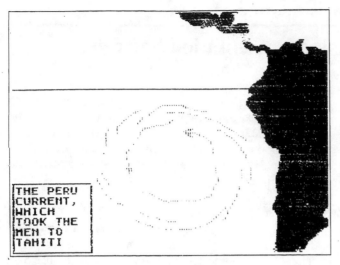

THE PERU
CURRENT,
WHICH
TOOK THE
MEN TO
TAHITI

Figure 2.

Produced by Patrick
Lake.

THE KON-TIKI
EXPEDITION
COVERED 4300
NAUTICAL MILES,
OR A DISTANCE
EQUAL TO THAT
FROM CHICAGO
TO MOSCOW.

Figure 3.

Step Five: The "Show"

Patrick walked into his class the next day with his disk and several pages containing miniature versions of the screens he had created. At my suggestion, he had written some key notes next to each screen image to help him talk about the 10 chosen screen events and places. When called upon, he went to the front of the room, placed his self-booting disk in the drive, and turned on the Apple IIe computer set up for him. Immediately, the opening screen was displayed on the smaller monitor as well as on the large color monitor seen by the complete class. He pressed one key and the first screen came up. Patrick was doing his book report!

By all accounts, Patrick "took over" the classroom for about an hour, answering questions and carefully explaining the significance of each event shown. The students were fully engaged and watching the screen. The teacher, the reluctant one, was impressed.

Step Six: The Outcomes!

Within the next two days, Patrick was asked to show the report to his Creative Problem Solving class. He was also asked to save the disk for the Parent's Night Open House later that month (he did this, setting the program to cycle automatically from beginning to end, then restarting, running this way during the evening).

The school's computer coordinator, hearing about the show, asked to see the disk. She immediately ordered 10 copies of the *Slide Shop* program for use by teachers in that building.

And I, a region-wide trainer responsible for teaching teachers how to integrate computers into their classrooms, smiled and showed Jenny, my third-grade daughter, how to create slides using the *Slide Shop*.

I am sure I will have another story to tell soon.

Daniel T. Lake, Onondaga/Cortland/Madison BOCES, Syracuse, NY 13221.

THE LOGO CENTER   Edited by Judi Harris, Molly Watt, and Sharon Yoder

Logo Writing: Illustrating Poetry

by Sharon Yoder and Connie Sue Bowman

Reprinted with permission from The Writing Notebook: Creative Word Processing in the Classroom, *April/May, 1988. For more information on* The Writing Notebook *contact P.O. Box 1268, Eugene, OR 97440-1268; phone 503/344-7125.*

Word processing is quickly becoming standard in high school English courses. While computer science students used to fill the computer lab, more and more students are now found working on writing papers and reports. Imagine, then, the disappointment of a 9th grade basic English class when told initially that their next unit, Illustrating Poetry, would not be on the computer! A compromise, however, was reached when the teacher agreed to give *LogoWriter* a try. Because *LogoWriter* allows both text and graphics on the screen at the same time without much programming knowledge, it seemed perfect for this project. Three class sessions were planned.

Session 1

LogoWriter was introduced: Students were shown how to start the program and how to use the word processor. Each student had a sheet of poems, at least one of which was to be copied using *LogoWriter*. With the help of the handout giving basic information, students went to the lab and entered the poem of their choice with little difficulty.

Session 2

This session began with a demonstration of stamping shapes. The student handout included a copy of the "Shapes Page." This special page includes 20 pre-designed shapes for the turtle. The steps needed to place a shape and stamp its image on the screen also were listed on a handout.

Session 3

Session 3 focused on how to create and use student-designed shapes. Each student had a handout explaining the steps necessary for creating these shapes. The last part of each of these three sessions was spent at the computer.

The intensity with which these students focused on illustrating their poems surprised everyone. In light of their previous experience with a standard word processor, entering poems on the first day was a routine task. Few students paid much attention to what they were typing. However, once they learned about shapes and began the process of illustration, the noise level dropped precipitously. It became very clear that most students were thinking very hard about the meaning of the poems in order to illustrate them in an interesting way.

One of the poems talked about mushrooms. Suddenly, groups of *LogoWriter* tree-shapes sprouted on several screens, where they clearly looked more like mushrooms than trees.

Other students labored to create high rise buildings to illustrate a poem about apartment houses. Many students came into the lab during their free time to work on projects. Two students spent literally hours illustrating a poem about Vietnam. And, with some assistance, they learned how to write a simple Logo program to animate a shape.

The students' responses were overwhelming. After a few anxious moments of "Can I really do this?", students moved forward eagerly into the realm of computers. Students whose experiences with the computer in junior high had often been negative now were clambering for computer time during class, during study hall, and after school. Here were students who were working together to perfect "their" poems, students who were learning to "put their heads together" to come up with a "superior" product. These same students whose handwriting, spelling, and composition limitations had hindered their progress in written communication in the past were now eager to—of all things—revise their work. They were much more receptive to the idea of revision when they saw their work on the screen and were shown the ease with which they could make additions/corrections/deletions, not only with text, but with the graphics they had used to illustrate their poems. They were willing to experiment with revision to find the best possible way to present the text and graphics of their poem. Fingers flew over the keyboards, and students exchanged ideas with other students in the process.

Student attitudes changed, too. Teachers in other classes reported that many of the students involved in this project were more concerned with detail and were taking more care (and pride) in what they were doing. Students were pleased to discover that they could, in fact, "hold their own" with the more advanced computer students seated near them in the lab. They overcame their apprehension, both of using *LogoWriter* and other programs. Students were proud of their accomplishments with the computer; they even bragged to their noncomputer-oriented friends about their prowess. Many a student completed *extra* classwork, just for the chance to continue using *LogoWriter*.

The *LogoWriter* poetry project was well worth the class time used. Although *LogoWriter* usually is associated with elementary students, there was no indication that these students felt that it was only for "little kids." The students gained valuable insights into their own capabilities. Teachers saw improved attitudes and quality of classwork. Both found a pleasant working atmosphere in the milieu of the computer lab. Certainly, it is a project to expand upon in the future.

[Sharon (Burrowes) Yoder, ISTE, Univeristy of Oregon, 1787 Agate St., Eugene, OR 97403.]

Copy Me! Using LogoWriter

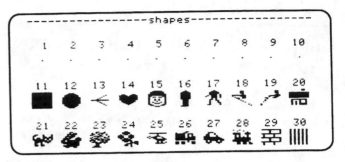

GETTING STARTED

1. Boot the LogoWriter Master Disk.
2. When "LogoWriter appears on the screen,
   - Return the Master disk.
   - Put in your scrapbook disk
   (Write the number here _____).
   - Press Return.
3. Use the arrow keys to choose NEWPAGE.
4. Press Return.
   You should see a page like this:

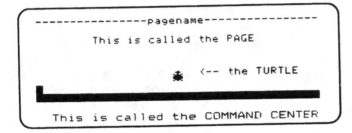

5. Choose a name for your page.
   Write it here: _____.
6. Type NP "(the name you chose goes here).
   Be sure the name appears at the top of the page.
7. Type HT (to hide the turtle).
8. Type Apple-U to go "UP" onto the page.
9. Now type the poem that you were given.

Here is a list of keys to use when working with this word processor.

```
----------------------------------------
               WORDPROCESSOR KEYS
----------------------------------------
From Command Center to Page:  Apple-U
From Page to Command Center:  Apple-U

Moving the cursor:

One space:  <--  and  -->
One line:   up-arrow  and down-arrow

Top of page:     Apple up-arrow
Bottom of page:  Apple down-arrow

Corrections:

Erase a letter:  Delete key
                 or Control/U
```

10. To save your work, press the ESC key.
11. To load your work, select it from the Contents Page.

STAMPING SHAPES

Boot LogoWriter. Put in your scrapbook and choose your page. Now you are going to learn to put shapes on the screen. Here are the shapes you can use:

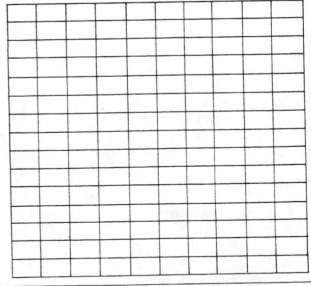

Moving the turtle:
1. Press Apple-9.
2. Use the arrow keys to put the turtle where you want it.
3. Press ESC.

Choosing a shape:
1. Make sure the cursor is in the Command Center.
2. Type SETSH number. ("number" is the number of the picture you want; SETSH 0 is the turtle.)
3. Type PD STAMP PU.

Repeat moving the turtle and stamping shapes until you are satisfied with your poem. (Use HT to hide the turtle when you are done.)

CREATING YOUR OWN SHAPES

Begin by booting LogoWriter as usual. Then, from the Contents page, choose SHAPES.

To **make your own shapes**, type Apple-F to "flip" the page. You will see the enlarged pictures. Use these keys to make your shapes:

To **move from shape to shape**:

Apple → to move to next shape

Apple ← to move to previous shape

To **move within a shape**, use the arrow keys to move up, down, right, and left.

To **change** a shape, use the space bar. Pressing the space bar erases or creates a "dot."

Here is a grid to use to design your own shape:

Writing and Computing: A Lab Affair

By J. Nicola Viani

In this article the author documents the steps he has used successfully to integrate word processing technology into the writing process. During several years of an enjoyable computing/writing relationship, Mr. Viani developed simple, efficient management strategies for both computer use and writing instruction. Mr. Viani's professional goal is to continue learning, to model an enjoyable instructional setting for others, and to reaffirm his support for the advancement of this essential technology in our schools.

There are three important factors that need to be addressed when managing a writing course in a computer lab: (a) the learning environment, (b) the students' keyboarding skills, and (c) the relationship between instructor and machine. It's comforting to know that, regardless of the software used, computers seem to have an unusual calming effect on children.

I stress to students and teachers alike that a word processing lab functions most efficiently as an editing tool rather than a compositional device. Our job is to go in prepared, and leave as quickly as possible. There are so many instructional uses for computers that we must all strive to maximize the efficiency of our scheduled visits.

Once students begin working in the lab, however, the urgency for time-management is alleviated by the absorbing attraction on the video screen.

Teachers excitedly remark how they'd never have anticipated the changes in student behavior that characterizes an electronic writing lesson. A student in my class one year had handwriting so unreadable that he dismissed spelling as irrelevant. Transferring his ideas to the computer screen where all letters are correctly formed, promptly triggered a connection between spelling and communication for him. That was the end of his spelling problem.

The importance of a serene atmosphere in a computer lab is reinforced when one realizes how easy it is to lose data. Considering the substantial investment in a lab, both financial and professional, it is paramount that respectful behavior be defined and consistently reinforced by all using the lab. A direct correlation between book bags and notebooks strewn about and the loss of important data and software exists in many school computer labs. Outdoor behavior should remain outside since an accidentally yanked power cord might result in serious repair bills.

Students' familiarity with the keyboard by the time they reach middle school is essential and should not be expected. In many elementary schools, youngsters are exposed to a teaching-unit that falls somewhere in the realm of "keyboard geography." The range of skills is extreme, and students who are unfamiliar with the keyboard must be taught. This is easily done at the beginning of the writing course, and twenty minutes of keyboard instruction handily compliments a daily word processing skill lesson.

I'm becoming increasingly convinced that language arts teachers must *demand* a keyboarding proficiency in the 25-30 words-per-minute range. This is not to suggest that language arts teachers must assume the sole responsibility for providing the instruction. It is clear, however, that as students gain speed entering data, the lab becomes free for other classes.

Finally, nothing is more imperative to a meaningful lab experience than a thorough understanding of the word processing program by the teacher. There is an endless list of unrelated elements that invariably go wrong at the absolutely worst possible time. "Murphy's Law" will prevail whenever there are large numbers of middle schoolers meddling with state-of-the-art technology. The solution is to learn the program and the machine before teaching students.

An unfortunate reality is that many educators are ill-equipped to handle the technology, neither for themselves personally nor within their classrooms. All too frequently curriculum guidelines that do address computer use merely suggest integrating a computer experience whenever possible, in lieu of stating specific technological skills to be addressed in a given course. Unfortunately preservice and inservice education courses haven't adequately prepared teachers for so important a responsibility. How long would parents tolerate an environment where students receive no PE, art, or music simply because the classroom teacher was uncomfortable teaching it?

The Setting

From 1982-1988, I taught in the middle school at the Canadian Academy, an international school in Kobe, Japan. Our school day consisted of eight 45-minute teaching blocks. My assignment in sixth grade was language arts for four blocks and social studies for two. Each 90-minute language arts block was dedicated to a literature-based reading program and the rest teaching the craft of writing.

When I checked the computer lab schedule, as luck would have it, there was a block free for both my morning and afternoon language arts sections. Armed with the hardware, I addressed the choreography of classroom and lab management. Exclusive of the pre-writing activity, approximately ten class sessions were necessary to complete a writing assignment. Each of those ten days is described below complete with directions included for both computer lab and classroom activities.

Day One—The Scoring Guide. Pass out a scoring guide that clearly states the expectations of the assignment and provides a valuable written copy of the instructions. The guides are divided into two components, primary and secondary traits, which focus on the two distinct features of the assignment. Primary traits outline the important features of writing that each student is expected to address (a) in their own writing, (b) while responding to other's writing, and (c) while scoring. There are generally four key objectives to each writing lesson, and those objectives must be phrased in a clear, measurable fashion.

I developed a scoring guide (see Figure 1) to use in evaluating the introduction component of the *I-Search* paper, a first-person research technique developed by Ken Macrorie. Subsequent lessons within the framework of the I-Search focus on the "body" of the search, the interview process, writing dialog, the conclusion, and the oral presentation of the experience. All together, there are six major components on which the students are graded. Each component has a separate scoring guide.

Another illustration of a scoring guide is one concerning poetry. An important unit in our Social Studies curriculum was studying Japan. In English, the students concurrently studied classical haiku poetry and were asked to write their own haiku, incorporating the elements customarily found in haiku of the master Japanese poets.

The primary traits for a haiku reads:

1. You wrote five original haiku poems based on a recent personal observation outside of class.
2. Your haiku dealt with some element of the natural world.
3. You remembered to create an air of surprise, astonishment, awe, or fascination, and focused on something unique or unusual.
4. The correct form for haiku was used, and you incorporated enough sensual references to create visual imagery.

Another assignment requires the students to write a set of simple instructions.

1. You wrote a set of instructions in paragraph form complete with a topic sentence, supporting ideas, and a "clincher."
2. You carefully indented your instructions, demonstrated the correct use of commas used in listing items and/or steps, and avoided employing brackets when a sentence would suffice.
3. You took special care to list all the steps in their proper order, and included "order words" to assist the reader.
4. Your instructions have no usage errors that might confuse the reader.

Secondary traits focus on the appearance of the assignment and how well it is edited. One full period is usually required to respond to questions about the scoring guide and make the connection with the pre-writing activity. If time permits, class time may be used to begin writing. For homework, students are required to finish a rough draft, due the next day, using dark pencil or ink and double spaced.

Day Two—The First Revision Session. I'm most comfortable teaching writing in "byte-sized" chunks. By keeping the length of the assignments reasonable, they usually are completed. The students' writing is submitted first thing in the morning, and two or three photocopies are made, depending on the number of participants in the response team. In class, we review the primary trait scoring guide and the students begin working in their response groups.

When first introduced to the writing process ten years ago, I developed a "script" to be followed by students in a response group that reassured me that the authors' were getting valuable feedback. Now, hundreds of classroom response sessions later, I'm convinced this script process works and authors are getting valuable feedback and maintaining ownership over their writing. In groups of three or four, the students labor over the primary traits, aware that what one gives, one also gets. It is extremely important that loyalty between students is qualified with substance, so I teach and reinforce an organizational technique for response sessions that closely resembles "PQP"—Praise, Question, & Polish (Neubert & McNelis, 1990).

Instead of the familiar "I really like it," responders are taught skills to communicate to the reader ideas about the piece of writing including: (a) what works, (b) why it works, and (c) what might be considered in the event of confusion. There is no way this part of the process can be over-emphasized; revision is the essence of student collaboration.

The value of the scoring guide is particularly evident during the evaluation process. Since all the students attempt to meet the expectations of the four-part scoring guide in their own writing, they similarly know what to expect in others' writing. If something is missing, they should catch it and alert the author, who quickly makes notes in the margins. After about 10 minutes everyone is on task and I can participate in small groups myself.

Day Three—Off To The Lab. We'll assume everyone had ample time to read their papers and absorb the feedback on Day Two. For the previous night's homework, each student was expected to either rewrite the piece or organize it into a readable fashion. Today's task is transferring the piece onto the word processor disk. It's imperative that students understand the instructions before they begin typing, because once they attack the keys it is improbable you'll ever regain their 100% attention in the event you forget something. For example, requiring an identifiable file name for a specific assignment makes searching students' disks a breeze. The key is making that identifiable file name unique.

For archival purposes, it may be worthwhile to save an entire class's writing on a particular topic onto one disk. There's trouble ahead, however, if everyone called their file "poem" or "autobiography." When another file with the same name is saved onto a disk, the previous file is replaced. This causes havoc if more than one student is sharing a data disk. One solution is to attach initials to the end of the file name (e.g. "autobio.NV" or "poem.NV").

Another lab strategy to consider is regular "saving-to-disk" sessions throughout the period. A colleague of mine uses this technique by assigning a student to set a digital alarm watch (yet another technological marvel) to signal when 10 minutes has passed. At the annoying beep, everyone saves, chats for a moment, and then resumes typing. It only takes a minute, and in the event a power plug is inadvertently kicked loose, considerably less data loss will occur. There are innumerable reasons why student data is lost on disks. One sure way to greatly reduce the number of disk failures is to carefully teach, reteach, and review the fundamentals of saving a file to disk.

Those 5.25" disks deserve their names: Floppy. Constant reminders to observe the red light on the disk drive while saving results in fewer headaches toward the end of the period when everyone is in a rush to get to the next class. Otherwise the tendency is to watch the screen while saving, the thumb expectantly poised over the drive's door anticipating a disk switch. All too frequently, the hand obscures the students' vision (of the red light), and the drive is opened prematurely. Another trick is having students save twice, once on their disk, and again on a classmate's disk. Some teachers require students to purchase their own "back-up" disks, a system that also works. Hold students responsible for producing a hard copy of their writing. If there's a loss of data with no back-up, the student is then obliged to retype the piece. As mentioned earlier, it's extremely important to establish and reinforce acceptable standards of behavior in the lab that are consistent with other classes. It is a polite practice to replace chairs under work stations, close disk drive doors, and recycle unwanted printing paper in the proper receptacle.

Perhaps even more important, though, is management of those students who finish early. For that reason, I keep a variety of computerized strategy activity disks handy (of course, they're all "educational games"). Quite a variety are available in the public domain, and I generally copy several onto the back of each student's data disk. I have had teachers question this practice fearing students will rush through a writing task in order to play a game. The natural consequences of submitting careless work seems to discourage the students from practicing poor study habits just to play the games. And who is to question the value of an occasional higher order thinking activity, anyway? Either way, arcade games they are not, and when students are finished saving their work, they merely flip to the back of their disks and shift gears. That allows me freedom to do screen conferencing as I wander throughout the lab.

The final task of the session is printing four copies; double spaced, wide margins, and identified with the author's name. If there are not enough printers to go around, assigning one or two students to designated "printing station(s)" expedites the process. I jokingly refer to this as "Valet Printing." While the author takes a breather, the printing crew quickly performs the printing routine, produces the product (the print out), maintains the printer's paper supply, and returns the author's storage disk, all with serious efficiency.

It's a good policy to have the students leave the word processor ON until they have a satisfactory printout, because revisions can be made far more quickly at their own work station than at the "printing station." If the computer is left on, the author will not be required to reboot the program and retrieve the file, time-consuming tasks which discourage some from ever making the change(s). We made it a point to recycle all the paper from the photo-copy room for printing rough drafts. Most printers accept single sheets as well as fan-folded paper, and considering the number of printouts this process generates, reusing the backside of scrap paper was successful. It also provided a relevant and timely lesson in conservation of natural resources.

Day Four—The Second Response Session. By now the assignment is nearly complete. Each student has amassed quite a collection of paper: (a) a rough draft from day one nicknamed the "sloppy copy," (b) the three photocopies used in class during day two's response session, (c) a rewrite, and (d) now four printouts. It is important to keep everything together since the final grade depends on completion, so reusable transparent sleeves can be used by the students as organizers. Day Four is spent in the second and final response session. By now I will have participated in several response sessions and conferenced with many in the lab. My homework is reading and responding to those I've missed or who had special problems to be worked out.

Day Five—Take a Break. This is as good a time for a break as any, particularly since there's always someone who's got to catch up (usually me). Students work on their revisions in the lab if they wish.

Day Six—Back To The Lab. The printouts from Day Four have been responded to, and today's the day for the final (primary trait) copy. The papers have yet to be edited. This is also the day we use Apple*Works* 3.0 integrated spell-checker, affectionately referred to as a "typo" checker since many "spelling" mistakes are actually typographical mishaps attributed to flying fingers. Bear in mind that other spelling checkers that accommodate a wide range of word processors are published by third-party software developers. Students print out two copies of their final pre-edited edition, one for the editing session in class the next day and one for me. For those students unable to complete the lab tasks, a contingency plan is necessary. Some work at lunch period, others before or after school, and still others at the discretion of teachers signed up in the lab who have machines available.

Day Seven—Editing Session. This is always fun because of the stamp pads. I ordered four stamps made. There's one for spelling, punctuation, usage, and sentence structure. The class is divided into four groups and each group is assigned a stamp "boss." I give each boss a stamp and 1/4 of the printouts from the previous day, and she or he distributes them to the editing partners. The group's job is to focus on their particular editing responsibility, although it's permissible to note other things. Anything suspect is circled. After the paper is read and editorial marks are made, it is stamped and collected by the boss. When all the papers are in, the pile is passed to another boss and the procedure repeated a total of four times. At session's end, the papers are covered with stamps and, hopefully, at least one circle for each stamp. The students make their corrections at home using a colored marker so their new additions will not be overlooked on this increasingly messy draft. The next day's lab session is far more efficient when each correction or revision colorfully stands out from the text.

Day Eight—Meanwhile, Back in the Lab. This session is quick and extremely important. All errors are corrected and the "final" printout is made. A dark printer ribbon, near-letter-quality printing, and special paper make for a truly enticing product. I request two printouts, and since the paper is due "today," the value of a word processor becomes evident. Minor changes, annoying typos, and the like are frequently noted at the last minute, easily corrected, and reprinted. I vividly remember when I was in sixth grade, angrily rewriting an entire piece in an effort to make one or two corrections. The final results of this additional rewrite were a couple of new errors. The likelihood of that happening when using a word processor is greatly reduced.

The students collect all their drafts, sloppy copies, printouts, revisions, and staple them neatly into a pile. Topping this off is the "cover contract" (see Figure 2), which assists students in monitoring their work as tasks are completed. The contract also keeps the students abreast of accumulated points earned. If all has gone well, each student should already have amassed 60 points out of 100, and that's before the papers have been scored. Here's the breakdown, taken from the cover contract: (a) AUTHORING COMPONENT— Rough Draft,10 points; 1st Rewrite,10 points; Final Copy, 10 points; and (b) PARTICIPATION COMPONENT—1st Revision,10 points; 2nd Revision,10 points; Editing Session,10 points.

Finally, each student's final copy and scoring guide are attached with a paper clip for tidy removal, and the whole packet slipped into the plastic sleeve, ready for scoring.

Day Nine—Judgment Day. For those teachers who are departmentalized, having students from different sections score each others papers can be enlightening. Here is a new set of papers the students haven't read or discussed in a response group. And in the case of some sixth graders asked to read grade eleven writings, there was absolute amazement at the quality of the work, not all of it positive.

On scoring day, I walk around the room and randomly pass out the thick plastic sleeves crammed with all the drafts and printouts. These are left face-down until all the papers are distributed. Then the reading begins. The first task is to have the scorer sign the scoring guide and from that point there is no stopping them. Since they have been living and breathing this assignment the past 10 days, they know what to look for, and by

golly, they find it. The papers are read carefully, merits and deficiencies noted, and the score totaled. Assigning letter grades to writing is relatively painless using the scoring guide. The significant ingredient here is the completion of assignments on time since so many people are dependent on everyone's participation. Generally, my assignments are awarded a maximum of 100 points, which allows easy transfer to letter grades. If students complete all steps of the process, they're awarded a minimum of 80 points for the assignment, which at many schools converts into the "B" range. Considering how much went into the task, that's a reasonable score. It's important to note that superior writing deserves and receives a higher score. Similarly, failing to complete components of the writing/scoring process reduces the score by 10 points for each omission. If a student is careless, the score reflects it.

It may first appear that quantity outweighs quality, but keep in mind there have been two response sessions, not to mention individual conferencing, to meet the primary trait goals. I have found the writing nearly always meets or surpasses my expectations due primarily to the collaborative process integrated in each project. To deal with authors who were ignoring the editing recommendations of their peers, everyone agreed to institute a "disrespectful oversight" penalty. If the scorer found an ignored secondary trait error that was previously circled or otherwise noted by a reader, editor, or responder, the author lost 10 points. The students also agreed this could be abused, so it was limited to one assessment per paper.

The primary and secondary scores are now totaled on the scoring guide, transferred to the cover contract, and the pile replaced into the sleeve. I record the scores, return the cover, and insert a copy into the student's writing folder. There are invariably instances in which a student feels they've been unfairly graded. As a compromise gesture, I also score papers on if asked, but only if the student agrees to average the two scores together.

Day Ten—Author's Chair. There's nothing quite like having the author proudly share his or her writing with the class, regardless of how many times it has been shared through the process. One copy is kept in the student's writing folder, properly identified in a table of contents glued onto the inside cover. The other copy is kept by the teacher to mount and display, to reuse in demonstration lessons, and always to cherish.

I recently was informed of the tragic death of a former student. Retrieving his writing from an anthology reunited us again, awakening memories of a writer finding his "voice." I shall always have those memories, facilitated by the ease of electronic data storage. Ten years ago I would never have had an entire term's anthology available to read through, but with a single 3.5" storage disk, I did. I've learned, and I'm grateful.

References

Neubert, G.A. & McNelis, S.J. (1990). Peer response: teaching specific revision suggestions. *English Journal, 79*(5), 952-956.
Macrorie, K. (1984). *Searching writing.* Boynton/Cook.

AUTHOR'S NAME _____

PRIMARY TRAIT SCORING GUIDE

(SCORERS: Please circle the score awarded)

5. **A** You clearly stated your topic and explained *why* you selected the topic you did. In addition, you shared an anecdote demonstrating your curiosity.

B You detailed *what you knew about your topic* when you began this project.

C You included *what you hope to learn* about your topic and added strategies of how you plan to conduct your search.

D Your paper is *written in your own words*, is *organized*, and is free of usage errors that might confuse the reader.

4. THREE OF THE FOUR factors for the "5" paper are present, but your paper is a bit weak in:

3. TWO OF THE FOUR factors for the "5" paper are present, and here is something to remember next time:

2. and 1. LATE and REALLY LATE (Talk to your teacher).

SECONDARY TRAIT SCORING GUIDE

(SCORERS: Please circle the score awarded)

Total the number of SECONDARY TRAIT errors and divide by the number of pages (rounded off to the nearest whole page). For example, 13 errors divided by seven pages = **1.85** or a score of **2** (also rounded).

3. Your paper had **NO** *(Hooray!)* typographic errors, was neat, and demonstrated correct capitalization, spelling, and end punctuation.

2. Each pages averaged a **FEW** *(1 or 2)* problems with typographic errors, neatness, spelling, capitalization, and/or punctuation.

1. Each page averaged **SEVERAL** *(3 or more)* problems with typographic errors, neatness, spelling, capitalization, and/or end punctuation.

SUM Of PRIMARY And SECONDARY TRAIT SCORES **X 5 =**   (40 max)
Please transfer this score to the cover contract.

Scorer's name _____   Scoring Date _____

*[**Note:** On the same line as the author's name, it is important to identify the scoring guide and the revision date. Rather than mass duplicating these, they are word-processed using Multiscribe for each assignment. The class debriefs after each writing task and makes suggestions for improving the experience for the next time. The changes are noted and the revision date changed.]*

COVER CONTRACT FOR _____

ASSIGNMENT: _____

I.   AUTHORING COMPONENT: **30 POINTS**

    ___ 1. Rough Draft (10 pts)

    ___ 2. Rewritten Copy (10 pts)

    ___ 3. Final Copy (10 pts)   Due:

II. **PARTICIPATION COMPONENT:**   **30 POINTS**

    ___ 1. 1st Revision Session (10 pts)   Date:

    ___ 2. 2nd Revision Session (10 pts)   Date:

    ___ 3. Editing Session (10 pts)
    (Please include the "edited" copies that were returned to you)

    Please check your "Editing Team"

    ___ Spelling (read backward)

    ___ Punctuation/Capitalization

    ___ Verb Tense & Subject/verb agreement

    ___ Sentence structure, run-ons, and fragments

III. **SCORING COMPONENT:**   **10–40 POINTS**
    (Please include your dated "Scoring Guide")

IV. **PENALTY POINTS FOR DISRESPECTFUL OVERSIGHTS:**
    (A single penalty may be assessed per assignment)   **(- 10 pts)**

TOTAL SCORE FOR THIS ASSIGNMENT
(100 points possible) _____

KEYBOARDING

If students are to be expected to use a word processor as part of the writing process, then it would follow that facilitating their interaction and skill with the keyboard, the primary input device of most computers is an important issue. Keyboarding or typing skill is no longer the exclusive domaine of the high school business education teachers, as many elementary and junior high schools have incorporated teaching this skill into their curricula. The questions of "How important is it to teach keyboarding?" and if taught "How should keyboarding be taught?" are addressed in the following articles.

Keyboarding—An Interview with Keith Wetzel

Reprinted with permission from Franklin, S. (Ed.).

A former elementary and middle school teacher, Keith Wetzel has conducted research on teaching writing and word processing to students grades 3-5 and is currently workshop coordinator for the Center for Advanced Technology in Education at the University of Oregon. Keith agreed to share his views on the subject of keyboarding with The Writing Notebook *readers.*

Keith, many people feel that touch typing is a fundamental skill students need before they can get the full benefits of word processing. What do you think?

With some hesitation I would agree. If teachers and students have a sufficient amount of hardware and software to make keyboarding training realistic—yes. If students are using the computer for an hour or less a week they should use a word processor or writing aid without worrying about keyboarding.

Recently I read Henry Becker's survey of computers in the schools. He found that in computer owning schools, the computer/student ratio nationally was 1 to 40. For each student to use the computer for 30 minutes a day, a 1 to 12 ratio is needed. I believe that in a situation in which there are a limited number of computers, keyboarding instruction should be ignored. A short amount of time—an hour, perhaps—may be used to acquaint students with the home row and where to place their hands. But if time is indeed precious, I recommend using it to do a class project where everyone makes a contribution, rather than using the time to teach keyboarding at the expense of other computer experiences.

How long does it take for students to become competent beginning touch typists?

This question is related to the goal of the keyboard instruction. If third, fourth, and fifth graders are to type as quickly as they can write by pencil, they will need 20 to 30 hours of instruction. In addition, new research has indicated that elementary students (after 20 hours of instruction) regress in their touch typing skills if they do not practice touch typing at intervals throughout the year.

What criteria should elementary students achieve to be considered adequate typists?

Truthfully, I wish the keyboarding question did not exist, because the real question should be: What experiences do students need to learn to enjoy writing and improve their writing? Clearly, the primary goal is not keyboarding, it's writing.

Now the problem is that if students are to benefit from the advantage of using word processing—ease of revision—they need to be able to use the word processor efficiently.

Without keyboarding instruction, upper elementary students will write at the keyboard at half the rate they write with pencil. Is this a problem? Yes. The physical part of writing—transcription—should be an automatic skill. Students should use their mental energy to think about ideas, how to express them, what goes next, the audience, and so on. When they have to add one more task to an already complete set of writing tasks, writing becomes more difficult rather than less.

Students in the upper elementary grades write with pencil at about 10 words per minute. Without keyboard training they write with the computer at a rate of 5 words per minute. Students should keyboard as efficiently as they write by pencil before they begin to use the computer for their daily writing. And then they should practice touch typing at intervals until their typing rate reaches 20 words per minute. Business education experts have indicated that students retain more of their newly acquired skills once they reach the plateau of 20 words per minute.

How do we decide when to teach kids to touch type? Is it a function of size of hand? Dexterity? Maturity? Attention span? Or can we base the decision simply on when students have access to the computer for word processing?

I would agree with the last comment. Students should receive keyboarding instruction just prior to actual use of the computer for writing.

If we lived in a world in which we could decide the optimal configuration, then the question of maturity would be more important.

I have read that children in grades K and 1 can keyboard as accurately and quickly as they can write by pencil. Intuitively this makes sense. I haven't measured this, but I've taught first graders to print, and I know how much they struggle with the direction of the letters, staying on the lines, and writing neatly.

I suspect that if keyboarding instruction started in first grade, a shorter amount of concentrated instruction would be required in the third and fourth grades. And in grades K and 1, nothing would need to be replaced in the curriculum Just as students practice tracing letters, they would practice the letter in another manner—saying, seeing, and pushing the correct key. This is a good research topic. I think it would be worth further investigation over a period of years.

There are a number of new keyboarding programs. How to the newer programs differ from the earlier programs?

Generally, the programs that are based on sound theory developed by the business educators are the best. I think we have moved passed the violent, Space Invaders-variety games that attempt to fascinate and entertain as well as drill.

Now we have programs that are more closely related to the typing instruction taught at the secondary level. These programs are in my opinion the best. They model correct posture and keystroking, and many of them offer excellent drill as well as opportunity to use an open screen, where the user can dictate spelling words and sentences.

It seems that it would be most desirable to teach keyboarding in a lab setting. Is this true? Can keyboarding be taught in a classroom with one computer?

Again, the one-computer-to-30-students classroom does not allow sufficient time for each student to practice every day for 20 minutes. Mathematically there is not enough time during the school day for each student to get on the computer. Remember, there are times during the day when students do not use the computer—lunch, movies, art, PE, regrouping for math, etc.

A lab usually allows teachers to set priorities such as—This year all third grade classes will use the computer for keyboarding during the second nine-week period, and then they will use the lab for writing during the third and fourth nine-week periods.

Should spelling and related writing skills be taught while teaching typing?

This is an interesting idea; however, to date I'm not aware of any teachers who have achieved this kind of integration. In typing instruction there is a standard progression for teaching the order of the letters; you teach the home row keys before you teach the keys you need to stretch to type.

On the other hand, if you were emphasizing c-v-c words in language arts, and during your keyboarding time you practiced short "a" words such as ad, add, dad, and sad, there would be an excellent opportunity for integration.

Do you see benefits to teaching touch typing to language disabled students?

Again, I don't know that I can generalize to all students with learning disabilities. I would definitely try it. I've seen several reports that testify to the success of word processing with children who have writing problems. However, keyboarding requires dexterity and motor-visual coordination, and it would be wise to see if a student with a particular problem would benefit from use of the keyboard. We know that there are some children who have more trouble learning to keyboard than others. I recommend trying it on an individual basis and proceeding if it is worth the amount of time needed to master the skill.

Can we turn keyboard instruction over to a computer keyboarding program, or is it important for teachers to model or demonstrate or otherwise deliver instruction in addition to the computer program?

The computer cannot watch the student perform. It cannot monitor whether a student strikes the key with the correct finger.

Philosophically I have problems with those who would replace teachers with machines. Learning includes much more than specific skills acquisition. Seldom do computers teach love of learning. Teachers include reasons, models, values, human interaction, and the human touch.

This point was illustrated in a research study at the college level: a group of college students received a computer-based typing program. They practiced without teacher assistance for an hour a day for 30 days. At the end of the training, the speed and accuracy of these students were compared to those who completed a teacher-based typing program. The skill levels of the students were similar at the end of 30 days; however, the computer-based students complained that their questions weren't answered, and that they didn't receive assistance when needed.

The components of a good school district keyboarding instructional program include: 1) collaboration in planning and implementing the program between business education (touch typing teachers) and elementary teachers; 2) elementary teachers who have sufficient training in the teaching of keyboarding to feel comfortable with the delivery of a new skill; 3) a scripted teacher's guide that makes direct instruction efficient; and 4) a good keyboarding software program.

What are the most important characteristics a school district should look for in a keyboarding instructional program?

My answer may not be the expected answer. I would not start with the software. I would start with the teacher training and the amount of student practice time demanded by any program that will work. Here are the questions I would ask:

1) Did teachers receive training to teach their students keyboarding, or are they beginning without training? Was this training done by business education experts? Do teachers feel competent to teach keyboarding?
2) Is there a sufficient time for each student to practice? And once the keyboarding instruction is complete, are the skills practiced at times in order to maintain the skill level?
3) Does the program include a record-keeping component (either a disk-based or a paper-based [graph] method of recording progress)?
4) Is there sufficient variety in the program? Does it combine teacher dictation, disk-based practice and nonviolent games?
5) Do students using the program meet your goals for the program? If students are to type at least as fast as they write by pencil, do they? Is there any research to suggest that following the program works?

Typing programs seem to emphasize technique, speed, and accuracy to varying degrees. Of these is there a priority teachers should be aware of as they instruct their students?

They are all related; however, the goal is for students to be able to use the computer for writing, for improving their writing, and to learn to think by revising and rewriting. Good technique is immaterial if students still type substantially slower than they write with pencil. If keyboarding does not become automatic, students will not spend their cognitive energy on the higher level task of communicating effectively.

Typing teachers especially feel that if kids learn to hunt and peck first, it will be harder for them to learn to touch type. Do you agree?

Several business education teachers have voiced this concern to me, while others have indicated that it is not of great concern to them. A major point is the extent of prior student keyboard practice. Those who were less concerned felt that the occasional computer use of elementary students was not a problem. I think that if students use the computer at least two hours a week, then they should have keyboarding instruction, and the instruction should be consistent with instruction they may receive at a later time, such as in business education courses.

There is a political issue about who should teach touch typing—typing teachers or classroom or English teachers. Do you have any thoughts on this?

I personally would like to have the teacher in the grade before the students come to me teach it! I think that language arts time should not be used for typing instruction.

An ideal place for keyboarding is in a computer literacy class. Some schools offer a computer literacy class for every sixth grader in the district. These classes include a wide variety of topics. I've found that this is an ideal place to teach it. About 20 minutes of the 50-minute class is then devoted to keyboarding instruction. The next step is to teach word processing and to practice the keyboarding skills in the word processing assignments. Database usage may follow and again, as students input data, they practice keyboarding skills. In this situation, selected computer literacy teachers receive training to teach keyboarding to all students. Language arts teachers teach writing with the computer as a tool, not keyboarding or the mechanics of word processing.

(1988). Making the Literature, Writing, Word Processing Connection: The Best of *The Writing Notebook* (2nd ed.). Eugene, OR: *The Writing Notebook.*

Elementary Keyboarding—Is It Important?

by Truman H. Jackson and Diane Berg

As computers become a common element in the elementary school, a major question posed is, "How do I make elementary students more efficient in the use of the keyboard?" The answer is, "Provide an appropriate instructional sequence in keyboarding."

In an early, informal analysis of student keying efficiency using the "hunt and peck" method versus keying efficiency after 15 hours of appropriate keyboarding instruction, students with instruction were judged to be approximately twice as fast as those who had no formal keyboarding instruction. This judgment was made by a computer science instructor who had some students in a programming class directly following their keyboarding instruction and some students who had not yet received keyboarding instruction. If a school has a computer education program with sufficient hardware, the decision to teach keyboarding has potential to either reduce the number of computers required in a school or allow students more productive time at the computer after only 15 hours of appropriate keyboarding instruction. From either perspective, increased efficiency or reduced cost, a formal keyboarding sequence makes sense. Therefore, a formal elementary keyboarding instructional program must be given consideration equal to other key computer decisions, such as hardware purchases and software selection.

What is appropriate keyboarding instruction? Answers to the following questions will help in the creation of a keyboarding instructional sequence which will provide each student an opportunity to develop reasonable keyboarding skills.

Are keyboarding and typewriting the same? Keyboarding, simply defined, is learning the correct manipulation of the keys on a computer/typewriter keyboard and using that keyboard for basic data input. Typewriting is the continued development of keying skills and the use of those skills to produce output in a variety of applications, such as in the creation of letters, memoranda, and reports.

Should keyboarding be taught? The incorporation of computers into the classroom and the introduction of application software in early elementary grades make reasonable keyboarding skills necessary. Using a computer without properly learning keyboarding skills will definitely hinder their future development.

Where should keyboarding be taught in the curriculum? Keyboarding should be taught just prior to required use of the keyboard for text entry, the inputting of words and/or numbers such as in keying word lists, creating sentences, entering programs, or using a word processor.

In early elementary (K-2), the goal of instruction may simply be to aid students in locating keys on the keyboard. But beginning at about the third grade level, formal development of correct keyboarding technique should be introduced, focusing on the alphabetic keys. Third grade students are physiologically ready to learn keyboarding and studies have shown that they can become keyboard proficient. At the upper elementary level, number and symbol/function keys should be introduced along with a simple-to-use text editor/word processor.

Where does the time come from for keyboarding instruction? In most cases, time for keyboarding instruction is coming from language arts. Since keyboarding has great potential to contribute to language arts skill development—learning new words and word definitions and creating spelling lists, sentences, and paragraphs—it is frequently the subject area into which keyboarding instruction is integrated. Social studies is another common area through which keyboarding instruction is offered.

How much time is needed for keyboarding instruction? Feedback from ongoing programs indicates that approximately 30 hours of instruction at the elementary level—15 hours in each of two consecutive grades or 10 hours each in three consecutive grades—provides the most successful teaching/ learning sequence. Twenty- to 30-minute class periods which meet every day work best for elementary students. Weekly 30-minute review sessions should continue throughout the year to help assure continued use of proper technique and keying skills.

What materials should be used? Both computer software and textbooks are available for keyboarding instruction. Since either set of materials can be used, hardware availability and instructor expertise tend to influence choice of materials.

Computer Aided Instructional (CAI) software for keyboarding has become more sophisticated. Some of the more recent software programs include instruction for correct technique; paced skill development where all input is monitored by keystroke, by word, or by line; speed reports beginning in early lessons; continuous, positive, relevant feedback; motivational devices such as games and printable progress reports; and an option for open screen keying where material keyed in may be printed. A combination of CAI software and a keyboarding textbook, which have coordinated lessons, provide the most desirable instructional media. Where both software and text are used, lines in each should be coordinated lesson-by-lesson so a student may switch from a computer to a typewriter at any time and can continue a lesson or drill using the same drill materials.

Several examples of software packages which incorporate

some or all of these criteria are: *MicroType, The Wonderful World of PAWS, MECC Keyboarding Primer, Alphabetic Keyboarding* and *Superkey. MicroType, The Wonderful World of PAWS*, with the coordinated text, *Computer Keyboarding: An Elementary Course* meet all of the above criteria. In *MicroType, The Wonderful World of PAWS*, special emphasis is placed on the use of integrated screen graphics to teach correct keyboarding technique, the area of instruction which is most critical for beginning learners. The program is based on sound pedagogical keyboarding instruction, while being fun and motivational for the user.

MECC Keyboarding Primer and *Alphabetic Keyboarding* also use integrated graphics to teach correct keyboarding technique. *Superkey* has a separate lesson devoted to technique instruction. The level of technique instruction varies among programs based on the age of student the program was designed to serve. *Alphabetic Keyboarding* is designed for grades seven through 12, so the technique instruction is more inclusive and goes beyond basic body, finger, and eye position. Each of these programs teaches correct manipulation of the alphabetic keyboard and also provides drill and practice for the development of basic keying skills. As instructor you must evaluate keyboarding software carefully to determine how you will use it to help meet the instructional needs of your students.

What equipment should be used? Either computers or electric/electronic typewriters, or a combination of both, may be used, but computers are generally preferred at the elementary level. Manual typewriters are inappropriate.

Does furniture size make a difference? Furniture is an important, often overlooked, consideration. Both table height and chair height must match student size to ensure that students can reach the keyboard properly. In cases where furniture does not match student size and cannot be modified or adjusted, cushions and footrests may be needed so proper body position is possible.

Who should teach keyboarding? Elementary teachers and high school typewriting teachers are teaching keyboarding at the elementary level. The keyboarding instructor should have a high interest in teaching keyboarding and have taken a methods course in keyboarding/typewriting. The methods course for business teachers should aid them in working with elementary-age students. Elementary teachers must learn keyboarding methodology and some may need to learn and/or strengthen their keyboarding skills. As the junior and senior high levels, a qualified business education typewriting teacher is the appropriate instructor.

What should be taught? Initial instruction should include correct keyboarding technique and the alphabetic keyboard. To maximize use of limited time, early learning should concentrate on correct manipulation of the alphabetic keyboard. Equally important is correct keyboarding technique, which includes body position, keystroking, and operation of the space, return, and shift keys.

What procedures should be used? The first two or three sessions should include orientation and then presentation of the home-row keys. Two new keys should be introduced each day thereafter. During the teaching/learning process, students must be monitored constantly and given immediate, appropriate feedback regarding what they are doing right and wrong. Students must be encouraged to make corrective adjustments immediately, particularly in technique, so bad habits are not formed. Understanding and using correct techniques are the most critical learning elements in beginning keyboarding. Early drills must be short, usually in the eight- to 15-second range. Speed, rather than accuracy, should be emphasized. Error correction should be allowed, using the back arrow. The development of keystroking sequences (chaining) should be encouraged as soon as key reaches are learned. A variety of activities and constant involvement of the instructor, in drills and in evaluation/feedback, are key ingredients which will contribute to the success of keyboarding instruction for both student and instructor. Activities should include, but not be limited to: teacher-called keystrokes (as in teaching of a new key), teacher-dictated words, student-called words (made up from the keys already learned), student composition based on presented phrases (e.g., Complete the following sentence), creation of poems, new-key learning exercises, skill reinforcement lines, appropriate skill reinforcement games, etc.

How should keyboarding performance be evaluated? Evaluation must focus on correct technique, the critical teaching/learning component of beginning keyboarding, through observation of students as they key. If a student is doing well, or if incorrect technique is being used, the teacher should tell him/her immediately: A technique check sheet, similar to that provided in the Teacher's Guide for *MicroType, The Wonderful World of PAWS*, page 12, would be helpful as an evaluation aid and in keeping track of student progress. When speed is checked, students should be encouraged to improve—try to type a little faster this week than last week. Self competition of this type is recommended, but competition between students—see who can type the fastest—is not appropriate. Error limits must be generous; generally, three or more errors should be allowed per line of type.

Should instruction be graded? A pass/fail grading system should be used. Letter grades should not be given since all evaluation (correct technique and keying skill) is done on a subjective basis. Rewards such as certificates, stars, stickers, etc., for various accomplishments should be given out daily and/or weekly to students. A reward system will help generate enthusiasm, build interest, and increase motivation. After the keyboarding unit, a certificate of completion should be given to each student.

Development of a keyboarding sequence based on consideration of each of these concerns will help assure the success of the program. And the success of your keyboarding program will add to the success of your entire computer curriculum.

For more specific information about the implementation of keyboarding, contact the authors. Truman H. Jackson, Business Education Program Specialist, Minnesota State Department of Education. St. Paul, MN 55101; Diane Berg, Instructor, Crestwood Elementary School, East Grand Forks, MN 56723.

Software

Alphabetic Keyboarding. South-Western Publishing Co., Cincinnati, OH.

The Electronic Keyboard for Personal and Business Use. Minnesota Curriculum Services Center, St. Paul, MN.

MECC's Keyboarding Primer. Minnesota Educational Computing Corporation, St. Paul, MN.

MicroType, The Wonderful World of PAWS. South-Western Publishing Co., Cincinnati, OH.

Superkey. Bytes of Learning Incorporated, Toronto, Ontario, Canada.

References

Beaumont, Crawford, Erickson, Ownby, & Robinson. (1985). *Computer Keyboarding An Elementary Course.* Cincinnati, OH: South-Western Publishing Co.

Minnesota Curriculum Services Center. (1984). *The Electronic Keyboard for Personal and Business Use.* St. Paul, MN: Author.

Keyboarding Skills: Elementary, My Dear Teacher?

by Keith Wetzel

I had high hopes for the computers-in-composition program I was evaluating last year. I imagined students eagerly writing more than ever before, taking the time to rework their compositions as they became more efficient in using the word processor. Although the eight- to ten-year-olds and eight teachers worked diligently, the program floundered. Students neither revised more nor wrote more using a word processor than they did using paper and pencil. And not only that—the students seldom reached the revising stage. Part of the problem was that each student had only 30 minutes per week at the computer, an unrealistic amount of time to achieve the program goals. However, clearly a bigger factor was that students worked inefficiently at the keyboard.

Students found the letters they needed with difficulty, and in so doing the flow of their thoughts was interrupted. I watched student after frustrated student scan handwritten notes for the last word typed, and then look down for the key that represented the first letter of the next word, look up at the screen to verify the letter and correct letter position—and then lose the place. Fingers would point and eyes would search from paper to keyboard to screen and back to paper. The cycle continued and the frustration grew.

When I realized that the problem was inadequate keyboarding skills, I reviewed the literature and found that other educators had noted similar concerns: Students wrote faster by hand than by word processor and hated typing (Gottschalk in Brady; 1984): furthermore, once they had typed their essays, students had little time for revising (Loud in *CCN Forum*, 1982). I found myself in general agreement. Although the third, fourth, and fifth graders that I observed did not hate typing, they did enter text at a slower rate than their handwriting speed, and they often did not reach the revision stage of writing. The fact is, students who can't type have a hard time using a word processor.

What happens when students *can* type? Students who type better are more enthusiastic about using the computer for writing (Daiute et. al., 1981) and computer programming (Stoker, 1984). Students who have adequate keyboarding skills use their time at the computer efficiently—that is, they can concentrate on problem solving or composing, rather than on the mechanics of typing. *Keyboarding is too important to leave to chance.* For these reasons educators should make sure that keyboarding is taught and learned.

Keyboarding Issues

The computer keyboard exists to accept and to enter information. Computer keyboarding skills are primarily typing skills, i.e., striking desired keys accurately and quickly, including the skills needed to correctly use special keys such as ESC and CTRL.

Educators wishing to make sound decisions about keyboarding curricula must address several questions:

1. What criterion ought to be set for keyboarding competence at the elementary school level?

Some authors suggest that students ought to type about 25 gross words per minute (gwpm) before using a computer application program (Kisner, 1984; Minnesota Curriculum Services Center, 1984). However, I believe students need varying degrees of skill (this will be described in more detail later); 25 gwpm is not a realistic entry-level goal. (Gwpm is figured by dividing total keystrokes per minute by five, with no adjustment made for errors.) Students need to type quickly and accurately enough to make relatively efficient use of the computer and to accomplish the purposes of the academic program.

"I watched student after frustrated student scan handwritten notes...and then look down for the key...up at the screen...and then lose the place."

Most fourth through sixth graders can copy from seven to 10 gross words per minute by hand, depending on the grade level (Groff, reported in Graham and Miller, 1980). Consequently, the criterion for adequate keyboarding skills should at least equal that suggested by the handwriting norms. I observed 26 third, fourth, and fifth graders using word processors with no touch-typing instruction. The average rate of transfer of text from paper to screen was 2.5 gwpm. This included a few students with some keyboarding skill. Those few who could type 7-10 gwpm did not scan the keyboard to locate each key, did not become frustrated by keyboard input, and did not lose their place on the screen or on the paper. I conclude that students who achieve 10 gwpm can make adequate use of the computer for tasks which require a significant amount of keyboard entry.

2. How much keyboarding is necessary?

The amount of time required for keyboarding instruction depends upon the computer application. Figure 1 illustrates my estimations of the keyboarding skill needed at the computer to accomplish various educational tasks.

The greater the amount of data entry, the higher the keyboarding skills required. Programs such as *Rocky's Boots* require no keyboarding skills—users work with a joystick, Mouse or KoalaPad. Drill and practice programs typically require students to use only a few keys; many times, for example, students select among options with a single keystroke. High-level keyboarding skills are required for entering computer programming code and for word processing.

Students acquire the "little" and "some" skill levels by learning how to move their fingers about the keyboard more quickly, starting from a base on the home row keys. To help students reach the "substantial" skill level, however, takes sustained time and effort.

3. How much time is needed for students to reach minimal proficiency in keyboarding?

Primary students can be taught the position of the home row keys and the correct finger for touching each key. This requires little additional instruction time. For example, when a reading lesson introduces a new letter, students can practice the letter on paper keyboards at their desks. If they can successfully use a computer for tasks that require a low level of keyboarding skill, they will be better prepared for keyboarding instruction when they enter grades three to five. This early preparation will become important to those teachers.

To effectively use a computer application requiring a "substantial" degree of keyboarding skills requires a keyboarding curriculum. Teachers and students must commit time daily to accomplish proficiency in entering code for computer programming or text for word processing. *Keyboarding instruction, however, cannot be integrated easily into the curriculum without replacing something*; the question of time is critical.

"Keyboarding is too important to leave to chance."

Typing studies in the elementary school serve as examples of the time frame needed. McClurg (1984) found two studies which reported the typing speeds of intermediate students: Fifth and sixth graders typed an average of 40 wpm after one year of one-hour-per-day instruction (Ray, 1977), and fifth graders typed an average of 22 gwpm after nine weeks of instruction at 45 minutes a day (Kercher, 1984). Lexie Hendersen-Lancett (1984) reports on the time required for teaching elementary-age students keyboarding and word processing skills:

> "Children have shown they can learn both touch-typing and word processing in as little as eight hours! This enables them to create stories on the computer at speeds of 15 words per minute. This is quite adequate."

Such reports strengthen the case for the effectiveness of a minimal, but definite time allotment for keyboarding instruction.

Based on a review of the research, most students in grades three through five will average 10 gwpm after receiving teacher instruction and practice on a microcomputer typing tutorial for 35 minutes per day for four weeks. If this schedule is extended to nine weeks, the average student will type 15 to 20 gwpm. Computer programming, database construction, or word processing can begin when students achieve 10 gwpm, which also gives them something to work toward. Students' speed and accuracy should continue to improve as they use the computer for academic tasks, especially if the teacher follows up on previous instruction and practice.

I recommend a keyboarding program which will accomplish this minimal goal (10 gwpm) in a relatively short period of time. Elementary teachers are under many competing pressures to teach more subject areas in the course of a day. A keyboarding program has merit, but it does not deserve 50 minutes of daily instruction for a year! The benefits do warrant 35 minutes a day for four weeks in the intermediate grades. Not only will the investment be repaid through more efficient use of time at the keyboard, that minimum level of keyboarding skill is *essential* to some activities.

4. Who should teach keyboarding in the elementary school?

Some business education teachers argue that only persons such as business education majors or minors should teach keyboarding skills (Kisner, 1984; Holmquist, 1983; Alexander and Dickey-Olson in Schmidt, 1983). Clearly, persons trained to teach typing should do the teacher training, but I think regular classroom teachers should instruct elementary students. Here the logistical problems and costs associated with using special teachers for keyboarding instruction must be balanced against the feasibility of such specialists training regular classroom teachers to do the instruction. Teachers who can type may be trained in as little as one day, and even those who do not type may be trained in as little as five weeks (Peggy Kennedy, 1984).

5. How should keyboarding skills be taught?

Keyboarding is usually taught by the touch-typing method. A common method of teaching keyboarding skills is the standard typing instruction offered in business education courses at the secondary level. Software tutorials such as *Typing Tutor* and *Microtyping*, and typing games such as *Mastertype* and *Type Attack* also offer keyboarding practice. Students use such software to learn to type on their own without benefit of formal instruction, although not necessarily with touch-typing techniques.

Researchers have examined microcomputer typing tutorial approaches which included only limited emphasis on touch-typing techniques. Schmidt and Stewart (1983) found that non-typing college students who received 10 hours of keyboarding practice on a microcomputer typing tutorial program achieved speed and accuracy rates commensurate with expectations for students in standard classes after 10 hours of instruction. Students in the study did comment on the inadequacy of the instruction regarding correct fingering and the too-quick introduction of new keys. The success of this approach may depend on the quality of the software used to teach or reinforce touch-typing skills.

Touch typing is important in the elementary school for several reasons. Beyond the beginner stage, touch typing methods are superior to two-finger hunt-and-peck methods (Stewart and Jones, 1983; Kisner, 1984). Gentner and Norman (1984) explain: "Touch-typing's major advantage comes when transcribing a manuscript; it eliminates the need to keep looking back and forth between the original and the keyboard." Business education teachers report that it is not easy to teach correct methods to students who have acquired improper typing habits (Stewart and Jones, 1983; Beverstock, 1984). Skills taught in the elementary school should be consistent with the skills students may subsequently need; for this reason I advocate the teaching of touch typing to elementary school students.

Degree of Keyboarding Skill Needed for Computer Applications

Application	Amount of Skill Required
Logic Programs —*Rocky Boots*	•
Art Programs —*Koala Pad*	•
Drill and Practice	•••••
Computer Programming —*Short programs*	•••••••••••••••
—*Long programs*	••••••••••••••••••••••••••••••••••
Word Processing	••••••••••••••••••••••••••••••••
	none *little* *some* *substantial*

Program Considerations

Hardware

Few schools have a computer for each student. Beal and others (1983) found in a survey of schools in Washington state that only 36 percent of elementary schools had computers, and in those which had computers the student/computer ratio was 184 to one. In a nationwide survey, Henry Becker (1984) found that in elementary classrooms where students used computers, each student used one for an average of 20 minutes per week. If machine time is this limited, there is no time—or need—to teach keyboarding. However, many elementary students now have much more access to computers.

Time

If school officials are planning to place computers in the elementary school, or already have a sufficient number, a keyboarding program may be needed. How much computer time must each student have to accomplish a significant task? The critical amount of time needed to make a significant difference, according to David Moursund (1984), is 30 minutes per student per day. Classrooms approaching this level of computer use should include keyboarding curricula.

Keyboarding Curriculum

The specifications for a keyboarding curriculum have emerged from the discussion of the five questions discussed earlier. Before embarking on a keyboarding program, however, educators should ask these four threshold questions:

- Has an academic area been identified that needs to be improved through the use of computers?
- Can the identified problem best be solved by a computer solution?
- Are enough computers available for students to achieve the goals of the program?
- Does the computer application require frequent and repeated use of most of the keyboard?

If answers to the above questions are "yes," a keyboarding program is needed. Figure 1 shows the amount of skill needed for specific applications, with a minimal keyboarding goal for each student of 10 gwpm using touch typing techniques as much as possible.

Principles of Keyboarding Instruction

Most texts and manuals agree on principles of keyboarding instruction. The Minnesota Curriculum Services Center (1984) indicates, for example, that:

1. Kinesthetic feedback in practice is important.
2. Watching fingers and keys in the early stages of learning is helpful.
3. Early emphasis should be on speed, not accuracy.
4. Knowledge of results helps develop skills.
5. Elementary students need to use several approaches in the early stages of instruction, e.g., teacher dictation of keys, games, and written drills.

Instructional Periods

Several sources suggest that instructional periods of 20 to 30 minutes are appropriate (Holmquist, 1983; Kisner, 1984; Minnesota Curriculum Services Center, 1984). After reviewing the research, I discussed the organization of a teaching period with keyboarding instructor Gale Daggett (1984), and observed her tutoring a student in keyboarding. I suggest this model:

Objective
A. Use correct keyboarding technique.
B. Use the *A* and *S* keys, and space bar on computer keyboard.

Suggested Activity
1.1 Students watch copy or screen rather than fingers or keyboard.
1.2 Teacher(s) or volunteer(s) demonstrate posture, arm and wrist position, and finger positions for home keys according to software or text used.
2.1 Teacher(s) or volunteer(s) demonstrate and students practice the *A* keyfinger and space bar and then the *S* keyfinger and space bar according to text or software used.
2.2 Students practice at desks as teacher monitors behaviors.
2.3 Continue to practice tasks via software and a variety of drills on the computer.
2.4 Practice real words as soon as possible.

Classroom or Computer Lab Organization

Elementary school computer(s) may be in the classroom or in a computer lab. Often the question is whether or not the computers should be divided equally among classrooms, where each classroom may have one or two computers—and perhaps just for part of a day. Both arrangements have advantages and disadvantages.

With a classroom arrangement:

1. The teacher presents a short lesson to the entire class on the skills to be practiced that day.
2. Students have a brief practice period at their desks.
3. Pairs of students practice at the computer throughout the day according to a schedule.

The advantages of a classroom arrangement are:

- Students do not need to leave the classroom to practice.
- The classroom teacher monitors student activities.
- One or two computers in a class can serve all the students.
- Nothing in the curriculum needs to be supplanted.

It should be noted that if students are regrouped out of their home classroom for much of the day, it is very difficult to schedule keyboarding practice.

The first two steps remain the same in the computer lab arrangement, but during step three all students practice at the same time. For example, if an elementary school has 13 comput-

ers in the lab and 26 students in the class, all students can practice in pairs at the same time. While one student works at the keyboard, the partner dictates words, monitors technique, and

---

"Students with adequate keyboarding skills can use their time at the computer efficiently...on problem solving or composing rather than on the mechanics of typing."

---

records scores. Students trade positions after three minutes of practice, with each student practicing for five periods of three minutes each. Typing tutorial programs require intense concentration, and distributed practice makes sense in this instance. However, the very best practice schedule is open to investigation. The advantages of a lab arrangement are:

- Students at the computer do not miss group instruction or disturb the class when they take turns.
- All students get a turn at the computer.
- The lab arrangement is the most efficient use of computer time (Becker, 1984).
- Practice comes immediately after teacher instruction.

In both arrangements the practice could be accomplished by a combination of tutorials and games.

Evaluation

A keyboarding program should have both formative and summative evaluation questions. Typical formative evaluation questions are: "Is the program being implemented as planned?" "Are students practicing according to the schedule?" "Is teacher training for the program adequate?" "Is the software working?" "What program problems are solved and which problems remain to be resolved?"

A typical summative evaluation question is: "What percentage of the students met the exit criterion of 10 gwpm?" Other summative questions regard the quality of the student technique and the accuracy of the typing.

Information gained from the formative evaluation helps improve the ongoing program; information gained from the summative evaluation helps determine whether the program has accomplished its objectives.

Recommendations

If frequent and repeated use of the keyboard is required to achieve program goals, students must be proficient at the keyboard. Keyboard technique should support, not hinder, achievement of problem solving or composing. But establishing keyboarding skills takes time. Is keyboarding instruction worth the time in the elementary school? The answer is found by balancing classroom time required to achieve keyboarding skills against the advantages gained by rapid keyboard entry of data now and later. If the program described here is followed, the time requirement is 20 days of instruction for 35 minutes a day—less than 12 hours. The advantages are:

- More efficient student use of computer time;
- Focused attention on the task to be accomplished, rather than on keyboarding mechanics;
- Early learning and accomplishment of touch-typing technique.

Keyboarding instruction is an investment in more efficient learning. I think the scale tips in favor of teaching keyboarding before grade six. Keyboarding is becoming an increasingly important issue. Educators in every school district should resolve it in advance.

Keith Wetzel, Center for Advanced Technology in Education, University of Oregon, Eugene, OR 97403.

Bibliography

Beal, Jack, Lynn Churchill & Conn McQuinn. "State of Washington Computer Use Survey." University of Washington, 1983 (mimeographed).

Becker, Henry Jay. "The Social Context of Microcomputers: It's Not Just a Matter of Good Software." Presentation at the *AERA*, New Orleans. April, 1984.

Beverstock, Caroline. "Computer Using Educators, Arizona State University Conference, 1984," *6* (8), 9.

Brady, Holly. "Who needs ten-finger typing?" *Classroom Computer News*, Sept. 1984, 64-5.

"CCN forum: Word processing." *Classroom Computer News*, 1983, *3* (3), 24-7 & 74-76.

Cowles, Milly, Martha Hedley & Mabel Robinson. *An Analysis of Young Children Learning Keyboarding Skills.* Bethesda, MD: ERIC Document Reproduction Service, ED 238542, 1983.

Craighead, Donna & Mary Ellen Switzer. "Is typing the key to computer literacy?" *Instructor*, 1983, *93*(2), 178-180.

Daggett, Gail. Keyboarding instructor, Eugene, Oregon. Interview July 3, 1984.

Daiute, Collette, et. al. "The Computer in the Writing Class: Problems and Potentials." Teacher's College Columbia University: 1981 (mimeographed).

Gentner, Donald & Donald Norman. "The typist's touch." *Psychology Today*, 1984, *18* (3), 67-72.

Graham, Steve & Lamoine Miller. "Handwriting research and practice: A unified approach." *Focus on Exceptional Children*, *13* (2), 1980, 1-16.

Hendersen-Lancett, Lexie. "Typing: To teach or not to teach." *COM 3*, 1984, *10* (3), 23-24.

Holmquist, Donna. "Business education: Some controversial questions." *Business Education Forum*, 1983, *37* (5), 3-4.

Kercher, Lydia. "Life-Skill Learning for Preadolescents." *Business Education Forum*, 1983, *37*(9), 4.

Kennedy, Penny. Formerly of Minnesota Curriculum Services Center, Whitebear Lake, MN. Telephone conversation, Nov. 9, 1984.

Kisner, Evelyn. "Keyboarding—A must in tomorrow's world." *The Computing Teacher*, 1984, *11* (6), 21-22.

Lindsay, Robert McDonald. *A Comparative Study of Teaching Typing Skills on Microcomputers.* Bethesda, MD: ERIC Document Reproduction Service, ED 220 597, 1983.

McClurg, Pat. "Keyboarding—An Issue in the Elementary School." University of Oregon, 1984.

Moursund, David. "The two-percent solution." *The Computing Teacher*, 1984, *11* (7), 3-5.

Ownby, Arnola & Heidi Perreault. "Keyboarding in kindergarten—is it elementary?" *Business Education Forum*, 1982, *37*(3), 19-20.

Russon, Allien & S.J. Wanous. *Philosophy and Psychology of Teaching Typewriting.* Chicago: South-Western Publishing Co., 1960.

Schmidt, B. June & Jeffrey T. Stewart. "Microcomputer typewriting in business education." *Business Education Forum*, 1983, *37* (6), 23-32.

Schmidt, B. June. *Keyboarding: The State of the Art.* Bethesda, MD: ERIC Document Reproduction Service, ED 236 352, 1983.

Stewart, Jane & Buford Jones. "Keyboarding instruction: Elementary school options." *Business Education Forum*, 1983, *37*(7), 11-12.

Sloker, John. University of Oregon, Eugene, Oregon. Interview, Nov. 9, 1984.

Sunkel, Mary Jane & Martha Coopa. "Typewriting: Teaching touch keyboarding on computer terminals." *Business Education Forum*, 1982, *37* (1), 18-21.

Wetzel, Keith. "Formative Evaluation of the QUILL Program." University of Oregon, 1984 (typewritten).

COMPUTERS AND THE LANGUAGE ARTS   Edited by Lynne Anderson-Inman

A Keyboarding Collection

Keyboarding instruction has been an important issue for teachers ever since the first computer entered public school. Initially the concern centered on whether or not keyboarding should even be taught to elementary students. With the increased use of word processing programs at the elementary level, keyboarding instruction came to be viewed as a must, not an option. The debate then moved on to issues such as when to teach keyboarding and how. Use of computers at the primary level raised concerns about too early an emphasis on formal typing skills. And a plethora of keyboarding programs have made the selection of teaching materials awesomely difficult, especially for teachers who have received little or no training to teach keyboarding. This month's column is a pastiche of short articles about keyboarding instruction. For the most part they are written by or with teachers who have struggled with the demands of teaching keyboarding and have some suggestions to pass on to others. In addition to the practical value of these suggestions, two new themes emerge. First, there is a growing emphasis on keyboard familiarization, helping students learn about the keyboard without requiring them to become touch typers. And second, there is increasing attention to the integration of keyboarding instruction with other aspects of the language arts curriculum.

Keyboard Familiarization: An Alternative to Touch Typing

by Jessica Kahn, Michelle Avicolli, and Kathy Lodise

When teachers introduce word processing to elementary school children, they usually find that the children have difficulty locating the desired letters on the keyboard. This makes writing at computers a slow, laborious process. Furthermore, when children spend much of their time searching for specific letters, they often loose their train of thought. One solution to this problem has been to teach the children how to touch type. This requires a considerable investment of time and effort and has met with mixed results. Another solution is to concentrate on keyboard familiarization, teaching the location of keys but not with an emphasis on "correct" fingering. This approach was tried and found to be successful by two elementary level teachers (3rd and 4th grade) involved in the "Microcomputers and Writing Development" study at the University of Pennsylvania.

Early in the school year both teachers distributed laminated photocopies of the IBM keyboard to each child. In addition, a giant facsimile of the IBM keyboard (3' by 5') was developed for demonstrations to the whole class. At the beginning of the day the teachers gathered their classes together and wrote 10 words on the chalkboard. The children were told to use the first fingers on each hand and pretend to "type" the words on their individual keyboards. Ten new practice words were given each day, including the teachers' names and the children's names. This afforded the opportunity to teach capitalization, spacing, and the period. Lessons were kept short, usually only five or 10 minutes at the start of the day. The children were told that learning the keyboard was their responsibility and that keyboard familiarity would make it easier for them to write at the computers.

After only a few days, one of the teachers found that four or five students who had become very quick at keyboarding grew

impatient when they had to wait for the rest of the class. To enable these children to work at their own pace, she changed the lesson so that the students could return to their seats when finished. To add interest for the quicker keyboarders, the other teacher disconnected the IBM keyboards from the computers and allowed some of the children to practice with these. Both teachers discontinued the keyboard familiarization lessons after six weeks, satisfied that the children had become sufficiently comfortable with the keyboard to use word processing programs for writing.

Classroom observations throughout the year by members of the "Microcomputers and Writing Development" research team indicated that the children, although not touch typers, were able to find the necessary keys fairly quickly. In interviews at the end of the year, the children were asked what their teachers could do to help future classes learn word processing. Almost every child mentioned the need to know where the letters are on the keyboard and indicated the practice sessions with the laminated keyboards had really helped.

We are not suggesting that touch typing shouldn't be taught. However, it is our belief that adding touch typing to the elementary curriculum only substitutes one set of mechanical difficulties (awkward finger reaches) for another (using pencil and paper). Touch typing was developed for use by secretaries so they could transcribe documents quickly. By memorizing the correct "reaches," secretaries were freed to look at notes or rough drafts instead of the keyboard. The situation is different for children word processing at a computer. Children are frequently composing as they type. If they look at the keys it does not slow them down to any significant extent. Furthermore, if they hit a wrong key, the error can be deleted simply and quickly. As the teachers in this study demonstrated, children need to know the location of the keys so they can write their ideas easily, but this goal can be accomplished without the pain of learning to touch type.

Dr. Jessica Kahn, Adjunct Professor, Beaver College, Glenside, PA 19038; Michelle Avicolli and Kathy Lodise, Upper Darby School District, Upper Darby, PA.

The "Microcomputer and Writing Development" study was funded in part by University of Pennsylvania grants from IBM and UPS to the Literacy Research Center. This three-year project was directed by Dr. Marilyn Cochran-Smith. Inquiries about the project can be directed to Dr. Cochrane-Smith, Graduate School of Education, University of Pennsylvania, 3700 Walnut Street, Philadelphia, PA 19104.

Computer Keyboard Cards:
Helping Young Children Get a Head Start
by Sandra Calvert and J. Allen Watson

Computers are rapidly entering school and home environments with the unspoken expectation that even very young children will be able to find the letters they want on the keyboard. In order to familiarize young students with the keyboard and facilitate their use of the computer, we designed special keyboard cards. Each keyboard card is drawn on a 5"x7" index card. At the simplest level, the card includes a picture, the letters of the word for that picture, and a graphic representation of the keyboard, scaled to the computer keyboard. The letters for the pictured word are highlighted in yellow. The cards are then laminated to make them more durable and less smudgeable by little hands.

We made keyboard cards for many words of interest to preschoolers: cat, dog, car, sun, turtle, and fish. Using Logo, a program was written to make the objects appear on the computer screen after the word was typed (Watson, Calvert, & Popkin, 1987). Sometimes the objects were programmed to move or make noises, creating an interesting learning environment for the children. When a child uses a keyboard card, the card is placed directly above the computer keyboard so that the letters on the card are in one-to-one correspondence with the letters on the keyboard. Then we teach the child to follow a straight line from a letter on the card to the same letter on the keyboard. Following the sequence of letters under the picture, and aided by the highlighted keys on the keyboard card, the children are taught to type each word.

Initial work using this approach has been promising. Children are able to follow the letters from the card to the keyboard and to press the correct keys. As they become experienced typing the words, we delete the keyboard from the card, leaving only the picture and the word. If this fading procedure is continued, removing more of the cues on the keyboard cards, the children are eventually able to type the words without any assistance.

Using this procedure, we helped 40 preschool children learn to type a set of 24 different words over a five-day period. The children used the cards individually in daily 20-minute practice sessions. Although some of the children learned to use the cards more efficiently than others, all of the children benefitted to some extent. On the fifth day we tested their ability to type the 24 target words independent of any cards. For children who were unsuccessful with a specific word or refused to try, we provided a picture and word card (without the keyboard). If still unsuccessful, we provided a keyboard card. On the average, children typed one word with no assistance, 22 words aided by picture-word cards, and two words using the keyboard cards. Clearly, the keyboard cards were instrumental in helping these young children become familiar with the keyboard and increase their competence with the computer.

Dr. Sandra Calvert, Assistant Professor of Psychology, Georgetown University, Washington, DC 20057; Dr. J. Allen Watson, Director of the Children and Technology Project and Professor of Child Development and Family Relations, University of North Carolina at Greensboro, Greensboro, NC 27412.

Reference

Watson, J., Calvert, S., & Polkin, L. (1987). Microworlds, sprites, Logo, and young children: A multipurpose software application. *Journal of Educational Technology Systems, 15,* 123-136.

Keyboarding Across the Curriculum
by Lynne Anderson-Inman

My daughter "did keyboarding" in the fourth grade. She did keyboarding in the same way she did Oregon history, the life cycle, and the solar system: as a separate subject, divorced from any meaningful context. Subsequent to her keyboarding instruction there hasn't been a single school activity requiring the skills she worked hard to develop. My daughter is now in the sixth grade. It has been two years since she "did keyboarding" and still she has not been asked to apply her keyboarding skills either during class time or out of class for a school assignment.

Although my daughter's experience may be atypical, it nonetheless raises an issue that teachers frequently face. Should keyboarding be taught if the curriculum does not reflect a need for it? Or, perhaps more importantly, if keyboarding *is* taught, how can it be integrated into the rest of the curriculum? I believe the answer to both questions requires a shift in perspective. *Keyboarding should not be viewed as a subject, but rather as a skill that is useful for learning other subjects.* Keyboarding should be taught and used "across the curriculum" in much the same way that reading and writing are taught and used across the curriculum.

The above suggestion is not entirely novel. Balajthy (1986), for example, has argued that the teaching of formal typing skills to elementary students cannot be justified unless these skills are meaningfully integrated into the language arts curriculum. For this to occur, teachers need ultimately to shift the emphasis of keyboarding instruction from the motor task (i.e., fast finger movement) to the language task. This shift happens naturally for teachers who have adopted word processing as an aid to composition instruction. For these teachers, keyboarding instruction is viewed as a means to an end, efficient use of the computer during writing activities.

In fact, keyboarding and word processing have been linked together so frequently and so consistently that some educators appear to believe that the only "purpose of keyboarding instruction is to enable students to benefit from the use of word processors" (Hunter, Benedict, & Bilan, 1989, p.25). Although this view is certainly more productive than one which results in teaching keyboarding as a separate subject, it is somewhat limited in scope. There are other domains in which teachers have found keyboarding instruction to be compatible with existing curriculum objectives.

Take spelling for example. Hollen (1987) added a keyboarding component to the spelling instruction received by 28 fifth-grade students. Students practiced their spelling words and took their spelling tests using a specially designed component of *Keyboard Now!* (Daggett). Results suggested that, for many of the low performing students, keyboarding practice on spelling words was an effective way to enhance their spelling accuracy. McClendon (1989) also found that keyboarding practice was helpful in improving the spelling scores of low performing students, especially when combined with a direct instruction approach to spelling. In both studies, the keyboarding component was felt to be highly motivating for the students, resulting in a positive attitude toward spelling practice. Interestingly, McClendon's students practiced their spelling words on laminated keyboards, not on computers.

There are, I believe, similar avenues for integrating keyboarding instruction and practice with most curriculum areas—certainly in the language arts and probably beyond as well. The time and effort required to learn efficient keyboarding skills is not insignificant. Keyboarding across the curriculum can help to amortize that investment, while at the same time enhancing student performance on existing objectives.

Dr. Lynne Anderson-Inman, Associate Professor, College of Education, University of Oregon, Eugene, OR 97403.

References

Balajthy, E. (1986). *Microcomputers in the reading and language arts.* Englewood Cliffs, NJ: Prentice Hall.

Hollen, D. (1987). *The effects of keyboarding on the spelling accuracy of fifth grade students.* Unpublished master's paper. University of Oregon, Eugene, OR.

Hunter, W.J., Benedict, G., & Bilan, B. (1989). On a need to know basis: Keyboarding instruction for elementary students. *The Writing Notebook, 7*(2), 23-25.

McClendon, S.L. (1989). First grade spelling success with keyboarding. *The Computing Teacher, 17*(2), 35-36.

Keyboarding Tips
by Ann Fidanque

In our district we teach keyboarding skills to elementary students in the third to fifth grades. Since younger students frequently use the computer prior to formal instruction on keyboarding, we've found that it is helpful to encourage good habits right from the beginning. Incorrect keyboarding techniques can be avoided in the early grades by teaching students (a) the division of the keyboard into right and left hand keys and (b) the correct fingers for pressing Return and Spacebar. Here are a few tips for familiarizing young students with these basic concepts.

1. Divide the keyboard vertically into halves using a bright colored piece of yarn, fastened top and bottom with tape. The purpose of the yarn is to separate those keys that should be pressed with the right hand from those keys that should be pressed with the left hand. Teach students that one hand cannot cross over into the other hand's half of the keyboard.

2. An alternative approach to separating left hand and right hand keys is the use of spare write-protect stickers. Create a line up the middle of the keyboard with the black stickers.

3. Teach the "teeter-totter" technique. Most games, even those for preschoolers, require players to use both the spacebar and the Return key. To develop to skill in pressing these keys, have students practice the teeter-totter technique by rolling back and forth between their right thumb and little finger. This technique can be practiced first on the table and then transferred to the keyboard.

Listed next are a few additional tips for students who are receiving formal keyboarding instruction.

1. Provide keyboarding practice using a word processing program. This enables students to be familiar with the features of a word processor by the time they have completed their keyboarding instruction. With the limited amount of computer time available for most students, each session should serve many purposes.

2. Print out the students' work as often as possible, even if they are still just typing isolated letters. The hard copy of their keyboarding practice is more reinforcing for students than any other reward a teacher can devise.

3. If timed tests are used to determine students keyboarding speed, it is recommended that the time periods be kept very short (i.e., 15 to 30 seconds). This encourages students to maintain their fingering technique while still pursuing an increase in speed.

4. Encourage students to practice keyboarding at home. A recent survey of 50 students taking part in a county-wide keyboarding contest for students in grades 4-8 revealed that 64% of the participants had computers at home. Furthermore, although games were listed by these students as their first choice for computer use, word processing and keyboarding practice followed close behind. There were no differences between the preferences of the boys and those of the girls.

Ann Fidanque, Eugene School District 4J, Eugene, OR 97401.

Keyboarding Instruction with Portable *Type-Rights*
by Cathy Carney

This article is a condensed version of a review that appeared in the April 1988 issue of *The Computing Teacher*.

Many schools find they have more demand for keyboarding instruction than can be satisfied with existing computer facilities. Crowded computer labs and minimal resources for new equipment can make it difficult for a school to meet the keyboarding needs of all its students. In Fairbanks, Alaska, fourth grade teachers at several of the elementary schools joined forces to solve the problem by purchasing classroom sets of *Type-Right*, an inexpensive ($30.40) laptop computer dedicated to teaching keyboarding. *Type-Rights* are supplied by Video Technology Industries, Inc., 380 Palatine Rd., Wheeling, IL 60090; phone 708/215-9700. This single-purpose, battery-powered computer is about the size of a detachable computer keyboard and includes keys for letters, numbers, shift, caps lock, and basic punctuation. The lightweight plastic box also houses a microchip programmed with nine drill lessons and two typing games.

The *Type-Right* units have a number of features that enhance their use for keyboarding instruction. First, they are small; enabling students to carry them to their desks, use them, and return them independently. A classroom set fits easily into two medium-sized cardboard boxes and can be stored unobtrusively in a crowded classroom. Second, they are sturdy. In Fairbanks, the units were shared between two classrooms. Students took them out of their cardboard boxes twice a day, used them at their desks, piled them back into the boxes, and carried to the classroom next door. No keys were broken, no screens were damaged. Furthermore, the machine turns itself off within a few minutes of nonuse to save battery life. Third, the keys are color-coded (dark gray keys alternating with light gray) to help students identify which keys are pressed with each finger. And fourth, buttons at the top of the unit will, if pressed, display a student's speed and accuracy .

Despite these useful features, many aspects of the *Type-Right* units provide barriers to effective keyboarding instruction. The feel of the keys is stiff, there are no raised dots on D and K keys, and the back panel holding the batteries occasionally falls off, tumbling batteries to the floor and creating confusion in the class. Furthermore, the LCD screen is on the same surface as the keys, making it difficult for students to avoid looking at their hands while typing.

More importantly, the sequence of the nine built-in lessons violates many accepted practices for effective keyboarding instruction. For example, the first lesson introduces *all* of the keys in the middle row at one time and the second lesson drills students on *all* keys in the third row. This ignores research that suggests students should thoroughly learn the home row keys *asdf jkl* before introducing any other keys. In addition, the program will not permit a typer to continue if an incorrect key is pressed. Instead, it will beep until the correct letter is found. Due to the difficulty of reading the eight-character screen this often proves to be impossible for students, resulting in the need to start again from the beginning of the lesson.

In spite of these difficulties, the teachers in Fairbanks found the *Type-Right* units to be an inexpensive and effective solution to the problem of insufficient hardware for keyboarding instruction in their schools. A little creativity eliminated most of the major flaws. Glue was used to put raised dots on the D and K keys, letters on keys were covered with tape or a folded paper screen, and the backs were taped to hold in the batteries. With respect to the software, the teachers adopted the sequence and examples found in other resources and dictated initial lessons to the students. The *Type-Right* units were set on Lesson 9 (which operates more like an open screen) so that students could copy the teachers' dictation. After students had learned all the home row keys and used them in dictated words and sentences, they were allowed to practice using *Type-Right*'s first lesson.

A 40-page manual was developed by the teachers incorporating their suggestions for taking advantage of the *Type-Right*'s strengths and minimizing the software's problems. The manual includes a reproducible student workbook and detailed day-by-day instructions for a six-week unit in keyboarding. A copy of this manual is available on request from the author at the Alaska Deptartment of Education. Please indicate if an Apple II or Macintosh disk copy would also be useful.

Dr. Cathy Carney, Office of Basic Education, 801 W. 10th St., Juneau, AK 99801.

COMPUTERS IN THE CURRICULUM: LANGUAGE ARTS

First Grade Spelling Success With Keyboarding

by Sondra L. McClendon

Can you imagine first grade students coming in from recess anxious to get started on their spelling lesson? I found that first graders who learn to keyboard increase their motivation to learn spelling. Spelling achievement improved dramatically for my low achieving students when keyboarding was added to the direct instruction format used to teach spelling. First graders are able to learn correct skills for keyboarding, and they enjoy having a skill that is usually reserved for junior high and high school students.

I conducted a study with my first grade class in the 1986-87 school year to see if keyboarding instruction could improve spelling. I taught the first half of the school year using the direct instruction method and the second half with a combination of direct instruction and keyboarding practice. The students in my first grade classroom were randomly assigned by the building principal and the kindergarten teachers. This group included two high achievers, eight average achievers, and eight low achievers.

With direct instruction spelling I say, sound out, and write the words as students listen and watch. They say, sound out, spell orally, and write the word on signal from me after I do each step. Then they cover the word, spell it again, check, and correct it. Students hear the words pronounced the right way, hear them sounded out correctly, and see them written the right way before they say them, sound them out, and write them. I followed this format for each phonetically regular spelling word.

For the keyboarding component I used *Keyboard Success* (Fidanque, et al., 1988) as a text. Materials used included a *Keyboard Success* teacher's manual, wall chart, laminated desk size keyboard templates, students manuals, overhead transparency of the Apple IIe keyboard, an ABC mastery coloring chart, and finger naming charts for each student.

Students learned at their desks since we had only one computer to be shared with three first grades making instruction on a computer impossible for every student. I taught the entire *Keyboard Success* program from September to January before those skills were used in Spelling. For the spelling lessons I worked with four students at a time. They had a copy of the instruction sheet and their keyboard models. I had a transparency of the instruction sheet for use on the overhead (see Figure 1).

The students touched on their own paper when I said, "Touch number one. Number one is *hat*. What word?" Students answered, "hat." I said, "Listen to the sounds in hat." I then said the sounds in hat and wrote the correct letters next to number one on the transparency of the instruction page. Then I said, "Now...your turn. Say the sounds in hat." Touching each letter in the correct order then I said, "First sound? Next sound? Next sound?" Students answered appropriately. I then said, "Get ready to type

hat. 'Fingers' (the signal to curve both hands above home row), Right hand, pointer finger over to *h*. Left hand little finger, *a*. Left hand, pointer finger up to *t*."

Students followed these directions to type the word hat. Then I said, "Spell hat." Students spelled the word orally. I covered my word and said, "Write hat." Students wrote the word hat. This was followed by students covering their word and spelling the word orally again as a group. From word two on, students orally reviewed each of the previous words while keeping their written work covered with the keyboard model. I then showed my word on the screen and had students touch under each of their letters to make sure they got them right.

Any missed word was marked through and rewritten the right way, right next to it. I asked the students not to erase mistakes but to draw a line through the word because I like to be able to see them help diagnose any student's problem. After the instruction was complete, students turned their papers over for the test. I said the words and students said them on signal. I said, "Write _____," and they wrote them and covered them. Sometimes we corrected words in group and sometimes I corrected them.

Instruction

```
1 ————————  9 ————————
2 ————————  10 ————————
3 ————————  11 ————————
4 ————————  12 ————————
5 ————————  13 ————————
6 ————————  14 ————————
7 ————————  15 ————————
8 ————————  16 ————————
```

Sentences

```
1 ————————————
2 ————————————
```

Figure 1.

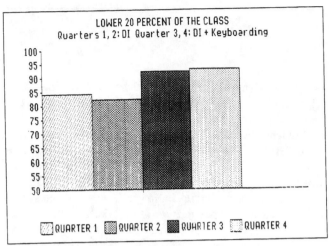

LOWER 20 PERCENT OF THE CLASS
Quarters 1, 2: DI Quarter 3, 4: DI + Keyboarding

☐ QUARTER 1 ☒ QUARTER 2 ■ QUARTER 3 ▨ QUARTER 4

Figure 2. In quarters 1 and 2, students copied the spelling words a number of times one day, completed workbook pages the next, took a pretest on Thursdays and a graded test on Friday. In quarter 3 I used direct instruction and in quarter 4, direct instruction plus keyboarding.

Irregular words were taught in much the same way but were spelled orally twice by me and then by students as I wrote them on the overhead transparency before the typing, writing, and correcting occurred.

I taught spelling using these techniques four days a week, 30 minutes for 10 words a day.

Results and Discussion

A review of spelling grades from September to January found them acceptable by a small margin. 15 of 18 spellers met the criteria—80% of the spellers achieving at least 80% accuracy on the final test each week. The other 20% were still below that level.

By February, when keyboarding had been incorporated for a month, all 18 students met this same criteria, and 16 of 18 students got 100% each week through the end of school. Weekly grades were compared. No cumulative test of the total amount of lists was given but words that had been missed by more than three students were put on the spelling list for the next week. Every four units of the book were reviewed in a Review Unit providing partial cumulative testing, although not every word from the four chapters was included in this unit.

Attitudes improved dramatically when the combined method was used during the second half of the year. The parents of one student in particular commented on the increased success rate in spelling after I added the keyboarding component. They were amazed at her success rate. Students said they liked being able to type because it was a grown-up thing to do. One of my students said he liked being able to type because he could practice his spelling words on the computer and use other computer programs better. The class seemed to enjoy spelling much more after learning to keyboard their words. They came in from recess

anxious to get started on spelling. I noticed this improved the transition time from recess to spelling. Instead of taking 10 minutes to settle down to work after a recess, they were ready to go to work in about three minutes.

I believe that the keyboarding component was the deciding factor in making this dramatic improvement. The students in the lower 20% of the spelling class at the beginning of the year improved their grades gradually from the first two quarters to an average of 90% accuracy for the final two quarters of the year (see Figure 2). Even the students who regularly met the criteria for success improved their grades some and their attitudes a lot. That made the teaching of keyboarding worthwhile.

The combination of verbal, visual, tactile, and written cues was most successful in raising the grades of the lowest achieving students, most of whom had previously shown a significant difference in their achievement test spelling scores and their academic success in spelling. I noticed positive feelings about spelling with keyboarding were profound with all students in class.

Recommendation

I was impressed with the improvement in my students' attitudes toward spelling class when I changed from teaching spelling with only the direct instruction component to using direct instruction and keyboarding. They enjoyed the activity, so were willing to stay on task better than previous classes. Besides this positive attitude toward spelling, students acquired valuable keyboarding experience they can use in the future. By June my first graders were fairly fluent typists needing less description when I modeled the letter for them to type. For instance, in February, I would say, "Right hand, pointer finger over to h." By June I could say, "Type h." This reduced the time needed for the spelling lessons. At this point they spent about the same amount of time on their spelling lessons after adding the keyboarding component as they did with direct instruction spelling by itself.

I did a "Brown Fox" handwriting evaluation at the beginning of the year but did not give one at the end. By June I observed that the students could type their words as fast as they could hand write them.

The *Keyboard Success* program is very easy to teach because of the scripted lessons. Each lesson outlines what materials teachers and students will need, new skills to be taught, and previously introduced skills to be reviewed. The 'teacher talk' is easiest to find if highlighted with a marker.

Teaching all 30 *Keyboard Success* lessons before incorporating them into the spelling curriculum is most important. Last school year I tried to add keyboarding as a component to Direct Instruction spelling before all the keyboard lessons were complete and students were confused to the point of frustration. After I removed keyboarding from their experience stress was relieved. In the future, I will again start keyboarding instruction the first day of school and continue until all 30 lessons are completed before applying them to spelling.

Keyboarding skills are valuable for students beginning in the first grade. In addition to spelling lessons, I believe keyboarding skills could be used to teach reading vocabulary words or to type math problems being solved. Keyboarding skills would also make story writing more fun for students. With only one computer per grade level, time for story writing is limited and students can take turns faster using good keystrokes.

Sondra L. McClendon, 410 N.W. Third, Pendleton, OR 97801.

Reference

Fidanque, A., Miller, S., Sullivan, G., & Smith, M. (1988) *Keyboard success.* Eugene, OR: ISTE.

The product reviews included here are given for two reasons:

1. *To give an indication of the variety and scope of software currently available which is applicable to computer use in writing instruction.*

2. *To provide a conceptual framework for critically evaluating any piece of educational software, especially those marketed for writing instruction.*

The power and sophistication of computer hardware and software continues to change so rapidly that it is imperative for those who intend to use these products, to look to current periodicals and professional journals for the latest information concerning product performance and applicability to educational contexts.

SOFTWARE REVIEWS   Edited by Linda Rathje

FrEdWRITER

FrEdWRITER
SOFTSWAP, San Mateo County Office of Education, 333 Main Street, Redwood City, CA 94063
Authors: Al Rogers, *FrEdWriter*—Paul Lutus, *Freewriter*
Subject: Word processor
Cost: $20; two disks, documentation and simple writing lessons included on disk.
Hardware Required: Apple IIe/IIc, modified II+; 1 disk drive; monochrome monitor; printer.
Reviewed by: Cathy Chemielowsi Carney, Computer Lab Coordinator, Ryan Middle School, Fairbanks, Alaska

FrEdWriter (Free Education Writer) is a public domain word processor available for a nominal fee from SOFTSWAP of California. Once you have the program you are free to copy and distribute it to anyone—but not to sell it. It is an enhancement of *Freewriter*, written by Paul Lutus of *Apple Writer* fame. Unlike much public domain software, its quality is as high as or higher than many commercial products.

The original *Freewriter* was a useful tool, but *FrEdWriter* incorporates significant improvements in its performance, documentation and educational usefulness.

The technical features one would expect from a basic word processor are found here, accessed through control characters: control-S for save, control-P for print, etc. Critics of such systems may be mollified by the on-line help screen available to help remember these commands. Pressing control-T brings up a tutorial which explains briefly each control code, and which can be exited at any point. This, coupled with the mnemonic control characters, makes the system very palatable to users I know.

Users of *Freewriter* will be delighted to learn that its major flaw has been corrected here; *FrEdWriter* will print from within the program itself. Furthermore, the writer can now choose to have the document printed to the screen first, to check for potential formatting errors. Those who have used a word processor with this capability can appreciate how much time and paper it saves. In addition to printing to screen, the printing options include such standard features as choice of line spacing; top, bottom, and left margins; page numbering and heading; and choice of page from which to begin printing.

The program recognizes whether it is in an Apple II or IIe/c environment, and loads the appropriate version. Apple II users need 64K of memory (a language card) in order to use the program. It is also highly desirable to have a lower-case display adapter, but I have known people to use the program on a II+ without this adapter. They simply press the shift-lock (esc-shift) before writing, and accept the printout in all upper-case letters.

On an Apple IIc, or IIe with 80-column card, text can be displayed in either 40- or 80-column format.

More sophisticated users who enjoy enhancing their writing through the various capabilities available on their printers will be delighted to know that *FrEdWriter* permits sending, at any point in the text, any number of control codes to the printer: foreign language sets, italics, boldface, or any other modification supported by their printer.

COPY AND COMPLETE THE FOLLOWING SENTENCE AS YOUR TOPIC SENTENCE:

My favorite place is_____.

My favorite place is the beach.

DESCRIBE HOW YOUR PLACE LOOKS.

The cold water splashes on the sticky sand. The birds dive through the water.

DESCRIBE THE FIRST THING OR PERSON YOU SEE WHEN YOU ENTER YOUR PLACE.

I see a lifeguard on a high stool. I also see people taking their dogs for walks along the shore.

My favorite place is the beach. The cold water splashes on the sticky sand. The birds dive through the water.

FrEdWriter's prompted writing option lets teachers create on-screen prompts or instructions for guided writing activities.

In addition to improved technical performance, *FrEdWriter* includes much more extensive documentation than *Freewriter*. There are four separate document files on disk, written by June Wedesweiler Dodge, which total 45 printed pages. They explain and give examples of the program features and list step-by-step instructions for the novice user. The user may either print these on paper to have as a ready reference or examine the files on screen when a question arises.

Because the people modifying *FrEdWriter* were educators, they did not stop with simply improving performance and documentation. An additional enhancement—prompted writing—is specifically designed for educational use.

In prompted writing, the instructor can create boxes of prompts which cannot be changed by the student. For example, a teacher may wish to encourage writing by storing the questions: "Who is your favorite hero?" "What does this hero do that makes you admire him/her?" "In five years, how will you be like that hero?" After each question, the student is to respond in complete sentences. The space between the questions expands to accommodate the answers.

The final product may be printed with or without prompts. If printed without prompts, and if the student has answered the questions in complete sentences, the resulting printout will be a complete story or coherent essay. Once students are accustomed to using prompted writing, they can further extend their writing/thinking abilities by creating their own prompts to help other writers.

The program may have weaknesses, depending upon what a particular individual wants. There are a few menus and credits that appear each time the disk is loaded, and the impatient user may find this annoying. Experienced computer users will doubtless find some features omitted which are present in other word processors. The graphics and calculator programs that were part of the original *Freewriter* disk are gone, so if you have a copy of *Freewriter*, you may wish to keep it.

Recommendations

Anyone with an Apple computer and without a word processor should obtain this disk immediately. Even if you will not use the program yourself, it is wonderful to be able to give free copies to students or to colleagues who have not yet discovered the virtues of word processing. Those who already have a first-class word processor may not see the need for it, if their uses are simply correspondence and writing papers. But if they teach and their students have access to computers, they will find the prompted writing features very useful. Furthermore, being able to print to the screen and to access the printer through control commands are quite useful features not found in every word processor. For the price, it can't be beat.

Publisher's Reply

FrEdWriter's ProDOS user interface is an improvement over the original *Freewriter* in that it shields users from obscure and confusing demands to enter "prefixes" and "pathnames," making normal disk management easy for all users.

The final version of *FrEdWriter* (Version 4) has the following additional enhancements: automatic line centering, improved printing features, all new documentation, and improved error trapping.

A Spanish *FrEdWriter* for the Apple IIe is also available. *Spanish FrEd* requires a character chip to display foreign characters on screen and comes with the purchase of a Spanish Wizchip from Hands-On Training Company, 4021 Allen School Road, Bonita, CA 92002, for $40 (quantity discounts available).

SOFTWARE REVIEWS   Edited by Linda Rathje

MultiScribe

MultiScribe
StyleWare, Inc., 6405 Hillcroft, Suite 201, Houston, TX 77081;
ph. 713/668-0743
Grade/Target Age Group: Grade four through adult
Subject: Word processor
Cost: $69.95; lab package prices available through the publisher.
Hardware Required: Apple IIe (128K), or IIc.
Reviewed by: Cathy Chmielowski Carney, Computer Lab Coordinator, Ryan Middle School, Fairbanks, Alaska

Does the worm of jealousy torment you while watching Macintosh owners print their writing in fancy font styles? Calm the worm. Try *MultiScribe* the word processor with fancy fonts for the 128K Apple.

An Easy and Efficient Word Processor

As a word processor, *MultiScribe* rates high. The writing tools most needed are provided: cut/paste clipboard, global find/replace, small and large cursor movements, and simple printer/interface-card setup. And since *MultiScribe* files can be saved as ASCII text, ProDOS telecommunications programs and spelling checkers can be used with them.

The features are easily and efficiently accessible. Pull-down menus and dialogue boxes (for messages and additional menu choices), similar to those on a Macintosh, simplify operations. Mac users will think they are using *MacWrite* and will immediately recognize the ruler-based formatting options for centering, justifying text, adjusting line spacing, and setting tabs, margins, and page breaks.

While the pull-down menus provide easy access for first-time users, experienced users can streamline their work by using the quick "open-Apple" commands corresponding to each option on a pull-down menu. After using a menu several times and seeing those onscreen prompts, it is an easy transition to using them directly. In addition to making the choices obvious—e.g., "S" for save—the authors include an appendix in the manual listing all open-Apple commands, their functions, and mnemonic clues for remembering them.

MultiScribe's Special Contribution

But to detail *MultiScribe*'s value as a word processor does not hint at its most important contribution. *MultiScribe* is special because it permits a writer to retain full word processing capabilities while simultaneously selecting, at any point in the writing, different type styles (fonts) in a range of sizes. Furthermore, what you see on the screen is what you get on the printer.

These features are not unusual for the Macintosh, but are very special for an Apple II.

The menu bar at the top of the screen contains the pull-down menu selections for adjusting font, size, and style. "Font" includes a variety of typefaces, some plain and straight, some curved and fancy. One font choice (Michelangelo) provides a set of 96 icons to enhance any writing. "Size" permits adjusting the chosen font from one to three times the original size, in increments of one half. "Style" offers such options as italics, underline, boldface, outline, or shadow, which can be incorporated into any font. My favorites are the "Upper case" and "Lower case" options, which change blocks of text into one case or the other.

Once font, size, and style are selected, any letters typed thereafter will appear on the screen in that form, until the options are changed. When editing, new material typed will take on the appearance of the surrounding letters, even if several different types have been used in the course of the writing. Changing the style of text already on the screen is a simple matter of highlighting text (using either the open-Apple and an arrow key or dragging the mouse); selecting a font, size, and style; and pressing an arrow key or clicking. The simplicity of this process encourages experimentation.

Figure 1. Michelangelo Fonts

Fonteditor

In addition to the 10 fonts provided on the disk, users can design their own (with up to 96 characters in each set) with the Fonteditor, as powerful and easy to use as the rest of the program. For those who want additional fonts without the trouble of creating them, it is safe to predict that StyleWare will soon be issuing new font choices.

Educational Uses

What does this program mean for schools? As a teacher utility, it competes with *Print Shop* for certain applications. *Print Shop* is perfect for making quick banners, posters and cards. But some announcements, seating charts, assignment sheets, and signs could be better designed using the flexibility of *MultiScribe* to place the desired stylized text in precisely the desired place on a page.

Teachers with diskfuls of tests, worksheets or handouts already created with *Apple Works*, *FrEd Writer*, *Apple Writer* or another ProDOS word processor, can use those files with *MultiScribe*. For example, *Apple Works* files can be saved as text (ASCII) files, loaded into *MultiScribe*, stylized, and then printed from within *MultiScribe*. Using this word processor, teachers can improve their printed instructional aids by highlighting important words and focusing student attention on critical sections through the ingenious choice of eye-catching fonts and icon graphics.

In addition to its value as a teacher utility, the program has exciting potential as a tool for motivating student writing. Our students used to enjoy making the medium match the message of their writing by customizing their poems and other special writing with Fontrix, a graphics-creating program. However, the need to switch disks and menus several times, and the danger of accidentally changing part of a screen, often confused and frustrated students. In *MultiScribe*, changing fonts is much simpler. Furthermore, any revisions are easily made, as the program automatically determines which font has been selected for an area and has additional entries appear in that font.

Students can easily alter the appearance of their text. A first grader showed the sound "Boom!!!" in lettering to match the meaning of the word. Story starters written in a font that matched the story's mood enticed students to finish a story. Students could now print their own name in special lettering to advertise their authorship. Teachers working to motivate student writing will daily find new ideas as they watch students experiment.

Additional Educational Features

Several other aspects of the program make it particularly attractive to schools. Though a teacher with a mouse will like using it with the program, schools without mouse peripherals will be glad that the program works with only a keyboard.

There is no copy protection on the disks—a boon to teachers concerned about crashed disks. If a jellied fingerprint deals a lethal blow to the working copy of *MultiScribe*, the teacher can immediately make a new copy from the original, and continue with class as planned.

Theft problems are reduced by the program's setup. Like *AppleWorks*, this is a two-disk program. A teacher can boot the program with disk 1, and then shelve it in a safe place. Disk 2 must remain in the drive, as it is frequently accessed, but the teacher need not worry unduly that disk 2 will "walk off"—it is useless without disk 1.

Support

The best part about the 250-page documentation is that it is rarely needed. In fact, any user familiar with *AppleWorks* or *MacWrite* can use the program without reading the manual. When the manual *is* consulted, its binding allows it to lie flat, making it easy to refer to while using the computer. The detailed index is handy. The table of contents clearly labels chapters as either chapters for learning about a feature, or reference chapters related to a feature. Summaries at the end of each chapter provide quick reference guides. And screen shots and diagrams are provided wherever helpful.

What the manual lacks is printout of what the various fonts and icons look like. Though the user can create a chart for reference, it would have been nice to find one ready-made in the manual.

A technical support telephone number available from 1:00 to 5:00 p.m. weekdays (Central Standard Time) is printed in large type on the back cover.

Limitations

Frequent and fluent writers may find this program too slow to use as their primary word processor. Because text is displayed on the graphics screen, the scrolling is slow. Frequent disk access, too, can be frustrating. And the memory requirements allow only seven to eight pages in memory at one time. (The latest version is compatible with extended memory cards, which would change this situation for those with the requisite hardware.)

Because it uses the printer's graphics mode, printing is slow on some printers. If the "simple" text printing mode is selected to speed up printing, you are no longer able to see on the screen exactly what will appear on paper.

The large cursor movements are somewhat less helpful that the corresponding movements in *AppleWorks*. For example, in *MultiScribe*, open Apple-9 moves the cursor to the beginning rather than the end of the last line. Thus, before adding new text, you must use small cursor movements to move the cursor to the end of that last line. Furthermore, all large cursor movements leave the cursor at the top rather than the middle of the screen. This means that additional scrolling must be done in order to see what comes before the cursor and revise the writing appropriately.

While it does not seem fair to call it a limitation, I cannot help but long for the ability to access the color-printing ability of the Imagewriter II through this program.

Recommendation

Anyone looking for a first word processor for home or school would not go wrong by purchasing *MultiScribe*—especially since the list price is only $70. I suspect that the major buyers, though, will be those who continue to do their word processing on the program they already have, and use *MultiScribe* to enhance those files or create handouts, posters, or announcements.

Teachers wanting to encourage student writing (and breathes there a teacher without this intent?) will find *MultiScribe* a potent ally. Students use it eagerly and easily, manipulating graphics and fonts to create a medium that portrays the message of their writing; to make the appearance consonant with the meaning.

The Macintosh earned its fame through permitting user to easily link linear, sequential text production with pictorial, holistic representations. Encouraging "left" and "right" brain hemispheres to work together in this way is an important goal for all educators. *MultiScribe*, using an Apple II, provides one simple, powerful, versatile way to reach this goal.

Publisher's Reply

Since Ms. Carney wrote her review of *MultiScribe*, StyleWare has announced a major update to the program—version 2.0. *MultiScribe* 2.0 offers a host of new features, including:

- Two near-letter-quality print modes;
- Headers and footers;
- The ability to delete files without leaving *MultiScribe*;
- A Page Setup command to allow users to set top and bottom margins and page length;
- A Select New Fonts command to let a user specify the path from which fonts are to be read;
- New print styles, including Wide, Tall, and Inverted; and
- The ability to install accessory programs produced by StyleWare.

These new accessories include:

- *Picture Manager*, which lets you put single or double high resolution pictures into *MultiScribe* documents. (Compatible with major graphics programs such as *Dazzle Draw* and *MousePaint*.)
- Desk Accessories, including full scientific calculator, clock, calendar, puzzle, and a control panel which lets you adjust sound and cursor speed and create up to 64 macros.
- FontPaks, each containing 10 new *MultiScribe* fonts, as well as an easy-to-use Font manager program which allows you to move fonts from path to oath and delete fonts from specific paths.
- *MultiScribe Spell Checker* for *MultiScribe* documents, with a 40,000-word dictionary.

MultiScribe 2.0 also supports all major memory expansion cards, including Applied Engineering's RamWorks and Apple's Memory Expansion Card, as well as "accelerator" cards such as Applied Engineering's Transwarp and Titan Technologies' Accelerator IIe.

Another new version of *MultiScribe*, for the Apple IIGS, includes a number of improvements. *MultiScribe GS* lets a user create as large a document as memory allows, and to open up to eight documents at one time. In addition to the font, size, and style options, *MultiScribe GS* lets you change the color of text and prints in color on the Imagewriter II. The Apple Laserwriter is also supported, allowing for the creation of near-typeset quality documents.

David Macdonald
Marketing Director

KidTalk/MasterType's Writer

KidTalk

First Byte, Inc., 2845 Temple Avenue, Long Beach, CA

Grade/Target Age Group: Preschool through junior high

Subject: Writing

Cost: $79.95

Hardware Required: 128K Macintosh

Reviewed by: Lynne Anderson-Inman, Ph.D., College of Education, University of Oregon, Eugene, Oregon

If you add synthesized speech to a program for word processing, what do you get? *KidTalk* is one of the first answers to this question. Designed for the Macintosh computer, *Kid Talk* incorporates the speech technology published earlier by First Byte as *Smoothtalker,* but in *KidTalk,* the synthesized speech of Smoothtalker's male and female voices are packaged as a talking word processor for children.

A Writing Tool

As a word processor, *KidTalk* has all the basic functions needed to manipulate text, and it employs the editing commands familiar to Macintosh users, e.g., cut, copy, and paste. Students write in a typical Macintosh "writing box" and are able to access any of seven pull-down menus, each accompanied by a picture.

Kid Talk is clearly easy to use. It is not, however, very flexible. Writers have the choice of three type sizes but no options as to the appearance of the font. Although this may seem to be a fairly trivial criticism, youngsters reared with a Macintosh have come to expect such features. Of greater importance is the program's lack of printer options. There is apparently no way to alter margins (other than using the space bar while writing) or even to underline. It can certainly be argued that such features are not necessary for young children. *KidTalk,* however, is billed as a program appropriate for students through junior high school and many of the suggested applications (e.g., stories, reports, plays, poems) could benefit from greater flexibility when it comes to printing.

A Talking Tool

But *Kid Talk* is not merely another word processing program. It's a writing tool that talks. And it does so without necessitating the purchase of any additional hardware. This is something many of us have been waiting for.

Kid Talk uses speech in two ways. First, the user is provided with verbal instructions on how to use the program, as well as ongoing assistance when needed. The program has a fairly extensive guided tour, in which its key features are explained by a parrot and demonstrated on screen. The guided tour is extremely well done, both visually and auditorially. My young

users of the program were able to grasp the basics from this tour, although it must be admitted that neither were novices on a Macintosh. An improvement would be to make the guided tour interactive. The youngsters were constantly reaching for the mouse, wanting to try what had been demonstrated without waiting for the tour to end.

Voice is also used to provide ongoing assistance. Writers who are unsure of how to accomplish some editing task, for example, can access the "SOS" picture menu for help. Explanations, with accompanying demonstrations, are both simple and clearly presented. This is one of *KidTalk's* best features, making it possible for even young users to become fairly independent on the word processor without the need for adult intervention when a question arises. In checking actual utility of this assistance I asked a seven-year-old novice user to "figure out" how to get rid of a specific sentence in her story (without using the delete key to remove it letter by letter). She quickly located the SOS menu and accessed the verbal directions on how to "cut." The directions were sufficient to teach the function, but she had to go back to listen a second time before accomplishing the necessary sequence of steps. Her response to this assistance? "I think most kids would find it easier to ask their parents." So much for independence!

The second way *Kid Talk* uses its built-in speech technology is really the most interesting: *KidTalk* has the ability to say anything the student writes. And for the vast majority of words written, what it says is correct. Child writers enjoy this feature immensely, feeling the added dimension of voice somehow makes their words really come alive. This feeling is enhanced through the many options available to control the synthesized sounds. The user can choose between a male or female voice and alter the volume, pitch, tone and speed. For words that *KidTalk*

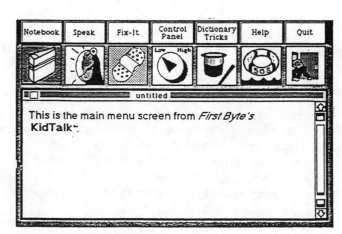

Figure 1. KidTalk Main Menu

does not speak correctly, the writer is encouraged to enter an altered spelling into the "sounds like" dictionary. For example, rewriting the word library as "lie brary" will get rid of the unwanted short "i" sound. Words derived from a foreign language are also problematic, so the manual warns that a word such as Chihuahua should be entered into the dictionary as "Chi wah wah."

Educational Applications

Of possible value for a wide range of students is the use of *KidTalk* as an aid to proofreading. Writers have the option of hearing a sentence immediately after it is written, or they can choose to hear a whole section of text at one time. Either way the auditory feedback can serve to highlight typographical errors and misspelled words, reveal grammatical inconsistencies, and prompt recognition of redundant word usage. Two of my test users found the speech function of *KidTalk* to be quite helpful in revising their compositions. The seven-year-old found she had spelled the word "might" as "migt" and the five-year-old recognized that she had started each sentence with "and."

Another interesting application for *KidTalk* is the development of talking stories or plays. Not only can writers control the characteristics of the voice (sex, pitch, tone, etc.) but they can also change these characteristics as frequently as desired while writing. This means, for example, that one voice can be used as a narrator and other voices for dialogue. In a similar fashion, different voices can be created for the various characters in a play. The writer's choices are saved along with the text, so that future "readings" of the story or play will incorporate the choices made.

A final application is, of course, as an aid to improving reading fluency. Paragraphs or stories can be typed into a file and then presented individually to students for reading practice. When unsure of a word or phrase, the student need only highlight it with the mouse, then have the computer say it by accessing the "Speak" menu. In this manner *KidTalk* might be easily integrated with the language experience approach to reading instruction as well as more skill-based or remedial approaches.

Limitations

For any of the above applications to be practical, accuracy in speech production is critical. In general, the voice quality in *Kid Talk is* intelligible and relatively few words are spoken inaccurately. That there are any inaccuracies at all, however, places some limitations on the program's use. Its utility as an aid to proofreading, for example, is somewhat hindered by the possibility that correctly spelled words might be targeted by the student as incorrect (and thus needing to be altered) upon hearing them mispronounced. The extent to which the program might actually encourage and reinforce certain types of spelling errors needs to be considered when structuring how the program is used.

Users of *Kid Talk will* probably debate whether or not the quality of the synthesized speech is adequate for instructional purposes. The reality of the situation is that you can understand the computer fairly well if you know what it is saying! Being able to read along with the voice helps tremendously. Even adults I shared the program with often could not make out what was being said if they were not looking at the screen. While listening to one of the stories provided on the disk I asked my five-year-old if she understood the words. Her reply was hopeful: "I got one of the words—beach."

Much can be done to improve the overall intelligibility if you type extra spaces between the sentences. Without these spaces the words and phrases seem to all blend into one continuous stream. Unfortunately, teaching students to type four spaces between sentences would result in negative transfer to other word processing programs, not to mention a printed copy with more blank holes than is aesthetically pleasing. This is probably trivial to fix programmatically, and I would recommend the publisher consider adding more sound spaces between sentences.

My last major concern has to do with the recommended age range. The program authors suggest an age range of preschool to junior high for *KidTalk*. *I* would estimate its greatest value is in the elementary school grades. Although preschool kids might find it fun for practice on letter names and sight words, most would probably not be independent in their use of the program. *KidTalk* would have greater value for this population if it contained an option for sounding words out phonetically, rather than spelling them letter by letter. The older children I shared the program with thought it was "cute, but not very practical."

A few other concerns will be mentioned briefly. First, it is sometimes irritating to have to wait for the computer to finish speaking. This was especially notable when accessing the help menus. Once children had the answers to their questions they wanted to return to work. The mouse and keyboard are inactive, however, until the computer has finished the predetermined discourse. Second, there is apparently no way to eliminate the voice. This could cause problems in the classroom unless earphones were available for the Macintosh. And third, the handbook, though generally well written, uses only male pronouns to refer to children. In a period of time when the issue of sex equity with respect to computer usage is widely discussed, it would seem appropriate to eliminate this vestige of sexist terminology.

Conclusion

Kid Talk is a very laudable effort. First Byte should be commended for integrating the Macintosh's capability for speech with a program that is well designed, easy to use and educationally relevant. For the computer to reach its potential as a learning tool, we need software designers willing to push the limits and explore the unknown. This is not easy, and products that go beyond the commonplace may have failings that limit their potential utility. That this is true with *KidTalk* does not diminish its importance as a significant milestone in educational software.

Publisher's Reply

When First Byte developed the Smoothtalker technology, it also committed considerable resources to produce pioneering and educationally exciting applications for children. We believe a program such as *KidTalk* is a look into the future, when computers cannot only talk, but listen.

Currently Smoothtalker is the highest quality, affordable speech synthesis technology on the market that does not require a board. It doesn't sound like your next-door neighbor yet (that doesn't seem to bother kids) but First Byte is committed to improving the speech quality and has a consumer policy for all products.

Kid Talk is the only educational speech product available that allows children the optimum control of being able to switch back and forth between a male and female voice within one document and manipulate the voice control of volume, pitch, tone, and speed. It may not be the type of word processor an older child would choose to use to format a term paper. It was intended to be a simple word processing program for creative writing. However, if the user is an experienced Macintosh pilot, s/he can boot with another program to access the finder level, move the file to a more sophisticated word processor, format the document and then move it back to *KidTalk* for proofreading as ordinary text.

MasterType's Writer

Scarborough Systems, Inc., 55 South Broadway, Tarrytown, NY 10591

Grade/Target Age Group: Grade four and above

Subject: Writing

Cost: $69.95 Apple version; $44.95 Commodore. Publishers will mail at no charge a back-up disk to purchasers returning the warranty card. Damaged disks will be replaced after the 30-day warranty for a $5 fee. The program Tutorial may be freely copied.

Hardware Required: Apple IIe (128K) or IIc, Commodore 64 or 128

Reviewed by: Cathy Chmielowski Carney, Computer Lab Coordinator, Ryan Middle School, Fairbanks, AK

Word processors abound, so what makes *MasterType's Writer* different? I found four intriguing features:

- It uses color to "filter" (hide) text;
- It has two adjustable text windows;
- It permits font-editing; and
- It allows sorting of numeric and alphabetic lists.

Working with Color

MasterType's Writer provides a color marking feature for identifying text to be displayed or hidden from view. The program's text filtering capacity works best with a color monitor, but it also works adequately without color, using variations in screen patterns to signal different colors. Selecting from the five color bars at the bottom of the screen, students can underline text as they type or underline text already on the screen. Once marked, selected text may be hidden or shown on the screen or printer at will.

This suggests a number of possibilities. A teacher could create writing activities with on-screen prompts which are hidden when the student prints the composition. When reading one's own or another's work, comments could be added using a different color, then either printed or not. An outline in one color could be printed alone or along with its text. Students working in pairs could each answer the same questions without seeing each other's work on the screen, then reveal both answers together for comparison and possible combination.

Using Text Windows

The program also has the ability to partition the screen into two windows, each of which can be edited, formatted, saved, and printed separately. I found this feature handy for viewing my outline in one window and writing in the other. Whenever I wanted to see a larger section of my outline or to view my writing on the entire screen, I adjusted the boundary between the two windows. It is possible to change, at any time, the size of the windows in relation to each other, or to move between windows with a single closed-apple keystroke.

There are other ways to use these windows, too. New ideas, tangential to the main topic, often come while one is composing or revising a piece of writing. Instead of losing these ideas, a user can regard window two as a notepad, jotting down ideas to be saved in a separate file and elaborated on later.

On-screen Typefaces

Another notable feature of this word processor is its special fonts. Students can have their writing appear on screen in one of seven different font sizes, ranging from 70-column type to very large letters suitable for young children or visually handicapped, to script. In addition, new fonts may be created. Children who have enjoyed editing the characters in *Fontrix, Gertrude's Secrets* or *The PrintShop Companion* will find the same satisfaction here. Some people who prefer a traditional writing tool over a typewriter or word processor because they like the freedom to create their own individual letters may find their styles supported here.

It is true that, no matter what the type style on the screen, standard characters will usually appear on the paper printout. But this program permits using the Imagewriter and a number of other printer and interface cards to print these fancy fonts in the form of a screen dump.

Sorting Text

One unusual feature in this price range is the inclusion of a sorting feature; paragraphs can be sorted numerically or alphabetically. I found this useful for quickly rearranging several paragraphs I had written. I simply numbered each, then selected Sort from the menu. In addition, material not in paragraph form (e.g., sections of an outline) can be identified as blocks of text by using special markers to designate the beginning and end. Treated as "records," they can also be sorted. Keeping an address file or list of names sorted this way would be simple.

Besides the above special features, the advertising touts this program as "easy to use," and it is. An inexperienced computer user can simply insert the disk, turn on the computer and write. The program recognizes and automatically formats blank disks used to save files. Since menus are accessible at the bottom of any screen by using the Escape key, there is no need to memorize control key sequences.

For the experienced user there are other options available. A number of menu choices can be accessed with control-key functions as well as menu selections, so frequent users need not always call up the menus. Files can be transferred to other word processors (e.g., *Bank Street Writer*, *AppleWorks*) by using a menu option to convert the *MasterType's Writer* file into ASCII form, and ASCII files from other programs can be transformed into *MasterType's Writer* files. A sophisticated user can define Macro keys that then become available each time *MasterType's Writer* is loaded.

Interactive Tutorial

For a beginning user, a most important feature will likely be the tutorial on the reverse side of the disk. It partitions the material into several easy-to-digest lessons, including how to delete text and switch between windows. At the beginning of each lesson, a few objectives are stated. After a short instruction, a review and quiz consolidate the learning. The sentence structure, vocabulary and large type permit even a young learner to follow the directions. Many of the lessons include a simulation of the word processor screen, so the user becomes familiar with it right away. The lesson which teaches the concept of word wrap —an idea newcomers to word processing often find initially confusing—is particularly good.

Both beginning and more experienced users should find the documentation helpful. The first few pages tell how to get started right away. The rest of the 100-page manual is arranged alphabetically, like a dictionary, with lots of cross references. The entry "Memory" has a paragraph of text, followed by the direction, "See also Erase, Files, Load, Resave a file, and Save." The manual ends with an index and an appendix describing the meanings of error messages.

Program Limitations

With good documentation, a friendly tutorial and a number of special features, is this the word processor for you? It depends.

In order to preserve ease of use, some flexibility is sacrificed. For example, there is little control of printer margins or line spacing. The program provides for only four global margin and line spacing parameters that can be saved as Setup specifications. Business teachers would need to carefully examine the limited range of formatting features available with *MasterType's Writer*. On the other hand, for most home and school use, this limited formatting flexibility may not be a serious handicap.

The text files are compressed and saved in a special format. In order to use these files with another word processor, such as *AppleWorks*, or to transmit files with a modem, they must first be converted to ASCII, using a menu option. If you will need ASCII files for either of these reasons, be sure you can make this conversion, and that you know how much time it will take, before buying this word processor.

The limitation I found significantly bothersome was not being able to move the cursor away from the bottom of the screen. In order to adequately revise a section, sometimes it helps to see what is below as well as what is above the cursor position. This is not possible, though, as the cursor always remains on the bottom line.

And the Apple version of this program only operates in a 128K IIe or IIc environment. This makes it useless to IIe users without the additional memory.

Recommendations

Elementary schools frequently have color monitors and may enjoy this program because it uses color to manipulate text. For use with young children, the enlarged type could be a deciding factor. If there is enough class time and computer access to allow children to experiment with creating and editing fonts, this feature is attractive. Some elementary teachers may use it because it can sort spelling words, student names or numbered test items.

With upper-grade students, using the second window for outlines or as a notepad for jotting random ideas while writing could be appealing. Using color for marking and filtering text permits students to comment on their own or each other's writing and could contribute to a rich process-writing environment. A print-to-screen (view) function—not available on all lower-priced word processors—saves on paper and time in formatting the final printout and could be particularly useful in schools, where there are often not enough printers for each computer and students need to be sure their writing is formatted properly before using printer time.

This program is also available for both the Commodore 64 and 128, though we did not review it. Owners of Commodores, who lack the array of choices available to Apple users, may be particularly glad to know about this inexpensive word processor. There are many word processor programs available for basic writing and revising. For teachers looking for ways to further assist their students in improving their organizing, thinking and writing skills, I recommend examining the special features available in *MasterType's Writer*.

Publisher's Reply
None.

SOFTWARE REVIEWS   **Edited by Linda Rathje**

Kidwriter/Story Maker/Bank Street Story Book

KidWriter

Story Maker

Bank Street Story Book

Kidwriter (Spinnaker), *Story Maker* (Scholastic) and *Bank Street Story Book* (Mindscape) are three programs that enable young writers to create illustrated stories. Students can "make" pictures or scenes and develop accompanying stories that can be read on screen or in print. The reviewers were able to work with children as they explored these programs, and have shared their observations.

Three programs for preschool and primary grades are also included this month. Reviewer Christine Chaille sees the two Joyce Hakansson programs *Ranch* (Spinnaker) and *Kermit's Electronic Storymaker* (Simon & Schuster) as "construction kit" or "electronic tinkertoy" activities which provide the young child with opportunities for self-directed experimentation. C & C Software has incorporated a management system in their *Letters and First Words* program, and reviewer Scott Turner, a first grade teacher, particularly appreciates the opportunity to make program modifications.

Last, but certainly not least, is Brøderbund's popular program, *The Print Shop*. Educators should definitely examine this versatile graphics program.

Kidwriter

Spinnaker Software Corp., 215 First Street, Cambridge, MA 02142

Grade/Target Age Group: Ages 6 to 10

Subject: Creative writing

Hardware Required: Apple II, II +, IIe or Commodore 64, IBM PC, IBM PCjr; Color monitor recommended; joystick optional; one disk drive

Cost: $29.95 (Apple), $29.95 (IBM), $26.95 (Commodore)

Reviewed by: Chrissie Forbes, Santa Clara Elementary School, Eugene, OR, Grades 1-2

Kidwriter is a combination word processor and picture maker for elementary-age children. It follows the teaching format used in many creative writing lessons: Draw a picture and then write about it. What child faced with the task of writing a story wouldn't be motivated by the fun of creating a picture on the computer screen? Any program using this format offers a potential writing tool of special consideration for the elementary teacher.

How It Works

Choosing from 99 objects, the child first creates a picture, selecting the size, position, and color for each object. One object is manipulated at a time and cannot be repositioned once the child adds the next object to the picture. When the picture is completed, seven lines remain on the screen to compose a narrative or description of the picture.

When a page is completed, the child may choose to: 1) make a next page to the story; 2) start a new story; or 3) store it on disk for later reading. Once a story page has been stored, it cannot be changed.

The commands needed for editing the text are not prompted on the screen but are easy to find in the manual. On the Apple IIe and Commodore 64, the cursor is controlled through the arrow keys. On the Apple II or II+ the cursor is controlled through the Control E, D, X, and S keys. Erasing is accomplished with the Escape key, one letter at a time. The child may insert letters or words, and the rest of the text will automatically move to the right. The Apple IIe and Commodore 64 versions are *very* easy to work. Young students can work independently, making it ideal for classroom use.

The commands for moving the objects in the pictures use the same keys used to edit on the Apple II or II+, which poses a serious problem for Apple II and Apple II+ owners. While Control E moves an object up higher on the screen, plain E erases the entire picture. While Control D moves the object to the right, plain D indicates that the child is done making the picture and ready to write the story. Once this D command is entered, changes cannot be made in the picture. My six-year-old daughter lost almost half of the pictures she made through this type of beginner's error. Choosing different keys for these commands or having an "Are you sure?" message could easily avoid these problems. (Apple IIe and Commodore 64 owners won't have this problem, because the picture objects are moved with the arrow keys.)

Strengths

Kidwriter is easy to use. I tried it out on my young daughter and her playmates, and with very little explanation they were busy taking turns drawing and composing. The short (10-page) manual was simple to follow. It was also easy to find all the commands that might be needed. With a couple of exceptions, the program displays all the commands that a child will need up on the screen at the appropriate time.

With the range of objects, colors, sizes, positions, and backgrounds to choose from, the picture-creating aspect of the program itself makes this an attractive product. Of course, if making a picture is all you're looking for, there are other more sophisticated (and more expensive) programs that allow for more creativity.

The manual is easy to use and any computer novice can experience mastery in no time. There are plenty of useful prompts and the user is asked to confirm all decisions to erase text.

Weaknesses

My daughter was frustrated by the accidental erasing of her pictures. A more glaring problem, from my viewpoint as an elementary school teacher, is the lack of editing options. Some children will want to write more than seven lines of text. When the seven lines are filled, the extra text is not automatically transferred to the next page of the "story." A sound beeps with each extra word and these words are lost. The program makes no allowance for the child who would like to write more and draw less. Also, once a child has developed a train of thought, it seems a shame to have to stop in mid-sentence to draw a new picture before being able to complete the idea.

In school (and at home) we try desperately to teach children that writing is a process involving many steps. We write, rewrite, write, and then rewrite again. We move sentences around. We change words. We add explanations and cross out unnecessary verbiage. We remember important information or even change a story's entire focus. Because this program doesn't allow the child to retrieve a page or an old story and make changes, it could reinforce the mistaken notion children get that writing is a one-step process. With all the attention given nationally to our children's inability to write and the need to teach these essential editing skills, I'm disappointed that *Kidwriter* doesn't provide for rewriting.

A final weakness of *Kidwriter* is the lack of a printing option. If a parent or teacher is hoping to print copies of a child's work for display or examination, then this program falls short. As a teacher I would insist on a program with a printing option so that my students could take their stories home.

Recommendation

Kidwriter was the first program to combine picture making and story writing. Newer programs are more sophisticated, but *Kidwriter* will give your child plenty of opportunity to "draw" pictures and compose stories. Because of its price, ease of use and motivating qualities, I recommend that primary teachers examine this program when considering combined word processor and picture-making software for elementary-age children.

Story Maker

Scholastic Inc., 2931 East McCarty St., P.O. Box 502, Jefferson City, MO 65102
Grade/Target Age Group: Ages 8 years and up
Subject: Creative writing and illustrated text editing
Hardware Required: Apple II+, IIe or IIc (64K RAM minimum), single or dual disk drive, KoalaPad, joystick or AppleMouse required.
Optional printers: Epson (with a Grappler card), ImageWriter or Scribe printer
Cost: Personal edition—$39.95 (one program disk, one picture disk, documentation)
Reviewed by: Heidi Imhof, Computer and Gifted Coordinator and Advisor to the Writer's Club, Connell Elementary School, North Franklin School District, Connell, WA

Story Maker is a text editing program for children, featuring the illustration capabilities of the KoalaPad, joystick, or AppleMouse. Students may draw their own pictures or choose predesigned pictures from a gallery of three picture disks: a general gallery disk containing animals, trains, etc.; and two specialized disks—one on science fiction and one on fantasy. Eight enlarged font styles allow students to select and change the typeface.

The program is driven from a simple menu. In making a new story students use the KoalaPad, joystick, or AppleMouse to select representative icons to type, select from the picture gallery, draw, erase, nip or clear pages, or exit. The same selection procedure is used throughout the program, simplifying instructions to the user.

Once a picture is selected, it may be "stamped" anywhere on a page. Students decide upon the size of their graphic (two sizes are available) and may nip each graphic 180 degrees. An UNDO function allows students to erase the last graphic stamped. For other changes there is an ERASE function that operates like an electronic pencil eraser.

I had some initial questions when I began working with this program: These concerns included:

- Use of a single disk drive;
- Younger students' ability to use the KoalaPad when making menu selections;
- Lack of flexibility in the number of words that can fit on a single "page";
- A few gallery pictures and one type style that appeared hazy and difficult to recognize on the screen;
- High cost of outfitting each writing section with a KoalaPad, AppleMouse, or joystick;
- The tedious job of designating the printer with each printing.

After using this program with our Writer's Club (grades four through six), nearly all my concerns were laid to rest.

It should be mentioned that Scholastic provides teachers with lots of assistance in using this program with students. In addition to thorough documentation, the school edition includes ideas for introducing *Story Maker* in your classroom, as well as a whole section of teaching activities. This activity section has some standard writing ideas—good ones you have probably seen before—but these ideas are well adapted for use with *Story Maker*. Scholastic is exemplary in providing activities which allow their software to be introduced smoothly and integrated soundly into the curriculum. Here's what I discovered in using this program with students.

First of all, *Story Maker* is highly motivating. After showing students some of the things I had produced, we began writing a story together. Students couldn't wait for their turn to write stories of their own. After I trained a sixth grader on *Story Maker*, he made appointments before school, during lunch, and after school to train the many students who were interested. Believing I had hit a fluke, I shared this program with groups of first through third graders with the same result. My first graders pored over the picture gallery cards (provided by Scholastic) and started their own stories while I worked one-on-one with each student at the computer. The KoalaPad section that I had worried about provided a good fine-motor, hand-eye experience for them, and they rose to the challenge, largely refusing my help. The letter and page size proved just right for primary students, who can become frustrated easily with the small print typical of many word processors. They made very careful and individual decisions about layout, and each story distinctly reflected its author. One first grader tried several locations, sizes, and directions before she was finally satisfied with her string of horses "running in a pasture."

The problem of disk swapping was a concern only to some of my fifth and sixth graders who are proficient on *Bank Street Writer* already. My sixth-grade trainer said, "It was worth having to change disks to get the pictures and backgrounds on *Story Maker*." Other older students thought they might use *Story Maker* for covers and illustrated pages and *Bank Street Writer* for the text of their stories.

The picture and type style that appeared hazy to me didn't trouble my students. After using the eighth type style once or twice, most students just opted to use one of the other, more

legible, type styles. Many students took advantage of the program's ability to switch fonts to add emphasis and interest to their stories. Pictures that were hard for me to discern were also no problem for my students. Although those brave few who decided to draw their own pictures learned how much mastery it takes to create a picture with the KoalaPad, experienced KoalaPad users were able to draw some great pictures.

In summary, my initial concerns were not valid for first through at least fifth grade. Experienced fifth and sixth graders generally recognized the tradeoffs and limitations, but were making sound decisions about appropriate use. However, I would still prefer using two disk drives, and would like to have *Story Maker* store the printer specification information.

Story Maker is simple to use, yet it takes good advantage of the computer's power. The ability to illustrate and write, with full layout control, gives children's creativity ample room for unique expression. Children can write and rewrite, as with most word processors, but can additionally redesign until they are content with their product. Scholastic has given us a fine word processing/storymaking program. After using it with children, I can heartily recommend it.

Bank Street Story Book

Mindscape, Inc., 3444 Dundee, Northbrook, IL 60062 Grade/
Target Age Group: Grades 3-9
Subject: Creative writing and drawing
Hardware Required: Apple II+, IIe or IIc with at least 64K of memory, one disk drive, monitor or TV (preferably color), joystick or KoalaPad
Cost: $39.95
Reviewed by: Lynne Anderson-Inman, Ph.D., College of Education, University of Oregon

---

Bank Street Story Book is a new addition to the recent outpouring of commercial software designed to encourage creative writing by combining text processing with computer graphics. In a field that has captured the imaginative and productive interests of so many software developers, one might easily assume that the resulting products are roughly equivalent and that no single contender will stand out as truly exceptional. After several weeks spent examining and comparing some of these new programs, I would like to suggest that *Bank Street Story Book* is definitely something special.

Like other programs of its genre, *Bank Street Story Book* allows the user to create a multi-page story which contains both pictures and words. The story can be saved on disk and then revised, read, or printed out whenever the user desires. What makes this particular program special is the range of artistic creativity and competence the program is capable of supporting, the sophistication of the word processing component, and the overall flexibility for mixing graphics and text in interesting and novel ways.

To create a picture, the user manipulates a "rubber band"

cursor controlled through a joystick or KoalaPad. Upon selecting LINE from a vertical bar menu at the side of the screen, the user is free to draw anything anywhere. Use of the joystick's buttons allows the cursor to be lifted from the graphic in progress and set down somewhere else on the screen. Although the width of the line is constant, it can be drawn in any of eight different colors. For smaller detail work, and greater control, the cursor span can be decreased in size. Pressing "G" (for "Grid") constrains the cursor to move only horizontally or vertically, especially helpful for younger users who enjoy creating pictures from basic geometric shapes. Sections of a drawing can be filled with any of 21 colors. To accomplish this the user selects COLOR on the horizontal bar menu and then uses arrow keys to "mix" two of the available eight colors. A press of the joystick button, and the desired color instantly fills the space targeted by the cursor. To make changes or corrections in a drawing, the delete key can be used to sequentially erase unwanted lines and colors.

To the novice joystick user, all of the above is somewhat foreign and awkward. Not having done anything of significance with a joystick before, I fumbled and fussed at great length before anything recognizable began to emerge. However, those familiar with the idiosyncrasies of this input device—even young children—seem to have no trouble adapting their already-acquired expertise to the specific demands of this program. When *Bank Street Story Book* was shared with some local second and third graders, those with previous joystick experience grasped the essential elements within a few minutes. The pictures are visually interesting and often quite stunning, especially those created by older users. Two sixth graders who experimented with the program were able to create some astoundingly sophisticated pictures; a sample story provided by the publishers indicates that a professional artist can go further yet. It's a credit to the designer that the program is easy enough for 7-year-olds, yet rich enough for adults.

To create a "storybook," however, the user needs more than an accessible graphics program. Without the ability to input text, there would be no story and hence relatively little academic value to the program. Unfortunately, this is where many such programs fall short. We still see products, for example, which accept only capital letters, do not accept the delete key, or use nonstandard procedures for altering text. *Bank Street Story Book* has avoided all of these traps. The word processing component on the program is sophisticated and easy to use. It has adopted the standard conventions for word processing programs (e.g., automatic word wrap, use of arrows to move cursor, easy insertions and deletions, etc.) and is even programmed to retain original text in memory, thus enabling revisions to be easily discarded if they are not felt to be improvements. The word processing component is accessible at any time in the process of creating a story by merely pressing "T" (for TYPE). A window appears which is then moved into place and expanded to the desired size with the joystick. A second pressing of "T" places the cursor at the top of the window, where it is ready to accept text.

From an instructional standpoint, the use of conventional word processing procedures in *Bank Street Story Book* is very desirable. Young students and those new to word processing may gain valuable skills through use of the program—skills that will later be transferable to other word processing applications. The corollary is equally true: Students with previous word processing experience find the program easy to learn because it uses skills they already have. As expressed by one sixth grader, "Heck, this is a snap!" The typeface used in the program is relatively small (by comparison to other programs), and this is an advantage. It allows the writer to put quite a bit of text on a single page if desired, and it facilitates using the text for labels or story dialogue.

As powerful and interesting as these two components of *Bank Street Story Book* are, it is their integration which truly makes this program exceptional. Initially the user will probably work on a picture and then write the text to go with it, or write the text and then draw the corresponding picture. It is possible, however, to go back and forth from graphic to text as often as the user wishes, i.e., drawing a portion of the picture, putting in some text, altering or adding to the picture, adding or deleting some text, and so forth. Unless given the command to FLIP, all of this will be on one "page" of the storybook being developed. When read, each page appears on the screen in the order created (i.e., the graphic is drawn before your eyes, spaces are filled with color, and the text appears in the sequence it was entered). When creatively designed, the end result is a story page which appears to come alive. With some judicious use of the WAIT command (requiring the reader to press a button for the next portion of the page to be revealed) and some well-planned deletions, the user is even able to create simple animation and the appearance of dialogue between story characters.

At any point in this process, the user can ask to read through the story being created or choose to move back and forth one page at a time and one story step at a time. This allows for later changes in the pictures and editing of the text. The tremendous flexibility built in to *Bank Street Story Book* has not resulted in a program which is difficult to use. It's a program that students can be successful with fairly quickly and then, as their experience builds, learn its finer features and capitalize on its depth. (Even second graders were fairly independent with the program by the second day and able to teach the essentials to their peers by the third day.)

The stories produced with *Bank Street Story Book*, when shown on the screen are unlike anything else students have ever been able to create. The writer not only controls the content but also, to some extent, the rhythm and pacing with which the story is read. Pages become dynamic entities which both captivate and motivate. Instead of using a computer to create replicas of traditional static pages, *Bank Street Story Book* moves the writer and the reader into a new electronic literary medium.

The potential classroom applications for *Bank Street Story Book* are many and varied, the most obvious being a tool to facilitate creative writing instruction. When using the program with young students, it was apparent that the drawing process served to stimulate their imaginations, especially when drawing curved lines (i.e., not in the "Grid" mode). After doodling for a while, their drawings began to look like something identifiable and, when prompted, they could write a few sentences to go with the picture. For teachers using the process approach to writing instruction, the program would work beautifully to generate ideas during the prewriting stage, while at the same time supporting the development and revision of students' written products. It is the program's capacity for accepting changes and facilitating corrections that seemed to intrigue the two sixth graders who tried it. Working as a team, they spent an entire afternoon creating a story and then perpetually revising ("improving") it. Some of these improvements resulted from experimentation with the program's graphic capabilities, but a surprising percentage were text-based modifications and additions. In fact, the original story had approximately doubled in size by the time they felt it was complete.

Other possible applications might build on the program's ability to print out students' creations. Teachers using the language experience approach to reading instruction could type in dictated stories to support students' drawings and then print the individualized storybooks for later rereading and fluency building. Other students could use the program to create an illustrated classroom newsletter or a project report, complete with graphs, tables, and maps.

It is always dangerous to write a review which doesn't appear to have taken a critical look at the program under examination. The enthusiastic and glowing praise of the above paragraphs may give the reader the impression that this is exactly what happened here. When beginning this review, however, I did have several areas of concern. First, the program's complexity made me wonder about its utility in the classroom: Would a teacher have time to learn and to teach students how to use it? Could the program be used by pairs of students or small groups? The first question was answered by the documentation. It is well constructed and well written. A tutorial is included to help teach the basic operations of the program quickly. Furthermore, on-screen help menus are easily accessible and another tutorial is included on the disk. The second question was answered by observations of my sixth grade testers. They obviously enjoyed cooperating on the creative process and learned more about the program because of their joint efforts. Integrating *Bank Street Story Book* into the classroom should pose no major problem to teachers already familiar with microcomputers.

A second concern centered on the apparent inappropriateness of the program for children in the primary grades, even though the publishers had targeted children as young as eight. After all, if I had some trouble manipulating the joystick and learning the program's idiosyncrasies, they would surely feel overwhelmed! Thanks to cooperative local teachers, some last-minute testing was done with second and third graders. Observation of these young users revealed they not only loved the program, but that they could learn it easily—even from their peers.

Only my third concern remains unresolved. I would like to have at least one simple, sample story on the disk that novices can identify with and younger children can read. I felt frustrated when my drawings were in no way comparable to those included as samples (even the samples created by children!). This concern may be more a reflection of my artistic talents (or lack thereof) than the program's limitations, but it is something to consider—especially when introducing the program to younger children.

Bank Street Story Book is clearly a program to explore and I recommend it very highly. It is one of those rare programs which continues to unfold as you use it. For teachers who value the role microcomputers can play in facilitating student writing, and who are looking for a motivating way to introduce or encourage the use of this new medium, *Bank Street Story Book* will undoubtedly become a useful and highly effective classroom tool.

SOFTWARE REVIEWS   Edited by Linda Rathje

Sensible Grammar

Sensible Grammer

Sensible Software, Inc., 210 S. Woodward, Suite 229, Birmingham, MI 48011; 313/258-5566
Author: David Long
Grade/Target Age Group: Junior High School through College
Subject: Writing, Proofreading
Cost: $99.95; includes a 3.5 inch disk and a 5.25 inch disk version of the program, plus an 88-page User's Manual. $299.95; school lab pack (10 disks, one User's Manual).
Hardware Required: Apple IIc, IIe (128K RAM)
Reviewed by: John Tenny, Instructor of Education, Willamette University, Salem, Oregon.

To understand what *Sensible Grammar* does, it might help to know what it doesn't do. It doesn't teach grammar; it doesn't check spelling; it is not a word processor or editor; it is not a prewriting aid; it is not a style checker; and it won't identify errors in sentence or paragraph structure, such as run-on or incomplete sentences, or disorganized or unclear paragraphs.

Sensible Grammar is a specialized proofreader. It is used on word processed writing and checks specifically for two things: punctuation errors and misused phrases. When the program finds a punctuation error, it provides an error message and allows the user to insert a marker in the document for later inspection and correction by the writer. When a "problem" phrase is found, the program offers alternative phrases as suggestions for replacement.

This after-writing tool checks for over 2,000 commonly misused phrases under numerous categories (see Figure 1) such as cliche, pompous, vague, redundant, etc. It will identify any phrase found in its list as a possible problem.

Sensible Grammar is a menu-driven program, with the main choices appearing across the top line of the screen. Subchoices are presented as you move the cursor to your selection.

The heart of the program is the PHRASES menu. Through this easy-to-use menu and the equally simple functions available, you can control the program as needed to meet specific writing goals. A teacher can examine, print out, or alter the existing phrases; add new misused and corrective phrases; and individualize according to curriculum needs or student sophistication. This flexibility makes the program powerful not only for the individual writer, but also for classes of students.

In the punctuation module, the program identifies repeated words, capitalization, abbreviation and punctuation errors. Punctuation errors include missing or unnecessary commas, misused dashes, and extra blank spaces. You can even set *Sensible Grammar* to expect one to four spaces after each sentence.

Getting Started

The program works with many of the most popular ProDOS word processor programs (*Apple Works, Apple Writer, Format II, Mouse Write, MouseWord, pfs: Write, Word Juggler, Word Perfect* and *Zardax*) through a Quick Setup option, or with ASCII files for those with other word processors. I tried this option with *FrEd Writer*, the public domain word processor, and it worked without difficulty.

The first step in running *Sensible Grammar* is to use the SETUP menu to identify your word processor, configure for your printer, and tell how many drives you have. Second, you can toggle the phrase lists on or off through the PHRASES menu. For example, you can focus on a particular type of faulty phrases (e.g., cliche), and the file will be checked only for those errors. This option could be very useful for individualizing the program for specific students or classes. Finally, using the CHECK menu, you decide whether to check punctuation, grammar or both. The default is to check both.

If you decided to check for "grammar" errors, the program then loads the phrase lists chosen and guides you through selecting a file to be checked. From there, *Sensible Grammar* will either step through the document error by error, or run through the automatic marking/printing option, according to your commands.

For every suspect phrase, the program offers one or more suggestions. By pressing the < S >UGGESTIONS key, you can see each suggested replacement in context, and accept a suggestion with the < R >EPLACE keystroke. If you don't care for the suggestions, < E >NTER lets you replace the highlighted phrase

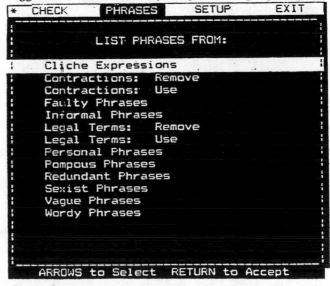

Figure 1.

with an on-the-spot correction. Also with single keystrokes, you can < I > GNORE the item, < P > RINT the line containing the error and *Sensible Grammar*'s suggestions, or < M > ARK the phrase, allowing you to insert a marker at the location of the error for later examination and/or correction, and move on.

If you are checking for punctuation errors, you can IGNORE, MARK and/or PRINT punctuation errors, but you cannot change them from within *Sensible Grammar*.

Strengths

- **Flexibility:** There are very few limitations to the ways a teacher can customize this program. The abilities to add and delete phrases, to add your own suggestions for replacement, even to add entirely new categories of phrases, make this an open-ended tool. Add the power to select which lists to check, and whether to print or mark the errors (or both). Then consider the ability to customize it for your printer and word processor. This flexibility results in a professional writing/teaching tool.
- **Simplicity:** Often programs that could be simple are made maddeningly complex. The opposite is true with *Sensible Grammar*. This is a powerful program that, through the use of menus and almost always obvious options, is quite easy to use. A half hour spent "messing around" with the menus and documentation will make you an accomplished user.
- **Documentation:** The documentation is extremely clear. The tutorial section (29 pages), and the reference section (35 pages), have plenty of screen shots to keep you on track; and the six appendices are straightforward. The two-page index covers all the basics.
- **Running other programs:** The EXIT menu allows you to access another ProDOS by simply highlighting the file name and pressing RETURN.
- **Extensive phrase list:** The supplied, 2,000+ phrases cover many commonly misused English phrases. There is no slang list, but there is an empty list titled "Personal Phrases" where additional phrases can be added.
- **Mouse support:** Although the program is set up to be controlled through the keyboard, you can use *Sensible Grammar* with the AppleMouse. There are scroll bars on some of the display windows that, with the mouse, let you jump to any page of the displayed information.
- **Hard disk and RAM disk support:** While the program is copy protected and cannot be copied onto another 5 1/2-inch disk, it can be copied onto a hard disk. The directions in the documentation are quite clear. As a hard disk user, I can attest to the decreased delay in access time. And for even greater speed and convenience, *Sensible Grammar* can be used with a RAM disk (using excess Random Access Memory for temporarily loading and running the program). To do this, you will need an expanded memory board and software to set up the RAM disk. For repeated use of *Sensible Grammar* during a single work session, this configuration would be the most efficient.

Limitations

- Spelling must be corrected first. Because the program checks for an exact match between its phrases and phrases in the document, spelling errors will camouflage other errors. Since students who have trouble with punctuation and faulty phrases often also have trouble with spelling, careful proofreading or using a spelling checking program before *Sensible Grammar* is a must.
- Punctuation errors can't be corrected on screen; the program only marks them for later revision. The disk is packed nearly full and since on-screen punctuation correction would require full screen editing capabilities, this was a necessary trade-off. Nonetheless, it would be nice to be able to do all the corrections during the same process.
- Individual phrase deletions. The teacher has the choice to either remove selected phrases permanently from the *Sensible Grammar* disk, or temporarily—until you are through with *Sensible Grammar* for the day. But if you want to start with a partial list (e.g., a list of 10 common cliches) and add to it throughout your teaching unit, you would have to re-enter the deleted phrases one by one. It would be more convenient to be able to toggle individual phrases for short-term exclusion.
- The printout is the only full record of errors. Since classrooms and computer labs have a limited number of printers, it would be advantageous to have a file generated on disk that contained both the mark showing the location of the error and the type of error, along with a list of suggestions. It would make off-computer editing easier, as well as providing a record of improvement for the teacher. This information is available in hard copy, if you are connected to a printer as you run *Sensible Grammar*. This is probably not a problem for personal use, but could be for classroom use.
- Setup parameters are not lockable. If this program were to be used in a lab setting, it would be preferable to make the settings for printing, phrase lists, etc., difficult for students to change.
- Backup policy. The program is copy protected. The first backup costs $5, when you return the accompanying program disk not compatible with your drives. After the 90-day free replacement period, replacements are $10. As one media specialist stated, "In our school, a program that has heavy student use can have up to four replacements per year. At $10 each, the program quickly becomes too expensive."

Recommendations

Writing is a form of communication, a method of passing ideas back and forth. Even the most boring writing "exercises" have, as an ultimate goal: the ability to communicate your thoughts clearly and accurately. Support tools—erasers, typewriters, word processors, and the now-emerging programs that assist in spelling, word selection, organization, style and "elimination of faulty phrases"—can be valuable aids to writers.

Such programs never overlook anything they're set to find.

They treat everyone the same; they don't evaluate the writer; and the user is not embarrassed when they find a mistake. And most important, they don't fix it for you; they just point you at something you might want to reconsider, then wait patiently until you make a decision. These tools can give us suggestions, help us step through complex processes of development, and remove the mundane proofreading chores. But we, the writers, must be the ones to say, "That's my message, and how I want to say it."

If you use an Apple computer for word processing and even occasionally find a cliche or sexist phrase creeping into your writing, consider buying this program. This objective proofreader will catch errors a writer can look at over and over without seeing. Its use could improve your writing while increasing your confidence and saving time.

If you teach in a discipline where students are assigned papers to be written on the computer, consider buying this program. Whether the assignment is in history, biology or psychology, the quality of the final product can be improved by conscientious and consistent use of *Sensible Grammar*.

And if a goal in your educational life is to improve students' ability to produce interesting and informative writing, consider buying this program. Let it aid students in this lower level of proofreading and revision; spend *your* time on organization and style.

Publisher's Reply

Sensible Grammar is designed to be a companion program to our *Sensible Speller* and therefore does not correct spelling. *Sensible Grammar* does check style in the sense of helping to make writing less pompous and more effective at communicating. It is the most innovative program of its type on the market today for the Apple computer.

Sensible Grammar now has an "autoload" feature for use with extra memory cards such as the Apple II Memory Expansion Card; Applied Engineering's RamWorks, RamWorks II and 2-RAM cards; AST Research's SprintDisk card; Checkmate Technology's MultiRam series of cards; and Legend Industries' E' and S' cards. If you do not have this feature and wish to update your present *Sensible Grammar* to the latest version, simply send us your disks and $15. Please specify if you prefer all floppies or all UniDisks or one of each format.

SOFTWARE REVIEWS

Edited by Linda Rathje

TimeOut Series

TimeOut Series
Beagle Bros Inc., 3990 Old Town Ave., Suite 102C, San Diego, CA 92110; ph. 619/296-6400.
Target Population: None stated.
Subject: *AppleWorks* enhancements.
Cost: *TimeOut Graph*, $89.95
TimeOut QuickSpell, $69.95
TimeOut SuperFonts, $69.95
TimeOut UltraMacros, $59.95;
TimeOut SideSpread, $49.95;
TimeOut FileMaster, $49.95;
TimeOut DeskTools, $49.95.
Hardware Required: Apple II with 128K. Additional memory recommended.
Reviewed by: Julie A. Poage, Software Review Editor, ICCE.

AppleWorks has become one of the most widely used computer programs, particularly in schools. With this one program, students can learn to word process, create and use databases, and place and analyze data in spreadsheets. But even with current upgrades, *AppleWorks* does not include some important features. With the introduction of Beagle Bros' *TimeOut* series, many enhancements can be accessed within *AppleWorks*.

The *TimeOut* series includes seven *AppleWorks* enhancements which can be installed on the *AppleWorks* disk. Two of these applications, *QuickSpell* and *Graph*, are of particular interest for classroom use and will be highlighted in this review.

TimeOut QuickSpell

QuickSpell is a spelling checker that can be accessed from any *AppleWorks* word processed file. To activate *QuickSpell* you simply press Open Apple-ESC and select the *QuickSpell* option from the *TimeOut* applications menu *QuickSpell* will search for the main dictionary file (the *Random House Concise Dictionary*, containing over 80,000 words) and a custom dictionary, then review the words in your file and lead you to the *QuickSpell* option menu.

This menu displays a list of all unrecognized and double words (i.e., the the) and presents several word replacement options. You can choose to correct individual words or the entire list. When a word selection has been made you will see the first word highlighted within the document. You then decide whether the word should be replaced, added to the custom dictionary, ignored for this document, or skipped; or you can request suggestions for alternative spellings. If suggestions are requested, a list of up to 29 will appear. Selecting the correct spelling causes all occurrences of the word to be automatically replaced.

When all of the highlighted words have been corrected or dismissed, *QuickSpell* automatically returns to your corrected *AppleWorks* document.

Strengths

Having a spelling checker easily accessible from an *AppleWorks* word processed file is a major improvement over other spelling checker programs. The user does not have to worry about saving, booting an additional program, or returning to *AppleWorks* to rewrite or print.

QuickSpell is very easy to learn. The commands are simple and the formal is very similar to *AppleWorks*. In fact, students who learn to use *QuickSpell* along with *AppleWorks* might not even realize they are using two programs.

Weaknesses

Beagle Bros has designed the *TimeOut* series for use with the Apple II family with 128K or more. Unfortunately, the dictionaries and the *QuickSpell* application cannot fit on one side of a 5.25-inch disk. I was using two 5.25-inch drives, so every time I wanted to spell check I had to make sure the disk with the application was in the drive. When *QuickSpell* was loaded and running it would immediately begin looking for the dictionaries, which were on a separate disk. An error message would come up, at which time I would place the dictionary disk in the drive and ask *QuickSpell* to try again. There seemed to be a lot of disk swapping going on.

While limits on disk and memory space were somewhat annoying on my 128K IIe, Beagle Bros strongly recommends that the *TimeOut* applications be configured to reside in RAM. With the addition of extra memory and/or the use of 3.5-inch disks there would be no need to swap disks at all. Unfortunately, many schools have not expanded their IIes beyond the basic starter system.

TimeOut Graph

The graphing capabilities of *TimeOut Graph* allow data in an *AppleWorks* spreadsheet to be presented in a variety of line, pie, and bar graphs. After you select *Graph* from the *TimeOut* option menu, a number of graphing selections appear.

First the graph type must be chosen. *TimeOutGraph* will produce nine different types of graphs, including regular or stacked bar charts, pie charts with an ability to "explode" part of the chart, line graphs, area or hi-lo charts, XY graphs (scatter grams), and point graphs.

After designating the graph type, the user identifies which data are to be plotted. Using simple cursor movements on the spreadsheet, up to six data ranges can be selected and then graphed. Selecting View from the *Graph* menu displays the current graph. Titles, legends, and grid lines can be added to improve readability and to clarify information.

Once a graph has been created it can be saved along with its formatting. It can also be printed using many different printers and printer interfaces, in several different sizes.

Strengths

While Beagle Bros has done a wonderful job of creating a graphing program that is simple yet extensive, the real power of *TimeOut Graph* is in its interactive capabilities. Because *Graph* is quickly accessible from an *AppleWorks* spreadsheet, it allows students an opportunity to make simple changes and view their effects. For example, when studying the effects of average litter size on rabbit populations students can manipulate several variables on the spreadsheet, view the graph, and watch the effect of each variable. Spreadsheet simulations can be created in a wide range of subjects including ecology, genetics, economics, political science, and more.

Students can use *TimeOut Graph* efficiently without extensive instruction. *Graph* instructions are simple, and teachers can set up and save the spreadsheet and graphing formats prior to student use, thus allowing students to concentrate on the concepts presented rather than the operation of the computer.

Weaknesses

Again, I was not able to load the *Graph* application into my IIe's memory. Therefore, every time I moved from a spreadsheet to a graph or from a graph to a spreadsheet the program had to access a disk. This process took several seconds, and to young users it could be somewhat frustrating. Using extended memory would eliminate this problem and speed up the entire graphing task.

Using *TimeOut* Applications with *AppleWorks*

TimeOut must be installed on an *AppleWorks* Startup disk before you can use it. Once *AppleWorks* has been prepared in this way, the *TimeOut* applications must be copied to a data disk. One disk will hold all of the applications, but extra disks may be necessary for dictionaries or additional fonts. If you are using 3.5-inch disks, Beagle Bros suggests putting all of the applications on the *AppleWorks* Startup disk.

Utilities that allow you to customize each application are included with *TimeOut* packages. For example, with the *TimeOut Graph* utilities you can configure your printer and printer interface, set the symbols and patterns used in graphs, request a box around a graph, and select fonts for graph titles. Beagle Bros has even included a data converter application, which allows you to quickly and easily transfer data between spreadsheet and database files.

The utility options also allow you to load applications into memory or dump applications from memory. If you have expanded the memory of your Apple (beyond 128K) then the *TimeOut* applications can be loaded directly into memory, enabling them to be used much faster.

Recommendation

Beagle Bros has done an excellent job with the *TimeOut* series. *QuickSpell* and *Graph* are two vital functions to *AppleWorks*. Students can now easily spell check their word processed documents without leaving *AppleWorks* and can take advantage of advanced spreadsheet applications with graphing capabilities. I strongly recommend these applications to any avid *AppleWorks* user. Here's a quick rundown of the other *TimeOut* programs:

TimeOut SuperFonts

SuperFonts produces Macintosh-quality fonts within *AppleWorks* word processed files. Fonts range from very small (6 point) to very large (127 point) and include special and foreign characters. *SuperFonts* allows you to print in a high quality mode or 50% reduction mode, and to easily insert graphics and pictures into your text. A number of styles (i.e., bold, italic, underline, shadow, outline, subscript, superscript, and inverse) can be used with any font. And a special page preview allows you to see exactly how the page will be printed. *SuperFonts* can be used with a large number of printers and printer interfaces.

TimeOut UltraMacros

UltraMacros can memorize any sequence of *AppleWorks* keystrokes and execute them at the touch of a key. It also adds mouse control to *AppleWorks* and other *TimeOut* applications. *UltraMacros* offers full IF-THEN-ELSE logic with string and numeric variables. A screen-saver feature blanks the next screen if a key hasn't been pressed for a while.

TimeOut SideSpread

SideSpread prints spreadsheets sideways from within *AppleWorks*. *SideSpread* sets no limit on the width of the spreadsheet, and it allows you to print all or part of a spreadsheet. A variety of fonts is available and high quality or 50% print mode is possible.

TimeOut DeskTools

Using *DeskTools* you can quickly access a calendar, calculator, notepad, dialer, envelope addresser, clock, clipboard converter, file encrypter, case converter, page previewer, word counter, and puzzle from any place inside *AppleWorks*.

TimeOut FileMaster

Now you can control your files or disks from inside *AppleWorks*. *FileMaster* allows you to copy, compare, and rename files or disks. You can also lock and unlock files, erase or format disks, display and print up 100 file names on the screen at one time, and quickly load and save any size RAM disks.

Publisher's Reply: None.

SOFTWARE REVIEWS   Edited by Linda Rathje

Ghost Writer

Ghost Writer
MECC, 3490 Lexington Avenue North, St. Paul, MN 55126;
612/481-3500
Author: Dr. Robert Bortnick
Grade/Target Age Group: Grade six through adult
Subject: Writing
Cost: $89; includes a program and back-up disk, and a 29-page Teacher's Manual.
Hardware Required: Apple IIc, IIe (64K RAM)
Reviewed by: Ruthie Blankenbaker, Director, Computer Curriculum, Park Tudor School, Indianapolis, IN.

Introduction

As woodworkers know, the quality of a beautiful piece of furniture only shows after finishing. So, too, the draft in progress is a rough piece that calls for finishing touches. Add, delete, substitute, reorganize: These are the rubbings which give written words the quality of perfection. MECC's *Ghost Writer* is a utility program that can help writers give their compositions these touches. It is designed for the "finishing touch" stages—as an electronic editor used to help communicate ideas more clearly.

Program Description

Designed for sixth grade through adult writers, *Ghost Writer* analyzes writing from several of the more popular word processors: *MECC Writer, Apple Writer IIe, Bank Street Writer, Milliken's Writing Workshop, Magic Window II* and *PIE Writer*. Using *Ghost Writer*, composers can receive a grade level estimate of the reading level of their writing and graphs of their sentence lengths. They can examine the unity and coherence of paragraphs and check the meanings of words often confused. Writers can also receive a listing of each word written and the number of times it was used. A final option identifies all "to be" verbs, prepositions, nominalizations (verbs used as nouns), and subordinating and coordinating conjunctions. All analyses can be reviewed either on screen or in print.

More specifically, the "Readability Test" gives a Fry grade-level estimate of the composition's reading level. Wisely, there is a suggestion that the readability level should typically be within a year of the writer's present grade level. Without this warning, students might interpret a high-grade reading level to mean quality writing.

The "Sentence Length Analyzer" shows students graphs which compare their sentence lengths to national norms. A word count per sentence is given in the right-hand margin and stars are placed by those sentences too long for all age levels. Students can quickly identify possible run-on or overly long sentences, or sentences which could be improved by combining.

The "Paragraph Outliner" prints out the first and last sentences of each paragraph. Sentences in between are displayed as dashes with punctuation marks. Subordinating conjunctions and some transition words are printed as they actually appear. This part gives students the opportunity to check proper use of transitions—both within the paragraph and between the paragraphs.

The "Homonym Checker" is useful to those who have difficulty determining "which witch is which." The program scans the text, identifies words often confused, displays the phrases in which they are used, and gives the various meanings of the homonyms. Writers can then determine whether they have used the correct word.

For students ready to give their writing close inspection, the "Clarity Checker" is an excellent tool. This module produces a listing of each sentence, identifying "to be" verbs, prepositions, subordinating and coordinating conjunctions, and nominalizations. Students often write in the passive voice, and their words are imprecise from the overuse of prepositional phrases and "bureaucratic" from the use of nominalizations instead of stronger verb forms. For example, it is common to read a sentence like: "There was a great deal of care in the application of her makeup." By pointing out the preposition overuse and the nominalization, the student can revise with a more precise, less academic and stronger sentence: "She applied her makeup carefully."

The final tool is the "Vocabulary Analyzer," which gives a list of words used with the number of times each appears. This module determines the percentage of the number of different words to the total number of words in a composition: The greater the variety, the higher the percentage. With this analysis students can easily spot overused words, and even those that are misspelled, vague, trite, imprecise, or nondescriptive.

After students have run all modules except the Paragraph Outliner and the Homonym Checker, a "Summary Report" recaps the evaluative information obtained from the other four *Ghost Writer* analyses.

In the Classroom

Ghost Writer worked for my 10th grade remedial writing students. They liked this quiet authority which pointed out ways to strengthen their writing—before I talked to them about it. *Ghost Writer* nestled into my students' writing process like a secret they didn't want to share. Running *Ghost Writer* they sometimes smiled, sometimes frowned, but always scratched out, typed over, dug through the thesaurus, worked with a classmate . . . and revised. Then they would put their revisions through another analysis to test their progress, and usually revised some more.

Ghost Writer, however, is not a program to place in students' hands without proper guidance. Students must first be capable of stating clearly focused ideas. They need interwoven and ongoing instruction in sentence combining and in elements of style, and experience with sentence and paragraph development to know how to revise using subordinating and coordinating conjunctions and transitions. Students must also realize that computers can neither fix poorly communicated ideas, nor make words, phrases, or sentences more precise.

I had given my students such direction for most of the school year when *Ghost Writer* became available. I therefore felt they were ready, both mentally and mechanically, for true revision; and I was curious to know whether an electronic editor could help them with their revisions.

I found introducing this program step-by-step worked well. Knowing that writers can't learn to do everything at once, I introduced one component of *Ghost Writer* at a time. Gradually, I led small groups to other parts of it when I felt they had mastered a particular point. Other times I took them back to combinations of *Ghost Writer* to teach another revision concept. For example, I gave them a printout of a writing upon which I had run the Sentence Length and Vocabulary Analyzer programs. I drew their attention to overly long sentences and imprecise words, having the class revise them into shorter ones by using more concrete vocabulary. When such analysis is used in combination with the other analysis modules, valuable interpretations can be made. Within about six weeks, nearly all of my students were independent users of *Ghost Writer*, a program they depended on to help them put the hard-rubbed finish to their prized pieces.

Strengths

Ghost Writer is a quick, uncluttered and valuable guide for revision. I like this program most, though, because it gives my students useful feedback. They often review their printouts much as they would view X-rays of broken bones: "So *that's* what's wrong. "Students gain a visible sense of the importance of sentence structure and word choice, and receive unbiased feedback about their writing. Used during the revision step in the writing process, *Ghost Writer* helps students make decisions about additions, deletions, substitutions, and reorganization. These are the heart of revision once ideas are well formed.

While *Ghost Writer* helps, there are ample warnings and suggestions that it *only* helps: "WARNING: You are the writer. *Ghost Writer* may make helpful suggestions. However, make a change only if you believe it communicates your ideas more clearly.... People, not computers, determine effective communication. "

I liked the options to output either to screen or to printer. For a particular point of revision (e.g., readability level), my students would have the *Ghost Writer* analyses output to the screen. For more thoughtful revision, they liked the hard copy.

Limitations

It's picky, but I must say the lack of cursor and/or response prompts on the start-up screens bothered my students and me. We are "technology trained" to see something blinking. Without this we felt lost. Another "mechanical" shortcoming is the fact that *Ghost Writer* does not work with ProDOS-based word processors. To run the analyses on a ProDOS file such as *AppleWorks* it must first be converted to ASCII. For writing classes, this conversion process is very time consuming.

And then there are the matters of interpretation. What exactly is a "Maturity Index"? The program determines this number from the ratio of the number of subordinating conjunctions to the total number of conjunctions used. I explained that greater use of subordinating conjunctions increased writing maturity levels. Later I noticed some students struggling unnecessarily to increase this level, with their writing becoming stilted. I had to remind them that they, not the computer, were the final authority. Others chose to think that a "Writing Maturity: 35" message meant they wrote like 35-year-olds, which caused hearty laughs.

Recommendation

For those who understand writing as a process, *Ghost Writer* is a valuable guide for the revision stage. Revision is the time when ideas are clarified for more effective communication to the reader. Words, sentences, and paragraphs are added, deleted, or changed.

With *Ghost Writer* students enjoy the challenge and experience the value of revision often difficult to achieve in a classroom. Instructors can concentrate on the higher-level aspects: audience, aim, purpose, and focus.

Before technology, fine tuning was labor intensive and time consuming. Close attention to both conceptual and mechanical details happened in only "hard-core" writing classes. But now computers count, identify, and analyze words. They can remove the drudgery and lend sophistication to writers—both novice and professional.

I like *Ghost Writer* because I can work with students to clarify their purpose, audience and focus. My students like *Ghost Writer* because it helps them better compose the ideas they are communicating. It is a quick, uncluttered, electronic editor we have come to depend upon for the finishing rub of revision.

Many writing teachers now accept the conventional wisdom of teaching "process, not product." And several recognize the value of word processing to aid this process. If you are one of these teachers, you would do well to take one more step, adding a valuable new dimension to writing instruction with MECC's *Ghost Writer*.

Publisher's Reply

Available November 1986, *Ghost Writer* will be enhanced to include a ProDOS version compatible with *AppleWorks* and several other ProDOS-based word processing programs. 128K memory will be required.

Pat Kallio
Public Relations Coordinator

SOFTWARE REVIEWS

Edited by Linda Rathje

Writer's Helper

Writer's Helper
Conduit, The University of Iowa, Oakdale Campus, Iowa City, IA 52242
Grade/Target Age Group: Grade 8 through college
Subject: Writing
Cost: $120 for one original and one backup copy of the Program Disk, plus one unprotected Work Disk; $240 for an Educator's pack containing four additional copies of the Program Disk.
Hardware Required: Apple IIc or Apple IIe, with 80-column card, 64K RAM; single disk drive; monitor. Printer recommended.
Reviewed by: Larry Lewin, Language Teacher on Special Assignment, School District 4J, Eugene, Oregon

Writer's Helper is not a word processor: It is a series of 22 mini-programs that help student writers *plan* what to write and begin to *revise* what they have written. As any composition teacher knows, these are two major obstacles for young authors. *Writer's Helper* begins with recognizing student problems and then proceeds to help overcome them.

Writer's Helper will work well for secondary and college teachers who apply the process approach, a four-step sequence of instruction that moves students from prewriting to drafting, editing, and finally publishing. While this method is widely popular at all grade levels, teachers who use it know the demands it makes on teaching time. Because each of the mini-programs in *Writer's Helper* can be learned in a few sittings, students can use it for individual instruction during prewriting and drafting, the two stages most neglected by current software.

Prewriting Activities

The first prewriting section includes mini-programs designed to help students consider alternative topics, purposes, audiences, and formats. Students can select any or all of these prewriting activities in any order.

One activity in this section is "Brainstorms," which allows students to freewrite three to 10 lines without the ability to delete. After assessing original typing speed, the program marks pauses in the flow with "...." until the writer continues. I liked how this encouraged my thoughts to continue flowing. After three to 10 lines have been written, the student can save them to his/her Work Disk, print them, or transfer them to a word processor for further work.

Another activity, "Lists," allows the student to type up to 10 possible writing topics in a few words or short phrases. "Lists" is included to prevent premature closure on the prewriting stage: Listing 10 potential topics increases the chance of discovering one that will be worth pursuing. This activity could be accomplished with pencil and paper, but most students prefer using computers.

A third prewriting mini-program in this section, "The Questioner," lists 20 questions, one of which may help the young writer find an interesting topic, such as, "Why do some people believe in astrology?" or "What is it parents should know more about?" These may trigger excitement for some students, but I found them to be uninspiring.

All three of these writing exercises had been used successfully for years before computers were available in the classroom. But *Writer's Helper* improves on them by merging them with a word processor. The *Bank Street Writer* or any other word processor that uses standard DOS 3.3 Applesoft text files can be used with *Writer's Helper* to expand work from these prewriting activities. This is a major strength of *Writer's Helper*.

In "Explore a Subject," another prewriting section, "Crazy Contrasts" compares a topic choice to something completely different in order to spur creative thought. For example, after I chose "Portugal" as my topic from an earlier "List," this mini-program asked how Portugal was like "an old shoe," "an iceberg," and "Donald Duck." I didn't get too far with these comparisons, but I need to work on my creativity.

A second way a student can explore a subject is by answering up to 20 questions designed by the teacher to stress key points about a subject. Teachers will appreciate the opportunity to tailor the software to their own writing assignments.

Third, exploration of a subject can be accomplished by selecting "Three Ways of Seeing." The student types in the name

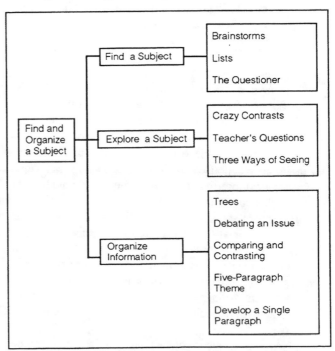

Chart of Programs in Find and Organize a Subject

of a subject, selects the appropriate label of "person, place, thing, event, idea, or activity," and answers 12 to 15 questions that look at the subject: 1) in isolation; 2) as a process of change; and 3) in relation to other subjects. I was stretched in my thinking about my topic as I answered the questions. While some answers were uninteresting to me, many served to make me look at my topic in new ways, which is a key goal of prewriting.

Writer's Helper can also be used to assist students with organizing their information after they have selected a topic and collected information about it. Five mini-programs which incorporate successful writing techniques are included:

- "Trees," an outlining procedure that helps the student categorize pieces of information about a subject;
- "Debating an Issue," which asks for both pro and con sentences about a subject;
- "Comparing and Contrasting," which asks for similarities and differences between the selected topic and a related topic;
- "Five-Paragraph Theme," which asks questions about a subject and reformats the sentence-answers into a rough draft; and
- "Single PSaragraph," which guides the student in developing either a descriptive or argumentative paragraph.

All these instructional methods have been used in writing classes, but *Writer's Helper* enhances them by adding the power of computer memory. For example, grouping information on a topic is accomplished neatly on the screen after the student enters the group names and lists the bits of information by number beneath them. This could be done on a worksheet, of course, but the computer does it much more quickly and neatly. Likewise, structuring information about a topic into a standard five-paragraph theme can be done by students, but how nice to have the computer do it for them.

Rewriting

Writing teachers agree that computers are most effective as tools for rewriting. They greatly aid revision by quickly and neatly inserting, deleting and moving text. Of course, word processors are dumb: They can't tell the author when and why changes should be made. But *Writer's Helper* provides students with initial reactions to their writing so they can begin to consider what inserting, deleting or moving should be done. It cannot tell students whether their writing is good or bad—that job is left for the much smarter teacher—but it can help them think about their writing in an organized way and help them find errors before the teacher does.

After students have written their first drafts on a word processor, *Writer's Helper* offers 11 mini-programs to help evaluate their writing (see Figure 1). The first menu choice in this section, "Paragraph and Sentence Analysis," will:

- List the first sentence of each paragraph for examination of transition words;

- Graph the number of words per paragraph for length variety consideration;
- List each sentence to show it in isolation from its neighbors for easier error detection;
- Determine readability level using the Fogg Index to compare it to the author's designated audience level; and
- Graph the number of words per sentence for length comparison (see Figure 2).

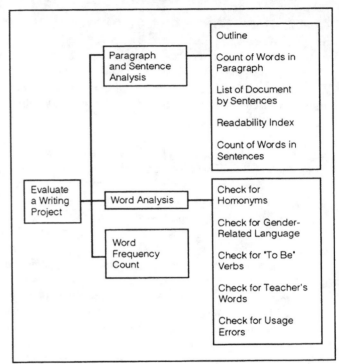

Figure 1.

Sentece Graph

Sentence	1:	***********12
Sentence	2:	***************************28
Sentence	3:	**********11
Sentence	4:	*************14
Sentence	5:	********************22
•		
•		
•		
•		
Sentence	47:	*******************21
Sentence	48:	*********************23

Figure 2.

This section is especially useful because it quickly and effortlessly provides the writer with data that indicates a possible need for more sentence variety, removal of run-on sentences, or elimination of sentence fragments. This reminds me of the "Sentence Opening Sheet" used in the *Stack the Deck* writing textbook series; the difference is that the computer does the counting for the students, which makes it more likely they will get the data they need to improve their writing. I am impressed.

The second choice from the "Evaluate a Writing Project" menu is "Word Analysis." Five mini-program word checkers are included: 33 homonyms, 25 gender-biased words, 59 usage confusions (e.g., farther/further, accept/except), and "to be" verbs (to check for passive construction). Though the teacher cannot add words to these four checkers, all the important ones are included. The fifth checker does allow teacher input: words the teacher wants to reduce (over-worked, trite words) or increase (specific vocabulary). *Writer's Helper* highlights a suspect word from any of the five checkers, lists the possible corrections, and marks it, if instructed, for later search and replacement in a word processor. The program does not include a spelling checker, however.

For paragraph analysis, the addition of an extra mini-program allowing the teacher input would improve *Writer's Helper*. Just as the teacher can create a list of topics or key vocabulary words for the student to consider in other mini-programs, the ability to do the same with paragraph characteristics would be helpful.

The last menu choice is "Word Frequency Count," which lists all the words in a piece of writing alphabetically, along with their number of occurrences. Because some words are inevitably popular (the, and, a), the student may exclude up to 20 words from the count, speeding up the computer's counting time. This word counter is a helpful self-evaluator: redundant words are exposed for the student before the teacher has to mark them in red ink; weak or boring words surface out of the camouflage of the sentence context; and even spelling or typographical errors are readily seen. This mini-program helps students edit their own papers independently.

Recommendation

Now that computers are increasingly available in the schools, teachers have been looking for ways to use them to assist with instruction. *Writer's Helper* is a welcome addition to writing instruction because it puts the new technology to good use: It helps students get started by guiding them through many pos-sible subject choices in ways the teacher would, and later helps them improve by providing feedback for possible revision in ways the teacher cannot.

I am impressed with this program's awareness of the process approach to writing: It offers 11 prewriting and drafting mini-programs that use the computer effectively instead of simply offering electronic worksheets. It also has 11 mini-programs that help teach how to edit for improvement. Because the program disk is resident, having four additional disks with the Educator Pack would be useful in a lab setting to increase its independent use.

The documentation presents in a clear, readable format the reasons for each section (with source material quoted), simple student procedures, and extended activities for the teacher to consider. The author also included ways to connect the programs to the study of literature, as well as specific suggestions for using the programs with writing assignments. Finally, the author wisely included a section in the manual on how to introduce a word processor to your class. He understands the writing process and has thought it through completely while designing the *Writer's Helper*.

When computer software can make the job of teaching kids how to write any easier, I will buy it. *Writer's Helper* will help the teacher of high school and college students in the areas of composition instruction. When considering *Writer's Helper* for use with your students, check the readability of text on the screen. Good readers, even middle or junior high school students, can use some or all of the 22 mini-programs. It has a 30-day money-back guarantee, so check it out.

Publisher's Reply

In May, Conduit will release a combined Apple DOS 3.3/ ProDOS version of *Writer's Helper* and an IBM PC, XT and jr version. Registered users of the *Helper* can upgrade to Apple DOS 3.3/ProDOS by sending all of their program disks to Conduit by September 1, 1986. There will be no charge for the upgrade.

SOFTWARE REVIEWS Edited by Linda Rathje

Story Tree

Story Tree
Author: George Brackett, Scholastic, Inc., 906 Sylvan Avenue, P.O. Box 2010, Englewood Cliffs, NJ 07632
Target Age Group: Ages nine and up
Subject: Writing
Hardware Required: Apple IIc, Apple IIe, Apple 11 Plus (48K), or Apple 11 (with 64K or Applesoft in ROM); IBM PC, IBM PCjr (128K); Commodore 64. One disk drive, monitor or TV, printer optional.
Cost: Retail edition, $39.95, includes Master Disk, Story Disk and User's Handbook.
Teacher's edition, $59.95, includes 2 Master Disks, 2 Story Disks, User's Handbook and Teacher's Guide.
Reviewed by: Lynne Anderson-Inman, Ph.D., College of Education, University of Oregon, Eugene, OR

Everyone loves a good adventure story, especially when the reader plays a role in deciding how the adventure will unfold. George Brackett's *Story Tree* capitalizes on this interest and takes it one step further. What could be better than *reading* "choose-your-own-adventure" stories? Well, *writing* them, of course! *Story Tree* lets you and your students do just that.

Story Tree is an exceptionally well designed piece of software that facilitates both the writing and reading of "interactive" stories, i.e., stories in which the reader makes choices determining the direction of events. Although an obvious application for a writing tool of this nature is in the creation of adventure stories, *Story Tree* lends itself to the development of other interactive genres as well. Provided as samples on the Story Disk are a somewhat silly jungle adventure in search of the magical Marigold Mine, a well researched and interesting article on the creature known as Bigfoot, and a mini database of extremely brief book reviews organized by topic. Each uses the program's capabilities in a slightly different way and together they help to illustrate some of its applications.

The *Story Tree* program takes its name from the branching capabilities of the stories that can be created with it. When writing with *Story Tree,* the writer has three options for linking pages together:

a) A story can CONTINUE from one page to the next, as it would in any story;

b) The reader can be given a CHOICE from among two to four options, with each option leading to a different series of events or type of information; and

c) The story can be made to branch by CHANCE, leading in one direction some of the time and in another for the remainder.

If used creatively and in combination, the resulting stories can be read and reread without being repeated in exactly the same sequence.

Designed for children as young as nine, *Story Tree* is a program that has been constructed with care. The main menu provides the user with four choices: (a) Read a story, (b) Work on a story, (c) Print a story and (d) Do disk work. Each choice leads to an appropriate submenu or a listing of the available stories, and ESCAPE always brings you back to the main menu. When reading a story, the user can elect to read it from the beginning or s/he can choose another place to start by browsing through the page menu. The latter is especially useful when rereading stories, as it allows curious readers immediate access to different events and alternate endings. It is also useful when editing stories, as the page-by-page access to different parts of a story helps the writer to locate pages needing clarification or story lines needing development.

When writing a story, the user is prompted through three operations for each page: (a) writing a page title (to allow access through the page menu); (b) writing text for the story; and (c) indicating how the page should be linked to successive pages, i.e., will it CONTINUE to another page automatically, branch by CHOICE or branch by CHANCE? After making a selection on the latter, the user is asked a sequence of questions which enables the program to create the appropriate connections between and among pages. For example, if branching by CHOICE, what choices are provided to the reader and to which page should each choice lead? Although the above may sound complicated, doing it is actually fairly simple, in large part because of the excellent prompts presented to the user on screen. For writers who haven't thought out all the details of a story (e.g., only one of three alternative choices has actually been conceptualized), temporary choice descriptions and page designations (letters or numbers, for example) can be used and then changed to something more descriptive when details have crystallized. As they are being created, all *Story Tree* stories are saved on a story disk, allowing for later reading or editing. Stories can be altered or expanded at any time, thus encouraging authors toward greater detail and increasingly complicated plots.

Story Tree stories can also be printed at any time. Two *Story Tree* pages are printed on an 8 1/2 x 11 piece of paper, and each section is marked with a page number. When cut and appropriately arranged, small books can be made from the printed pages. The capacity to print out stories is useful to students in at least two ways. First, it allows stories to be shared with family and friends. Second, having a printed copy enables the stories to be read and reread when the student is not near a computer, thus extending the educational value of the program and promoting the transfer of learned skills to noncomputerized settings. The reinforcing nature of the printed stories would be enhanced, however, if an optional large print mode were available. It is important for young students, as well as for older students with reading and writing problems, to see a big payoff for such a big investment of effort.

Suggestions for Use

In preparing this review I used *Story Tree* with two students (ages 9 and 14), and I talked with teachers who had used the program with small groups of students or entire classes. The following suggestions for using *Story Tree* represent a blending of ideas from these experiences and discussions.

1. Prior to introducing *Story Tree*, it seems best to ensure that students have had experience with "choose-your-own-adventure" stories. Teachers found that students who had had previous exposure to this type of story in book form approached *Story Tree* enthusiastically. Those who had not had this exposure were often unclear as to why a story should be read more than once, and were more confused about the structure of *Story Tree* stories, especially when writing them. If grouping students for work on *Story Tree*, take into consideration their experience with this type of writing. Students with little or no experience with "choose-your-own-adventure" stories should be grouped together, otherwise they tend to be overwhelmed by their more enthusiastic and confident peers and usually end up as passive participants in the creative process.

2. Collect, swap and exchange *Story Tree* stories created by students. One of the best ways to be introduced to *Story Tree* is for students to read sample stories, either in pairs or as a small group. Although sample stories are provided on the disk, they are not appropriate for all levels of students and are not written by children. The 14-year old I shared the program with felt the stories were too juvenile, and went on to create a complex James Bond-type spy story. The nine-year old felt Magic Marigold Mine was funny but complicated, and she couldn't identify with the report on Bigfoot at all. One of the best features of *Story Tree* is that it will support a wide variety of story types on an unlimited number of topics. Developing a library of stories for students to explore prior to writing their own will help to show off the program's possibilities and broaden its use.

3. Before writing *Story Tree* stories, it is especially helpful to teach students to map out or flowchart the sequence of events or information. This can be introduced using experiences from students' lives (to help convey the idea of choices and the impact of choices made on future events) and then by translating these experiences into the terminology used in the *Story Tree* program. The manual provides an excellent tutorial on how to write *Story Tree* stories and uses a mapping technique to illustrate the different types of page connec-

tions. Most teachers found this helpful in teaching students how to plan and keep track of their stories. (See Figure 1 for the map used in this tutorial.) In general, those students who took the time to map out their stories were able to finish them; those who did not often ended up in confusion.

4. Integrate the use of *Story Tree* with practice on word-processing skills. Built into the program is an excellent and easy-to-use word processor. It can be used to introduce students to the principles of word processing or as an alternate arena in which to apply already learned word-processing skills. Although most of the word-processing commands in *Story Tree* are fairly standard, teachers will need to pay special attention to those that differ from word-processing programs students are already using.

5. If using *Story Tree* in a classroom setting, provide students with a five-minute warning before the end of the period. There is no way a page that is being worked on can be saved before completion. This means that in order to save any text that has been written, the student must also designate the type of page connection and the destinations for each option before being able to stop. This requires some time—hence the need for a five-minute (or longer) warning.

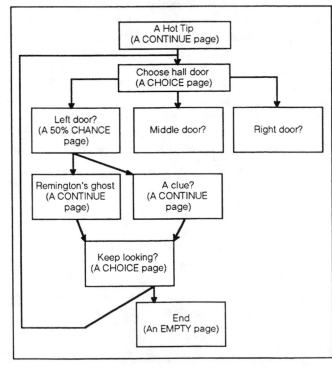

Figure 1. Mapping the sequence of events when writing Story Tree stories.

Other Applications

Story Tree is not limited to the language arts or English classroom. And even in these classrooms, the program is not limited to the development of stories. The Teacher's Manual which accompanies the educational version of *Story Tree* does an excellent job in suggesting other uses for the program and even includes guidelines for creating special types of "shells"—frameworks of pages linked together for specific purposes. A sampling of these other applications is enough to highlight the underlying potential of *Story Tree*

In the area of social studies, for example, groups of students could use the program to write an imaginary tour of another country or another era in time. Information could be organized around specific topics, as well as by location or date, allowing readers a different experience each time they took the "tour." In science, students might write a description of the circulatory system as seen from the "inside." Different branches of the descriptive report would address different branches of the system. A class poem could be generated using the random poetry shell, a framework that takes advantage of the branch by chance option. Each student writes a rhyming couplet on the same theme. When entered into the shell, the poem can be read and reread many different times with many different results. As a final example, the program can also be used to generate on-screen multiple-choice learning activities. Choosing the correct option leads to a "right answer" page and then on to another question. All incorrect choices lead to explanatory pages with individualized corrective feedback and then a return to the original question. It is suggested that students might develop these learning activities as well as play them. Although I was unable to find teachers who had implemented any of these ideas, or others from the manual, the ideas appear to be instructionally sound.

Making a Good Program Even Better

I've yet to see a software program that couldn't be improved upon in some way, and *Story Tree* is no exception. What is already a very good program can be made even better. The following suggestions for improvement come from teachers and students who have used the program extensively and therefore build on an in-depth appreciation for everything *Story Tree* already provides.

1. It would be helpful if *Story Tree* would automatically map or flowchart a story as it is being created. Younger writers, and those with special learning problems, often become "lost" in their stories, not being able to sort out which pages went with which story lines. Being able to consult a map of the story in progress would help to minimize this confusion and concentrate student energies on the writing process.

2. Students should have the option of seeing page titles on the printed version of their stories. As currently printed, page numbers are substituted for page titles. Since the pages are identified by title and not by number on screen, this substitution makes it extremely difficult to cross reference the printed version with the on-screen version. When editing, students often use the printed version to keep track of undeveloped story lines or to identify pages needing modi-

fication. Inclusion of page titles on printed stories would facilitate this aspect of the editing process.

3. It would be educationally helpful if *Story Tree* stories would allow use of the commonly available spelling checker programs. Teachers have become increasingly convinced of their value in promoting good spelling habits, and many teachers now encourage the use of such programs on all student writing. There is no logical reason why *Story Tree* stories should be an exception.

4. And finally, students should be directed to develop title pages for their stories. Although there is nothing to prevent the creation of title pages for *Story Tree* stories, there is no mention of title pages in the documentation and no examples provided on the disk. In the eyes of my nine-year old tester, "real" stories have title pages. Providing directions for their creation would be an easy and valuable addition to the program.

Overall Recommendation

In summary, I recommend Scholastic's *Story Tree* very highly! It is a well designed program that is educationally sound and fun for students to use. Furthermore, it is extremely versatile. It could find a comfortable home at many different grade levels, and teachers will discover interesting applications in a number of content areas. Because of its flexibility, it is appropriate for classrooms with a wide range in student ability and can be used quite successfully with special needs students. It is appropriate for students to use independently, but equally effective if used with students in pairs or in small groups.

Of equal importance to teachers should be the fact that students like *Story Tree* and once the basics are learned will often spend their own time embellishing stories begun in class. This seems to be true even for populations of students traditionally turned off to writing. One of the teachers interviewed for this review related that he had several ninth grade boys come into his computer lab daily, on their own time, in order to write with *Story Tree*. These boys taught themselves the program and then spent approximately an hour a day, five days a week, for six to eight weeks writing and rewriting their stories. Any writing software that elicits that kind of commitment deserves to be looked at seriously!

Acknowledgment

The reviewer would like to thank the teachers of Eugene School District 4J who shared their students and their experiences using *Story Tree*. Special thanks go to Tom Layton, computer teacher at South Eugene High School, who graciously shared ideas arising from his use of *Story Tree* with students who have special learning needs and also provided many of the suggestions for improving the program.

Publisher's Reply: None.

COMPUTERS AND THE LANGUAGE ARTS   Edited by Robert Shostak

Creating Software for Classroom Specific Needs
by Diane Siverstein

How often have you wished you could have a particular piece of computer courseware to enhance a specific lesson or help instruct a particularly difficult concept? But you either had no money to buy the product you wanted or the product itself had not yet been developed which could meet your specific needs. Then someone suggested that you write the program yourself using an authoring language (because a programmer you are not). What a great idea you thought—until you found out that learning the authoring language would be almost as difficult and time-consuming as learning a programming language. Well, maybe you ought to try the Electric Poet. *Although it lacks the branching capabilities of the more sophisticated systems on the market I found is far easier to use and versatile enough to produce effective teaching materials for specific classroom lessons. As a matter of fact children in the intermediate grades can learn to use the system very quickly. In the article which follows Diane Silverstein describes how simple it is to use the program and includes a brief example of one of its many applications.*

Speech-language pathologist Barbara Newman of Ft. Lauderdale, Florida, needs a special piece of software. She explains, "My students practice pronouncing particular sounds by reading long lists of typewritten words. It is a tiresome, repetitive, but essential, task. I could stimulate their interest by using color and animation on a personal computer to highlight the sounds they are practicing."

Judy Lessne, a reading teacher at Meadowbrook Elementary School, asked me, "Do you know if there is a program that teaches the hour and minute hands on a clock? Now that digital clocks are so prevalent, my students need more explanation than ever before. I haven't been able to find a clock program anywhere that does an adequate job." These teachers have special needs which are not being satisfied by available software. But there is an easy solution to their problem. They can design their own teaching materials, and you can, too, with *Electric Poet*, an authoring system currently distributed by IBM. *Electric Poet* meets your needs because it is content oriented. The system allows you to provide your own content in a simple programming environment. *Electric Poet* gives you the opportunity to produce professional quality teaching materials without being a computer whiz. Since the program does the technical work, you do not have to learn programming to create exciting and colorful presentations of your subject matter.

The program was named *Electric Poet* because it emphasizes the meaning of words by coloring and animating text. You don't need to be a professional artist to design interesting graphics because *Electric Poet* uses text graphics, which are quicker and easier for amateurs to master. You don't get

sidetracked into complicated graphics programming, but you can support and enhance your words with colorful animated drawings. If you like to stretch your imagination, you can think of yourself as a cartoonist who concentrates more on content and less on artistic detail. And, naturally, a teacher's main focus is the subject matter at hand. To give your information more visual appeal, you change the color of your borders and put blocks of color around your text instantly. And if you really want to capture your students' attention, you can animate your words by moving letters around the screen. You can further jazz up your animation by playing appropriate sounds and music. It's Pac Man with meaning!

Before you jump to the conclusion that all this razzle dazzle requires math know-how or a high level of programming skill, relax. *Electric Poet* is a beginner's program, simple enough for a teacher who has never used a computer to learn without any special training. To accomplish this, you have to understand only eight master commands. They give you complete control over the color and time of appearance of your lesson on the screen. The *Electric Poet* command system walks you through the commands you need to issue, and each is issued with a single keystroke, highlighted in color for your easy selection. Speaking of coloring your words and graphics—when you want to select a color you don't have to guess how it will look, because a color pad diagram appears in the lower left corner of the screen. Colors are numbered to correspond to the function keys, so they are also selected with a single keystroke. After you choose a color, the color pad disappears from the screen.

Animation is just as quick. You put time delays between the appearance of your letters, words, sentences or paragraphs by designating in seconds and tenths of a second how long it will be before the next change occurs on the screen. Then *Electric Poet* automatically times and animates your text.

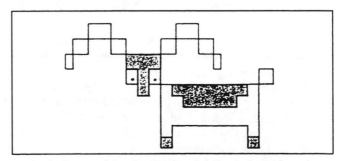

And what would an instructional program be without interaction? *Electric Poet* lets your students provide simple input. You can ask students to type a response (such as their name) and then automatically use the response in your lesson, or you can instruct the program to ask a question and check each input for accuracy. Sometimes you want to give a student more than one chance to type the correct answer; you can give students up to nine tries to match the correct answer before the programmed lesson continues. You can even stop the program when students' incorrect answers indicate they are not ready to continue. To check students' progress, instruct them to press the "Print The Screen" key to make a copy of the screen on which their answers appear, or to save the entire lesson on a data disk. While you survey your students' individual responses, you can examine their test results to evaluate the strengths and weaknesses of your own teaching materials. And as your students and classes change, you may want to update your programs with *Electric Poet's* easy one-step-at-a-time editor (which, again, is operated with single keystrokes). You can delete, insert, or change any command. The editor works like a tape recorder with fast forward, rewind and play functions, allowing you to review your programs at faster or slower speeds than the viewing speed you set for your students. You can make a single change in an instant or really spend time creating a master lesson.

Here is a good example of how lo use *Electric Poet* to help you leach a lesson in poetry. The lesson's objective is to enable students to see the effect of rhyme scheme in a poem, a difficult concept for many students to grasp. Although they see the words on the printed page and hear the sounds as a poem is read, these two stimuli are not always connected to produce meaning. With the help of *Electric Poet* you can display the rhyme scheme in matching colors that visually call out the matching rhymes. This way, students can both hear and visually distinguish, with ease, the rhymes in a poem. Once you have accomplished this part of the lesson, you may go on to explore how the rhyme scheme and rhythm contribute to the total meaning of the poem.

Let's use a poem by Alfred Lord Tennyson called "The Eagle" to demonstrate how easy it is to prepare your own lesson material using *Electric Poet*. Once you understand how to display this poem, you can choose any poem and follow the format in this example. You can also use color to show other elements of poetry such as meter, will give you the step-by-step commands to issue lo *Electric Poet*.

1. Place the program in your disk drive and turn on your computer.
2. When the Master Selector Page appears, select the Screen Clear command. This will automatically erase the screen where you will type your lesson .
3. Next select the Delay Pace command. We want a pause after each line of the poem appears on the screen to give the student ample time to read it. Select 3.0 seconds, and it will be automatically inserted each time you move the cursor to the next line on the screen.
4. Now you are ready to type the poem. Select the Type Text command. A clear screen appears with a flashing cursor. If it is not already there, move the cursor to the upper left corner of the screen.

5. Select the color green by pressing F10, F3, and the Enter key.
6. Type this poem:

The Eagle
He clasps the crag with crooked hands;
Close to the sun in lonely lands
Ringed with the azure world he stands.

The wrinkled sea beneath him crawls;
He watches from the mountain walls,
And like a thunderbolt he falls.

7. You will notice that the lines in the first stanza rhyme. To show the rhyme, select the color orange by pressing F10, Fl and the Enter key. Move the cursor over the "a" in "hands" and type "ands." Now move the cursor over the "a" in "lands" and type "ands." Finally, move the cursor over the "a" in "stands" and type "ands." These three words now stand out in orange.
8. The second stanza follows the same form; the last words in each line rhyme with each other. To show this rhyme, select the color green by pressing F10, F7 and the Enter key. Now move the cursor over the "a" in "crawls" and type "awls." Repeat the process by moving the cursor over the "a" in "walls" and typing "alls," then move the cursor over the "a" in "falls" and type "alls." These three words stand out in green, in contrast to the orange ones in the first stanza and the black (on the printout) of the rest of the poem. The AAA BBB rhyme scheme is now completely visible to the student, a graphic illustration traced on the brain to match the auditory impression of the words' sounds. What you have done is to follow the first rule in good teaching: Show, don't tell.
9. Move the cursor to the top of the page. Select the color cyan (light blue) by pressing F10, F6 and the Enter key, and type "RHYME."
10. Press the Enter key, and when the Master Selector page reappears, select Delay Once. We want the poem to remain on the screen for five seconds, so select 5.0.
11. To save the screen you have typed, select Halt Save and type the name "Rhymes" followed by the Enter key.
12. Now, to view your lesson, select Review Recite, sit back, and watch the lesson material you created appear on the computer monitor.

This is just the beginning. You can use *Electric Poet* as a simple word processor to write and illustrate stories, create grammar lessons, and produce an endless variety of lesson material to be used on and off the computer. The opportunities are as vast as the capacity of your imagination.

Diane Silverstein, 3347 Oak Drive, Hollywood, FL 33021.

Computer Use in the IBM "Writing to Read" Project

by Brian Cleary

We teachers are a persistent lot—forever trying to discover new ways to teach more, faster. John Henry Martin is one example. He has devised an ingenious plan, "Writing to Read," to teach reading through writing.

Martin, now a retired educator, was frustrated at standing by helplessly while children painfully groped with the inconsistencies and complexities of the English language. A five-year-old has a repertoire of 2,000 to 4,000 words in his vocabulary. As you well know, this same five-year-old has the ability to express very complex ideas orally. The challenge for Martin was to *use* this knowledge that beginning readers possess.

A phonemic alphabet is introduced to young children. Using this alphabet, children are taught to write anything that they can say. While Martin is the first to admit that this is not a new concept, he has implemented the project using the latest technology. He started in 1977 by introducing Selectric typewriters into the curriculum. Since 1981 the personal computer has taken over a big role in the "Writing to Read" program.

The IBM Personal Computer that is currently being used is equipped with voice output and color graphics. The PC plays an integral part in the program. The ten primary computer cycles consist of three key words each. Other words are formed by using the basic sounds of the key words.

The computer program relies heavily on repetition. The computer says the word and asks the student to repeat it. The computer then instructs the child to spell the word out loud. Finally, the computer asks the student to type the word on the keyboard.

With consistent use of the phonemic spelling system, children can write anything that is contained in their rich vocabulary. Martin contends: "As children develop their writing proficiency, they will discover and become able to cope with the [spelling] inconsistencies …and adjust their phonemic writing to textbook spelling."

I recently visited a number of schools where this program is being piloted. My first impression was one of awe. The language-rich environment approached idyllic. One corner of the room housed four IBM PCs. Next to them stood a row of Selectrics. The other side of the room had various activities that involved all the senses of these young children. There was a table where students were busily writing in their "work journals," although these journals looked conspicuously like basal workbooks. Another part of the lab housed a collection of children's classics on cassette tape. Children followed along in the book as the story was read to them. The bulletin boards were covered with typewritten stories. I was convinced on first sight that these children were making great gains in the vicious world of percentile ratings.

I was impressed by everything except the capacity in which the computers were being used in this setting. Upon closer examination of the software, I found many inconsistencies. Why couldn't I understand the word that was coming from the computer? Did I have a bad connection? After more examination I was convinced that the voice output was of poor quality. It just didn't sound right.

One particular lesson I listened to was introducing the phoneme "w." The voice asked the student to repeat each sound of the word in isolation. *W-a-g-o-n*. The "o" sound was a distinct short "o" sound such as you might hear in the word "hot." The problem arose later when the computer pronounced the word "wagon." The "o" in wagon does not have the short "o" sound when it is surrounded by "g" and "n." It is in fact controlled by them. I see inconsistent messages being sent to the student—the same inconsistencies that John Henry Martin is trying so hard to avoid.

The program did keep track of student miscues. After a predetermined number of mistakes, the program looped the user back to the beginning of the program. It didn't branch to an alternative review of the missed words. The program unmercifully subjected the students to the same lesson again.

I like to think that one role of the computer is that of an aid to the teacher, possibly a tool that will free the teacher of mundane clerical duties. The personal computer can be utilized as a tracking device. Many computer programs will record missed items and keep a running total of the student's progress. In short, good educational courseware helps manage a classroom. This particular program did none of the above. A very unruly chart comes with the program. The teacher is instructed to track each student's daily progress on this form. I found it hard to believe that this paper work wasn't being recorded by the program.

The major point in question here is whether or not the computer is being used appropriately. Is its full potential being exploited in this program? I commend the attempt at trying to use voice output as an enhancement to this program, but the synthesized voice just isn't clear enough.

As educators it is imperative that we use computers to their maximum. We must demand that the software use the full capabilities of the computer. The education field will be held accountable by the public that literally is spending millions of dollars a year on hardware and software acquisitions. The public will, and rightly so, demand results for their investment.

I personally feel the "Writing to Read" program has great potential. I like the idea of children having early successes in their writings. I like the idea of a rich language arts environment. I also feel that computers can play a very important role in this program. I just hope that the software that supports the program can take advantage of the many unique capabilities of the computer.

Brian Cleary has taught at the primary level and is interested in computer applications for reading and writing. He is currently in the computer education program at the University of Oregon.

The Children's Writing and Publishing Center

The Children's Writing and Publisning Center
The Learning Company, 6493 Kaiser Dr., Fremont, CA 94555; 800/852-2255.
Subject: Writing, Desktop Publishing.
Grade/Age Levels: Age 9 and up.
Cost: School Edition (2 program disks) $79.95; Lab Edition (6 disks) $139.95.
Hardware Required: Apple IIe (128K), IIc, or IIGS (5.25" and 3.5" versions), dot matrix black/white or color printer. IBM/ Tandy and compatibles (384K) version available spring 1989.
Optional Hardware: Color monitor and mouse.
Reviewed by: Beverly Krieg and Mary Carucci, Modesto City Schools, Media Center. 426 Locust Street, Modesto, CA 95351; 209/576-4106.

How long has it been since you've been able to load a new piece of software into your computer, and without reading the documentation obtain a product with which you were pleased? *The Children's Writing and Publishing Center* is one of the friendliest pieces of software we have come across in a long time. This sophisticated writing tool is recommended for ages nine years and up. In addition, teachers use this introductory desktop publishing program for many of their own needs.

Program Description

We used Apple hardware with and without a mouse, with and without color monitors, and using 5.25" disks. The 5.25" version has a double-sided Program disk and a double-sided Picture disk. The 3.5" version has the Program and Picture files on one disk. Both education packages contain a Template disk that contains sample files and formats to accompany the teaching activities. The home edition contains only a sample letter.

The user begins by selecting one of two formats, Story or News, or by retrieving saved work. All selections can be made from icons or text in the main menu (see Figure 1). The Story (Report, Story, or Letter) format creates a single column of text and graphics up to four pages per file. The News (Newsletter) format creates a two-column, single page file (see Figure 2).

The screen layout is consistent. The top center of the screen designates your current location within the document. Under the title is the menu bar and icons/text for user choices. Keystrokes highlighted at the bottom of the screen keep the user apprised of which keys to press. The open apple-? provides Help from any user screen.

Headings—Once a format is selected, the user chooses whether or not to have a heading. The heading uses one quarter of the available writing area. Both graphics and text can be placed within the heading. There are eight fonts, two of them available only in upper case (see Figure 3). Text may be typed, edited, underlined, and justified left or center. The documentation advises the user to first place the pictures and then the text, but we found either could be adjusted at any time. Just one caution: If text in the heading overlays the graphic, that portion of the graphic will not print.

Graphics can be selected by name or number from the Picture disk, which contains 137 full-color pictures and 22 predesigned headings. The Picture disk art is divided into subject categories: Adventure, Animals, Going Places, Holidays, People, Sports, and Things. A picture is selected (see Figure 4) and then moved into position. It can be flipped into four different orientations. The picture can be moved or deleted while in the Picture menu.

Graphics can also be imported from a compatible DOS 3.3-formatted disk containing binary graphic files. A list of some compatible disks is provided in the back of the manual. It includes, among others, *PrintShop Graphics Library-Holiday Edition* and *PrintShop Companion* from Brøderbund; *Minipix* disks 1 & 2 from Beagle Brothers; and 23 disks from the *Graphics Library* of the Big Red Computer Club. Using those other graphics library disks was frustrating. However, we were successful with the *PrintShop Graphics Library disks* 1, 2, and 3, with a little work. We booted the *PrintShop* program (IIe version), loaded a picture in the graphic editor, and saved it to a formatted DOS 3.3 disk. This became a compatible graphic.

When finished with the heading, the option Next allows access to the Body. At this time it is appropriate to save the work in progress. Using the File option, disks may be formatted and files saved, listed, or deleted. From the Print option, you may print, change setup, and test the printer. The New User Messages guide you through the process, and can be suppressed. If you want to print before saving, the program prompts for a save.

Body—Creating the body of the document is done in the same manner as the heading. The same icons and options are available. Fonts may be changed at any letter or word. However, text typed in one font cannot be changed without deleting and retyping. Fonts used in the News format are half as high and wide as the same font in the Story format. Therefore, the same amount of text can be presented in the one-page News format as a four-page Story format. In contrast to the heading procedure, the manual suggests creation of text and then insertion of graphics. When graphics are inserted, text reformats, flowing around the picture. The cursor may be moved about the screen quickly for viewing or editing with open apple-Arrow key commands. Cut and Paste commands are included for editing.

The screen lets the user know when the bottom of the column or page has been reached and moves on if there is any space available in the four-page file. A handy feature is the open apple-V (View) command to see how the entire file is laying out (see Figure 5).

Both the school and lab editions have a comprehensive teacher's guide. It contains scope and sequence charts for curriculum integration, on-line and off-line activities, and blackline masters. The Ready Reference card is very useful.

Printing

Most people will be quite pleased when they look at the printer setup section. The program has drivers for 29 models of printers from Apple, Citizen, Epson, Okidata, Panasonic, and Star. Interface card selections number 44. The printing options include varying the number of copies, printing a border, printing the entire document in bold, stopping between pages for single-sheet feed, printing page numbers, and changing the beginning page number. The printed colors are strong and vibrant, even when using a slightly tired four-color ribbon. We especially like the mahogany/brown achieved by the color mixing available on the ImageWriter II.

Classroom Uses

Students can use *The Children's Writing and Publishing Center* to write book reports, publish school newsletters, produce reports in any subject area, and learn how to write. Teachers can use it for parent communication, to showcase student work, post assignments, and design bulletin board instructions. The program is highly appropriate for cooperative learning groups and is easy enough to use that individuals or small groups of students can work independently of teacher guidance.

For those wanting to get started quickly with minimal documentation, the manual provides a first-time user's sample letter to guide them through the program's basic features.

The Children's Writing and Publishing Center is extremely useful in the one-computer classroom. The program is easier to run with a double-drive system, but is quite manageable with one drive.

Kindergarten and first-grade teachers can use the program as a teaching aid because of the large clear text that is created, even on the Apple IIe.

Strengths

The Children's Writing and Publishing Center is not a full-blown publication program, but it has all the features many of us need to produce a report or newsletter—and for students to use without confusion. The program has marvelous on-screen prompts, and extremely useful Help screens. There is no hunting around for the proper disk to use when you are ready to add your picture or headings, as the dialog boxes tell you exactly on which side of which disk you will find your graphics.

The teacher's guide, on-line and off-line activities, and blackline masters are very well done. The manual really starts from scratch, telling the teacher what skills are needed before the student can use the program. *The Children's Writing and Publishing Center* is a writing tool. The documentation states

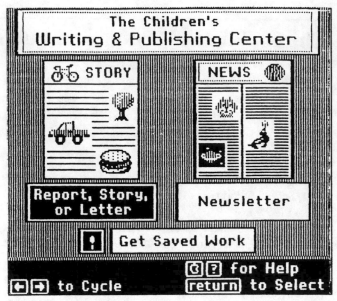

Figure 1. Main Menu

which computer skills, word processing skills, and writing skills are required, and which will be developed while using this program. Activities are suggested for all levels of users, including students with few keyboarding skills. The blackline masters enable electronically-shy students to become comfortable enough to create their own documents. The material is comprehensive, pleasantly displayed, and nonthreatening.

We found elementary students could more easily manage the disk handling of this program than any other desktop publisher we have used.

Weaknesses

The primary frustration with this program comes from trying to incorporate compatible graphics from other disks. Not only is reformatting necessary with some graphics libraries, but graphics from other disks only print in black, even when they appear in color on the screen. If you wish to print with color, we suggest you use the graphics supplied with *The Children's Writing and Publishing Center*.

Additionally, there are slight flaws in the WYSIWYG. Text or graphics near the bottom of a page may actually print on the next page. Graphics that appear at the top or bottom of a paragraph of text may print into adjoining paragraphs.

Recommendations

We love this program and give it an "A." *The Children's Writing and Publishing Center* program is easy enough for a third grader to use with success. It produces a product that a teacher can be proud to display. We feel this software will promote the use of computers as writing tools, and allow more individuals to become more creative.

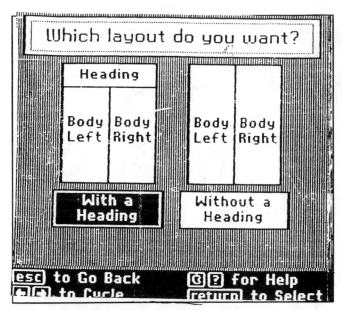

Figure 2. The News (Newsletter) Format

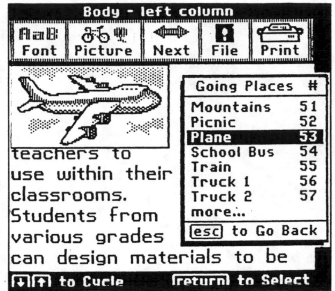

Figure 4. Graphics Selection

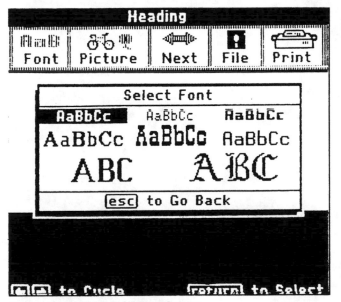

Figure 3. Heading and Font Selection

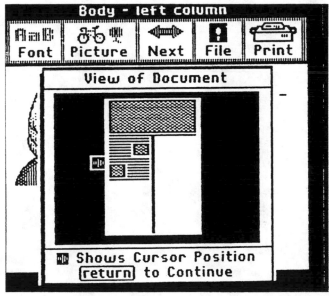

Figure 5. Open Apple-V (View) Command (Shows Layout)

Publisher's Reply

It is gratifying for us to see such a thorough and positive review of our newest product, *The Children's Writing & Publishing Center*. We spent many months testing this program with children, parents, and teachers to make it as enjoyable and easy to use as we possibly could, without letting the program grow too large for a 128k Apple IIe or IIc.

One point in the review we do want to clarify is how easy it is to use *Print Shop* compatible pictures. Any compatible picture disk that is not copy protected can be used as easily as the picture disk we supply with the program. A list of disks we have tested and know will work is provided in the Teacher's Guide of the School Edition. This list includes many inexpensive public domain titles. In addition, any single high resolution graphic image can be converted to a format usable by *The Children's Writing & Publishing Center* using the "capturing graphics" function of the Graphics Editor+ found on the *Print Shop Companion* program.

—The Learning Company

SOFTWARE REVIEWS

Type-Right Keyboard

Type-Right Keyboard
Video Technology Industries, Inc.
400 Anthony Trail, Northbrook, IL 60062; ph. 312/272-6760.
Grade/Target Age Group: Nine years old and older.
Subject: Keyboarding.
Cost: $29.50. Includes a 56-page course book.
Hardware Required: Four C batteries.
Reviewed by: Cathy Carney, Eighth Grade English Teacher, Ryan Middle School, Fairbanks, AK.

Writing and revising with a computer demand good keyboarding skills, especially if students have limited time on the computer. However, in order to first learn and then practice keyboarding skills, students need ongoing access to computers or typewriters on which to practice. Here in Fairbanks, Alaska, several of our elementary schools had to decide whether to commit their limited number of classroom computers for keyboarding instruction or to provide minimal keyboarding instruction in order to have computers available for activities such as word processing, problem solving, and database applications. One solution now being implemented is to provide instruction through the use of classroom sets of *Type-Right*s, inexpensive lap-top computers dedicated to teaching keyboarding.

Description

This single-purpose computer is a light (about two pounds) plastic box, the size of a detachable computer keyboard. The keyboard includes all the letters and numbers, space bar, return key, shift keys, caps lock, and a few common punctuation marks. The box also houses a microchip programmed with nine keyboard drill lessons and two typing games. As letters are typed they appear on an eight-character LCD screen above the keyboard. Next to the small screen are five buttons which select power on-off, bring up the menu of lesson choices, select a typing game to play, display the speed of the last selection typed for Lessons 6-9, and display the accuracy of the last selection typed for those same lessons.

A removable back panel encloses four C batteries (not included). There is no provision for an AC adaptor. The price for batteries must be added to the cost of each unit. Purchasing four rechargeable batteries and a unit to recharge them will double the price of each unit. Alternatively, standard alkaline batteries can be purchased at one-third of the cost. Whichever type of battery is used, the batteries will last a long time. A fully recharged set will serve the average classroom through several weeks of keyboarding practice, averaging a half hour per day for six weeks. The standard alkaline batteries last much longer than the rechargeable

ones but need to be replaced. We have not yet decided which system for powering the units is most cost-effective.

A 56-page course book comes with the unit. Its spiral binding and extra-rigid covers allows it to be placed upright, like an A-frame. An audio-cassette tape is also included, which repeats the introductory information—exactly as presented in the course book.

Results of Using *Type-Right*

This year we have used *Type-Right* to help teach keyboarding in three Grade 4 classrooms. In previous years, the involved teachers spread keyboarding instruction throughtout much of the year. That was the only way, given our limited number of computers and lab availability, to provide students with enough access to keyboards to learn and *practice* typing skills.

We were delighted with the results of using *Type-Right*. We are able to teach a whole classroom of students how to keyboard in six weeks and to use their limited computer time for word processing effectively for the rest of the year. Furthermore, each word processing session reinforced correct keyboarding habits rather than encourage the development of hunt-and-peck methods.

The children were enthusiastic about their experiences. They loved having their own computers, portable enough for them to carry around and use at their desks for group instruction, or to use for individual practice whenever they had spare time.

Valuable Features

The major advantage we found in using the *Type-Right* was obvious: Increased access to a real keyboard increased student success in learning to keyboard. Other advantages became apparent over several weeks.

- The units are small. Though the keyboard is full sized, so the transfer to using a full-function computer is easy, the complete unit is barely larger than the size of the keyboard itself. This permits students to independently pick them up, take them to their desks, use them, and return them. Their size also allows a classroom set to be stored unobtrusively in a crowded elementary classroom. A set fits into two medium-sized cardboard boxes which can be hidden under a table or in a corner.
- They are sturdy. Because two of our adjoining classrooms were both using them, fourth grade students took them out of their cardboard boxes twice a day, used them at their desks, piled them back into the boxes, and carried them to the classroom next door. No keys were broken, no screens were damaged.

- The original packaging—a heavy cardboard box and styrofoam—provides protection from even more jarring conditions. When shipping the keyboards from school to school within the district, we package them in these original containers. The boxes are easy to re-use and they provide excellent protection in the school mail.

- If some accident inadvertently turns on the power, the machine turns itself off again within a few minutes of nonuse, to save battery life.

- Several features directly support good practices for teaching typing. The keys are color-coded (dark gray keys alternating with light gray) to identify which are reached with a given finger. At the top of the front panel, near the LCD screen, are two buttons: *speed* and *accuracy*. After completing a section in Lessons 6 through 9, students can press one of these keys to learn how accurately or fast they typed. Once a student has learned all the keys, two simple games are available with the press of another key. With only an eight-character display the games are not very sophisticated, but they did induce our students to practice keyboarding skills at every opportunity.

... many aspects of Type-Right *provide barriers to effective keyboarding instruction.*

Problems

Despite these use features, many aspects of *Type-Right* provide barriers to effective keyboarding instruction.

Several physical aspects of the hardware frustrated our students. The feel of the keys is stiff, making it physically tiring for little fingers to press them for 20 or 30 minutes. Noting if the caps-lock key is on or off is difficult, as there is no light indicator and the position of the key does not change. The back panel holding the batteries has occasionally fallen off as the students were handling the machines, tumbling the batteries onto the floor and creating confusion in the class.

Because the screen is on the same surface as the keys, it is difficult for students to avoid looking at the keys when they are looking at the screen. This leads to the habit of watching their fingers rather than truly using *touch* typing. Also, the touch-typing aid of raised dots on the D and K keys is lacking.

The most difficult problems for us to overcome were caused by the built-in software. Several components of the program violate most accepted practices for effectively teaching keyboarding.

With other programs, keys are usually introduced in a logical sequence—either the common letters first so students can learn to type words at a very early stage, or starting with home row keys and then all the keys reached by a specific finger of the home row. In contrast, the first lesson of this software introduces all the keys in the middle row at one time, without any preliminary instruction or partial sets of letters. Neither the documentation nor the software pays attention to successful instructional models which drill students extensively on the home row keys *asdf jkl;* before introducing the other second-row keys.

The second lesson drills on all the letters of the third row. The third lesson drills on all the letters of the first row. These drill lessons are based on random letters from the targeted row appearing on the LCD screen and remaining there until the student correctly types that letter.

Typing words, including using the space bar and return key, is not done until Lesson 6, after all the letters have been introduced. In contrast, good typing teachers introduce real words much earlier in the instructional process.

When words are introduced, they are used in very lengthy selections, difficult for a beginner to complete in even 15 minutes. Furthermore, the text presented in the student typing books is written in print far too small for young typists. The lines are easy to confuse with one another, making it likely that children will lose their place as they look back and forth between the text and the screen.

The shift key is not introduced until after numbers have been taught in Lesson 4. Then Lesson 5 introduces the shift key *and* reviews the number keys. Few elementary teachers, interested only in preparing students for word-processing, want to spend the time needed to make sure students can type numbers as fluently as letters.

But perhaps the major software limitation is the fact that the program will not permit a typist to continue if the wrong letter is pressed. It will only beep until the correct letter is typed. Thus students who lose their place cannot continue practicing until they have found it—which proved impossible for many given the eight-character screen window. Instead, they needed to start again from the beginning of the lesson. This severely frustrated the nine-year olds. Since no speed or accuracy score can be obtained until a section is completed, children sometimes went days without being able to see a score. A less serious concern is the lack of any record-keeping system for tracking students' progress.

Fixing the Problems

As disappointed as we were with these problems, we were able to compensate for the major flaws.

Fixing the hardware was relatively easy. Providing raised dots on the D and K keys requires only a tube of glue or two circle-hole reinforcers. In fact, putting those circle reinforcers on all eight home row keys for a few days was a convenient way to introduce students to setting their fingers correctly on the keyboard.

Covering the keyboard—but not the screen—with a folded paper tent helped wean students from watching their fingers. Next time we will cover each individual key with masking tape or stick-on dots. Tired fingers were soothed by having students stretch their fingers and arms periodically—a good practice whenever teaching motor skills. The inability to determine the position of the caps lock became less of a problem as students learned to identify and fix the situation. Although the batteries continued to fall out of the back panel more often than we liked, they were easy to replace. Taping the backs solved this problem.

> *Schools without access to sufficient keyboards on which to teach typing may find* Type-Right *an inexpensive and effective solution.*

Fixing the software problems required more ingenuity. Our teachers chose a book designed to teach elementary computer keyboarding, *Computer Keyboarding, An Elementary Course* (1985) from South-Western Publishing, and dictated the lessons in the book to students. In general, they followed the book's sequence of introducing keys. Because the *Type Right* lessons will not permit any letters to be typed except those expected by the computer, the students set the computer on Lesson 9, which operates more like an open screen, in order to copy the teacher's dictation. The computer would beep occasionally when set on Lesson 9 and used this way, but this sound never proved a distraction.

When students had learned all the home row letters in this way and had used them in dictated sentences, only then did they drill on the home row using *Type-Right*'s first lesson. A similar pattern was followed for the other lessons.

Frequently, teachers altered the sequence of introducing keys used by the South-Western keyboarding book. This was necessary so the students could learn the keys they would need for the next drill section in the *Type-Right* units.

The recommendations given in the *Type-Right* documentation for the speed and accuracy that should be obtained before moving to the next lesson were unreasonably high, and we ignored them.

Because there is no built-in record keeping system, students copied their scores into their journals. Keeping this daily record and watching their scores improve motivated them to work hard.

Recommendations

I would not recommend these units to a school which has easy access to computers. Good typing software, far more sophisticated than the software built into this unit, is available.

Schools that can't find access to sufficient keyboards on which to teach typing may find *Type-Right* an inexpensive and effective solution. However, rather than depending on the software or documentation that comes with these units to carry the burden of instruction, teachers must borrow extensively from other materials to teach keyboarding effectively.

Conclusion

We believe the effort put forth by teachers in designing lessons to use with the *Type-Right* units, and the constant contact between teachers and students in direct instruction were the major factors in helping students successfully learn to keyboard.

As stand-alone units to give to students, expecting them to learn typing, *Type-Right*s are quite inadequate. But in the hands of a creative teacher they can be invaluable to a school that wants to teach keyboarding yet lacks sufficient keyboards. As always, the effectiveness of this software/hardware will be determined by the creativity and experience of the classroom teacher using it.

Postscript

As four different teachers used a classroom set of this equipment for six weeks each, we developed, tested, and constantly revised written materials to accompany them. In these materials strategies are outlined to minimize the software problems and take advantage of the *Type-Right*'s strengths. We now have a 40-page manual which includes a reproducible student-workbook and provides detailed day-by day instructions for a six week unit in fourth grade keyboarding using the *Type-Right* and the typing book mentioned in the review. However, materials could easily be modified to use any typing book. For a copy send $5 (to cover reproduction and shipping costs) to the above address. Indicate whether you want the material in print, on a Mac disk in Microsoft *Word* format, or on an Apple disk in an *AppleWorks* or test file.

Publisher's Reply: None.

SOFTWARE REVIEWS   Edited by Linda Rathje

Listen to Learn Version 1.01

Listen to Learn Version 1.01
IBM Corporation, P.O. Box 1328-W, Boca Raton, FL 33429-1328.
Authors: Rosegrant & Cooper.
Grades/Target Age: Grades K-6.
Subject: Talking word processor.
Cost: $195 (speech synthesizer not included).
Hardware Required: IBM PC/XT/AT/PC Convertible/PCjr/Model 30/Model 25/Personal System 2 with at least 128K of memory; one disk drive; IBM PC or PCjr Color Display or color TV with RF modulator; ECHO PC speech synthesizer and serial adapter or IBM Speech Adapter. Printer and earphones recommended.
Reviewed by: Judi Harris, Curry School of Education, University of Virginia, Charlottesville, VA.

"Words have weight, sound and appearance. It is only by considering these that you can write a sentence that is good to look at and good to listen to."
—*W. Somerset Maugham 1938*

An idea appears as a sentence on the computer's screen. Your fingers pause, your body reclines in the chair, and your eyes scan the verbal architecture of a newborn phrase. You check vocabulary, grammar, tone, voice and rhythm. Does this printed construction clearly represent the idea? It certainly looks like it does; but how does it sound? You read the sentence aloud. Perhaps that is all that is needed to guide the necessary revisions. If not, you seek an audience to listen to the words: your cat, your spouse, your tape recorder, your mirror.

Today there is yet another option. You can be the audience as your computer pronounces the phrase you have synthesized.

Talking word processors are now an affordable reality. *Listen to Learn* was designed by a teacher to address the special needs of young writers. (It is also marketed by Scholastic for the Apple II series as *Talking Text Writer*).

Author Theresa Rosegrant describes *Listen to Learn* as "a program that combines word processing with synthesized speech to help children learn how to write and read" (Rosegrant and Cooper, 1986). Users can hear their writing read by word, line, letter, or page at self-selected intervals as each word is typed or after an entire section is crafted. This helps children identify phonetic spelling errors, adjust word choice and sequence, build their vocabularies, and be an active audience for their own writing.

Program Description

Listen to Learn is a simple but elegant 40-column word processor. It has only two screens, and the most frequently used options are shown in the margins of each display. The directory screen appears when the program is booted. The titles of all files stored on the data disk are then listed, and the user selects an existing file to work on or creates a new one by adding another file name to the list.

The edit screen appears after the file is accessed. It is blissfully free of complicated option prompts, displaying only a status/error line, the file name and page number, the text area, and a menu line. All displayed program options are mnemonically logical. For example, to erase a line, the menu line prompts with an "Erase line" (Ctrl-E) key combination. Pressing the F2 key will cause the menu line to scroll, displaying additional selections. General on-line help is always available when the user presses the F1 key.

Listen to Learn can speak what is written on the screen in four ways. The word at the cursor can be pronounced, the sentence containing the cursor can be spoken, or the whole page of displayed text can be read aloud when the user presses one of three function keys (F4, F5, or F6). The program's Speech option can also be invoked so that the user hears his or her words pronounced each time the space bar is pressed.

Program Strengths

The program has two exemplary features. The first is that irregularly spelled words can have correct pronunciations entered and stored (e.g., through). This facility seems to have been written mainly for the teacher's use, but its operation would not discourage a student who enjoys playing with phonemes. Two different types of pronunciation codes can be used to improve speech: phonetics and phonemics. Using phonetics, the user can enter the word as it would be spelled phonetically. Phonemics, on the other hand, are 48 codes that can be entered when finely tuned pronunciation is desired. For example, phonemics include symbols for aspirated h's, double vowels, and hard g's. A user-defined dictionary is included in the program and can be accessed from just one file on the files disk, allowing classes to share word definition.

Listen to Learn is simple, but it is not limited in terms of the word processing needs of elementary-aged children. It has standard, well-explained word processor functions such as block copying, moving, deleting, double-spacing, and text justification. Disk management commands are limited to renaming, erasing, and copying files. Printing can be done from either screen, with an option to produce primary-style, large type.

The documentation that accompanies the program is clearly written, well organized, and manageable (approximately 80 pages long). It includes several pages of suggestions for program integration into language arts processes and addresses considerations for populations with special needs. These tips are written from a decidedly linguistic, language experience orientation, which is refreshing to see in computer support materials. The manual could be used by fourth, fifth, or sixth grade students, but it is slanted toward adult readers in its presentation. Overall, the emphasis of the written materials is upon the use of the program rather than its specifications. *Listen to Learn* is a methodologically realistic, powerful tool. Its simple operation and adaptability demonstrate the authors' careful attention to design detail as well as their child-centered philosophy. This is obviously the creation of experienced teachers who attend carefully to children's language development. This program could do much to further that growth in a most motivating way.

Program Limitations

Many of the inconvenient aspects of *Listen to Learn* seem to be due to hardware limitations. The function key options are difficult to commit to memory, and the documentation's Special Keys summary chart is incomplete and difficult to find. Teachers who plan to use this program with their students would be well advised to make and distribute their own options charts.

The speech synthesizer I used (the PC Convertible speech adapter) was difficult to hear under normal, less-than-silent classroom conditions. I recommend earphones for classroom use.

The program exit options proved confusing to some users. There are only two: E, which saves and exits to the directory screen; and S, which saves the file and stays at the editing screen. Most users expected the exit function to return them to DOS. There is no alphabetic option for that in this program—a Ctrl-F7 key combination is required. This makes it difficult to lose files, but also hard to use another program after quitting this one.

Several teachers who have used the program point out that synthesized speech, unlike digitized speech, is initially very difficult to understand. Yet, they add children become accustomed to the robotic voice rather quickly, and there is little age-related difference in this ability. Though only a few of the teachers I interviewed had worked with digitized speech (formed by recording a human voice as opposed to synthesizing the sounds electronically), those who did expressed a desire to use a digitized talking word processor. It should be noted, though, that digitized speech is far more expensive and initially more time-consuming to use on the microcomputer at this point in its technological development than synthesized speech.

The program's documentation would be even more successful if it included more than five pages of pedagogical suggestions. The authors obviously have a lot to say that could assist an educator in rethinking his or her way of helping children to explore language, but their philosophy is sketched in skeleton form only at the back of the manual, presented as if it were an afterthought. The excellent learner-based design of the program belies the implications of placement and length of instructional suggestions in the documentation.

Recommendations

The introduction of talking word processors is a milestone in instructional computing history. It ranks in potential learner empowerment with the advent of the touch-sensitive graphics tablet and the more recent data projection panel.

The capability of a learner to hear his or her written communication spoken as it is typed opens up new doors for student-centered, experiential, computerized language arts environments. Yet the most exciting peripheral devices can do little more than attract passing fancy without user-appropriate applications software. *Listen to Learn* takes full advantage of advances in technology without forgetting the needs of learners and facilitators. It would be a creative addition to any school software library.

Publisher's Reply: None.

SOFTWARE REVIEWS   Edited by Linda Rathje

Springboard Publisher Version 1.1

Springboard Publisher Version 1.1 (5.25" disks).
Version 2.00 now available.
Springboard Software, Inc., 7808 Creekridge Circle, Minneapolis, MN 55435, ph. 612/944-3915.
Subject: Integrated Desktop Publishing.
Cost: $139.95.
Hardware Required: Apple II with at least 128K memory; one disk drive; printer. A second disk drive, RAM disk or hard disk, and mouse recommended. 1 Mb RAM required in version 2.00.
Reviewed by: Mary Neiter, Math and Computer Science Teacher. Laurel Middle School, Laurel, MT.

Desktop Publishing has been the craze of late and *Springboard Publisher* is an impressive attempt at desktop publishing for the Apple II family. As a Macintosh/*PageMaker* user I was eager to get my hands on *Springboard Publisher* and check out Springboard's many promises.

Program Description

Springboard Publisher is an Apple II program that combines page layout, word processing, and graphics in one package for the purpose of producing professional-looking documents. Each of these applications displays a different mode, or viewpoint, of the page. At any time users can switch modes without leaving the current page.

The text mode is used for word processing. Text can be entered directly onto a page or imported as an ASCI text file or a file from *AppleWorks* or *Bank Street Writer*. Text mode shows a page at actual size: users see the entire width of the page but only about one-third its length.

Text automatically wraps around from line to line, from column to column, and from page to page. If the page layout is changed, the text adjusts itself to the new layout. The appearance of the text can be varied using any of the character formatting options including fonts (Gothic, Sans Serif, or Serif), style (plain, bold, italic, underline, outline shadow, superscript, subscript, and inverse), size (9 to 72 points), and spacing.

Graphics mode is used for graphics creation or importing clip art. In this mode users see a slightly enlarged view of the page to show how illustrations will look when printed. *Springboard Publisher*'s Graphics mode contains an excellent paint program with full drawing capabilities. Users may import clip art from Springboard's *Works of Art* and *Clip Art Collections* and most other Apple II graphics applications.

Once text and graphics have been created the page mode is used for layout and design. Layout is the process of arranging the elements of a page, including:

- page margins: the white space around the outside of the page
- text frames: rectangular areas created for special text such as a heading, quotation, or caption
- graphics frames: rectangular areas created for illustrations
- regular text area

In page mode, users see a reduced version of an entire page, making layout much easier. The regular text area can be divided into as many as nine columns.

Text and graphics can easily be moved, creating a professional looking final product. All layout commands also work in the text and graphics modes.

Strengths

Overall *Springboard Publisher* is a valuable program with a number of strengths. Program features such as integrated applications (i.e., graphics, text, and layout all in one program), pull-down menus, mouse control, multiple pages, and WYSIWYG (what you see is what you get) are definite pluses.

Each mode also offers a number of effective features. The page and text modes include automatic text wrap, the ability to change the number of columns from page to page, and rulers which can be set for inches, centimeters, or pixels. Users may put patterned borders around frames, define gutter widths, and have columns of different sizes on one page. One very nice surprise is the international character set allowing users to write in eight different languages.

In the graphic mode text can be added horizontally, vertically, or diagonally, and there is a zoom mode for pixel editing. Additional graphics features include the ability to mirror, invert, trace, skew, distort, and change the perspective of images.

One of the greatest strengths of *Springboard Publisher* is the reference materials included with the software. The Desktop Reference card is laminated, colorful, easy-to-read, and loaded with valuable quick reference information. The tutorial included in the Getting Started manual is an easy-to-follow, informative, step-by-step lesson in creating a first document. New users are sure to find the program easy to learn if they start with the tutorial. The Reference manual gives more detail on the program features and also includes complete descriptions of additional features. Both manuals are extremely well written, clear, descriptive, and explanatory. The author, John Hickman, should be congratulated. I also appreciated the on-screen help function, even though I was not able to access it every time I wanted help.

The additional disks available for *Springboard Publisher* may also be considered strengths. Users may purchase three different volumes of clip art, style sheets, additional fonts, and a laser printer driver.

Weaknesses

The publisher's promises and time delays should be noted as weaknesses. *Springboard Publisher* was promised to be on the shelves months before it was actually available. When the first edition was released it was only available on 3.5 inch disks. Regular 5.25 inch disks followed several months later. The public should not be subjected to this form of false advertising. Discussion of works in progress and hopeful new products is reasonable, but promise dates and failure to deliver is not acceptable.

For me, *Springboard Publisher* was a hardware nightmare. When I first booted the master program, the initial title screens looked great but the first dialog box was totally unreadable. I checked the manual for requirements. My Apple IIe enhanced to 128K was all that was required. After further manual scanning, a long-distance phone call, a trip to a local computer store, and a thorough reading of my Extended 80-Column TextCard manual, I learned that *Springboard Publisher* uses double high-resolution graphics (which is actually a strength) and I needed to install a jumper on the two Molex type pins on the extended text card in order to obtain the double high-resolution display. (However, this procedure only works on Apple IIe's with the Rev B main logic board, identified by a B as the last letter of the part number on the logic board.)

One of Springboard's claims is that *Springboard Publisher* is usable in schools, because it runs on the Apple II family. The only requirement is 128K of memory. However, using an extended text card with a jumper on a Rev A Apple IIe makes the computer inoperable. Rev A Apple IIe's cannot display double high-resolution graphics. Ironically, all the computers in my school are Rev A, therefore I can't use *Springboard Publisher* at work.

My next obstacle with *Springboard Publisher* was the Startup. When I get a new piece of software I like to dive in and see what I can do without a manual. Then I go back and proceed through the manual step-by-step, or feature-by-feature. My first reaction to this program was favorable in that it started with clear on-screen directions. Unfortunately, I soon got to a message saying my disk was write protected, but it did not tell me what to do next. After re-booting and trying again, I started to search the manual for help. The manual recommends making a backup first: the addendum says you must make a backup first, because you need to do setup on the backup disk rather than the original. Once I made a backup and got through the set-up procedure, I found the program features to be familiar and easy to use (much like Aldus *PageMaker*).

Probably the most important weakness of this program is its slowness of operation. Without a mouse, without a second disk drive, and without additional memory, *Springboard Publisher* is just too cumbersome. I fought with slow text entry, problems with pointer movement, slow program response, and a ridiculous amount of disk swapping.

My version of *Springboard Publisher* operates from three double-sided 5.25 inch disks. In addition, users create a scratch disk and a data disk, bringing the total number of disks to eight. The scratch disk temporarily holds the document you are working on, freeing up the computer's memory to allow the use of program features. However, the program is so large the computer is continuously accessing disks during regular operation. The one-page document I created using the program tutorial should have taken me less than one hour from layout to printing. It took me five hours. At least eighty percent of this time was spent swapping disks and waiting for the program. Traditional word processing, cut, paste, and photocopying, would have been much easier and much more efficient.

The disk swapping examples are numerous. In editing text, to insert one letter, I had to swap disks twice, type the letter, and swap once more. To scroll through the document using the scroll bar, I had to move the pointer, and swap disks six times. To go from text mode to page mode, I had to swap disks 18 times! Unfortunately, a second disk drive would not have alleviated the problem. Most of the swapping is between a program disk and the scratch disk. But there are technically six different program disks. A second disk drive would help, but there would still be a large amount of disk swapping required for program operation. Using the 3.5 inch disk version would definitely speed things up.

Recommendations

Springboard has done an excellent job creating an easy-to-use, integrated desktop publishing program for the Apple II family. This program will work more quickly on an Apple IIGS, but I would not recommend the program for users with only a 128K Apple IIe. Version 2.2 is advertised to be three times as fast but that doesn't solve the disk swapping problem, and I am curious to know if the new version is really faster on the IIe or just the IIGS.

I also recommend a mouse. The keyboard commands are clear and effective, but a mouse is much more efficient in an environment where pointer/cursor movement and control is crucial. Graphics created via keyboard rather than a mouse are crude and must be edited pixel by pixel.

Springboard Publisher is a great desktop publishing program for the personal user with the adequate hardware configuration and some knowledge of layout and design. I would not recommend this program for general classroom use, but see it as very useful in the publishing curriculum (journalism, school paper, etc.). Journalism teachers craving a Macintosh with *PageMaker* have an attractive alternative with an Apple IIGS and *Springboard Publisher*.

After reading my review of *Springboard Publisher*, version 1.1, Springboard graciously sent me version 2.00. As with most updates, version 2.00 has corrected many problems. However, most of the weaknesses outlined in the original review still exist. Text entry and editing are faster with version 2.00, and some of the disk swapping has been reduced. Version 2.00 required only two disk swaps to scroll through a document (six swaps with version 1.1), and only three swaps to go from text mode to page mode (18 swaps were required with version 1.1). On the other hand, with version 2.00 it took me ten disk swaps to go back to text mode from page mode, and 27 disk swaps to save!

Springboard Publisher is still an excellent integrated desktop publishing program for the user with the adequate hardware configuration (128K and RAM disk or hard drive). Version 2.00 is a bundle of value, including the *Springboard Publisher* laser driver package, sample style sheets and newsletters, and coupons for a free *Works of Art* package and $125 off the purchase of an Applied Engineering RAM disk. Graciously, Springboard will upgrade the *Springboard Publisher* for only $20.00.

Publisher's Reply

While we regret the inconvenience caused by delays in bringing this advanced software to market, *Springboard Publisher* has in fact been available since April 1988 (May 1988 for the 5 1/4" format). The current version (2.00) has been available since September 1988.

Springboard Publisher 2.00 is a significant advance beyond the older version reviewed here. As the reviewer points out, the user must have an adequate hardware configuration to get the most out of *Springboard Publisher*. *Springboard Publisher* 2.00 requires 1 megabyte of memory in order to operate. This memory eliminates the slow mechanical disk access and manual disk swapping noted in the review. Apple IIe and IIGS users will all benefit from improved speed in version 2.00. even if they were already using a large RAM disk with version 1.1.

Springboard Publisher 2.00 also includes an improved startup procedure. The program is not copy-protected, and it has always been our strong recommendation that a backup copy of the disks be made before installing.

With version 2.00 and the proper hardware, *Springboard Publisher* brings advanced Mac-like desktop publishing to the Apple II family of computers.

Tom Kuder
Product Manager
Springboard Software

PROFESSIONAL LITERATURE

The professional literature in the fields of computer education and of language arts provides new and important information concerning the use of computers in writing instruction. In addition to the articles included in this book, the following articles are suggested reading for anyone interested in computers and writing instruction.

RESEARCH WINDOWS

Research Windows Highlights

by Betty Collis

This month's "Research Windows" highlights five studies, four of which were presented at the National Educational Computing Conference, held in San Diego, June 4-6, 1986. Three of the studies describe valuable insights into word processing and writing, the fourth relates to gender differences in attitudes about computers, and the fifth discusses the lack of impact of a simulation program on concept learning.

Writing Errors with Word Processing

Daiute, C. (1986, June). *Instrument and idea: Some effects of computers on the writing process.* Paper presented at NECC '86, San Diego. (Daiute's address is Harvard University, Graduate School of Education, Cambridge, MA).

Do junior high students make and correct different types of errors and make different types of revisions when they use word processors compared to when they use pens? Is their writing more error free? Daiute introduced 31 students to keyboarding and word processing and observed their use of a word processor over a school year, where each student had at least one class period per week at the computer. She compared computer and pen writing from each student and found that students had the same initial error rate in each medium (crossing out words in pen as readily as they used the computer editing features), but corrected a higher percentage of errors on computer than by pen when they worked on subsequent drafts. More importantly, they made different types of errors in the two media. Using a computer was associated with more mechanical errors (mostly punctuation errors, possibly related to the positions of the punctuation keys or to the 40-column display present in this study), more sentence fragments, and more "empty" words than pen writing. Daiute suggests that the empty words may resemble speech more than traditional writing and that "the production mode of the computer (with its fluid and malleable text)" may be in some ways more like the production mode of speech than it is like pen writing. This has many implications, particularly in studies where writing samples from the two modes are directly compared.

Reading Efficiency and Word Processing

Haas, C. & Hayes, J. R. (1986). "What did I just say?" Reading problems in writing with the machine. *Research in the Teaching of English 20*(1) pp. 22-35.

Reading is an important part of the writing process. This study explored the possibility that reading is slower and less efficient on the computer than from print and that this has an impact on writing with a word processor compared to writing with pencil and paper. The researchers, using university students who were all experienced in word processing, found that readers apparently had better "spatial memory" of the location of specific sentences within a multi-page document when it appeared in print than they did when they read it on a monitor. Readers, on the average, could find a particular sentence in 13 seconds in a printed manuscript, but took 32.7 seconds to find the same sentence in the same text presented as a word processing file. The study also found a considerable advantage in speed and accuracy for paper and pencil over word processing when students were asked to reorganize a disordered text. The paper and pencil advantage disappeared, however, when students used a large (19") high-resolution, black-on-white display for their word processing. These are valuable findings; they suggest that some aspects of computer-displayed writing may make revision less productive when done on the computer than when done with traditional tools. The researchers conclude by suggesting teachers may want to encourage students to make use of hard copy rather than on-screen text for revision and editing when using a word processor without "advanced" screen displays.

Collaborative Writing and Word Processing

MacGregor, S. K. (1986, June). *Computer assisted writing environments for elementary students.* Paper presented at NECC '86, San Diego. (MacGregor's address is Department of Administrative & Foundational Services, Louisiana State University, Baton Rouge, LA.)

In this interesting study, 100 sixth graders participated in various writing environments: paper and pencil, independent use of a word processor, working in pairs at a word processor, and using "writing-prompting" software. Students' writing was appraised with paper and pencil before and after the 10 weeks of treatment. Word processed pre- and post-study samples were also obtained from the computer groups. Children using the computers showed significantly greater improvement in measures of writing mechanics, spelling accuracy, word usage and narrative length than the children using only paper and pencil. Children using the story starter program did indicate more instances of cause and effect relationships in their writing than did the other children, but also had more instances of run-on sentences. Most interesting are the results when children working in pairs at the computer are compared to other children. Children working in pairs at the word processor made fewer mechanical errors than children working individually, and this differential was maintained in the paper and pencil post-test, which was written independently by all the children. However, the paper-and-pencil narratives of children who had worked in pairs were significantly shorter when they wrote independently than were the narratives of children who had worked independently all along. This may suggest both positive and negative developments associated with collaborative writing on the word processor, and that a mixture of both types of experiences is probably desirable.

December/January 1987-88

Grade Two and Word Processing

Poner, R. (1987). *A Report on the Project "Word Processing the Writing Process and Revision Strategies in Young Children."* Unpublished manuscript, Macquarie University, New South Wales, Australia.

This carefully done study describes the use of word processing by 26 children throughout their second grade year. These children had already been regular users of word processors throughout first grade, and in addition had the support of a research assistant who worked with them at a classroom computer for three days a week throughout the second grade. The total amount of time spent at the computer for individual children ranged from 1.5 hours to 20.5 hours. A control group was compared to the computer group with respect to reading and spelling. Despite the extensive use of word processing in the presence of a supportive 'second teacher' no differences were found at either the beginning or the end of second grade for these two groups. Members of the computer group, however, indicated they made more changes in meaning and structure in their writing by the end of the year than did the control group (data obtained from interviews with the children); however, the computer groups teacher emphasized revision to a greater degree than the control group's teacher. The majority of the computer group children indicated it was easier for them to make changes with a word processor than with a pencil and that they preferred writing at the computer compared to writing with pencil and paper.

This study is yet another example of the difficulty in designing a realistic investigation of the benefits of word processing compared to non word-processed writing on the development of language skills; confounding variables are many and likely to influence any conclusions. The researcher acknowledges this and emphasizes the critical interrelationship between the teachers instructional strategies, the classroom writing environment, the level of development of the young child's literacy skills, and his or her use of word processing. Despite his inability to provide the sort of justification for word processing that many people continue look for, this study provides a contribution to the word processing literature through its case studies, its careful examination of individual children's keyboarding strategies, and its consideration of nine "revision profiles" that may help to clarify measurement of growth in revision skills in young children. Also, the study notes the importance of drawing in the early stages of writing. For more information on this 64-page report, contact Dr. Porter at the School of Education, Macquarie University, New South Wales 2109, Australia.

Functional Communication

Riel, M (1984). The Computer Chronicle Newswire: A functional learning environment for acquiring literacy skills. *Journal of Educational Computing Research, 1*(3), pp. 317-337.

Third and fourth graders with learning difficulties were involved in the development of a "newspaper" made up of articles written by the children in various schools and sent among the schools on computer disks. When they began their experiences, students used an "interactive writing system" which helped them decide what to write, but later wrote without prompting. After three months of newspaper involvement, their performance on a task involving writing a composition improved in a variety of ways in both quantity of writing and number of words used to describe activities, but more importantly in their approach to writing.

After experiencing some computer prompting and contributing for three months to the newspaper disks, the students "picked up their pens" and "began writing," without complaining or needing teacher suggestions as to their approach to writing.

Riel makes the interesting observation that when the students first began the experience, they entered a 98-word "joke section" for the newspaper in the same amount of time that they composed 24-word stories, important because it demonstrates that the limited length of these early stories was not due to a lack of computer or typing skills, but that "the students simply did not know what to write." She also notes the importance of students working cooperatively on writing and experiencing writing as a form of functional communication. Even without the "interactive writing system," This experience of sending a "newspaper disk" to each member of a group of participating schools seems an excellent idea for teachers to consider.

Recopying Errors

Levin, J. A., Riel. M., Rowe, R. D. & Boruta, M. J. (1984). Muktuk meets Jacuzzi: Computer networks and elementary school writers. In S.W. Freedman (Ed.), *The acquisition of written language: Revision and response.* Hillsdale, NJ: Ablex.

Rowe compared data from 10 sixth grade students who had completed four writing tasks. These involved writing two stories, one by hand and one on a word processor, and then rewriting the stories for a final copy. He found that the children wrote more with pencil (average length 101.9 words) than they did on the word processor (58.8 words). There were 14.2 errors in the first paper and pencil drafts (0.14 errors/word) and 7.3 errors in the first word processed drafts (0.12 errors/word). In the rewritten versions, the students corrected 43 percent (6.2) of the paper drafts errors and 78 percent (5.7) of the computer draft errors.

Most importantly, however, the students made an average of 5.5 new errors when recopying on paper with pencils, but using the computer, only an average of 0.4 new errors were introduced. Thus the final drafts using pencil still contained a large number of errors (0.10 errors/word) whereas the word-processed second drafts were virtually error free (0.03 errors/word). This study concludes that rewriting pencil and paper drafts for elementary school students may even have a negative value in terms of improving a piece of text, "since new errors are introduced at about the same rate as old errors are corrected." Here is another valuable point to use in encouraging word processing for young writers.

February 1988

Speech Synthesizers and Writing

Borgh, K., & Dickson, W. P. (1986, April). *The Effects on Children's Writing of Adding Speech Synthesis to a Word Processor*. Paper presented at the Annual Meeting of the American Educational Research Association, San Francisco.

The *Talking Screen Textwriter* is a word processor that includes a speech synthesizer and allows the writer to choose to have letters, words, sentences, or longer sections of text spoken aloud. The program has been used with children who have communication disorders, but the use of spoken feedback during writing may facilitate the writing process for regular writers, both for motivational reasons and because "hearing the computer 'speak' their written words may encourage children to take an audience's perspective on their work" (p. 3). In order to examine the impact of this spoken feedback on writing, 48 students from two second-grade and two fifth-grade classrooms wrote two stories under a spoken feedback condition and two stories using the same word processor but without spoken feedback. The order in which the children experienced the writing conditions was randomly assigned as were picture stimuli which were used as the story starters for each writing episode. There were no significant differences in length of written composition or quality of writing for stories written with spoken feedback compared to stories written without spoken feedback. There were also no significant differences in the quantity or type of editing that occurred when students had the program read or reread the entire text. However, there was significantly more sentence-level editing when students received spoken feedback after writing an individual sentence. Overall, when spoken feedback was compared to no spoken feedback and when editing categories were combined, "Regardless of grade level, school, or sex, children did between three and seven times mote editing under the spoken feedback condition" (p. 13). Editing occurred both for "lower-level" grammatical errors and for "higher-level" content-related errors. When interviewed, 40 of the 48 children indicated that they enjoyed writing better when the computer "talked" than when it didn't; they did

not, however, indicate they were thinking more about making changes for a specific audience when they heard the spoken feedback than they did when they wrote silently.

These results are encouraging, especially as the type of voice synthesizer used in this study can be obtained for only about $200. The results suggest we look more carefully at utilizing the computer's capabilities that allow children to experiment with the interrelated roles of reader, writer, and listener. For more information, write to the authors at Child and Family Services, University of Wisconsin, Madison, WI 53706. Also, see the chapter on Speech Technology and Reading in the book by Blanchard, Mason, and Daniels mentioned in the introduction to this column .

April 1988

Zurn, M.R. (1987). *A Comparison of Kindergartners' Handwritten and Word Processor-Generated Writing*. Unpublished doctoral dissertation, Georgia State University, Atlanta, GA.

In contrast to our results with the SLD population, Zurn observed 67 children in three kindergarten classes who were involved in a Writing to Read project for three months. She compared a handwritten and a word-processed writing sample done by each child and found a clear difference between the two samples: The word-processed writing had more words used, more different words used, and contained more complete thoughts (T-Units) than the handwritten samples. However, there was no difference between the samples on a holistic rating that evaluated the child's overall writing stage development. The word processor "increased the children's fluency, but did not enable them to write at a more complex grammatical level" (p. 74). Zurn notes that using the keyboard "did not turn out to be a source of problems" (p. 83), and the computer proved to be especially helpful in making children more aware of word boundaries (through the ease of adding spaces) and of directional principles, as often their handwriting would begin at the middle of the page and then continue anywhere they could find space. Especially interesting for those involved in analyses of the Writing to Read program, the children showed no tendency to make use of the core set of words emphasized in WTR. Only 13% of the word-processed samples and 6% of the handwritten samples contained more than one of the 40 core words, supporting the criticism that the words chosen for emphasis in WTR are irrelevant to the children in their natural use of language. Contact Dr. Zurn through the Department of Early Childhood Education, College of Education, Georgia State University, Atlanta, GA 30303, for more information on this well-done study.

Gerlach, G.J. (April, 1987). *The Effect of Typing Skill on Using a Word Processor for Composition*. Paper presented at the annual meeting of the American Educational Research Association, Washington. DC.

Many people claim that lack of typing skill can be a deterrent to young children's effective usage of a word processor. Gerlach divided 19 fourth grade students into two groups, one of which completed fifteen 25-minute typing tutorial lessons. All children had the same instruction, and after the typing lessons were completed all were introduced to the same word processor. They used it over a three-month period during which writing samples were collected. Contrary to expectations, there were no differences between the typing tutorial children and the hunt and peck children on any of the variables looked at in the study: length of essays, number of revisions (either at the surface level or the phrase level), and attitudes about typing and writing with a word processor. The result concerning revision is not surprising, as numerous studies have emphasized the importance of instruction on revision strategies, and these children all had the same instruction about revision. However, it was unexpected that lengths of writing samples and attitudes about typing and writing with a word processor did not differ between the groups, indicating again that writing as a process transcends in complexity the tools we use to do it with, and that simple conclusions about writing are not appropriate. For more information, contact Dr. Gerlach at Indiana University of Pennsylvania, University School, 104 Davis Hall, Indiana, PA 15705.

Application of Word Processing Skills to Writing
Wolf, D. P. (1985). Flexible texts: Computer editing in the study of writing. In E. L. Klein (Ed.), *Children and computers* (pp. 37-53), New Directions for Child Development, no. 28. San Francisco: Jossey-Bass.

Four children aged 11 and 12 and four adolescents between 13 and 15 were studied as they used word processors over a two-month period. Although all of the students could perform local editing tasks, the younger writers did not seem to consider the chain of problems that a local revision could cause throughout a text. Also, when the students were asked to expand their stories, the younger writers inserted new entries only at the beginning or end of the stories or at paragraph boundaries, whereas the older writers "thickened or embroidered" text throughout their stories. The younger students tended to use word processing tools for line-by-line proofreading whereas the older students "widened their window of writing that they can consider as connected text." This is a valuable observation; the sheer existence of the capacity to perform global editing is of little use to students unless they are first taught "to think in terms of large-scale changes and to make such changes with an eye on the resulting ripples of effects throughout their texts."

COMPUTERS AND THE LANGUAGE ARTS

Retooling for the Future: The Latest and Greatest Resources on Computer-Based Reading and Writing Instruction

by Lynne Anderson-Inman

The beginning of the school year is a time for renewed commitment to the curriculum and to the needs of students. Fresh from a couple of months away from the classroom, the new academic year looks promising and you have energy to try something innovative. Perhaps a book or two might point the way. The last two years have brought a tremendous increase in information on computer applications for teaching reading and writing. Listed below are some of the best resources published recently, with comments to help you choose the book most appropriate for your interests and needs.

This annotated bibliography is divided into three sections: (a) books whose primary focus is computer applications to reading instruction, (b) books whose primary focus is computer applications to writing instruction, and (c) books whose primary goal is to promote the integration of language arts software into the curriculum.

READING INSTRUCTION

Two types of resources are included in this section. The first two books provide an overview of computer applications for reading instruction and includes suggestions for classroom implementation. The last two books provide a survey of the literature in this field, with questions for educators to explore and lists of resources for further study.

Using Computers In the Teaching of Reading
Strickland, Feeley, & Wepner, 1987

Adopting the conceptual framework of computer as tool, tutor, and tutee (Taylor, 1980), the authors of this volume provide teachers with a very classroom-oriented text. Computer applications appropriate for fostering growth in reading and other language arts are described and discussed in relation to their function: that is, as a *tool* to assist the teacher or student, as a *tutor* to provide instruction or practice, or as a *tutee* in language-based problem solving. For example, in discussing the computer as a tool, the authors describe the use of word processing programs within a Language Experience Approach (LEA) to reading instruction, the use of teacher utility programs to generate word games and puzzles, the use of readability formulas to estimate text difficulty, and the use of databases for information retrieval and research.

Two subsequent chapters focus on the use of the computer as a tutor in reading instruction: the first with an emphasis on drill and practice, the second with an emphasis on "interactive learning." Divided by grade level, the text in this section is largely composed of software descriptions illustrating use of the computer as a supplementary instructional aid in the reading curriculum. The chapter on computer as tutee completes the triad of functions. In this last section the authors suggest that programs enabling learners to direct the computer (e.g., those that facilitate creative expression or language-based programming) work to enhance the reading and thinking strategies of their users.

Overall, the book is an excellent introduction to the use of computers in teaching reading, especially for teachers at the elementary level. The authors have taken considerable trouble to intersperse the text with anecdotal accounts of students and teachers using the suggested strategies and software programs. These vignettes help bring the content alive and focus attention on real-life classroom applications. The book, however, does not have much to say about the use of computers in content area reading instruction. Furthermore, discussions on such important topics as keyboarding and speech-based software are extremely limited. Ironically, two of the book's strongest contributions are outside the tool, tutor, tutee framework. An introductory chapter provides readers with a research-based overview of the reading process, concluding with an important list of instructional guidelines for using computers as an integral component in this process. And in a concluding chapter on issues and trends, the authors take a firm stand on software piracy, offering realistic suggestions for educators and schools in order to prevent the illegal copying and distribution of purchased programs.

The Computer in Reading and Language Arts
Blanchard & Mason, 1987

This book is actually a special issue of the quarterly journal *Computers in the School*. The 10 articles are contributed by professionals in the field of reading instruction and together form a solid body of literature discussing major trends and issues. Each article integrates significant research related to the topic and explores classroom implications for computer-based instruction of reading and language arts. Some of the articles provide the reader with a conceptual framework for organizing the field. For example, there are articles that: (a) survey the use of the computer as a language arts tool, (b) examine computer technology in relation to different theoretical models of the reading process, (c) explore the future of computers in the language arts curriculum, and (d) suggest the types of software appropriate for holistic language arts instruction.

Other articles are more specific in scope: a discussion of two instructional design issues in computer-based reading (reinforcement and instructional objectives), a list of suggestions for integrating computer technology into a district's language arts program, and an essay on estimating text difficulty using computer-based readability formulas. Two of the articles focus on applications appropriate for a specific population: young children and students learning English as a second language. Interestingly, one of the best articles is a creative and thorough review of research examining the effects of word processing on the quantity and quality of student writing, on student attitudes toward writing, on composing behavior, on collaboration, on revision, and in relation to reading within the revision process.

The volume is an excellent blend of scholarship and practical application. It is appropriate for both teachers and teacher educators with an interest in exploring the current thinking and available resources for integrating computer technology into the reading and language arts curriculum.

Computer Applications in Reading, 3rd edition
Blanchard, Mason, & Daniel, 1987

For educators wanting to pursue any topic related to the use of computers in reading instruction, this book is a must! The third and greatly revised edition of a book that first appeared in 1979, this volume is a compilation of annotated references to research, implementation ideas, exemplary programs, and professional opinions. The book is arranged by topic, with articles and chapters cited chronologically under each topic. Preceding the annotated bibliography for each topic is a brief overview of the subject outlining major variables and describing the current state of the art.

It is surprising how much information is packed into this one reference book. What is also surprising is how up to date the discussions and citations are. When the slow process of book publishing teams up with a field that seems to be changing overnight, this is not an easy task. The sense of being current is conveyed through the large number of recent references and the authors' choice of organizing topics. Many of the topics are to be expected: computer based instruction in reading, evaluating reading software, word processing and reading, readability formulas, computer managed instruction in reading, and so on. Other topics are more forward looking. For example, three of the most intriguing chapters explore topics mentioned only superficially in most other texts (and then frequently lumped together in a section labeled "future trends"). These chapter topics are: (a) the use of speech technology to produce effective reading instruction, (b) factors that affect the legibility of electronic texts, and (c) the potential influence of interactive videodiscs and other forms of optical technology.

This book is easy to read and easy to use. The annotations for listed articles and chapters are clearly written, providing readers with direction and insight into the available literature. The book is designed for self-learning educators in pursuit of more in-depth information on selected topics related to a wide range of computer applications in reading instruction.

Reading and Computers: Issues for Theory and Practice
Reinking, 1987

Until the publication of this book it was difficult, if not impossible, to grasp the major theoretical issues and existing research base relevant to computer applications in reading instruction. This vol-

ume is the first serious effort to establish a common groundwork for educators interested in what the data suggest about this growing field. *Reading and Computers* is the collaborative effort of 17 major thinkers, writers, researchers, and educators. Each has devoted considerable energy to synthesizing a body of research relevant to the field and discussing the implications of this research for the future. The recommendations and questions that emerge from these discussions should be of critical importance to a broad range of professionals: reading educators, researchers, curriculum specialists, software developers, and teachers.

The issues addressed in this book are divided into three sections: theoretical issues, research issues, and instructional issues. In the first section, the authors lay a foundation for understanding the ways in which computer based reading is different than reading from a printed page. Critical to this discussion is an examination of variables affecting text legibility within a dynamic electronic environment. The second section surveys the ways in which computers have influenced reading research, both as a process and as an area of study. The chapters in the third section suggest instructional implications of computer based technology for the reading curriculum and for training reading specialists. In two of these chapters the use of speech output as an enhancement to the process of learning to read is examined.

Although the book does not assume much entry level knowledge, its content will be of greatest interest to those already acquainted with classroom applications of computer based technology. The content of this book is both mind expanding and forward looking. For educators who find that many resources simply review familiar material, this book is guaranteed to be something different. For educators interested in a glimpse of the issues to be tackled in the next decade, this book is a telescope to the future.

WRITING INSTRUCTION

The process approach to writing instruction has been widely adopted by teachers across the nation. All three resources listed in this section support the process approach and provide practitioners with useful ideas for teaching writing within a word processing environment.

A Practical Guide to Computer Uses in the English/ Language Arts Classroom
Wresch, 1981

The focus of this book is somewhat broader than writing instruction, as it also includes chapters on using the computer for teaching grammar, spelling, vocabulary, and literature. The book's strength, however, lies in its description of computer applications at the various stages of the writing process. Adopting the process approach to composition, the author explores a variety of practical computer uses for students during the stages of prewriting, writing, revising, and editing. Because the word processor is central to a computer based writing program, Wresch first examines essential features of this writing tool and suggests numerous activities for introducing and using a word processor.

Subsequent chapters describe computer applications to help students during prewriting (questioning programs, outliners, and databases) and during revision and editing (spelling checkers and style analyzers). As a natural follow-up, Wresch provides an overview of programs that integrate features supporting all stages of the writing process into a unified software package. Building on this foundation, the author gives some interesting examples of "new forms of writing": interactive stories, dialogue stories, and programs that allow writers to combine text and graphics. Also included is a chapter on using computers to generate poetry and to appreciate the patterns and styles of different poetic forms.

Although the book is clearly designed for the novice computer user, there are many excellent ideas for teachers already experienced in the use of computers for writing instruction. Interspersed throughout the text are numerous screen shots from exemplary software programs and substantial text excerpts illustrating the features under discussion. These enable the reader to grasp the concepts and suggestions easily while also encouraging readers to examine the software more closely. Some discussions are more cursory than would be ideal. For example, the discussion on revision fails to explore the use of the computer for conferencing and peer feedback, and the discussion on keyboarding doesn't provide teachers with sufficient direction to be useful. The book is appropriate for teachers at all grade levels, although many of the suggested strategies are best suited for students in middle and high school English classes.

Teaching Writing with a Word Processor, Grades 7-13
Rodrigues & Rodrigues, 1986

This booklet is one in a series of publications cosponsored by the National Council of Teachers of English (NCTE) and the ERIC Clearinghouse on Reading and Communication Skills, a federally sponsored information center and database of exemplary programs, research reports, and related information. Drawing on these resources, the authors have written a booklet designed to bridge the gap between research and classroom practice. Their stated purpose is to demonstrate how word processing software can be used as the key element in a program to teach writing as research suggests writing should be taught.

The first section of the booklet provides a quick review of research on composition instruction as well as recent research examining the effects of word processing on student revision, student attitude, and student approaches to the writing task. The remaining sections explore the implications of this research for practice, recognizing that writing instruction in a word processing environment is somewhat different than traditional writing instruction and that instructional strategies often needed to be adapted when implemented using a computer. An important contribution is the authors' emphasis on "lesson files," disk-based directions or prompts to the student designed to teach or practice key aspects of composition within a word processing environment. Numerous sample lesson files are provided, as well as detailed instructions on creating lesson files. Also

included are helpful suggestions for adapting such familiar strategies as conferencing, journal writing, collaborative writing, and research papers to computer based writing environments.

The booklet is well written and heavily directed toward classroom application. Although the text assumes readers have a basic familiarity with word processing, it is clearly designed for teachers of English and composition. Even teachers who have not yet introduced word processing into their writing curriculum will find the suggestions and examples easy to implement if they decide to do so.

Making the Literature, Writing, Word Processing Connection: The Best of The Writing Notebook
Franklin, 1987

For a potpourri of interesting and immediately useful ideas, this book is a gold mine! Drawn from previous editions of the *Writing Notebook*, this carefully edited volume bursts with the energy of writing teachers and students across all levels of the curriculum. For example, tucked into its pages are ideas for using *LogoWriter* to celebrate holidays, tips for teacher-designed composition materials, a reproducible peer editing worksheet, topics for process writing research, a report on publishing a multischool electronic newspaper, techniques for using imaginative writing to teach about social conflict, a look at poetry instruction in a cooperative learning environment, and suggestions for using the computer to promote pen pals around the world.

The glue that binds these and other diverse offerings together is a commitment to the creative use of technology in support of an integrated curriculum for ensuring literacy and a sense of global citizenship. Exemplifying this commitment is Jon Madian's "Thanks for Teaching Me," an article that describes his experience teaching a poetry workshop to Navajo high school students. Woven into the narrative of his teaching and the poems the students produce is both an affirmation of the students' heritage and a vision for cultural integration through literacy. The title comes from a poem written by one of the participating students, who says:

"Thanks for teaching me. You made me feel good. You made my brain come alive. You made me smart. You made me think. You made me write what I want."

The Writing Notebook is a journal dedicated to promoting the "wise use of technology toward humane ends," and this collection of articles contains a wealth of ideas for teachers who support that goal.

CURRICULUM INTEGRATION

Reading, Writing and Language Arts: Curriculum Software Guides
Apple Computer, Inc., 1987

Finding the right software to achieve a specific goal within the existing curriculum is not an easy task. The task, in fact, is frequently so frustrating that many teachers have given up on meaningful integration of CAI into their language arts program. The curriculum software guides published by Apple Computer are an answer to this problem, at least for teachers using Apple II computers in their classrooms.

The primary intent of these guides is to assist teachers in identifying and selecting software that matches their existing instructional objectives. In the areas of reading, writing, and language arts, Apple has produced two guides: one focusing on software appropriate for use in Grades K-6, the other for Grades 6-12. The two guides follow identical formats, each containing three major sections. Section I contains Curriculum Skills Matrices for six subject areas in language arts:

- Spelling;
- Vocabulary;
- Punctuation and grammar usage;
- Reading/literature;
- Writing/composition; and
- Study skills.

Exemplary software is listed alphabetically within the matrix for each subject area, followed by indications as to its type (drill, tutorial, simulation, etc.), the major concepts or content coveted in the program, and then the major processes or applications expected of the user. By selecting the curriculum elements (concepts and/or processes) that most closely match a teacher's objectives, a list of potentially appropriate software can be generated fairly quickly.

Section II is provided to assist teachers in finding out more about the products that pass this initial screening. Section II is an alphabetical listing of product descriptions, including such information as price, accompanying support materials, average lesson length, and sources in which a more detailed, evaluative review can be found. This section can, of course, be used independently of the matrix to look up information about any software package whose title is known.

Section III, the purchaser information chart, can be used to further elaborate on product information by identifying the publisher's policies on backups, networking, disk replacement warranties, and so forth. Because it lists the software alphabetically, arranged by publisher, it can also be used to find a given program if only the publisher is known.

Together the curriculum software guides allow teachers to identify appropriate software and access more information

about them in any of three ways: by curriculum objectives, title, or publisher. Without a doubt this is an important first step in providing teachers the assistance they need in order to find and use software relevant to their goals. It is, however, only a first step. As with any paper-based publication, the guides are quickly out of date, therefore not terribly helpful with respect to the newest programs on the market. (Perhaps Apple will consider marketing a disk-based guide that can be more easily updated?) Furthermore, the information available should be seen as only a screening device. Nothing can substitute for actually previewing a software package. What looks good on paper may not look good on your classroom's computer!

Dr. Lynne Anderson-Inman, Associate Professor, College of Education, University of Oregon, Eugene, OR 97403.

References

Apple Computer, Inc. (1987). *Reading, writing and language arts: curriculum software guide K-6*. Cupertino, CA: Apple Computer, Inc.

Apple Computer, Inc. (1987). *Reading, writing and language arts: curriculum software guide 6-12*. Cupertino, CA: Apple Computer, Inc.

Blanchard, J.S., & Mason, G. (Eds.) (1987). The computer in reading and language arts. *Computers in the Schools, 4* (1) New York: Haworth Press.

Blanchard, J.S., Mason, G., & Daniel, D. (1987). *Computer applications in reading, third edition*. Newark, NJ: International Reading Association.

Franklin, S. (Ed.) (1987). *Making the literature, writing, word processing connection: The best of The Writing Notebook.* Eugene, OR: The Writing Notebook.

Strickland, D.S., Feeley, J.T. & Wepner, S.B. (1987). *Using computers in the teaching of reading*. New York: Teachers College Press.

Reinking, D. (Ed.) (,987). *Reading and computers: Issues for theory and practice*. New York: Teachers College Press.

Rodrigues, D. & Rodrigues, R.J. (1986). *Teaching writing with a word processor, grades 7-13*. Urbana, IL: ERIC & NCTE.

Wresch, W. (1987). *A practical guide to computer uses in the English/language arts classroom*. Englewood Cliffs, NJ: Prentice Hall.

BIBIOGRAPHY

This bibliography is reprinted with permission from The Use of a Computer-Facilitated Conferencing Technique to Encourage Revision in Children's Writing, *an unpublished doctoral dissertation by Jane Ritter.*

Dr. Ritter was awarded the national Phi Delta Kappa Outstanding Dissertation of the Year Award for 1987-88 for Phi Delta Kappa's District I.

Afflerbach, P. (1985). Overcoming children's reluctance to revise informational writing. *Journal of Teaching Writing, 4,* 170-176.

Applebee, A., & Langer, J. (1983). Instructional scaffolding: Reading and writing as natural language activities. *Language Arts, 60,* 168-175.

Applebee, A., Lehr, F. & Auten, A. (1980). *A study of writing in the secondary school* (Final Report NIE-G-79-0174). Urbana, IL: National Council of Teachers of English. (ERIC Document Reproduction Service No. ED 197 347)

Bartlett, E.J. (1982). Learning to revise: Some component processes. In M. Nystrand (Ed.), *What writers know: The language, process, and structure of written discourse* (pp. 345-363). New York: Academic Press.

Beach, R. (1986). Demonstrating techniques for assessing writing in the writing conference. *College Composition and Communication, 37,* 56-65.

Beaverton School District. (1986). *Analytical trait writing assessment* (2nd ed.). Beaverton, OR: Author.

Benson, N.L. (1979). The effects of peer feedback during the writing process on writing performance, revision behavior, and attitude toward writing (Doctoral dissertation, University of Colorado at Boulder, 1979). *Dissertation Abstracts International, ?,* 1987A.

Bereiter, C. & Bird, M. (1985). Use of thinking aloud in identification and teaching of reading comprehension strategies. *Cognition and Instruction, 2,* 131-156.

Berkenkotter, C. & Murray, D. (1983). Decisions and revisions: The planning strategies of a publishing writer, and response of a laboratory rat—or being protocoled. *College Composition and Communication, 34,* 156-172.

Birdsong, T.P., & Sharplin, W. (1986). Peer evaluation enhances students' critical judgment. *Highway One, 9*(1), 23-28.

Boone, R.A. (1986). The revision processes of elementary school students who write using a word processing computer program (Doctoral dissertation, University of Oregon, 1985). *Dissertation Abstracts International, 47,* 155A.

Bracewell, R., Bereiter, C., & Scardamalia, M. (1979, April). *A test of two myths about revision.* Paper presented at the annual meeting of the American Educational Research Association, San Francisco.

Bridwell, L.S. (1980). Revising strategies in twelfth grade students' transactional writing. *Research in the Teaching of English, 14,* 197-222.

Bridwell, L.S., & Duin, A. (1985). Looking in-depth at writers: Computers as writing medium and research tool. In J.L. Collins & E.A. Sommers (Eds.), *Writing on-line: Using computers in the teaching of writing* (pp. 115-133). Upper Montclair, NJ: Boynton/Cook.

Bridwell, L.S., Johnson, P., & Brehe, S. (in press). Composing and computers: Case studies of experienced writers. In A. Matsuhishi (Ed.), *Writing in real time: Modelling production processes.* New York: Longman.

Bridwell, L.S., Nancarrow, P.R., & Ross, D. (1984). The writing process and the writing machine: Current research on word processors relevant to the teaching of composition. In R. Beach & L. Bridwell (Eds.), *New directions in composition research* (pp. 381-398). New York: The Guilford Press.

Bridwell, L.S., Sirc, G., & Brooke, R. (1985). Revising and computing: Case studies of student writers. In S. Freedman (Ed.), *The acquisition of written language: Revision and response* (pp. 172-194). Norwood, NJ: Ablex.

Britton, J., Burgess, A., Martin, N., McLeod, A., & Rosen, H. (1975). *The development of writing abilities.* London: Macmillan Education.

Bruffee, K.A. (1979). The Brooklyn plan: Attaining intellectual growth through peer group tutoring. *Liberal Education, 69,* 447-468.

Brunner, J.S. (1966). *Toward a theory of instruction.* Cambridge: Belknap Press.

Bryson, M., Lindsay, P.H., Jorman, E., & Woodruff, E. (1986, April). *Augmented word-processsing: The influence of task characteristics and mode of production on writers' cognitions.* Paper presented at the Annual Meeting of the American Educational Research Association, San Francisco.

Burkland, J., & Grimm, N. (1986). Motivating through responding, *Journal of Teaching Writing, 5,* 237-247.

Calkins, L. M. (1980). Children learn the writer's craft. *Language Arts, 57,* 207-213.

Calkins, L.M. ((1983). *Lessons from a child: On the teaching and learning of writing.* Portsmouth, NH: Heinemann.

Campione, J. (1981, April). *Learning, academic achievement, and instruction.* Paper presented at the Second Annual Conference on Reading Research, New Orleans.

Clifford, J. (1981). Composing in stages: The effects of a collaborative pedagogy. *Research in the Teaching of English, 15,* 37-53.

Collier, R. (1983). The word processor and revision strategies. *College Composition and Communication, 34,* 149-155.

Collins, C. (1985). Interactive literacy: The connection between reading and writing and the computer. *Collegiate Microcomputer, 3,* 333-338.

Comprehensive Tests of Basic Skills. (1981). Monterey, CA: McGraw-Hill.

Daiute, C. (1981). Psycholinguistic foundation of the writing process. *Research in the Teaching of English, 15,* 5-22.

Daiute, C. (1983). *Writing and computers.* Reading, MA: Addison-Wesley.

Dickinson, D. K. (1986). Cooperation, collaboration, and a computer: Integrating a computer into first-second grade writing program. *Research in the Teaching of English, 20,* 357-378.

Dunn, S., Florio-Ruane, S., & Clark, C. M. (1985). The teacher as respondent to the high school writer. In S. W. Freedman (Ed.), *The acquisition of written language: Response and revision* (pp. 33-50). Norwood, NJ: Ablex.

Dyson, A. (1984). Learning to write/learning to do school: Emergent writers' interpretations of school literacy tasks. *Research in the Teaching of English, 18,* 233-264.

Elbow, P. (1973). *Writing without teachers.* New York: Oxford University Press.

Elbow, P. (1981). *Writing with power.* Oxford: Oxford University Press.

Emig, J. (1971). *The composing processes of twelfth graders* (Report No. 13). Urbana, IL: National Council of Teachers of English. (ERIC Document Reproduction Service No. 058 205)

Ericsson, K. A., & Simon, H. A. (1980). Verbal reports as data. *Psychological Review, 87,* 215-251.

Evans, B. (1986, April). *The integration of word processing and composition instruction in fifth and sixth grades.* Paper presented at the annual meeting of the American Educational Research Association, San Francisco.

Faigley, L., & Witte, S. P. (1981). Analyzing revision. *College Composition and Communication, 32,* 400-414.

Faigley, L., & Witte, S. P. (1984). Measuring the effects of revisions on text structure. In R. Beach & L. S. Bridwell (Eds.), *New directions in composition research* (pp. 95-108). New York: Guilford Press.

Fischer, O. H., & Fischer, C. A. (1985). Electrifying the composing process: Electronic workspaces and the teaching of writing. *Journal of Teaching Writing, 4,* 113-121.

Flavell, J, Friedrichs, A., & Hoyt, J. (1970). Developmental changes in memorization processes. *Cognitive Psychology, 1,* 324-340.

Florio-Ruane, S. (1986, April). *Taking a closer look at writing conferences.* Paper presented at the annual meeting of the American Educational Research Association, San Francisco.

Flower, L., & Hayes, J. R. (1977). Problem solving strategies and the writing process. *College English, 39,* 449-461.

Flower, L., & Hayes, J. R. (1980). The cognition of discovery: Defining rhetorical problems. *College Composition and Communication, 30,* 21-32.

Flower, L., & Hayes, J. R. (1981). A cognitive process theory of writing. *College Composition and Communication, 32,* 365-387.

Flynn, E. (1984). Students as readers of their classmates' writing: Some implications for peer critiquing. *The Writing Instructor, 3,* 120-128.

Fox, R. (1980). Treatment of writing apprehension and its effects on composition. *Research in the Teaching of English, 14,* 34-49.

Freedman, S. (1981). Influences on evaluators of expository essays: Beyond the text. *Research in the Teaching of English, 15,* 245-255.

Freedman, S., & Sperling, R. (1985). Written language acquisition: The role of response and the writing conference. In S. W. Freedman (Ed.), *The acquisition of written language: Response and revision* (pp. 106-130). Norwood, NJ: Ablex.

Gantry, L. A. (1980). Textual revision: A review of the research. Southwest Regional Laboratory Technical Note. TN 2-80/11. Los Alamitos, CA, SWRL.

Gere, A. R., & Stevens, R. S. (1985). The language of writing groups: How oral response shapes revision. In S. W. Freedman (Ed.), *The acquisition of written language: Response and revision.* (pp. 85-105). Norwood, NJ: Ablex.

Graves, D. (1975). An examination of the writing processes of seven-year-old children. *Research in the Teaching of English, 9*, 227-241.

Graves, D. (1979). What children show us about revision. *Language Arts, 56*, 312-319.

Graves, D. (1983). *Writing: Teachers and children at work.* Portsmouth, NH: Heinemann.

Harris, J. (1985). Student writers and word processing: A preliminary evaluation. *College Composition and Communication, 36*, 323-330.

Hayes, J. (1978). *Cognitive Psychology: Thinking and Creating.* Homewood, IL: Dorsey Press.

Hilgers, T. (1984). Toward a taxonomy of beginning writers' evaluative statements on written compositions. *Written Communication, 1*, 365-383.

Hilgers, T. (1986). How children change as critical evaluators of writing: Four three-year case studies. *Research in the Teaching of English, 20*, 36-55.

Hillocks, G., Jr. (1984). What works in teaching composition: A meta-analysis of experimental treatment studies. *American Journal of Education, 93*, 133-170.

Intentional Educators, Smith, F. E., & Bank Street College of Education. (1982). *Bank Street Writer* [Computer program]. New York: Scholastic.

Kintsch, W. (1974). *The representation of meaning in memory.* Hillsdale, NJ: Lawrence Erlbaum.

Kroll, B. M. (1978). Cognitive egocentrism and the problem of audience awareness in written disclosure. *Research in the Teaching of English, 12*, 269-281.

Lapidus-Saltz, W. (1981). The effective feedback script: A peer response procedure. *The Writing Instructor, 1*, 19-25.

Larsen, D. (1985). *Recording Wordstar* [Computer program]. Minneapolis: University of Minnesota, Academic Computing Services and Systems.

Lytle, M. J., & Rankin, R. (1987). *Computer writing attitude scale.* Unpublished manuscript, University of Oregon, College of Education, Eugene.

Matsuhashi, A., & Gordon, E. (1985). Revision, addition, and the power of the unseen text. In S. W. Freedman (Ed.), *The acquisition of written language: Response and revision* (pp. 226-249). Norwood, NJ: Ablex.

McKensie, L. & Tomkins, G. (1984). Evaluating students' writing: A process approach. *Journal of Teaching Writing, 3*, 201-211.

Michaels, S., Ulichney, P., & Watson-Gegeo, K. (1986, April). Social processes and written products: Teacher expectations, writing conferences, and student texts. Paper presented at the annual meeting of the American Educational Research Association, San Francisco.

MicroPro International. (1984). *Wordstar* [Computer program]. San Rafael, CA: Author.

Moffett, J. (1983). *Teaching the universe of discourse.* Boston: Houghton Mifflin.

Murray, D. (1978). Internal revision: A process of discovery. In C. Cooper & L. Odell (Eds.), *Research on composing: Points of departure* (pp. 85-103). Urbana, IL: National Council of Teachers of English.

Murray, D. (1979). The listening eye: Reflections on the writing conference. *College English, 41*, 13-18.

Nold, E. (1981). Revising. In C. H. Fredericksen, & J. F. Dominic (Eds.), *Writing: The nature, development, and teaching of written communication* (pp. 67-79). Hillsdale, NJ: Lawrence J. Erlbaum.

Palincsar, A. & Brown, A. (1984). Reciprocal teaching of comprehension-fostering and comprehension-monitoring activities. *Cognition and Instruction, 1*, 117-175.

Perl, S. (1979). The composing processes of unskilled college writers. *Research in the Teaching of English, 13*, 317-336.

Pufahl, J. (1984). Response to Richard M. Collier, The word processor and revision strategies. *College Composition and Communication, 35*, 91-93.

Rogers, A. (1986). *FrEd Writer* [Computer program]. San Diego: Computer Using Educators Softswap Project.

Rohman, G. (1965). Pre-writing: The stage of discovery in the writing process. *College Composition and Communication, 16*, 106-112.

Rohman, G., & Wlecke, A. (1964). *Pre-writing: The construction and application of models for concept formation in writing.* (U.S. Office of Education Cooperative Research Project No. 2174). East Lansing, MI: Michigan State University.

Rosenshine, B.V., & Furst, N. (1973). The use of direct observation to study teaching. In R. Travers (Ed.), *Second handbook of research on teaching* (pp. 122-183). Chicago: Rand McNally.

Russell, C. (1983). Putting research into practice: Conferencing with young writers. *Language Arts, 60*, 333-340.

Scardamalia, M., & Paris, P. (1985). The function of explicit discourse knowledge in the development of text representations and composing strategies. *Cognition and Instruction, 2*, 1-39

Searle, D. & Dillon, D. (1980). The message of marking: Teacher written responses to student writing at intermediate grade levels. *Research in the Teaching of English, 14*, 233-242.

Selfe, C. (1985). The electronic pen: Computers and the composing process. In J. L. Collins & E. A. Sommers (Eds.), *Writing on-line using computers in the teaching of writing* (pp. 55-66). Upper Montclair, NJ: Boynton/Cook.

Shaugnessy, M. P. (1977). *Errors and expectations: A guide for the teacher of basic writing.* New York: Oxford University Press.

Simon, H. & Hayes, J. (1976). Understanding complex task instruction. In D. Klahr, (Ed.), *Cognition and instruction* (pp. 269-285). Hillsdale, NJ: Lawrence Erlbaum Associates.

Sommers, N. (1978). Response to Sharon Crowley, Components of the process. *College Composition and Communication, 29*, 209-211.

Sommers, N. (1980). Revision strategies of student writers and experienced writers. *College Composition and Communication, 31*, 378-388.

Sommers, N. (1982). Responding to student writing. *College Composition and Communication, 33*, 148-156.

Sommers, N. (1985). COMMENT: Word-processing: A response to David G. Hale. *The English Record, 36*(2), 20-21.

Sommers, N. (1986a). The effects of word processing and writing instruction on the writing processes and products of college writers. (Doctoral dissertation, State University of New York at Buffalo, 1986). *Dissertation Abstracts International, 46*, 2064A.

Sommers, N. (1986b). What I really meant here ... Measuring writers' revisions: Problems, scales, uses. *The English Record, 37*(2), 8-10.

Stein, N. L. (1983). On the goals, functions, and knowledge of reading and writing. *Contemporary Educational Psychology, 8*, 261-292.

Stein, N. L. (1986). Knowledge and process in the acquisition of writing skills. In E. Z. Rothkopf (Ed.), *Review of research in education* (pp. 225-258). Washington, DC: American Educational Research Association.

Sudol, R. A. (1985). Applied word processing: Notes on authority, responsibility, and revision in a workshop model. *College Composition and Communication, 36*, 331-335.

van Dijk, T. A. (1980). *Macrostructures: An interdisciplinary study of global structures in discourse, interaction, and cognition.* Hillsdale, NJ: Lawrence Erlbaum.

Wertsch, J. (1980). The significance of dialogue in Vygotsky's account of social, egocentric, and inner speech. *Contemporary Educational Psychology, 5*, 150-162.

Witte, S. P. (1985). Revising, composing theory, and research design. In S. W. Freedman (Ed.), *The acquisition of written language: Response and revision* (pp. 250-284). Norwood, NJ: Ablex.

Woodruff, E., Lindsay, P., Bryson, M., & Jorman, E. (1986, April). *Some cognitive effects of word processors on enriched and average eighth grade writers.* Paper presented at the Annual Meeting of the American Educational Research Association, San Francisco.

Put the Future of Education in Your Hands…

Pick up David Thornburg's latest in visionary theory and
explore the social and technological trends shaping education.

Edutrends 2010—Restructuring, Technology, and the Future of Education

Thornburg examines the recent flurry of teacher bashing, moving from the reasoning flaws of those who would dismantle U.S. public education to the change process necessary for educational restructuring for the 21st century.

He proposes a way to think intelligently about the future while we reshape education to meet the needs of our society.

Education, Technology, and Paradigms of Change for the 21st Century

Learn unique patterns of thinking that encourage students to go above and beyond the three Rs. The technologies of calculators, computers, laser discs, and video games converge with new concepts of learning and intelligence to provide unprecedented opportunities for all students. Let this progressive. book lead you toward a future filled with new paradigms.

International Society for Technology in Education
1787 Agate Street, Eugene, OR 97403-1923
Order Desk: 800/336-5191   Fax: 503/346-5890

Make This Step Your Next Step.

You've got your new Mac. Now what?

You want to know what those cute icons mean. You need to find out how to use that mouse-thing-a-ma-jig.

You'd like to know how to "empty the trash," and it'd be great to understand exactly what the "chooser" chooses.

By following the footsteps in ISTE's *Macintosh Step by Step*, you'll pick up on all these basic Macintosh operating procedures, plus more—from finding the "power" button to demystifying the little Apple menu in the upper left corner.

And it also teaches you the theory behind Mac file storage and the importance of backing up your data on a regular basis.

In all, you'll find that this simple, illustrated guide will lead you on your way toward becoming a Mac user—not just a Mac owner.

Just call today and make your next computing step a step in the ISTE direction.

All you need is the right tool...

With either *HyperCard for Educators* or *LinkWay for Educators* as an introduction to the interactive world of hypermedia, you can learn to build libraries of knowledge suitable for both classroom and personal use.

If you have basic computer skills, you can follow the simple tutorials and start using buttons, fields, backgrounds or base pages, stacks or folders to make your data and images come alive in your classroom.

By starting with the foundation that these books provide, you'll be on your way to using sounds, images, and animation to jump-start your curriculum in no time!

Take advantage of the organizational tools computers provide.

Call ISTE to order and begin building your *HyperCard* or *LinkWay* skills today.

ISTE Books & Courseware Order Form

Name _____

School/Business _____

Address _____

City _____ State _____ Zip/Postal Code _____

Country _____ Phone _____

☐ Yes! I'm presently an ISTE member. Membership number must be included to receive discount.
My membership number is _____ (Discount does not apply to initial membership fee.)

Occupation

Grade Level: ☐ all (K-12) Specific grade level _____
☐ Teacher (350) Subject _____
☐ Administrator (320) Title/Position _____
☐ Higher Education (360) Title/Position _____
☐ Federal/State Government (310) Title/Position _____
☐ Educational Information Resource Manager (IRM) (320)
☐ Technology Coordinator (340)
☐ Other _____

Payment Options

☐ **Payment enclosed.** (Make checks out to ISTE.) Non-U.S. orders must be pre-paid with U.S. funds or credit card.
  ☐ VISA ☐ MasterCard ☐ Discover Card Exp. Date _____

  ☐☐☐☐☐☐☐☐☐☐☐☐☐☐☐☐

☐ **Purchase Order enclosed.** (Please add $2.50 for order processing. P.O. not including $2.50 fee will be returned.)

☐ **C.O.D.** for U.S. Book orders only. You will pay UPS the total upon delivery (check or cash—ISTE will add $2.75 order processing).

Shipping & Handling for Books & Courseware

$0-$15.99 (subtotal) .... add $3.25
$16-$45.99 (subtotal) $4.50
$46-$75.99 (subtotal) $5.50
$76-$100.99 (subtotal) $6.50
$101 or more .... 7% of subtotal

Do not include *additional site license fees or subscription costs* when computing shipping rates.

Non-U.S. orders for Books & Courseware are sent surface mail. If you want your Books & Courseware order shipped AIRMAIL, please check here. ☐ ISTE will bill you the additional shipping charge.

GST Registration Number 128828431

ISTE Books, Courseware, & Nonmember Subscriptions

Qnty.	Title	Member Unit Price	Nonmember Unit Price	Total Price

BOOKS & COURSEWARE SUBTOTAL	
Add Shipping, based on Books & Courseware SUBTOTAL	+
Add $10 S & H for Don't Copy that Floppy	+
Add Additional 5% of SUBTOTAL if shipped to PO Box, AK, HI, or outside U.S.	+
Add 7% of SUBTOTAL for GST if shipped to Canada	+
If billed with purchase order, add $2.50; If COD, add $2.75	+
	=
Membership Total from other side	+
TOTAL	=

MAIL this form to:
  ISTE, 1787 Agate St., Eugene, OR 97403-1923 USA
FAX this form with credit card or P.O. information to: 503/346-5890
PHONE your credit card or P.O. order to:
  ISTE Order Desk: 800/336-5191